Regulating globalization

Regulating globalization: Critical approaches to global governance

Edited by Pierre de Senarclens and Ali Kazancigil

United Nations
University Press

TOKYO · NEW YORK · PARIS

United Nations University Press
United Nations University, 53-70, Jingumae 5-chome,
Shibuya-ku, Tokyo 150-8925, Japan
Tel: +81-3-3499-2811   Fax: +81-3-3406-7345
E-mail: sales@hq.unu.edu   general enquiries: press@hq.unu.edu
http://www.unu.edu

United Nations University Office at the United Nations, New York
2 United Nations Plaza, Room DC2-2062, New York, NY 10017, USA
Tel: +1-212-963-6387   Fax: +1-212-371-9454
E-mail: unuona@ony.unu.edu

United Nations University Press is the publishing division of the United Nations
University.

Cover design by Mea Rhee

Printed in India

ISBN 978-92-808-1136-0

Library of Congress Cataloging-in-Publication Data

Regulating globalization : critical approaches to global governance / edited by
Pierre de Senarclens and Ali Kazancigil.
     p.   cm.
  Includes index.
  ISBN 978-9280811360 (pbk.)
  1. Globalization. 2. Democracy. 3. International organization. 4. International
cooperation. I. Senarclens, Pierre de. II. Kazancigil, Ali.
JZ1318.R436   2007
303.48′2—dc22   2007005048

Contents

List of contributors vii

List of acronyms ix

1 Introduction 1
   Ali Kazancigil and Pierre de Senarclens

2 The United Nations as a social and economic regulator 8
   Pierre de Senarclens

3 The significance of statehood in global governance 37
   Ali Kazancigil

4 Financial globalization, "global governance" and the erosion
   of democracy 69
   Virgile Perret

5 Trends in global economic governance and the emerging
   accountability gap 93
   Ngaire Woods

6 Rule-making in global trade: The developmental challenge 118
   Miguel F. Lengyel

7 Regionalism and global governance: An appraisal 150
    Louise Fawcett

8 Regionalization and globalization: Two concomitant dynamics
    in need of coherent institutions 177
    Yves Berthelot

9 Developmental and environmental policies: Past trends,
    present issues, future prospects 205
    Yohan Ariffin

10 Can global governance make globalization more legitimate? ... 249
    Jean-Marc Coicaud

11 Conclusion.. 275
    Pierre de Senarclens and Ali Kazancigil

Index 281

List of contributors

Yohan ARIFFIN, Senior Lecturer in International Relations at the University of Lausanne, Switzerland. He has been a visiting fellow at the London School of Economics, the Victoria and Albert Museum in London and the Institut d'Etudes politiques in Paris. Most recent publication (with Pierre de Senarclens): *La politique internationale. Théories et enjeux contemporains* (2006).

Yves BERTHELOT, Economist, Senior Research Fellow, City University of New York Graduate Centre, NY, USA and at the United Nations Institute for Training and Research (UNITAR), formerly Executive Secretary of the Economic Commission for Europe (UNECE). He edited *Unity and Diversity in Development Ideas: Perspective from the UN Regional Commissions* (2004).

Jean-Marc COICAUD, Head, United Nations University Office to the United Nations, New York, USA, formerly fellow at Harvard University and New York University Law School. Latest publication: *Beyond the National Interest* (USIP Press, 2006).

Louise FAWCETT, Fellow and Lecturer in Politics at St Catherine's College, University of Oxford, UK. Her latest book (with Monica Serrano) is *Regionalism and Governance in the Americas* (2005).

Ali KAZANCIGIL, Political Scientist, Secretary-General of the International Social Science Council, Paris, France; formerly UNESCO's Assistant Director General for Social and Human Sciences. His latest book (with G. Hermet and J.F. Prud'homme) is *La gouvernance: un concept et ses applications* (2004).

Miguel F. LENGYEL, Political Scientist, Executive Director of the Latin American Trade Network (LATN) and Senior Researcher at the Facultad Latinoamericana de Ciencias Sociales (FLACSO/ Argentina). His latest book (with Vivianne Ventura-Dias) is *Trade Policy Reform in Latin America. Multilateral Rules and Domestic Institutions* (2004).

Virgile PERRET, Teaching Assistant at the Institut d'Etudes Politiques et Internationales (IEPI) of the University of Lausanne, Switzerland. He is working on a doctoral thesis on the tension between financial globalization, democratic regulation and citizenship.

Pierre DE SENARCLENS, Professor of International Relations, University of Lausanne, Switzerland. His latest books are *Mondialisation. Théories, enjeux et débats* 4th edn, 2005, and with Yohan Ariffin, *La politique internationale. Théories et enjeux contemporains*. He worked for several years with the UN system and is presently Vice-President of the Swiss Red Cross.

Ngaire WOODS, Director of the Global Economic Governance Programme and Dean of Graduates at University College, Oxford, UK. Her most recent book is *The Globalizers: the IMF, the World Bank and their borrowers* (Cornell University Press, 2006).

List of acronyms

AA	Agriculture Agreement of the WTO
ACN	Andean Community of Nations
ACP	African, Caribbean and Pacific (countries)
AD	Anti-dumping
ADB	Asian Development Bank
AMF	Asian Monetary Fund
APEC	Asian Pacific Economic Cooperation
ASCM	Agreement on Subsidies and Countervailing Measures of the WTO
ASEAN	Association of South East Asian Nations
ATC	Agreement on Textiles and Clothing of the WTO
BWI	Bretton Woods institutions
CAC	Codex Alimentarius Commission
CAO	Compliance Adviser/Ombudsman
CARICOM	Caribbean Community and Common Market
CBD	Convention on Biological Diversity
CDEAO	Communauté des Etats d'Afrique de l'Ouest
CDM	Clean Development Mechanism
CENTO	Central Treaty Organization
CGIAR	Consultative Group of International Agricultural Research
CMEA	Council for Mutual Economic Assistance
CSCE/OSCE	Conference/Organization of Security and Cooperation in Europe
CSFs	coordination services firms
CSOs	civil society organizations
CSR	corporate social responsibility
ECA	[UN] Economic Commission for Africa

ix

ECAFE	Economic Commission for Asia and the Far East
ECE	[UN] Economic Commission for Europe
ECLAC	[UN] Economic Commission for Latin America and the Caribbean
ECOSOC	Economic and Social Council
ECOWAS	Economic Community of West African States
EEC	European Economic Community
EFTA	European Free Trade Association
EPTA	Expanded Programme of Technical Assistance
ESCAP	[UN] Economic and Social Commission for Asia and the South Pacific
ESCWA	[UN] Economic and Social Commission for Western Asia
EU	European Union
FAO	[UN] Food and Agriculture Organization
FCCC	Framework Convention on Climate Change
FDI	Foreign Direct Investment
FTA	Free Trade Agreement
FTAA	Free Trade Area of the Americas
G-20	Group of Twenty
GATS	General Agreement on Trade in Services
GATT	General Agreement on Tariffs and Trade
GCC	Gulf Cooperation Council
GEF	Global Environmental Facility
GHG	greenhouse gases
HIPCs	highly indebted poor countries
IADB	Inter-American Development Bank
ICO	Islamic Conference Organization
ICRC	International Committee of the Red Cross
ICT	information and communication technology
IFC	International Finance Corporation
IFRC	International Federation of the Red Cross and Red Crescent
IGOs	intergovernmental organizations
ILO	International Labour Organization
IMF	International Monetary Fund
IOSCO	International Organization of Securities Commissions
IP	Intellectual Property
IPCC	Intergovernmental Panel on Climate Change
IPR	Intellectual Property Rights
ISO	International Standardization Organization
ISS	interstate space
ITC	International Trade Center
ITO	international trade organization
IUCN	International Union for the Protection of Nature
LAFTA	Latin American Free Trade Association
LATN	Latin American Trade Network
LDCs	less/least developed countries

MDG	Millennium Development Goals
MERCOSUR	Southern Cone Common Market
MIGA	Multilateral Investment Guarantee Agency
MSF	Médicin sans frontières
NAFTA	North American Free Trade Agreement
NEPAD	New Partnership for African Development
NGLS	[UN] Non-Governmental Liaison Service
NGOs	non-governmental organizations
NIEO	New International Economic Order
OAPEC	Organization of Arab Petroleum Exporting Countries
OAS	Organization of American States
OAU	Organization of African Unity
ODA	Overseas Development Aid
OECD	Organisation for Economic Co-operation and Development
OEEC	Organization for European Economic Cooperation
PAFTA	Pan-Arab Free Trade Area
PBR	Plant Breeders Rights
PCT	Patent Cooperation Treaty
PfPs	Partnerships for Peace
PPP	polluter pays principle
PRSPs	Poverty Reduction Strategy Papers
QELRO	Quantified emission limitation or reduction objectives
S&D	Special and Differential Treatment
SAARC	South Asian Association for Regional Cooperation
SADC	Southern Africa Development Community
SCM	Subsidies and Countervailing Measures Agreement of the WTO
SEATO	South East Asian Treaty Organization
SPS	Sanitary and Phytosanitary Measures
TBT	Technical Barriers to Trade
TIR	Transport International Routier/International Road Transport
TNCs	transnational corporations
TPS	transnational public space
TRIMs	[WTO] Agreement on Trade-Related Investment Measures
TRIPs	[WTO] Agreement on Trade-Related Intellectual Property Rights
UDEAC	Union des Etats d'Afrique Centrale
UMOA	Union Monétaire Ouest Africaine
UNCTAD	United Nations Conference on Trade and Development
UNDG	United Nations Development Group
UNDP	United Nations Development Programme
UNEP	United Nations Environment Programme
UNFPA	United Nations Fund for Population Activities
UNHCR	United Nations High Commissioner for Refugees
UNICEF	United Nations International Children's Emergency Fund
UNWRA	United Nations Relief and Works Agency
UPOV	International Union for the Protection of New Varieties of Plants

UR	Uruguay Round
URA	Uruguay Round Agreement
USTR	United States Trade Representative
WFP	World Food Programme
WHO	World Health Organization
WIPO	World Intellectual Property Organization
WMO	World Meteorological Organization
WSF	World Social Forum
WTO	World Trade Organization

1

Introduction

Ali Kazancigil and Pierre de Senarclens

This book is about the governance of globalization. It is at once analytical, critical and normative. It has retrospective and prospective dimensions. The first is needed, for the present cannot be understood or the future usefully imagined without taking into account a number of relevant past developments. In the context of this book, the prospective dimension, which is partly normative, consists of an attempt to outline the future shape of global governance and, in this respect, to formulate recommendations for action and policy without however indulging in post-modern or post-structural speculations, which can often confuse discourse with reality and be detached from empirical evidence. This approach takes into account historical experiences and political theory, as well as perennial elements such as the state, sovereignty, legitimate authority, political community, citizenship, and the unequal distribution of political, economic, social and cultural resources. Otherwise, it would not be possible to reach a critical understanding of globalization and its governance as they are, or to produce knowledge that is relevant to formulate action aimed towards the introduction of new patterns and directions. To be sure, much of the architecture of renewed global governance remains to be "invented", and, to be meaningful and meet a large degree of consent, such innovations should necessarily be rooted in and grow out of political processes and agency at national and international levels.

This volume, like most multi-author volumes, offers the advantage of a variety of viewpoints, but at the cost of a weaker coherence than that found in single-author books. However, the team of authors share a

Regulating globalization: Critical approaches to global governance, de Senarclens and Kazancigil (eds), United Nations University Press, 2007, ISBN 978-92-808-1136-0

number of hypotheses and a convergent understanding of concepts, and what unites them can be summarized as follows: global governance involves an ensemble of actors – such as sovereign states, intergovernmental organizations, transnational corporations (TNCs), non-governmental organizations (NGOs) and social movements – who, in various degrees, participate in policy- and decision-making procedures and international regimes aimed towards the regulation of economic, financial, commercial and technological globalization. At the core of the latter lies a largely deregulated capitalism, mainly dominated by financial flows and markets – the so-called shareholder capitalism. Globalized processes are fostered and de-territorialized by powerful information and communication technologies, as well by means of transportation, which facilitate mobility and shrink distances. Globalization is also effectively supported by neoliberalism, which, since the collapse of communism, is the only surviving hegemonic ideology in today's world. It is urgent to start making progress towards a different globalization and its governance. They should both be rendered legitimate by obtaining the consent of the majority of the world's populations. Sovereignty, which is the principle around which the political community, citizenship, democratic regimes and civil societies have been built, cannot be ignored. Much as a well-regulated capitalist market is the better tool for creating economic growth, the democratic state is the better mechanism to provide security, social and political integration and redistributive justice, as well as maintain a balance between the diverging interests of social classes and enhance public interest over corporate interests. Thus, statehood is a *conditio sine qua non* for a legitimate global governance.

The purpose here is not to idealize the sovereign state. The concept of sovereignty has evolved in the course of history, from the Age of Absolutism to the contemporary welfare state. The latter's democratic regulatory functions, which aim at satisfying the individual and collective needs of citizens, require in certain respects international cooperation mechanisms and the devolution of the state's prerogatives to international or transnational bodies, some of which have supra-national powers and capacities. Thus, both in traditional multilateralism and in global governance, the sovereign state is still the major actor.

Statehood, which is a central concept of this book, is not to be equated with the sovereign state. It involves the latter, but rather refers to the politics of public good and public interest, the state being the structure or the tool providing the space and conditions for sustaining these principles and, more generally, the democratic regimes.

In order to build a legitimate global governance, such elements of statehood – that is, democratic politics, the public good and public interest, and some forms of citizens' participation, which so far mainly remain within the frontiers of the states – need to be projected onto a transnational public space. It is within such a space that states would have to share their sovereign prerogatives with other states, as well as with a number of non-state actors, if progress is to be made towards democratized and accountable global governance. So far, states have, to a limited extent, entered into such shared arrangements in economic and financial fields, collective security, environment, international humanitarian and criminal law within the framework of the post-World War II multilateralism. Here, one encounters a foundational contradiction which makes it so difficult to advance towards a more rational and equitable world order: not only are sovereign states reluctant to transfer onto the transnational space certain elements of democracy and statehood needed to enhance global governance, but they are unable to agree on even the minimum amount of reform necessary to make the existing multilateral architecture a more effective one. The most recent evidence in this respect is the striking failure of the United Nations (UN) summit held in September 2005, the purpose of which was to render the composition of the Security Council more relevant by enlarging its membership. Some of the chapters in this volume explore ways of overcoming such contradictions, which prevent traditional multilateralism from adjusting to evolution in the configuration of the world order.

The chapters of this book do not adopt a systematic anti-globalization stance. They do not deny that a properly regulated globalization may bring economic and social progress for all, provided that it gives as great a policy priority to equitable redistribution mechanisms as to economic performance and profit making. They observe that the current neoliberal globalization, which does not meet the consent of the majority world, lacks legitimacy and thus sustainability. It creates discontent, to use the expression of Joseph Stiglitz, because it benefits only a minority of the world's countries and people. Its actors favour private interests and a technocratic, rather than a more democratic, participatory and accountable global governance. Economic and financial actors, particularly the TNCs, play a dominant role in it without having a legitimacy do so, while political actors – sovereign states and elected governments – which possess the legitimacy to govern globalization, often acquiesce to acting as logistic bases for these powerful economic forces, putting societies and social cohesion at risk. The ideological paradigm of globalization is effective in persuading public opinion and the media that the "market society" – involving unlimited competition between corporations and countries, concentration of wealth, consumerism and privatization of public services – is the best path to progress and increased well-being.

This remains to be seen. In the meantime, we get greater inequalities, declining democratic regimes and a declining sense of solidarity within and between societies, as well as continuous environmental degradation.

Globalization has turned upside down the principles of multilateral cooperation and the institutional architecture to govern the international system, which were established in the wake of the Second World War. The mechanisms and organizations have nowadays become quite inadequate to deal with the economic and social challenges, foster development and human security, reduce inequalities and poverty, as well as coping with the resulting injustices and violence. Yet, the universal political and legal principles, as expressed in the UN Charter, the major conventions and resolutions dedicated to justice, human rights or economic and social progress, still provide a legitimate normative framework for global governance. They have been neglected by the powerful actors of neo-liberal globalization. Their reactivation is necessary if globalization and its governance are to serve the common good and operate to the benefit of humankind as a whole.

A fundamental tenet of this book is that this sort of legitimate global governance can only be brought about if it is based on statehood and the principles of democratic and participatory politics. This means that an institutional configuration is required in which public interest prevails over corporate interest, with the sovereign state recovering its role as the unrivalled mechanism for political and social integration, and with an effective trade-off between economic growth and social cohesion, as well as between the instrumental role of the market and the emancipating role of democracy.

Turning now to the contents of the book, Chapter 2, by Pierre de Senarclens, presents a historical account and critical assessment of the international institutional architecture – that is, the UN organizations and the system of multilateral co-operation, established in the immediate aftermath of the Second World War. He explains in some detail the reasons why this architecture has become an ineffective instrument, and outlines the conditions for reforming multilateralism. He then makes proposals for actions and policies in this respect, especially concerning the new shape and responsibilities to be entrusted to the UN, and, in particular, its highest decision-making body, the Security Council, by extending its membership and fields of intervention beyond collective security and peace-keeping to human security in economic, social and environmental areas, and to improving its rules and operative methods.

Ali Kazancigil devotes the following chapter to discussing the role of statehood in global governance, which he considers to be a crucial element in giving priority to the political and public dimensions at the expense of the currently predominant bias towards private interests and technocracy. He discusses the conditions for projecting, beyond national boundaries, certain elements of democracy and participation to politicize global governance. He considers that there are two ways of advancing towards better global governance: the first is the reformist approach, aimed at improving multilateralism and ending up with an enhanced version of the system of inter-state cooperation established after 1945. This, indeed, would already be a significant achievement, paving the way for further progress. However, historical experience, including the UN summit of September 2005, shows that a process that involves sovereign states exclusively cannot go very far in renewing global governance. The second approach is a more ambitious, transformative one. Sovereign states, assisted by the intergovernmental organizations, which are their instruments, will still be at the centre of it. This is unavoidable as states remain the major, although no longer the only, international actors. However, in addition to states and the powerful TNCs, other actors that participate in the transnational public space, such as NGOs and social and citizen movements, are also players in the process through appropriate, interrelated national, regional and transnational mechanisms. Thus, Ali Kazancigil formulates proposals for action and policy towards establishing such a transformative process in order to achieve an alternative governance of globalization.

In Chapter 4, Virgile Perret provides a critical analysis of the growing role of the private sector in the current global financial regulation. In his view, this is leading to an erosion of democratic principles at the national and transnational levels, as well as affecting the patterns of public–private interaction in most developing countries. The economic and financial order established after 1945 was based on the principle of public control. With the rise of globalization, this control was increasingly transferred to private or quasi-private authorities, including the privatization of global financial governance. He contends that there is also a political rationality underlying these developments, which reflect the struggle for comparative advantage between the states, as analysed by the regulationary theory of economics developed by French economists such as Michel Aglietta. Virgile Perret concludes his chapter by formulating proposals of reform in the international financial architecture.

In Chapter 5, Ngaire Woods, too, is concerned with the implications of private forms of global economic regulation and governance, particularly from the perspective of accountability. She analyses the growing role of corporations through arrangements such as the Global Compact, different sorts of NGOs and expert groups and networks that reinforce the technocratic nature of the current global governance. She then identifies the conditions for enhancing accountability and transparency in global governance and formulates proposal for action in this direction. She considers that states and intergovernmental organizations are important actors for inputting the much-needed public good element. She also notes the spaces that intergovernmental organizations (IGOs) such as the International Monetary Fund (IMF) and the World Bank have been trying to create in order to involve, admittedly to a limited degree, local and international NGOs in their operations.

Miguel Lengyel's argumentation in Chapter 6 relates in many ways to the two previous chapters as he discusses the public–private dynamics in the specific context of global trade regimes – the Uruguay Round and the current Doha Round – and their implications for development strategies. He links them to WTO's trade-related rule-making and discusses the gains and losses of the developing countries. His proposals for crafting new institutional arrangements towards more efficient global trade governance encompass the national and transnational levels through the regional level, which he considers to be very important. In this respect, his chapter relates to those of Louise Fawcett and Yves Berthelot.

The increasingly important roles of regionalism as a policy goal and regionalization as a trend in globalization and global governance is a fact. The next two chapters deal with this phenomenon, in complementary ways.

In Chapter 7, Louise Fawcett argues that the development of regional structures in different parts of the world, with the European model being the more advanced one, is a central element in the management of globalized world order. She takes a long, historical view of regionalism, exploring the issues of regional governance and its articulation with global governance in different experiments of regionalism, including obstacles they meet, such as sovereignty and hegemonic states. She then discusses the conditions for overcoming them.

Yves Berthelot, in Chapter 8, stresses the complementarities between the dynamics of regionalization and globalization. He analyses the dynamics of regionalization, and compares its strong and weak points with those of globalization. He makes a case for regional approaches within globalization in areas such as industrial development and global finance, and makes proposals for regional and global institutions, their interactions and articulation. In this respect, he assesses the experience of the UN Regional Commissions.

In Chapter 9, Yohan Ariffin critically addresses one of the most sensitive problematiques of global governance, which is the ambiguities and contradictions of the international regimes concerning the interrelations between environmental and developmental policies. He argues that such regulatory frameworks, which he analyses in a detailed and precise manner, are not particularly favourable to the least developed countries. The main reason for his scepticism is that the forces that shape the patterns of global environmental governance are overwhelmingly associated with corporate interests in the northern hemisphere. He concludes the chapter by outlining ways of resisting such dominant trends and makes some radical suggestions, such as abolishing the Global Environmental Facility (GEF).

Jean-Marc Coicaud deals with a central concern in Chapter 10 that is common to all the chapters of this volume – namely, can globalization and its governance be made legitimate and, if so, how? He argues that legitimacy requires coherence between the norms and agency in global governance. He considers that human rights, both as benchmarks for good global governance and as the normative framework for global policy-making, are the crucial elements in closing the gap between principle and practice and, thus, in legitimizing globalization and its governance.

In the concluding chapter, Pierre de Senarclens and Ali Kazancigil provide a summary of the problems analysed and the proposals formulated for action and policy-making towards better global governance in the chapters of this volume.

On behalf of all the book's authors, we would like to extend our gratitude to the institutions and colleagues who contributed in so many ways to this project. The United Nations University (UNU), UNESCO's Management of Social Transformations (MOST) Programme, and the University of Lausanne provided generous financial support. The three workshops at which the papers were discussed and revised took place at the Château de Coppet, on the shores of Lake Leman, Switzerland, the UNU Headquarters in Tokyo, Japan, and at St Catherine's College, Oxford University, UK. We owe a particular debt to the UNU, which included our project in its Peace and Governance Programme and has published the book under the imprint of the UNU Press. Our thanks also go to the Rector of the United Nations University, Professor Hans van Ginkel, the Publications Officer, Scott McQuade, and Yoshie Sawada of the Peace and Governance Programme, for their effective and friendly support throughout the project.

2

The United Nations as a social and economic regulator

Pierre de Senarclens

It is widely recognized that globalization entails an increasing inter-dependence between societies and therefore a growing states depen-dence on multilateral negotiations and decision-making processes at the international level. The volatility of capital and of monetary markets, the pollution of the global environment, international migration and pan-demics are some of the transnational issues that impact on the capacity of a state to promote its national interest autonomously. No government can pretend to fulfil its main security and welfare functions indepen-dently. People who enjoy security and social welfare usually benefit from good public policies that are the consequence of responsible gov-ernment, as well as of sophisticated regimes of regional integration and international cooperation. On the other hand, violent conflicts, mass dep-rivation, or even some of the worst aspects of environmental decay, are generally closely correlated with bad governance at national and interna-tional levels. This reality is not new, but globalization has precipitated a new demand for international regimes, or even for the devolution of the state's prerogatives to regional bodies.

Politics status quo and, in particular, power politics of course play a major role in the socio-economic problems of our time, as well as in every aspect of the dynamics of globalization. Nonetheless, most social scientists tend to agree that, contrary to the premises of orthodox realist thinking, intergovernmental organizations have their own internal dy-namics and political autonomy, which make them actors of world politics. They play an important role in international politics, in particular by con-

Regulating globalization: Critical approaches to global governance, de Senarclens and Kazancigil (eds), United Nations University Press, 2007, ISBN 978-92-808-1136-0

tributing to the definition of international norms, by producing data and analysis, by influencing state agenda and policies, by supporting regimes and by implementing operational programmes, while constantly interacting with the media and NGOs. In other words, the most obstinate problems created by the dynamics of globalization – in particular, social polarization and the misery of poor countries – does not result solely from the dynamics of power politics, but are also determined or shaped by the current structures and processes of international governance.

The role of the UN system is therefore at stake.[1] Although it plays a relatively minor role in influencing the major players of the globalization dynamic and is far from being the sole mechanism of intergovernmental cooperation, it remains the symbol of the international community. It offers an essential forum for multilateral diplomacy. It assumes an important role in the conception and promotion of international norms and in the quest for collective security. It is also a source of economic and technical assistance for numerous underdeveloped countries. There is obviously a sizeable gap between the principles and ideals of the UN system and its capacity to deliver. The inconsistency of the Security Council – that is to say, primarily of its permanent members – is obvious since the most terrible poverty abounds in many countries racked by civil wars or violent political conflicts. Moreover, the UN and its specialized agencies, which have an important mandate for promoting economic, social and cultural progress, are obviously not in a position to make a significant contribution in these areas. The tragedy of mass misery and social polarization at the international level, the rapid degradation of the natural environment, the growth of pandemics and humanitarian emergencies are some of the symptoms of the failure of the UN, not only as an institution representing its member states but also as a system of bureaucracies devoted to international cooperation in influencing and implementing development policies and strategies. It is even legitimate to wonder whether the UN and its specialized agencies are in any way adapted to the conditions of the twenty-first century.

The uncertainty, which weighs on the type and form of its commitments in promoting welfare and in fighting poverty, is not new. This chapter aims at putting within a historical context the structural limitations of the UN system as an institutional model for present global governance. It will attempt to elucidate the political and institutional obstacles that have initially weakened its capacity to fulfil its mandate in economic and social affairs. It will also show how the UN's original failures and structural problems affected the development of its system and engendered a singular type of multilateralism wherein rhetoric and symbolic politics play an immoderate role that affect its modus operandi, its capacity to deliver and its aptitude for reform. The chapter will conclude by proposing a new image of world governance that would be more adapted to the present challenges of globalization.[2]

Original institutional defects

The maintenance of peace was the main objective for the foundation of the United Nations Organization, and the Security Council was conceived as the principal organ of the new organization. However, the founders understood that the new international order could not be built on the traditional notion of collective security alone. They realized that governments could no longer successfully achieve their aims in the areas of security without strong international cooperation aimed at promoting economic progress and social welfare, although they were aware that the UN could not interfere directly in the social fabric of its member states. They intended to fight unemployment, and to promote social progress and better standards of living through greater freedom. It was widely recognized within the Western world that that peace and reconstruction, economic growth and development should be based on higher industrial and agricultural productivity, the expansion of international trade, free access to raw materials and the return to monetary stability. States should therefore play a decisive role in solving economic and social problems by adopting anti-cyclical policies aimed at fighting unemployment and recession, mastering the dynamics of the capitalist system, narrowing the gap between rich and poor, and striving to protect workers and their families from the risks of sickness, accidents, unemployment and old age. These goals and means were reflected in Article 55 of the United Nations Charter.

The architects of the post-war world were able to reach a formal consensus on these economic and social objectives, but they had no common practical vision of the institutional mechanisms or the strategies needed for their promotion and implementation. Following the hegemony of the Anglo-Saxon allies, the International Monetary Fund (IMF) and the World Bank were first created as a result of the Bretton Woods meetings in 1944. As these organizations were intended to deal with issues that were politically very sensitive, the US government managed to incorporate a voting right in their statutes that would ensure its control over their management and policies. Later on the UN and its other specialized agencies were established at the San Francisco Conference of 1945. Following a principle that transposed the model of parliamentary democracy to the international level, it was decided that every state would be represented within most of the organs of this new system on an equal footing.

A very complex structure of specialized agencies was therefore established, each having its own constitutional body, its own more or less precise sector-based mandate and its specific programmes aimed at promoting the welfare of member states. There were immediately clear cases where mandates overlapped – for example, between the UN itself and the International Labour Organization (ILO). Soon after the creation of the UN system, five regional economic commissions were established. Adding to an already very complex structure, further programmes – such as the United Nations Relief and Works Agency (UNWRA), United Nations High Commissioner for Refugees (UNHCR), the United Nations International Children's Emergency Fund (UNICEF) and, later, the United Nations Development Programme (UNDP) – were set up and endowed with separate boards, each developing its own programmes and budgets independently of the principal organs and all competing for the scarce financial resources provided by the rich countries.[3] Moreover the budgetary resources of the UN differed greatly from those of the Bretton Woods institutions, whose assets came from industrialized countries and the financial market. Although the Economic and Social Council (ECOSOC) was theoretically in charge of coordinating this area, it never received the necessary political and financial support to do so. Its mandate quickly became unclear and even impossible to fulfil, especially where relations with the General Assembly and the other specialized agencies were concerned. From 1948 onwards, the issue of coordination among the different parts of the system and the need to concentrate its resources were questions frequently raised by member states. In its resolution 310 (IV), the General Assembly complained of "the proliferation of activities and the multiplicity of programmes". It underlined that "the resulting excessive numbers of sessions and meetings as well as the creation of subsidiary organs" were placing a severe burden on the human resources of member states (Taylor, 2000: 106–7). The specialized agencies developed their own intellectual traditions and corporative logic. This structure was not simply a hindrance to coherent development actions; it also involved the consumption of a considerable amount of human and material resources. The UN system was therefore not designed to engage in coherent action on a large scale, and this institutional weakness was bound to affect its capacity to design and contribute to the implementation of coherent strategies in the socio-economic field.

Politics and propaganda

The difficulty of achieving coherence came not only from institutional constraints but also from political obstacles. As a matter of fact, the diversity of national interests and the determination of each state to preserve its sovereignty largely explain this particular architecture of governance of socio- economic matters. The Cold War was not only responsible for the breakdown of collective security but also contributed to the failure of the UN in the field of economic cooperation and development. The Marshall Plan was launched outside the UN, and economic aid thus became an aspect of defence strategy. It manifested the will of the United States to rebuild a liberal European economy and to integrate this project into a worldwide struggle against the threat from the Soviet Union and the growth of communism. The establishment of the Organization for European Economic Cooperation (OEEC), the Council of Europe and, subsequently, the European Community (EC) also reflected this strategy. These new institutions gave their own impetus to the development of the welfare state based on a respect for political pluralism and the rule of law and human rights, leading to the rapid economic, social and cultural progress of Western Europe, and were therefore bound to marginalize the UN system. At the same time, and especially after the failure of the International Trade Organization (ITO) in the American Congress, trade negotiations were also pursued outside the UN system, essentially between highly industrialized capitalist countries. With the Marshall Plan and the growing influence of the Bretton Woods institutes (BWIs), in particular the World Bank and the General Agreement on Tariffs and Trade (GATT), the most significant aspects of the international political economy escaped the orbit of the UN.

It soon became evident that the USA and its allies rejected the idea of using the UN as an effective instrument of cooperation. They could not accept its cumbersome decision-making process and the eventuality of being overruled by a majority of weak and often undemocratic states. For these reasons, the UN system was kept at a distance from the multilateral mechanisms, and this enabled the rich industrialized states to harmonize and implement their socio-economic policies. More specifically, the UN remained on the sidelines of negotiations and decisions relating to major monetary, financial and commercial issues. In addition, the upsurge of McCarthyism in the USA meant that the ideal of an independent, international, public function lost ground.

These political constraints were the most serious obstacles in the effective pursuit of collective security and universal social welfare. The UN became the centre of a very particular multilateral diplomacy whose principal function was to give government representatives an opportunity to deliberate, interact on a personal level, ritualize through complicated procedures and ceremonials the manifestation of their state sovereignty, maintain through rhetoric and propaganda their own national authority and their international legitimacy, find ways and means to play out their conflict on a symbolic level, and also to benefit occasionally from the programme resources allocated by the system.

The promotion of liberal values

This very particular form of multilateralism, however, did not prevent the UN and its specialized agencies from carrying out extremely valuable work on the definition and promotion of legal norms. They were the custodians of the liberal principles and ideals of the UN Charter and were legitimized to defend, promote and interpret these norms. Their secretariats were at that time largely dominated by the Western world. Moreover representatives of the USA and its allies had a pre-eminent influence on the agenda and deliberations of the UN system. This was particularly true in the field of human rights. The adoption of the Universal Declaration of Human Rights by the General Assembly on 10 December 1948 was a landmark in the history of humanity. It reflected an extremely progressive definition of human rights. States, in association with intergovernmental organizations, were required not only to protect individual liberty, but also to promote and implement a variety of economic, social and cultural rights. From then on the Universal Declaration established the moral and legal standards by which to judge political legitimacy, influencing national legislation and contributing to customary international law. It was also in 1948 that the United Nations adopted the Convention on the Prevention and Punishment of the Crime of Genocide. During the following years it prepared the two Covenants on Human Rights, which were adopted by the General Assembly in 1966 and which came into force ten years later.

While the first debates at ECOSOC and the UN General Assembly were initially devoted to economic and social issues of the industrialized states and to their reconstruction needs, the development of "backward" countries was not long in taking centre stage among the concerns of the UN. As early as 1946, the Temporary Social Commission on Social Affairs stated:

At least half the peoples of the world are living, by no fault of their own, under such poor and inadequate conditions that they cannot, out of their own scarce resources, achieve decent standards of living. The deep gulfs existing between the standards of living of different nations and peoples are, in the opinion of the Commission, a main source of international discontent, unrest, crisis and are causes of wars ultimately endangering and devastating countries of high as well as low standards of living. (Senarclens, 1988: 90–1)

The theme of the widening gap between the developed and the less developed countries, linked to that of the growing interdependence between the different parts of the world, appeared in the very first documents about development and technical assistance produced by the UN Secretariat. The gravity of the problem and its alarming nature were stressed, as well as the challenges it posed to the international community. Variations on this theme multiplied over the following years.

Development became a major issue in the ideological and political battles of the Cold War. It was the catchword for promoting Western policies and strategies towards the poor countries of the southern hemisphere, colonial dependencies and newly independent countries. It was seen as a global process aimed at transforming the whole world along the path followed by the industrially advanced societies and largely understood as the spreading of a Western "way of life" to the rest of the world. This political project was supposed to resolve the contradictions between existing imperial structures and the principle of self-determination and between archaism and modernity. Ideas about development put forward by the UN reflected the political, social and cultural concepts, which prevailed in Anglo-Saxon academic circles or among the civil servants of progressive Western countries. It was thought that late industrialization required a significant degree of government intervention and therefore the creation of a modern state with an effective administration. It necessitated agrarian reform, planning and reduction of social inequalities. It was obviously impossible to count on the invisible hand of the market to accomplish this process. In the "backward" regions, the economy was based on agriculture. Productivity was low, conditions of health and hygiene were deplorable, illiteracy widespread, and the low level of education and technical training made progress almost impossible.

In 1949, during his inaugural speech, President Truman launched his famous Point IV Program, a technical assistance project for underdeveloped countries. It aspired to show the way to a future of "abundance and liberty". The UN followed suit. In May 1949, the Secretariat published a new report entitled *Technical Assistance for Economic Development.* It laid down some of the basic principles of UN multilateral aid. It stated that development in each country must grow from that country's particular needs, desires and potentialities. It also underlined that technical assistance was intended to help the underdeveloped countries to help themselves. This purpose could not be achieved unless the countries concerned were themselves willing to take vigorous action to establish the internal conditions upon which sound development depended. As a result of President Truman's initiative, ECOSOC established in August 1949 the Expanded Programme of Technical Assistance (EPTA). It involved all the specialized agencies in these assistance programmes, particularly the International Labour Organization (ILO), the Food and Agriculture Organization (FAO), the World Health Organization (WHO) and bodies such as the Regional Economic Commissions and UNICEF. It remained grossly under-financed.

It was also thought that material progress would encourage the blossoming of the cultural and institutional conditions necessary for development. In order to achieve "conditions of stability and well-being", great importance was attached to "the modernization of production methods", which meant, above all, "bringing the tools of modern technology within the reach of all the people". In order to achieve this, it was necessary to ensure a "rational, effective and comprehensive utilization of labour, tools, technical means, energy and capital": industrialization was to play a decisive role in this process. No issue turned up more frequently in the work of the UN than the ability of science and technology to leapfrog over the classic stages of development and to move from backwardness to modernity. The need for sociocultural transformation explains the role attributed to experts in the development process. The notion of technical assistance was based on the assumption of a universal paradigm, of an economic, social, cultural and institutional norm, applicable to all peoples on earth. The experts replaced the missionaries of former times with the aim of achieving the potential of the newly independent states. They were going "on mission". They were sent "into the field". They contributed to "realizing the potential" of the countries concerned. The language of the official reports on assistance was infused by the messianic ideals. The projects were diverse. They included advice given to governments for making an inventory of their resources, for helping them to create a "good administration", for setting up legislative structures, employment services, teaching and public health systems, agricultural programmes or the management of civil aviation. They involved the sending out of an army of technicians for training purposes and the allocation of fellowships. As technical assistance demanded significant social, cultural and institutional changes in the countries concerned, it became obvious that the application of these "rational" and "technical" norms had political implications. The emphasis was on the institutional processes, the requirements of a rationalist and materialistic culture, the values and educational norms that favour the progress of science and technology and the role of the public authorities.

In fact, the technical assistance projects of the UN always remained poorly funded: in 1954, they were mostly financed by voluntary contributions that amounted to US$15 million. This was a far cry from the approximately US$14 billion invested in Europe under the Marshall Plan. Development assistance was indeed more an ingredient of the rhetoric of the "Free World" than a reality. Certain voices were raised among the Latin American and Asian representatives contesting the structures of international trade and requesting large amounts of economic aid. In 1949, M.K. Rao submitted to the Sub-Commission on Economic Development a project to create a UN Administration for Economic Development. In 1952, the representative of Chile, Hernan Santa Cruz, asked the General Assembly to create a Development Fund but encountered the opposition of the US government who had no intention of supporting the UN's work in economic and social development. It refused to listen to any discussion about such a fund knowing that it would have to bear most of its financial burden. The US government preferred to emphasize the need to create a climate favourable to private investment in the developing countries and therefore favoured the mechanisms of Bretton Woods, which it controlled. However, the World Bank, which drew most of its resources from the financial market, had been rather slow in espousing the development agenda. Most of its projects were in infrastructure. The Bank definitely favoured private over public projects and it was not concerned with social issues (Kapur, 1997: 9). It took the US government several years to "kill" the project for a Development Fund, which was finally buried in 1957 after numerous studies, expert committees and UN resolutions. Nevertheless, in 1958 the United States did not oppose the creation of the United Nation Special Funds, with some resources at its disposal to finance pre-investment activities. In 1965, this programme was amalgamated with the Technical Assistance Programme to form the UNDP (Senarclens, 1988: 98–99).

The work of the UN Secretariat in economic and social affairs has also carried weight. It took the form of statistical data, analyses, periodical reports and reviews and publications dealing with all aspects of the economic and social development of humanity. This work tended towards the promotion of new ideas in the legal, social and economic fields, and also towards the creation of institutions which would serve to make these ideas a reality. It benefited from the advice of economists such as Hans Singer, Gunnar Myrdal, Raoul Prebisch and Philippe de Seynes. It managed to produce a series of excellent reports, including *The Economic Development of Latin America and Its Principal Problems* (1948), *National and International Measures for Full employment* (1949), *Measures for International Economic Stability* (1951), *Measures for the Economic Development of Under-Developed Countries* (1951). This last report had the benefit of advice from renowned economists, among them two future Nobel Laureates: Arthur Lewis and Theodore W. Schultz. UN documents of this period stressed over and over again the importance of government stability, the maintenance of public order and respect for the law. The organization strongly insisted on the structural obstacles to be overcome by underdeveloped countries in the face of market dynamics.

It underlined the necessity to help them to counter the degradation of their terms of trade. The reports called for price stabilization for commodities and the mobilization of public development assistance in order to increase the agricultural productivity of underdeveloped countries and to encourage their industrialization. From its origins in 1949, under the leadership of Prebisch, the Economic Commission for Latin America (ECLA) promoted a provocative analysis of the structural obstacles to the development of capitalist countries, insisting on the degradation of their terms of trade.

The contestation of the Third World

National independence movements and the arrival of newly independent states at the forefront of international politics increased the UN concern about development. In the 1960s the General Assembly was more than ever an instrument of the propaganda war between the "free world" and the Soviet bloc. At a time when the balance of terror forced the superpowers to play out their conflicts in Third World countries, and while the gulf between the industrialized and the developing countries was growing, it was widely felt at the UN that much greater effort would be needed to assist the newly independent and rebellious nations. President Kennedy launched the Alliance for Progress project in Latin America, which was soon reinforced by the Peace Corps. It was mainly a question of halting the advance of "Castroism" south of the Rio Grande and promoting economic and social change, democracy and the growth of the multinational corporations. On 9 December 1961, again on the initiative of President Kennedy, the General Assembly proclaimed the period 1960–70 to be the First Development Decade. The resolution proclaiming this Decade was strongly imbued with the ideas that were in vogue in the American administration at the time. Development, as conceived by the United States and its allies, was clearly associated with an economic growth primarily based on market expansion and foreign direct investments. The resolution especially recommended states "to adopt measures which will stimulate the flow of private investment capital for economic development", and therefore to create a climate favourable to the expansion of the capitalist system. However, it also supported the need to establish "well conceived and integrated country plans". This proposition was consonant with the technocratic ideas, fashionable at that time, both in the governments of the Third World and in those of the industrialized countries. Each country was supposed to attain, as a minimum aim, an annual increase in GDP of 5 per cent by the end of the Decade. This was to be made possible through international trade, as well as with the support of foreign capital, both private and public. This resolution assigned the same importance as before to the traditional objectives of technical assistance: eradication of illiteracy, hunger and disease – conditions "which seriously afflict the productivity (*sic*) of the people of the less developed countries". As before, the economic policies that really affected development were being worked out on the fringes of the UN and its specialized agencies, particularly by the IMF, the World Bank and GATT, and within the regional institutions for economic and political cooperation, such as OECD and the European Economic Community (EEC). The UNDP's resources increased fairly regularly, but towards the middle of the 1960s its budget was still only US$50 million. The United States and its allies were also investing more in their own bilateral assistance, which brought them obvious economic and political benefits, than in support for multilateral UN projects.

The Western hegemony within the UN was shaken in the 1960s by the admission of new member states coming mostly from Third World countries. The process of decolonization considerably enlarged the General Assembly with new states whose socio-economic foundations were shaky and whose rulers had few inclinations towards Western concepts of law and politics. These changes did not improve the climate of UN meetings, or those of the specialized agencies. In the debates of the ECOSOC and of the Second Committee of the General Assembly, there were growing arguments against development strategies based upon liberal philosophies. The developing countries were always more vocal in requesting significant international structural changes to facilitate their industrialization and, in particular, measures to improve their terms of trade. These demands gave rise to the United Nations Conference on Trade and Development (UNCTAD) held in Geneva from 23 March to 16 June 1964, and then to the creation of a permanent UNCTAD organization. Its agenda was, to a great extent, the work of the Argentine economist, Raül Prebish, former Secretary-General of ECLA and it was to dominate more or less the UN's future agenda for development. Prebish emphasized the adverse effects of the long-running deterioration of the terms of trade between the "centre" and the "periphery". The International Development Strategy proclaimed by the General Assembly on 24 October 1972 took up the concerns of Third World countries, the so-called Group of 77, as expressed in UNCTAD, such as international agreements on trade in raw materials, constitution of regulatory stocks, together with the establishment of a preferential system for exports from developing countries.

From this time on, the General Assembly played a dominant part in the policy orientation of the resolutions and programmes of the UN and it firmly adopted a Third World point of view. There were not only impassioned attacks on imperialist Western structures by delegates from "non-aligned" countries, but also the persistent polemics of Soviet propaganda with regard to the United States and its allies. At the beginning of 1974, during the extraordinary session of the General Assembly, representatives of the Third World thought that the day of reckoning had come when they managed, with the support of the socialist countries, to pass a major resolution on the New International Economic Order (NIEO). This resolution, which reflected the growing influence of the oil-producing countries following the 1973 war in the Middle East, was a new departure from the mainstream liberal conception of development that had previously dominated the agenda of the UN. It was very much in line with an authoritarian conception of the state and full of recriminations against imperialism and structural dependency that prevented the development of Third World countries.

The debates and resolutions of the UN system as a whole were from now on regularly confronted with all sorts of broader political issues, such as the elimination of colonialism, the occupation of foreign territories, Zionism, apartheid and racial discrimination, which representatives of the Western world did not consider to be directly relevant to progress in the matters being discussed. The General Assembly and its subsidiary organs, such as ECOSOC, became endless talking shops used by the representatives of member states to indulge in a Manichean propaganda war. Most of the specialized agencies followed the same trend.

The lack of Western support, coupled with a growing ideological heterogeneity in the UN, resulted in an increasing tendency to turn away from functional activities and encouraged governments to invest more than ever in a symbolic and discursive role at the UN. Without the financial resources needed to fulfil their mandate, the UN and its specialized agencies fast became a rather rigid bureaucracy with little ability to change. This inertia was made worse by the constraints inherent in the inequitable geographical distribution, which was the basis for recruitment policies in the various secretariats. The number, the length and the confusion of their resolutions increased, and the same discourses and resolutions were repeated within the different agencies. In 1974, M. de Guiringaud, the French foreign minister, warned the General Assembly "of the risk of passing so many resolutions, with little hope of being implemented, ever longer, repeating themselves, dealing with the same subjects in quasi similar terms, while being practically unreadable and often not read, even by those who have supported them" (Senarclens, 1988: 148). In 1975, the General Assembly adopted 180 resolutions. Most of the texts were long, incoherent, badly structured and repetitive. In the following years, the number of resolutions continued to increase, reaching 252 in 1982. This development went hand in hand with a rise in the production of reports on all possible socio-economic issues. What was then perceived within the so-called Western world as the "politicization of the UN" eroded its capacity to adhere to the liberal principles of the Charter and led to a process of bureaucratic stultification. Irrelevance calls for irrelevance. A growing part of diplomatic activity within the UN boiled down to trying to get the presidency of a committee or a meeting, or pushing for the appointment of a national of a given state within the secretariat.

The UN Secretariat managed, nevertheless, to organize a number of world conferences, preceded by regional and expert meetings – such as the Stockholm conference on the environment (1972), the Rome conference on nutrition (1992), the Bucharest conference on population (1974) and the Mexico conference on women (1975). Their preparation mobilized governments, experts and the media and therefore contributed to raising awareness of, and focusing world opinion on, major social issues and the political challenges they represented. However, their final resolutions and plans of action lacked coherence and precision and their adoption very rarely reflected a common political will on the part of member states to implement their own rhetorical commitments.

From NIEO to neoliberalism

Towards the end of the 1970s, Western governments took up the theme of human rights and humanitarian values and so launched within the UN system, as in other fora, their ideological attack on repressive states. During his administration (1977–81), President Carter included the promotion of human rights as an important aspect of his foreign policy, more particularly in US relations with the Soviet Union and with Latin America. Margaret Thatcher's appointment as Prime Minister of the UK, followed shortly by the election of Ronald Reagan as President of the United States, were to have important repercussions on the UN, just as they would have on world politics. Their arrival on the international scene amounted to a paradigm shift since they exploited the crisis of the welfare state and the dire effect of authoritarian and tyrannical governments in the southern hemisphere that were undermining the ideological concepts which had influenced development strategies since the end of World War II. Under the spell of the new American hegemony, states were invited to downscale social programmes and to promote the self-regulatory functions of the market. In this context, public development aid lost ground, because it was associated with the type of government intervention that was supposed to impede market dynamics. From then on, the expansion of the market and foreign direct investments tended to be seen by most OECD countries as the best instrument to promote economic growth and social progress. Donor countries were inclined to abandon post-war development strategies.

The debt crisis that engulfed most of Latin American and African countries favoured the promotion of neo-liberal ideology and programmes in the southern hemisphere. It was managed by the BWI whose structural adjustment programmes encouraged the developing countries to embrace "market forces". In return for new loans, which allowed them to service their debt, governments concerned were encouraged to undertake stabilization measures and structural adjustments. In accepting these recommendations they agreed to limit their budget deficits and therefore to freeze social expenditure, including that on health and education. They were to follow sound macro-economic policies and to support the easing of restrictions on trade and the deregulation of capital markets. They had to privatize services and state-controlled enterprises and to repeal various protective measures, which applied to local industries. They modified national laws on foreign investment, liberalized those concerning the repatriation of capital, profit and dividends by abolishing all discriminatory measures in these areas. They offered multinational corporations much better conditions for investment and competition than had been the case previously.

This new power shift, as well as the political and ideological climate of the 1980s, naturally affected the UN system. It was in this context that the US government began to distance itself further from the UN system. In 1983, it decided to leave UNESCO, followed shortly by the UK. Moreover, the US started delaying payment of its contributions to the regular UN budget as a lever to pressurize the organization to follow American ideological positions. The secretariats had no choice but to reflect the dominant liberal thinking of the OECD countries. From then on, all the reports, studies and statistics produced by the UN, with the help of consultants and Anglo-Saxon academic circles, showed that the neo-classical paradigm was, without doubt, the right one. There was very little room for dissenting voices, although the hegemony of these liberal conceptions did not prevent UNCTAD from expressing criticism of the BWI's stabilization and structural adjustment programmes, stressing in particular the immense obstacles, facing the Least Developed Countries (LDCs) in their efforts to join a world market economy. Its annual *Trade and Development Reports* became somewhat critical of the structural obstacles affecting the developing countries. In 1987 UNICEF published *Adjustment with a Human Face* which did not contest the fundamental market orientation of the BWI, but requested that it also took account of the need to meet the vital needs of the people. The report underlined that adjustment policies had resulted in worsening health among the poor, with rising malnutrition and falling school attendance.

The illusory consensus on poverty

The crumbling of the Soviet Empire and the liberalization of the Chinese economy contributed to the expansion of globalization. From then on it became almost impossible to contest the dynamic and, indeed, the benefits of market forces. If the end of the Cold War opened an opportunity to revitalize the role of the Security Council, it did not enhance the effective role of the UN in economic and social matters. Monetary, financial and trade negotiations and policies that had a decisive effect on global economic issues – on the fate of developing countries in particular – continued to be negotiated within more restricted institutional fora such as the G7, the Bretton Woods institutions, the OECD and the major players of the WTO.

However, the end of the Cold War favoured the UN as an agenda-setting institution whose role was to promote liberal values and democratic regimes and, in the 1990s, the UN organized a series of important world conferences on specific socio-economic issues – in particular, on the environment, human rights, social development, habitat, food and nutrition, and the status of women. The final resolutions of these conferences called for important action programmes. In 1992, UNDP launched its *Human Development* reports which reformulated the notion of the basic needs that the ILO had promoted in the 1970s. It promoted indicators of human development, such as liberty, gender equity and human rights and social justice. It emphasized the benefits of a healthy and well-educated population and the advantages of good national governance. The expansion of private enterprises and of communication and information technologies were supposed to go hand in hand with individualism, utilitarian profit-driven behaviour and the wide-ranging acceptance of the human development indicators, which prevailed in the industrialized countries. While supporting the neo-classical approach of the Bretton Woods institutions, the UNDP promoted a discourse on the relationship between human rights and socio-economic progress. It was not always very precise in defining the international policies and strategies to be followed in order to reach these objectives, although the *Human Development Report 2005* courageously denounced the "hypocrisy and double standards" that characterized the rules-based multilateral trade system, underlining that the growth of international trade had brought little profit to the majorities of countries for which "the globalization story is one of divergence and marginalization" (UNDP, 2005: 116). Today, most of the UNDP operational engagement is in the field of governance aimed at creating a political and normative environment favourable to socio-economic progress in the developing countries.

The industrialized countries have remained adamant in their support of policies that would redress the structural international obstacles to development and in their determination to provide the material assistance necessary to fight mass poverty. In fact, the resources of the UN and its specialized agencies for development assistance tended to decrease in the 1990s and the UNDP budget also declined. At a time when budgetary restrictions affected public development aid, OECD governments were subcontracting their aid policies to NGOs, which received an increasing share of these resources. NGOs were considered to be more efficient for aid purposes than intergovernmental organizations as they were supposed to have only minimal running costs while able to call on the services of dedicated personnel, full of common sense and goodwill. Most of the UN agencies were compelled to cope with a lack of funding and so more and more they sought the help of business circles and the big North American foundations, adopting new promotional methods by, for example, calling on personalities from the media, such as film stars, to obtain the funds they so badly needed. In 1999 the Secretary-General launched the idea of a UN–business partnership, the so-called "global compact", aimed at receiving support from multinational corporations for the protection of internationally proclaimed human rights, together with protection of the environment and the transfer of technologies, but at the risk of allowing them undue influence over the UN's social agenda.

As the dynamics of globalization tended to increase the marginalization of the so-called least developed countries and an escalation of civil wars, Western governments and public opinion manifested a tendency to see the problems of the poor countries of the southern hemisphere through the looking-glass of charity. A growing part of Overseas Development Aid (ODA) was directed towards humanitarian objectives: between 1990 and 2000, the amount of official humanitarian assistance nearly tripled to become more than 10 per cent of ODA. The OECD countries provided billions of dollars in humanitarian aid, and the agencies that implemented their programmes injected more money into Africa than the World Bank (Macrae, 2002: 9). UNDP and UNICEF were devoting a growing part of their operational capacity to them. The UNHCR budget increased, with the OECD countries financing 97 per cent of it. This commitment was made within the framework of a security policy that was intended to prevent refugees from flooding into Europe, and other destabilizing migratory movements. It also served to contain the flood of Kurdish refugees into Turkey in 1992, and to limit population displacement during the civil war in Yugoslavia. At the same time, humanitarian assistance was increasingly politicized as it became an integral part of peacekeeping or peacebuilding operations and was simply part and parcel of Western efforts to change the economic and social policies of the least developed countries. In Kosovo, as in Afghanistan and in parts of Africa, the UNHCR's operations were broadly influenced by the political choices of the US and its allies.

In 2000, the 55th session of the General Assembly produced a consensus on a set of ambitious social and humanitarian goals with the proclamation of the Millennium Development Goals (MDGs). On this occasion, 147 heads of state and government, together with the representatives of all the member states, adopted a resolution requesting the UN to reduce by half, in the following 15 years, the proportion of the world population living on less than a dollar a day, as well as the number of people going hungry and without access to clean drinking water. They also made a commitment that all children should be able to finish primary school, and that girls and boys should have equal access to all levels of education. They promised to reduce the mortality rate among children under five by 75 per cent, to eradicate or halt the HIV/AIDS epidemic, malaria and other pandemic illnesses, and to improve, by the year 2020, the lives of at least 100 million people existing below the poverty line. In the Millennium Declaration, and in the subsequent plan for its implementation proposed by the Secretary-General, the importance of a global approach and a coherent strategy for the whole of the UN system was reaffirmed.

This vast programme had the merit of establishing precise targets, but the question remained as to how to define a coherent strategy to reach them and, in particular, what was the specific role of states, markets and intergovernmental organizations in this development process. The MDGs were much more focused on the symptoms of mass misery than on the development strategy that would help to diminish or eradicate them. In addition, the UN Secretary-General made it clear that none of the objectives laid out in this Declaration could be met without a significant increase in resources (A/56/326). In 2002, at the UN conference on development in Monterrey, Mexico, the United States and their allies agreed to increase their development aid.

Although the amount of Overseas Development Aid is presently rising, the implementation of these UN objectives is most uncertain. As in the past, the mechanisms of global governance remain sectorialized and highly detrimental to most developing countries. The Doha Round (2001) of negotiations linking the multilateral cooperation on trade with development issues, has been very slow in delivering its promises. Trade barriers detrimental to poor countries have not been reduced while, at the same time, agricultural subsidies have increased and commodity prices have further declined. Moreover "rich countries have aggressively pursued rules on investment, services and intellectual property that threaten to reinforce global inequalities" (UNDP, 2005: 113–14). The

UN system continues to have a wide range of economic and social functions, without sufficient resources to carry them out. From time to time, it mobilizes human and material resources to aid victims of war, famine or natural disasters and to alleviate their suffering. Some of its agencies have specific functional mandates – for example, in the areas of population, health, food and agriculture – and their secretariats handle an enormous expertise that serves universal values and international legal norms but, sadly, these sector-based commitments do not form part of a consistent overall strategy for development. Today, about 6.5 per cent of development aid from the OECD countries is channelled via the UN system. The UNDP's regular budget of around US$800 million does not compare favourably with the hundreds of billions of dollars which the American Congress and the European Union committed in 2003 for war, reconstruction and humanitarian aid in Iraq.

Education has remained a good example of the gap between rhetoric and reality. The number of children out of school is estimated today at about 115 million, but in addition there are a very large number of dropouts and there is no way of knowing how many children leave school without learning to read, write or count. A recent report of the Joint Inspection Unit of the UN, written by Doris Bertrand, comes to the conclusion that 50 per cent of children in the developing countries are "out of education". In recent decades there have been a large number of regional and international conferences resulting in ambitious plans of action that have never been implemented. Again in 1990, UNESCO, UNICEF, UNDP, UNFPA (United Nations Fund for Population Activities) and the World Bank convened a world conference on Education for All. The resulting action plan predicted that in the following decade all school-age children and adults would receive basic functional education. This commitment was reaffirmed in April 2002 at the World Education Forum in Dakar, where even more precise and targeted objectives were fixed for the following 15 years. And yet UNESCO's Approved Programme and Budget for 2002–2004 provides US$46,746 million for education, to which must be added an equivalent amount for staff costs. UNICEF, for its part, spent US$201 million on girls' education in 2002. The World Bank lending for education in 2002 amounted to US$1,384 million. It has twelve times more financial resources for education than UNESCO and education represents 7 per cent of bank loans (Bertrand, 2003: 14).

Reform: the past and future of an illusion

International society today is faced with a variety of circumstances that are very different from those which determined the creation of the UN and its specialized agencies. One has to recognize that the UN system has become increasingly irrelevant to face the major challenges of our time. In addition to the problems created by the enormous mass of poor, illiterate and insecure people suffering from inadequate health provisions, some of the major contemporary challenges of global governance include the rapid degradation of the natural environment, recurrent natural disasters, the growing importance of international migrations, unemployment and under-employment, the spread of major pandemics (in particular HIV/AIDS), the significant number of "failed" or fragile states, civil wars, minorities struggling for autonomy or independence, and criminal and terrorist networks. Although the various UN bodies still participate in the development of international order by promoting universal principles and values, promoting international law, analysing socio-economic world problems and setting the agendas for important international negotiations, they bring only a small contribution to the most urgent needs of the weak and poor states. The *raison d'être* of several UN agencies, funds and programmes has run out of steam, to a great extent, because most governments are having to seek recourse in other bodies, sometimes private, to carry out the tasks originally entrusted to these organization.

The reform of the UN has been on the agenda of the General Assembly for a long time, although the most recent debate has been concerned mainly with the Security Council. The US government has been particularly vocal, regularly denouncing the ossified structure of the UN and requesting administrative reforms along the lines of new public management. It has called for improved supervision of budgetary resources, the establishment of a "result-based budgeting", a better concentration of programmes, the discontinuation of inefficient ones, and a sunset provision for ongoing projects. It would be laborious to enumerate and comment on all the different proposals that have been made on the reform of the UN system in recent years. From the 1970s onwards, the number of studies and reports dealing with reform – coming from the Secretariat, governments, private institutions and academic circles – has greatly increased. All these proposals have been aimed at strengthening the UN's capacity for action in social and economic matters by improving the coherence among the programmes of the specialized agencies and by rationalizing the decision-making process of the UN system. Another concern, which has often been expressed within the different proposals, is how to avoid the duplication of debates and resolutions in the General Assembly, ECOSOC, UNCTAD and in the specialized agencies. Western governments have regularly complained that the same questions have been raised year after year within the General Assembly and that they have also appeared on the agendas of different bodies of the UN. The idea of establishing an Economic and Social Security Council was expressed by Maurice Bertrand in 1995 and reiterated several times in different reform proposals, with the aim of creating at ministerial level a restricted forum for debate on the major questions affecting international economic cooperation.

In 1997, the Secretary-General put forward new proposals for improving coordination between funds and programmes of the UN. To this end, the United Nations Development Group (UNDG) was established as a coordinating mechanism between the UNDP, UNFPA, UNICEF and the World Food Programme (WFP). In addition, the coordination of activities among the various specialized agencies, and between them and the BWI, has been enhanced in order to ensure the coherence of aid programmes for the developing countries. In practice, this has given a new lead to the Bretton Woods Institutions in promoting, through the Poverty Reduction Strategy Papers (PRSPs), their specific development agenda within the most vulnerable and indebted countries, since the most endowed organizations call the tune. However, the General Assembly has consistently stalled when confronted with the necessity of tackling more structural reform and the 60th session of the General Assembly closed without the heads of states and governments finding a consensus on these necessary institutional changes.

In spite of this failure, nobody can dispute the fact that the UN structural problems tend to erode its capacity of being an effective instrument of international cooperation. In 2004, the Report of the Secretary-General's High-Level Panel, *A More Secure World*, criticized the General Assembly by asserting that "Its norm-making capacity is often squandered on debates about minutiae or thematic topics outpaced by real-world events. Its inability to reach closure on issues undermines its relevance. An unwieldy and static agenda leads to repetitive debates" (A/59/565). The Secretary-General has also referred to the unsatisfactory way in which the General Assembly works,

> In the General Assembly, where all states are represented on the basis of sovereign equality, their sheer number has helped produce an agenda crowded with items that either overlap or are of interest to only few states. Repetitive and sterile debates crowd out the items that really matter. Decisions can often be reached only on a lowest-common-denominator basis and, once reached, command little or no attention beyond the confines of the General Assembly Chamber (A/58/323).

The Secretary-General recently pointed out that the number of meetings held under the auspices of the different organs of the UN has dramatically increased in recent years. He also stressed that there had been an "excessive" number of official reports. In 2000–2001 there were

15,484 meetings to which nearly 6,000 official reports were submitted. The Secretariat, as well as diplomats, is overburdened by this trend. He went on to say that "Member states, especially the small countries, find it difficult to cope with the mountains of paper that need to be absorbed and acted upon. The Secretariat itself is struggling to keep abreast of the growing number of reports, requested by the various intergovernmental bodies" (A/57/387).

Governments frequently add to the confusion in the various UN programmes by adopting, at major international conferences, the type of blanket resolutions which may be used to justify almost any programme. Since its foundation, the system has never stopped expanding, with the multiplication of all sorts of committees and sub-committees, the development of new administrative structures including programmes, funds and different organizations. Each major conference sees the birth of new commissions (the latest being the Peace Building Commission established by the World Summit on the occasion of the 60th anniversary of the UN), and, consequently, the setting up of new administrative structures, the proliferation of which is subsequently roundly condemned by these same governments responsible for this expansion. The latest example of this institutional incoherence is the fight against HIV/AIDS. The Joint United Nations Programme on HIV and AIDS, UNAIDS, which was recently established, has been given responsibilities which should normally fall within the framework of the WHO mandate. Subsequently, the Global Fund, dedicated to the same goals, has been created outside the UN. The particular procedures, rhetoric and rituals of the UN, the incessant reproduction of formalistic meetings, redundant reports and repetitive innocuous resolutions entailed, result in the continuous proliferation of new bodies. In the meantime, as it has been suggested, key negotiations on trade, finance and monetary policies take place among a very limited number of countries whose representatives have a recognized expertise in the subject matter under consideration.

This negative trend is largely due to the size and heterogeneity of its instances. Contrary to a widespread myth, the decision-making process within the UN system does not reflect an equal and universal representation of "international society" since it grants in principle the same procedural rights to Vanuatu and Monaco as it does to India and China. In more restricted bodies, such as the ECOSOC or the Executive Board of Specialized Agencies, the process of deliberation and decision-making is also flawed by the large number of states represented on them. Regulatory procedures in the UN and its specialized agencies are often erratic. The appointment, or renewal of appointment, of heads of agencies, funds and programmes are essentially politically motivated. Their constitutive bodies have difficulty in supervising their budgets and programmes and are even less able to contribute substantially to the definition of these programmes. The Fifth Committee of the General Assembly, which is supposed to supervise administrative and budgetary matters, is widely considered as part and parcel of the problems to be solved in this respect. This criticism of the General Assembly applies equally to many other constitutive bodies of the UN system. The ECOSOC was supposed to be the principal UN organ for coordinating humanitarian and development decisions and programmes within the system as a whole, but it has never been able to fulfil this mandate. The tripling of its original composition has further affected its role. Most of its deliberations are superfluous to those pursued in other instances of the UN or in the system as a whole. It is not unusual for the member states as a whole to fail to agree on the substantive work and the policy orientations of a given organization and thus to leave it adrift in a permanent state of crisis.

This political and institutional irrelevance has contributed to the marginalization of the UN in the field of economic and social affairs. In 2004, the High-Level Panel on Threats, Changes and Change (A/59/565) had to recognize that "the decision-making on international economic matters, particularly in the areas of finance and trade, has long left the United Nations and no amount of institutional reform will bring it back". While the modus operandi of most instances of the UN results in the proliferation of insignificant consensual resolutions that every government is free to interpret or disregard, the Bretton Woods institutions have the capacity to promote and implement coherent economic strategies that have a profound impact, not always positive, on the development of poor countries, but with little participation of the representatives of these countries within the decision-making process.

Under the present circumstances, governments and their representatives are therefore inclined to attach more importance to the formalities of UN multilateralism than to its substance. They use it to defend the diplomatic prerogatives associated with a traditional conception of state sovereignty. They preserve the rituals of lengthy and tedious negotiations and, in so doing, they encourage a surreal political rhetoric, which diverts the international organizations from their sector-based functions. They tend to invest in the symbolic and rhetorical aspects of the various UN bodies and even of some of its specialized agencies. They use them to put forward their own ideological agendas as fora for diplomatic exchange, and to ensure the presence of their representatives on the various commissions and ad hoc committees. This particular form of multilateralism is a serious obstacle to constructive dialogue and to the implementation of concrete programmes of action. It contributes to the crisis in the legitimacy and accountability of the UN system. Diplomats in New York and Geneva are indeed regularly overstretched by the obligation to attend a daily load of different meetings on a great variety of topics. It is particularly burdensome for poor countries whose limited number of representatives have to rush from one meeting to another, with little possibility of making a substantive contribution to the debates and unable able to absorb the enormous number of reports published by the secretariats. Since part of this multilateralism is devoid of substantive issues, governments tend to dispatch junior diplomats to these meetings. Lacking clear instructions, and sometimes even the appropriate technical competence, these representatives have little inclination to take the content of programmes seriously. They also devote time and energy to promoting the appointment of their representatives to various UN bodies, or to the chair of one of these bodies, rather than to the substance of the debate. The frailty of checks and balances within the system is also due to the fact that the positions taken by diplomats in international fora are not subject to scrutiny by the media or national parliaments.

The accelerating regional integration processes and globalization, together with a dramatic increase of non-governmental actors, seem destined to marginalize even further the role of the UN in international regulatory mechanisms. Globalization tends to favour an increase in the number of non-governmental regulatory systems. In the dominant discourse, business enterprises, banks and private consulting firms are being associated with institutional structures of governance (see Perret, Chapter 5, this volume). Certain NGOs, in particular, are able to provide human and material resources of a better quality than those dispensed by the UN. They are also gaining a reputation for the promotion of legal norms and political values. At a time when intergovernmental bureaucracies are under constant fire, the NGOs have the advantage of less cumbersome administrative structures, enabling them to recruit qualified personnel at short notice. Their composite nature and the diversity of their objectives also ensure a certain ideological pluralism. They offer an institutional alternative which offsets the weight of states and intergovernmental organizations. Unfortunately, the proliferation of NGOs active within the broad mandate of the UN, often with the financial support of the system, has increased the difficulty of achieving coherence and coordination in the economic, social and humanitarian fields.

The most frequently recurring explanation for these failures is the lack of political will – or, preferably, the conflicting political will – of its member states. It is evident that the UN system cannot perform as it should when states are reluctant to provide the necessary resources for promoting its goals, or when they are not committed to implementing the resolutions they have solemnly accepted. In fact, most states, and in particular those which contribute the major part of the UN budget, seem disinterested in making the system an effective instrument for deliberation and action. In the present political circumstances, avenues for any substantial structural changes within the UN system as a whole seem to be blocked. The World Summit organized on the occasion of the 60th anniversary of the foundation of the UN is another manifestation of this reality. A significant reform would require a revision of the UN Charter, and such a revision has little chance of getting through the General Assembly, especially at a time when the US government and many others, for different reasons, are adamant in their refusal to embark on such a process.

The developed countries suffer little from the failure of this global governance; they even benefit from it. They have established complex, economic, sociocultural and political links among themselves. They have set up fairly predictable trade agreements, as well as certain – although not always very reliable – regulatory mechanisms for monetary and financial flows. They have frequent consultations and endeavour to harmonize their positions within restricted institutional mechanisms such as the OECD, the Basle Committee or the Group of 10 (G10) of the IMF. The European Union is a sui generis integration process, the complexity and institutional impact of which goes without saying. One result of these developments is that the role of international politics among the most advanced capitalist countries has changed radically. In the meantime, most significant multinational negotiations usually take place at the level of heads of state or government, or at ministerial level and among government representatives, who have both considerable authority and political influence. The leaders of the major industrialized nations, members of the G8, get together regularly to discuss important international matters – in particular, money, finance, the environment and terrorism.

The failure of the UN system has a much greater impact on poor countries – in particular, on the least developed ones – than on industrialized ones. Most of the poorer countries are highly dependent on intergovernmental aid for their development, and on the WTO and Bretton Woods institutions in particular, especially as their regional cooperation mechanisms are in their infancy. At the same time, they have little influence on the policies of these organizations, which determine part of their own socio-economic conditions (see Woods, Chapter 6, this volume). Nevertheless, most governments of the developing countries are reluctant to support a reform of the UN because of the fear that it would accentuate their marginalization in the deliberation and decision-making processes, as well as in the sphere of symbolic politics that exists within the system. They rightly resent the idea of establishing a new system dominated by the major economic powers whose national interests and policies might infringe on their own. They prefer the institutional status quo that provides them with a political platform, allows them to participate in multilateral debates and provides international civil service posts for their citizens, rather than a new and more efficient mechanism of deliberation that would accentuate their marginalization.

The reform of the operational capacities of the UN resembles the squaring of the circle. It should be aimed at conciliating its universal character and mandate while centralizing its decision-making processes in order to ensure its efficiency. Large meetings are obviously not an adequate multilateral environment for any decision-making process concerning important strategic issues such as financial and monetary issues. However, the operational aspects of development strategies require the participation of all the governments and social forces directly concerned. As a matter of fact, most of the reform proposals arise from technocratic premises that are contrary to the very nature of the international politics at play within the UN. It is difficult to resist denigrating its strange conference diplomacy as futile because of its rhetorical, idealistic and ritualistic characteristics, but one should not forget that illusion is an integral part of politics, and consequently of international politics. In other words technocratic reforms proposals could be interpreted as a specific illusion that denies the illusory nature of institutional politics.

Prospect for a new global governance

It is certainly misleading to envisage the reinforcement of the centralized institutions and law-enforcing mechanisms as the only way to meet the challenges of globalization. It is reasonable, nevertheless, to aim at creating a new architecture whereby decentralized regimes of cooperation along functional or regional lines would support more centralized but open and responsible decision-making structure. In any case, the negotiation and decision-making procedure at the global and regional levels will have to be thoroughly reviewed to take better account of the way in which political and economic forces are moulding the international scene, and also in order to ensure the participation of the poorest countries.

It is difficult to make any conjecture about the future evolution of the UN system, especially at a time of deep ideological, political and institutional crisis. The United States has launched a strong and systematic attack against the UN that is part of their defiance of multilateralism and of their inclination to confuse their national interests with the common good of the world. Yet no other major powers, or for that matter the European Union, are showing any intention to take up the challenge of reinvigorating and reforming the system. The UN decline is obvious in the growing normative and operational roles of major NGOs, in the increasing importance of regionalism, and in the surge of new mechanisms of deliberation among the major economic and political powers, such as the G8 and G20. What will be the consequences of, on the one hand, a new power configuration influenced by China and India and by the enlargement of the European Union, or, on the other hand, by the ever-mounting anarchy in sub-Saharan African countries? Will universalism, as defined within the Charter and human rights instruments, be definitively brushed away by mounting religious and conservative ideologies?

One way of thinking about reform is to imagine a world in which the universal institutions have to be thoroughly reconstructed because of tragic circumstances, such as those which called for the establishment of the League of Nations or indeed of the United Nations itself. This prospective exercise is problematic because it requires a representation of the future, in particular of the power configurations and of the predominant ideologies that are, by definition, inaccessible. There is, nevertheless, a certain heuristic value in underlining some of the major defects of the current global governance.

If one were to start from scratch, it is probable that the actual UN system would not be reinvented as it is today. The new global governance would most probably reflect the new power configuration influencing international society and the dynamics of regional integration, in particular within Europe. It would also continue to give a prominent role to national governments in shaping their economic and social development strategies, but it would also reflect the changing nature of state sovereignty that entails new areas of functional cooperation between national bureaucracies and a declining role for traditional diplomacy (see Kazancigil, Chapter 4, this volume). However, large-scale institutional reforms of global governance will certainly entail a major transformation at state level and, in particular, in the working practices of ministries dealing with foreign affairs. It is also likely that innovative methods of governing and supervising international organizations would have to be found.

Multilateral diplomacy at the universal level dealing with global issues would remain but its modus operandi would be different from the present UN General Assembly. It could consist of periodic world conferences, aimed at defining universal principles and norms, as well as specific regimes of intergovernmental cooperation. The real challenge of any new global mechanism, apart from its budgetary resources, would be to reconcile in its structures the participation of the major powers with a fair representation of the more vulnerable countries, while giving a voice to representatives of a selective number of important NGOs.

The Security Council could be maintained but enlarged, with additional permanent representation of the major powers and a shifting selection of representatives from the developing world. The European Union could have only one representative. One could also envisage along these lines a new Trusteeship Committee, which would become responsible for the reconstruction of countries which had gone through a period of civil war or persistent violent troubles. This new council could also examine cases brought by minority groups or indigenous peoples and draw the attention of the Security Council to internal conflicts which threaten the integrity of a state.

As there is close dialectical relationship between peace and well-being, the Security Council could have an evolving composition, like the Council of Ministers of the European Union, where different ministers meet regularly according to the matters under deliberation. Alternatively, a new Economic and Social Security Council could be established that would take over the G8 negotiations, enlarging them to a broader representation of a regional character. It would have to take account of the way in which political and economic forces were moulding the international scene, while ensuring the real participation of poor countries in the decision-making processes that affected their development. Most specialized agencies would not be re-created as such, with their current independent constitutive bodies, but would be redefined as specialized administrations answering to the same global political organization. The mandate of the latter would be to increase international liquidity, harmonize regional monetary systems, oversee balance of payment problems and to manage the thorny problem of debt crisis, taking into account the responsibilities of the lender countries. It could be responsible for the management of a new Fund for Sustainable Development whose budget would be financed not only by contributions from the member states, but mainly by international tax contributions. Its secretariat would have all possible means available for analysing the challenges posed by sustainable development and for channelling to the least developed countries the financial resources necessary for their economic and social progress. Its independence with regard to the member states would be much better protected than is the case today. It would also avoid any interference in humanitarian emergencies, leaving the field to the NGOs – in particular, the International Committee of the Red Cross (ICRC), the International Federation of the Red Cross and Red Crescent (IFRC), Médicin sans frontières (MSF), and other reliable organizations.

In all likelihood, the future mechanism of governance would require the establishment of new debating and decision-making procedures, based on the representation of regional or sub-regional groups of states. Indeed, one way of restricting the hegemonic control of intergovernmental institutions by major powers, of limiting states that are tempted to indulge in unilateral actions, and of containing the concentration of transnational economic actors that affect democratic participation at different levels of governance, would be to set up institutional and political checks and balances at the regional level (see chapters by Berthelot and Fawcett, this volume). In any case, building and defending an international order based on the United Nations' universalistic principles would require a redefinition of the relationships between states and regional institutions. Moreover in order to ensure some ideological and doctrinal pluralism within the new institutional system, consultative mechanisms would need to be established at the global and regional levels whose main functions would be to promote the participation of NGOs in the supervision of these new institutions. It is difficult to give a more precise image of the relevant institutional transformations, as they would result from any ongoing struggles, but it is more than likely that they would differ considerably from those set up at Bretton Woods and San Francisco.

Notes

1. In this article the UN system does not include the Bretton Woods institutions.
2. Historians and political analysts have shown little interest in the UN system, its internal workings, its administrative structures and its various activities. There are a number of studies of the Bretton Woods institutions and, in particular, of the World Bank. In sharp contrast, works on the UN, its funds, programmes and specialized agencies are frequently of an edifying nature and carry the imprint of official bureaucratic positions. This lack of interest is, to a large extent, due to the complexity of the system, the incomprehensible overlapping of its bureaucratic structures and the essentially discursive and esoteric nature of its activities.
3. Rosemary Righter was quite correct when she wrote: "in setting out to design a network of institutions for post-war order, the UN's architects assumed that the creation of organizations custom-made for different forms of cooperation would simplify the task ahead. Nobody foresaw that in the following decades, this principle would be carried to such extremes that the UN would acquire a complexity beyond the grasp of all but a handful of specialists, and quite beyond the control of national bureaucracies" (Righter, 1995: 43).

REFERENCES

Barnett, M. and Finnemore, M. (2004) *Rules for the World. International Organizations in Global Politics*, Cornell: Cornell University Press.

Emmerij, Louis, Joly, Richard and Weiss, Thomas (2001) *Ahead of the Curve? UN Ideas and Global Challenges*, Bloomington: Indiana Press.

Kapur, D., Lewis, J.P. and Webb, R. (1997) *The World Bank. Its First Century*, vol. I, Washington: Brookings Institution Press.

Macrae, Joanna (ed.) (2002) HPG Report 11, *The New Humanitarianism: A Review of Trends in global Humanitarian Action*, ODI, April.

Righter, Rosemary (1995) *Utopia Lost. The UN and the World*, New York: A Twentieth Century Fund Book.

Senarclens, Pierre de (1988) *La crise des Nations Unies*, Paris, PUF.

Sharp, Walter (1969) *The UN Economic and Social Council*, New York: Columbia University Press.

Taylor, P. and Groom, J.R. (2000) *The UN at the Millennium*, London: Continuum.

Toye, John and Toye, Richard (2004) *The UN and the Global Political Economy*, Bloomington: Indiana University Press.

United Nations Development Programme (UNDP) (2005) *Human Development Report*, New York: UNDP.

3

The significance of statehood in global governance

Ali Kazancigil

Introduction

Both neo-liberal globalization and its regulation through biased and non-accountable global governance create discontent (Stiglitz, 2002). Globalization is effective in generating growth, but it also creates inequalities and poverty in a great number of countries (Wade, 2003; Ocampo, 2005). The governance of globalization has been giving higher priority to serving the rich and powerful countries than the majority of nations, while, at the same time, fostering corporate interests over public interest.

In this chapter, we shall critically analyse the structural, political and ideological factors which have produced and legitimized such biases and deficiencies. We shall then explore the two ways – the reformist and the transformative processes – of advancing from the current private interest-oriented global governance, established and supported both by the powerful states and the market forces, to a global governance that is structured around statehood, participation and accountability. Such global governance is necessary to regulate globalization effectively towards a legitimate and sustainable process, blending economic efficiency, redistributive justice and sustainable development. The problem is not the globalization process in general, but its dominant neo-liberal features, and inadequate regulation.

A central argument in this analysis runs against a fallacy which is quite widespread in global studies, political and corporate circles and the

Regulating globalization: Critical approaches to global governance, de Senarclens and Kazancigil (eds), United Nations University Press, 2007, ISBN 978-92-808-1136-0

media. It consists in arguing that: a) globalization and the sovereign state have been maintaining antagonistic, zero-sum relationships; and b) the expansion of the globalization process has resulted, as a long-term and irreversible trend, in the weakening of the sovereign state, although this trend affects differently the various categories of states. Globalization and its apolitical regulation favouring neo-liberalism is supposed to have a bright future, while sovereignty is doomed, and with it the state. Such definitive views on the prospects for the state are vastly over-stretched (Putzel, 2005). We might add that, if they were confirmed, this would also mean the end of democratic politics. However, the above fallacy is not borne out by the historical facts and empirical evidence, as we shall see below. On the contrary, the state is still the more powerful transnational actor, and some effects of globalization strengthen its role (Weiss, 2005).

Undoubtedly, the current cycle of globalization is more powerful, in many ways, than the previous occurrences through a unique combination of political agency, ideological hegemony, shrinking time and space. This is thanks to powerful information and communication technologies (ICTs) and means of travel, as well as the penetration by market logic and forces of social relations and life-spheres. However, this reality cannot hide the fact that globalization started to expand in the late 1970s as a result of the political decisions and public policies of a limited number of major states, which still continue to support it. The speed and intensity with which globalization thrived was in fact correlated with the very active policy support it was given. The rest of the interstate system had no other choice than to accept it, more or less eagerly.

There are lots of variations and uncertainties concerning the impact of globalization, but one point is certain – namely, the determinant role of the state and its public policies in capturing the beneficial effects and mitigating the destructive impact of globalization. In fact, within the contemporary world system, the capitalist world economy and the interstate system have long been articulated and interdependent (Wallerstein, 1979, 1986). Interrelations between economic and financial globalization and sovereign states have not diverged from this pattern: they continue to sustain and reproduce each other through variable combinations of global and domestic dynamics. In this sense, globalization can be interpreted as an upward change of scale in such interrelationships (Bayart, 2004).

Therefore, the analyses which claim that globalization is a process operating in an economic and financial sphere more or less dissociated from, and even antagonistic to, politics, sovereignty and the state are not accurate. Globalization, and the globalized capitalist markets which constitute its substance, neither operate nor are sustainable on their own. In the absence of public regulation through accountable global governance, they produce distortions which weaken the legitimacy of the world order and democratic regimes (Dervis, 2005; Held, 1995). Globalization must be tamed by democratic politics and legitimate global governance (Kazancigil, 2003).

It is thus necessary that a basic tenet of global governance is statehood, with public regulation concerned with general interest and equity. This in itself requires the participation and consent of state, interstate (intergovernmental organizations (IGOs)), and non-state agents which are active in the transnational scene, the role of the state being a central one.

A hegemonic paradigm to legitimize the neo-liberal globalization and shareholders' capitalism

During the last two decades of the twentieth century, there was a far-reaching and lasting paradigmatic transformation in the way global economic and social models, processes and policies were represented and hierarchized. The neo-liberal ideology became hegemonic and was highly effective in directing people's understanding and representation of two interrelated areas, one concerning globalization and the other structural changes in global capitalism, induced and encouraged by globalization.

In the first area, the hegemonic paradigm was successful in legitimizing a representation of globalization in which the predominance of free markets and their agents over democratic politics and political agency appeared as an incontrovertible, inescapable, almost natural phenomenon, beneficial in the long run to every society and every individual. The historically falsified claim (Polanyi, 1957) that the economic and financial spheres are autonomous and dissociated from society was promoted with success. This paradigm provided the ideological framework for globalization as well as for global governance, which is responsive to the need of private interests.

Under this skilful global ideological drive, undoubtedly one of the most effective in modern history, the hegemonic outlook shifted from a social democratic one, founded on a balance between economic efficiency and higher-order principles of redistributive justice and solidarity, to neo-liberalism and social Darwinism. This was driven by ruthless rules of competition between individuals, corporations and states, conceived as the survival of the fittest, with an instrumental approach to social and human relations. The requirements of the capitalist economy prevailed over those of democratic politics and social cohesion. Theories and policy prescriptions of the neo-Keynesian or regulationist schools – which consider that the economy is part of society and culture, as well as that economic policies should be adjusted to social requirements – were discarded. Monetarist theories and policies became the policy-makers' gospel.

The powerful and lasting impact of this hegemony operated at cognitive and lexical levels. For example, the meaning of socio-economic reform has been inverted. Until the 1980s, it designated policies and measures aimed at full employment and improving the welfare of the majority through a social regulation of capitalism. Such a definition of reform, and the public policies it inspired, is now regarded as anti-modernist and populist. Reformism under the hegemonic ideology of globalization amounts to liberating capitalism and financial markets from public regulation, destroying the welfare state (the neo-Conservative slogan in the USA is "starve the beast"), turning public services into commercial activities, implementing socially regressive policies, dismantling labour legislation, indifference to unemployment, or providing precarious jobs and low wages, which has induced the creation of a new socio-professional statistical category: the working poors.

The additional wealth that is generated has never "trickled down" automatically, as it is claimed by the neo-liberal hegemony. It can only do so through redistributive regulation, which is perfectly possible, but rejected by the hegemonic ideology. In the meantime, the Schumpeterian "creative destruction" processes seem to continue indefinitely instead of leading, largely thanks to technological advances, to a new cycle of prosperity and well-being as Schumpeter had theorized. But could the Austrian economist have foreseen that, in the early twenty-first century, the corporate agents and states that support them would be short-sighted and self-serving enough to foster a capitalist model under which the world seems condemned to an endless destructive phase?

The second area where the legitimating efforts of the hegemonic paradigm were remarkably successful concerns the current configuration of the capitalist system, referred to above, dubbed the "shareholders" capitalism. It replaced, over the last decade, managerial capitalism and Fordism. Public opinion has been persuaded, against all available evidence, of the favourable consequences of this important shift in global capitalism. Yet, managerial capitalism was, to a certain extent, concerned with productive and job-creating investments, and social questions such as decent employment rates and conditions, as well as wages. It accepted the legitimacy of public regulation.

The shareholders' capitalism, which blossomed within neo-liberal globalization, is quite different. It is dominated by financial interests. The main priority of its corporate agents' has been obtaining the highest possible profit rates and levels of "return on equity", buying back their own shares, investing their profits in stock markets and distributing them to shareholders. Shareholders' capitalism is also beset by numerous scandals of corporate corruption and misbehaviour. Such a capitalist model is completely dissociated from social concerns, despite certain initiatives such as corporate social responsibility (CSR) and a "Global Compact" alliance with the UN, which are image-building communication strategies rather than a serious consideration of the social question.

Indeed, shareholders' capitalism is not committed to what constitutes the main social legitimacy of capitalism – that is, taking risks in order to contribute to economic growth and general welfare. This dysfunctional form of capitalism has trapped many developed countries into low growth rates. To come out of this trap, profits that are generated should be invested in productive and job-creating activities, and real wages increased to foster purchasing power. Instead, the top priority is given to corporate profit rates – which, in 2004, reached their highest level since the 1970s in the G7 countries as a whole and, in the USA, since the 1929 crash. These profits are not used as productive capital (after 2000, such investments fell in the USA and most EU countries), but distributed to shareholders and used in corporate self-financing (the rates of the latter are over 100 per cent in the USA, UK, Germany and Japan).

Thus, current capitalism faces both an equity (the distortion of the balance between the shares of the capital and the labour, and profits and wages, in national income), as well as an efficiency problem (the low growth trap). Certain economists argue that by maintaining such patterns shareholders' capitalism is destroying itself (Artus and Virard, 2005; Hoang-Ngoc and Tibel, 2005). Prominent corporate leaders and CEOs have elaborated on the adverse effects of "shareholder dictatorship" (Peyrelevade, 2005).

In the southern hemisphere, ideological hegemony and the policies it has inspired have also taken their toll even more severely than in the north. Neo-liberal orthodoxy had no concern with the specific requirements of different economies, emergent or developing. Under the recipes imposed by the Washington Consensus in the 1980s and part of the '90s, the already inadequate social security mechanisms collapsed (Berr and Combarnous, 2005). Close to a hundred severe financial crises struck emerging and developing countries (Stiglitz, 2002). The number of least developed countries (LDCs) has kept rising, many of them are also labelled by another of those unpleasant acronyms behind which lies a hideous reality: HIPCs – Highly Indebted Poor Countries. The long list of "LCDs/HIPCs" is a telling indicator of the distortions and failures of the global order.

Contrary to the claims of the hegemonic paradigm, globalization carries benefits to only a handful of rich countries and a limited number of emerging countries. Less than 20 per cent of the world's population, including the more prosperous classes in the southern hemisphere, has access to financial and educational resources, ICTs and mobility. To the "majority world", particularly many small or failed states, globalization means powerlessness, more poverty and greater inequality. While, on aggregate, the world's economy generates more and more wealth, almost half of its population lives on less than two dollars a day and, despite a global food surplus, some 800 million people suffer from malnutrition. Certain critical analysts of globalization go as far as claiming that collectively "we are involved in an immense crime against humanity through the upholding of the present global economic order" (Pogge, 2003, 2002). There is ample evidence showing that the world needs "A Fair Globalization, Creating Opportunity for All" (World Commission on the Social Dimensions of Globalization, 2004).

To conclude, the hegemonic paradigm is essentially the output of a powerful ideological effort undertaken by certain sovereign states at the centre of the world system, working hand in hand with corporate interests, in order to justify and provide legitimacy for neo-liberal globalization and its biased governance amongst citizens, the media and public opinion throughout the world. This ideological representation is, of course, far from reflecting what is happening in the real world, but such a misrepresentation is precisely its goal.

The sovereign state and neo-liberal globalization: allies or adversaries?

A considerable social science literature, theorizing the decline and modifications in the role and capacities of the state, was produced from 1970 onwards (Keohane and Nye 1971, 1977). It contested basic postulates of the realist theory of international relations, such as the quasi-monopoly of sovereign states on the international scene and the primacy of strategic and military objectives over economic issues. It argued that economic interdependence required cooperation and legitimacy within the world society, rather than power relations, conflict and use of force between empires and sovereign states. It contended that the economic and financial globalization process seemed to confirm theories on the decline of the sovereign state. Seemingly in support of this, a variety of non-state entities – such as non-governmental organizations (NGOs) and social movements, transnational corporations (TNCs), global private regulatory authorities (see this volume, Perret, Chapter 4 and Woods, Chapter 5), and ethnic and terrorist networks – emerged as global agents, efficiently using the resources of globalization and contesting the monopoly of the state at the international level.

Such developments have been analysed as a weakening of the sovereign and territorial character of the state, reducing the significance of its boundaries. It has been theorized that world politics has entered a period of turbulence through a split between multilateralism, which is a state-centric system, and transnationalism, a multicentric system in which non-state actors tend to become dominant (Rosenau, 1991; Rosenau and Czempiel, 1992). Others have argued that the state has lost much of its sovereignty and influence in the economy and that the globalized financial markets and TNCs have overpowered it (Strange, 1996).

Two different developments have been taking place at the transnational level. On the one hand, the all-powerful Westphalian sovereign state has been undergoing quite far-reaching changes over the last couple of decades, and it has been facing serious challenges and competition from other types of agents on the transnational scene. But the basic assumptions of the realist theory, concerning a world order characterized by power relations and conflicts between empires and nation-states, continue to be valid. On the other hand, institutional arrangements and patterns of behaviour have emerged and gradually expanded over the last five or six decades, based on cooperation and legitimacy; this seems to point to the possibility of a transition from a world system to a world society. Such developments are far from having invalidated the realist theory's assumptions. Still, they are there to stay, with corresponding norms, operational principles and an institutional architecture that encompasses the multilateral cooperation arrangements with the UN, its specialized agencies, funds and programmes, the Bretton-Woods institutions, the WTO, regional organizations and banks, and the International Criminal Court (see this volume, de Senarclens, Chapter 2).

However, the emergence of a transnational space of cooperative norms and behaviour does not eliminate questions about the validity of the thesis regarding the irreversible domestic and international decline of the sovereign state. From the readily observable evidence indicating that the non-state agents have gained considerable influence on the transnational scene at the expense of the sovereignty of the state, can it be concluded that the balance of power has decisively shifted in favour of the former? The answer should be in the negative. The thesis of the decline, and ultimately the demise of the state, is a teleological one. It belongs to the category of value judgements that denigrate the state, and which are as irrelevant in social scientific analyses as the ones that sacralize it. They should be neatly distinguished from the issue of the contemporary crisis and transformations of the state, which deserves serious inquiry (Bobbio, 1998).

Beyond the sovereign state as an ideal type, the existing states display empirically a wide range of disparities. From the point of view of the domestic and external capacities of states to exercise their sovereignty, and assessing their role in global governance, there are empirically documented variations between the strong, the relatively strong and the failed states. The first and third categories are a minority, while the second constitutes a majority in the interstate system. Another relevant categorization distinguishes between the regulatory state, concerned with social issues, and the competitive state, giving priority to supporting market forces. In reality, almost all states display a mix of these two categories. Some are more on the regulatory side, such as France and Germany, others more on the competitive side, such as the USA, UK or Ireland. The exceptions are the failed states, which have neither regulatory nor competitive capacities.

The empirical plurality of states, as well as the wide differences between them, is accompanied by a feature they all share (except the failed ones): the territorial state is the locus of popular sovereignty and representative politics. As Clifford Geertz once asked, "What is a state, if it is not a sovereign?" (2004). The use of the state in singular form as an ideal type in parts of this text is not a denial of the variations between states and their capacities; it refers to this common characteristic, which is of the highest importance in discussing the role of statehood in global governance. Indeed, without sovereignty, there can be no political organization, citizenship, democracy, civil society, or participation in global governance. If there were doubts about this, remembering the disaster resulting from the destruction of the Iraqi state by the USA–UK invasion should be enough to dispel them.

To what extent does globalization challenge sovereignty – that is, the capacity of the state to act and exercise power internationally and domestically? In fact, since Jean Bodin first theorized sovereignty in the sixteenth century as the "ultimate and perpetual power" of the state, which no obligation could limit, this concept was gradually relativized, starting with Grotius in the seventeenth century, in the framework of international legal rules transcending the sovereign rights of individual states. Much progress was accomplished in this respect in the twentieth century, with remarkable developments in international law, particularly international humanitarian law. Consequently, a progression from an international "anarchic" system to a world "society", where cooperation and "soft power" would decisively gain ground against the use of force, seemed to be within reach. In this context, the kinds of questions debated were: is the sovereign state still the dominant agent on the transnational scene? Does the distinction between the domestic and external spheres keep its analytical relevance? Is world politics moving from the Hobbesian and Weberian models to a Kantian cosmopolitanism, granting that in some countries, the Durkheimian anomia dominates? The destruction of the Twin Towers on 9 September 2001 created a different context for such debates. If the reaction of the USA to this tragedy had a lasting significance, compounded by the illegal preventive war in Iraq in March 2003, it would be that globalization did not lead the sovereign states to adopt post-Hobbesian patterns as regards the use of force at the international level. The situation is different in respect of the socio-economic dimensions of sovereignty.

Sovereignty and its utilization by states need to be deconstructed. In strategic and military areas, the classical prerogatives of sovereignty and the monopoly of the state on the international arena are preserved, except in the case of failed states. The picture is different in the governance of national socio-economic systems in relation to globalization, where the state sovereignty has been reduced, and with it its capacity to perform one of its fundamental functions, as well as a central element of its legitimacy: enhancing the welfare of the citizens and preserving the social cohesion.

Why? Is it out of obligation and against their will, or as a matter of policy choices that sovereign states, which keep their monopoly in diplomatic, strategic and military matters, have been making concessions on their economic and financial sovereignty? Both should be the answer. To exercise its sovereignty, as well as perform its basic functions of external and domestic security, justice, redistribution, provision of public service in education and health, or infrastructure-building, the state is in need of resources, provided by the economy. Thus, it has a stake in having an efficient economic system from which resources are transferred, mainly through fiscality.

The state and the market, politics and the economy, have always been intertwined from the early stages of the emergence of the capitalist system. The neo-liberal claim that the market economy and economic development took place in the West without, or despite, state intervention is an ideological argument. It is inconsistent with the historical experience of the earlier (in the West) and the later (in East Asia) success stories of economic development (Ha-Joon 2003; Hausmann and Rodrik 2002; Gerschenkorn 1966). The denial of the role of the state and arguments in favour of its retreat from socio-economic matters means ignoring "the developmental lessons of history and the perverse impact liberalization has had on peace and security" (Putzel 2005). Because of its uncritical acceptance of the hegemonic ideology, the World Bank shared such a denial of historical evidence in the 1980s, but later admitted the importance of statehood in development in the 1990s. Such historical evidence is so clear that even the promoter of the "end-of-history" fairy tale, Francis Fukuyama, came round to recognizing the important role of the state (2004). Indeed, since the nineteenth century, and according to historical circumstances and the perception of their interests, states have oscillated between interventionism and non-interventionism in the economy. After two world wars and a disastrous period in between, the post-World War II era, from 1945–1975, was characterized in the West by the development of the welfare state and a capitalist economy subjected to public regulation.

Since the late 1970s, the world economy has again become disembedded. Starting with the USA and the UK, and followed at different degrees by the other Western states – and gradually by other world states, including developing countries and, as of the early 1990s, former communist countries – public policies have given priority to the requirements of the market economy over social concerns. While, in the aftermath of World War II, public policies had kept a relative equilibrium between the conflicting interests of capital and labour, from the 1980s the balance tilted in favour of capital. States relinquished a good measure of their economic sovereignty and deregulated the financial markets and labour markets. *The Economist*, which can hardly be suspected of being anti-capitalist or alter-globalist, reported that "Capitalists are grabbing a rising share of the national income at the expense of workers", and that according to the calculations of UBS, a Swiss investment bank

> [I]n the G7 economies as a whole, the share of profit in national income has never been higher ... labour's share of the cake has never been lower ... Over the past three years American corporate profits have risen by 60 per cent, wage income only by 10 per cent ... In 1979–2000, the real income of the poorest fifth of American households rose by 6 per cent, while that of the top fifth rose by 70 per cent (and of the top 1 per cent by 184 per cent) (12 February 2005; 16 July 2005).

Despite growing inequalities and unprecedented levels of corporate profits in North America and Europe, taxation on corporations has been drastically reduced. In Europe, over the last fifteen years, the average rate of such taxation has been cut by 33 per cent.

The consequence of this so-called "fiscal revolution", implemented in the name of the requirements of global competitiveness, is that the public services in education, research and health have been less and less capable of fulfilling their missions. Their purposefully provoked decline was then interpreted as a proof of their inefficiency and justification for their privatization. The current interest for introducing the "flat tax" system, in which a billionaire and a minimum wage-earner would be subjected to the same rate of income tax, is yet another manifestation of the disdain for public good, redistributive justice and, ultimately, a threat for democratic societies.

Renouncing the social regulation of capitalism meant regressing to a situation characterized, in the words of Karl Polanyi (1957: 250–1) as "the utopian experiment of a self-regulating market" and "the economic system lay(ing) down the law to society". This amounted to ignoring the lessons learned from the tragic historical experiences of the twentieth century. Of the three competing systems of the past century – communism, fascism and democracy – only democracy has survived (Mazover, 1998). In this success, the welfare policies introduced by the democratic states in the wake of World War II played a significant role. Instead of reforming the welfare states, though, in order to adapt them to changing conditions, the current policies have been trying to eliminate them, thus putting democratic regimes at risk.

Such public policy choices are obviously not guided by historical awareness, but by hegemonic neo-liberal ideology, as well as a cynical cost-benefit analysis. At their origin, there is the "conservative revolution" of the late 1970s – that is, the decision of taking radical action to overcome the cyclical crisis of the capitalist economy that followed the upwards cycle of the 1945–75 period (Artus, 2000).[1]

In addition to the requirements of capital accumulation, states needed the fiscal resources drawn from an efficient economy. They also decided to actively support corporate interests. Responding to such necessities was therefore considered to have priority over the democratic, symbolic and social costs of relinquishing portions of their economic sovereignty and social regulation capacities. The price to be paid in terms of social cohesion proved to be very high, but this dimension was not then, and is not nowadays, a dominant concern of the present-day neo-liberals, who do not seem to share the ethical scruples of the nineteenth-century liberals, such as John Stuart Mill or Benjamin Constant (see Coicaud, Chapter 10, this volume, on ethical issues in globalization and its governance).

Neo-liberal policies and deregulation measures, which reduced the regulatory functions of states and accelerated the globalization process, were not imposed by some higher authority upon the Western states as of the late 1970s, but purposefully decided by them, exercising their rights to give away segments of their sovereignty to global markets. On the whole, such public policy choices have not only been a departure from social progress founded on the welfare state, but also from the nation-state built on popular and democratic sovereignty. It was a blow to social cohesion, as well as the political community and citizenship.

It appears, therefore, that the "retreat" and relative incapacitation of states in globalization and global governance, has been organized and constructed in conformity with the interests of certain social classes and economic agents. As a result of the policy options they have taken, states have started to act, not as defenders of the interests of their citizens, but as logistic bases to foster the global competitiveness of their TNCs, at the expense of the welfare state and well-being of their populations. As Martin Wolf has noted (*Financial Times*, 6 February 2002), the current shape of globalization is due to the fact that governments consciously and voluntarily abandoned it to the rule of market forces. In the competitive state which prevailed over the regulatory state, the trend towards the privatization of certain public functions is the result of ideological preferences more than economic criteria (Hibou, 1999). The claims that the necessities of global competition did not allow states to improve social conditions, and obliged them to reduce welfare policies and public services, looked more like self-justification than anything else. Private health and retirement systems do not appear to be sustainable in the long run, and the social benefits of wage-earners are in jeopardy, as happened in the case of the Enron bankruptcy. The "social state" is weakened by the reduction, excessive rationalization and privatization of public services. Economic policies continue to give priority to fighting inflation, even when the latter is quite low, at the expense of promoting a balanced economic growth and employment.

The so-called "powerlessness" of the state in the context of economic globalization is a selective proposition. When the issue is rising unemployment, precarious jobs or the working poor, state authorities confess their helplessness in the face of the unavoidable reality of our time – the necessity to increase the competitiveness of the nation's economy – adding that very soon things will improve on the labour market. But when it comes to salvaging influential corporations, suddenly the same state recovers its power and resources: witness the billions of dollars Japan has poured into avoiding the bankruptcy of its heavily indebted private banks, or France's efforts to rescue a major bank, Crédit Lyonnais, or the transnational corporation, Alstom. The deregulated global financial markets escape state control, because this is accepted by the states. When necessary, major powers feel free to depart from the sacred principle of free markets and financial orthodoxy, which they keep preaching to developing and emerging countries. For example, despite the rhetoric that markets decide the value of currencies and governments are unable to do anything about it, the value of the dollar goes up and down according to the preferences of the US government. Or, industrial countries protect their agriculture and industries in various ways. All this is written in the history of globalization, as it has developed over the last decades as a joint venture between sovereign states and corporate interests, often at the expense of wage-earners. The neo-liberal form of globalization is neither the result of historical determinism (de Senarclens, 2000), nor a natural phenomenon beyond human control, but an outcome of agency. Arguments such as Margaret Thatcher's that "there is no alternative" to this type of globalization, which became a media acronym – TINA – were pure demagogy. On the contrary, neither the influence exercised by global markets over democratic politics, nor the socio-economic "retreat" of the state are unavoidable, but a matter of public policy choices.

The upshot of this is that, although the sovereign state has been undergoing changes at the global and domestic levels, the demarcation line between the two spheres is becoming increasingly blurred, and its role remains a central one. However, the state no longer holds a monopoly and various non-state agents compete with it on the transnational scene. To refer to classical works, if the transnational scene is no longer monopolized by sovereign states, as analysed by Raymond Aron (1962), it is not dominated by networks of non-state agents either, as predicted by Karl Deutsch (1968). Although contested, obliged to adapt itself to new global contexts, and less overwhelmingly dominant than before, the state still keeps its specificity and remains more than a *primus inter pares* vis-à-vis non-state agents. The state could, if and when it wishes, regulate globalization differently. The notion that the state is stripped of its power in the globalization process is, to a great extent, an exaggeration as far as the strong states are concerned (Weiss 1998) Major states situated at the centre of the world system, having opted for neo-liberal globalization, could equally decide, if they so wished, to regulate it along more democratic and equitable lines. The fact is that they do not wish to, at least not yet. As a result, global governance remains non-accountable, technocratic and heavily biased towards private interests.

The situation is different for developing and emerging economies. The legal principle of the equality of sovereign states does not translate into reality, the interstate system being marked by huge inequalities. Roughly 30 states enjoy a good measure of freedom of choice and action. This group gathers the "rule makers" in the globalization process, which they regulate to their benefit, through their own assemblies (G8) and the international and regional IGOs they control (IMF, World Bank, WTO, OECD). They promote neo-liberal agendas that are to their advantage, but display reluctance to support measures towards greater global equity, such as increasing public funding for development and eliminating barriers against developing countries' exports. According to IMF's *World Economic Outlook 2005,* 29 countries with 15 per cent of the world's population receive 55 per cent of the world's income. On the other hand, the remaining 165 or so of the least developed and developing countries, together with the majority of emergent countries, where 85 per cent of the world's population lives, receive 45 per cent of the world's income. They are the "rule takers", and have only limited or no freedom of choice. They just have to play the game as per the rules set by the states at the centre of the system. The cost of failing to conform to the current rules of globalization is too high to risk. However, within this category there are considerable variations. Southern "Whales", such as China, India and Brazil, have a greater capacity to resist. The weak and small states are helpless. Relatively strong medium-sized countries can resist partially and occasionally, such as Malaysia's introduction of currency exchange control during the Asian financial crisis in 1997.

However, this picture is changing fast and soon some of the big emerging countries, particularly China, may join the club of the "rule makers". Indeed, in 2005, the combined output of emerging and developing economies, measured at PPP (purchasing-power parities) overtook that of the developed countries and rose to above half of the global total. This seems to be a long-term trend, since their overall growth rate is higher, and in 2005 they accounted for more than half the global GDP increase in current dollar terms (*The Economist*, 21 January 2006).

The spaces and agents of global governance: interstate space and transnational public space

The transnational scene is currently structured through the interrelations and tensions between the interstate space (ISS) and the transnational public space (TPS).

On the ISS, the principle agents are sovereign states and the dependent ones are the inter-governmental organizations (IGOs). ISS is characterized by formal equality and real inequalities and stratification. It is relatively homogenous in legal terms, but empirically there are huge differences amongst the states and their capacities. The IGOs also yield various degrees of power and resources, according to the preferences of the major powers.

A major demarcation line on the ISS runs between the states from the northern hemisphere and those from the southern hemisphere. The 1999 street demonstrations in Seattle were instrumental in disrupting the WTO conference, but its failure was mainly due to the resistance of the states from the South. The same scenario was repeated at the WTO conference in Cancun, Mexico (September 2003), where a much better organized and vocal southern coalition was formed. These countries refused to discuss the northern agenda on free trade and investments, unless the southern agenda on eliminating agricultural subsidies and protectionism in the USA and the EU were taken equally into account. They also came up with an articulate agenda for reforming multilateralism. In fact, although the historical importance of the emergence of non-state actors on the global scene is not to be underestimated, the central tensions and effective political contest at the global level are still those which oppose the northern states, which by and large control the global agendas, and support southern states which aim at participating in agenda-setting, and which have been achieving some results in this respect. Brazil was particularly effective in 2004–5 in modifying certain global agenda items, particularly at the WTO, towards eliminating the protectionism of rich countries in agricultural trade.

The North–South opposition cropped up again at the WTO conference in December 2005 in Hong Kong, the third in the "Doha Cycle" of free-trade negotiations. The pressures of the southern G-20 led the USA and the European Union to accept the elimination of all their agricultural subventions by 2013. But there are still uncertainties on how they will do it, especially since in exchange the northern countries have asked the developing and emerging economies to eliminate all protectionist measures against their industrial exports (see Lengyel, Chapter 6, this volume, on trade and development issues).

A further complexity in such North–South alignments and their impact on global governance is that some emerging economies, such as Brazil and India, have some interests that coincide with the North. Thus, these two big southern powers are part of a G-6 in the WTO talks, in which the other members are the USA, the European Union, Australia and Japan.

The legal perspective is useful in assessing the shifting roles of the state and statehood in global governance. Since World War II, sovereign states developed a world order through the UN Charter and a wide range of legal instruments and declarations (see de Senarclens, Chapter 2, this volume). The foundational elements of this world order are the collective security system, international humanitarian law and socio-economic development. Legal instruments were adopted – such as the Universal Declaration of Human Rights (1948), the two UN Covenants of 1966 (one on political and civil rights and the other on socio-economics rights), as well as numerous other texts. The international humanitarian law progressed further with the adoption of legislation on genocide and crimes against humanity, the establishment of ad hoc international tribunals on Nazi crimes, ex-Yugoslavia, Rwanda and Sierra Leone, and finally the creation of the International Criminal Court. These efforts have obtained limited success, but their influence in introducing norms of civilized behaviour in international relations and fostering multilateralism cannot be underestimated (Thakur and Malcontent, 2004). After all, the sovereign states' resort to armed conflict outside the UN collective security system has become an exceptional occurrence.

In the area of human rights, the progress was real but far from being satisfactory. The 1948 Universal Declaration had established them as an indivisible whole, but the fact that in 1966 the political/civil and socio-economic/cultural rights were split into two distinct instruments weakened their indivisibility, with socio-economic rights remaining largely neglected. In a similar fashion, in the architecture of the UN, financial matters have been separated from social issues and attributed to the so-called Bretton Woods institutions (IMF and World Bank) controlled by Western powers through a weighted voting system. The UN international development strategies proved to be ineffective, partly because of different approaches and ideologies prevailing in the UN and the Bretton Woods institutions. The creation of the World Trade Organization (WTO) in 1995 as a successor to the General Agreement on Trade and Tariffs (GATT) further consolidated the dissociation of the commercial issues from the social ones. Things were made worse by allowing the WTO to extend free trade regimes, such as the General Agreement on Trade in Services (GATS) and Trade Related Intellectual Property Rights (TRIPs) beyond commercial services to education, culture, science, health, environment and intellectual property rights.

It appears therefore that norm production at the transnational level develops quite unevenly. The normative space of human rights expands much more slowly than the normative space relating to markets. There is no World Court of Human Rights. In contrast, WTO's organ for the Settlement of Disputes, which has unparalleled international enforcement powers that are better than those of the UN Security Council, functions like a true world trade court. These two transnational normative spaces are disjointed and unhierarchized. The International Court of Justice, which could introduce some synchronization, is entirely dependent on the discretion of the states.

The sovereign states ceased to be the exclusive source of international law. Deregulation measures which accompanied economic globalization led, in fact, to redeployment towards new forms of regulation produced through governance procedures by a multiplicity of public and private agents, the states being one of them, even if they remain more powerful than non-state partners. The regulation process is fragmented as a compilation of micro-strategies and sectoral decisions, producing temporary ad hoc reversible norms and rules (Badie, 2000). Therefore, at least in economic, financial and commercial matters, international law is not entirely identified with the sovereign state. This is one of the more important modifications in the traditional role of the state in the international realm, partly due to its own policy choices, as discussed earlier. It points to the uncertainties of new modes of global governance, the institutions of which are yet to be invented – an issue which will be discussed below.

The transnational public space (TPS) has emerged more recently on the global scene. Its agents are the non-state actors, characterized by extreme heterogeneity, problems of legitimacy and representation, as well as inequality between the transnational corporations (TNC) and the non-governmental organizations (NGOs). Through the actions of such non-state entities, the TPS was gradually formed over the recent years, especially since the street demonstrations during the WTO conference in Seattle in December 1999. The TPS has gained strength through recurrent massive manifestations protesting against the current neo-liberal globalization on the occasion of G8, IMF, World Bank, WTO and European Union meetings.

Beyond protests, the TPS has also developed a capacity to re-think globalization and formulate alternative proposals for its governance, particularly through the World Social Forum (WSF). The WSF, which also has an important symbolic function as the platform representing the underprivileged populations, originated in 2001. Initial meetings were held in Porto Alegre, Brazil, and later in Mumbai, India, Bamako, Mali and Caracas, on the same dates as the gatherings of political and corporate leaders at the Davos World Economic Fora. The TPS and its agents are having a considerable impact in the international media and gaining sympathy in national public opinions. Global regulatory arrangements, which previously were confined to interstate space (ISS), are now being penetrated and influenced by the ideas generated and actions organized by TPS agents.

Some analysts qualify such developments as the emergence of a global civil society. However, comparisons should not be pushed too far between the relations that the ISS and the TPS entertain in global governance, on the one hand, and the interactions between the state and civil society in national governance, on the other. Indeed, at the transnational level there is no central sovereign authority and precisely for this reason the TPS is not yet, and has little chances of becoming, a global civil society. Nonetheless, the non-state agents which are active in global governance matters manage to establish links with national public opinions and carry major global issues into local public debates much more effectively than earlier. The governments feel the impact of these pressures, which influence to a certain extent their discourse and, in rare cases, their actions. The voice of the TPS reaches them through the mediation of national public opinions. The TPS plays an important role in promoting the public good in global governance. Certain non-state actors on the TPS promote statehood and public interest in global governance more actively and effectively than sovereign states turned into competitive states, having decided to abandon some of their regulatory capacities.

A major problem of the TPS is the difficulty of identifying the nature, legitimacy and representativeness of its agents. Some, such as Oxfam,

Amnesty International, Human Rights Watch, or Médecins Sans Frontières, are legitimate and represent important visible and vocal constituencies. Others are much less commendable, such as the governmental NGOs (GONGOs), and NGOs created by the mafias to further their growing criminal activities, thanks to global deregulation and fiscal paradises tolerated by the major powers. Another problem of the TPS in its initial stages was that it had been set up mainly by northern non-state agents. Indeed, independent NGOs and social movements existed in rather small numbers in the southern hemisphere in the initial stages of the TPS. This, however, has been changing rapidly, particularly since the emergence of the World Social Forum and southern NGOs are now more vocal and influential. The strategic importance of the WSF is not only in its being an autonomous emancipatory space, generating alternative ideas on global governance from Southern perspectives and fostering debates, but also in its being the first articulate attempt to organize and give coherence to the TPS (Sen, Anand, Escobar and Waterman, 2004).

The relations between the ISS and the TPS are partly complementary and partly conflictual. As already noted, the NGOs working towards a more democratic global governance and equitable globalization are naturally favouring public interests. It would be contradictory for them to be systematically against statehood. They oppose the competitive biases of states aiming at fostering neo-liberal globalization, but support their actions in favour of a social regulation of the latter.

Another fault line on the TPS runs between the democratically oriented NGOs and TNCs. As global non-state agents, The TNCs have their own agenda, which is not focused on advancing from technocratic to accountable global governance, but on securing that at the global level private interests continue to prevail on public interest and on maximizing profits and gaining larger shares on world markets. A growing number of business corporations adopt norms of equitable trade and corporate social responsibility (CSR) to acquire legitimacy through claims of better practices in social and environmental fields. Given the pressing demands from consumers, NGOs, the media and labour unions, they feel that the management of reputation and image risks has become a strategic challenge. There are several public and private international and national bodies which articulate the issues and activities, or generate specific norms on CSR, such as the UN Global Compact Initiative, UN Human Rights Commission (2005/69) ILO, OECD, International Organization for Standardization (ISO 2600), Global Reporting Initiative (SA8000), and the Institute of Social and Ethical Accountability.[2] But, such developments are unlikely to compensate for the negative impact of the current globalization and economic policies, promoted by the same TNCs

(Zammit, 2003). One reason for this is that the CSR movement is still a relatively marginal one among the TNCs, but this may change over time. The more important factor is that the TNCs resist strongly against the introduction of binding norms of CSR and accountability, advocating rules based on voluntary action.

TNCs regularly participate and exercise strong influence on global policy-making, something they have long been doing in national governance. They are also influential actors in the economic and financial IGOs. They are official UN partners in the Global Compact, play a major role in the Codex Alimentarius Commission, or in the telecommunications field, the International Telecommunication Union (IUT) has several hundred corporate members.

On the NGO side, the latter had earlier obtained a status with the UN Social and Economic Council and the specialized UN agencies, and later the IMF and the World Bank also established links with them. But their participation is rather marginal. Although they have long had a status at the UN and its agencies, the NGOs have limited direct influence on global decision-making. Their participation has been enhanced by the multi-stakeholder arrangements introduced by Kofi Annan. The report he commissioned on United Nations–civil society relations, which was drafted under the leadership of the former president of Brazil, Fernando Enrique Cardoso, formulated proposals to make the UN a more outward-looking global convener of diverse constituencies. However, in the documents and resolutions produced by the UN such as, for instance, the Commission on Sustainable Development, the inputs proposed by the NGOs are seldom, if ever, taken into account.

So far, the TPS has been able to score results on certain global issues through the activism and proposals of NGOs, social movements and the WSF. Its strongest impact has been on raising awareness in public opinions and in shaking the self-assurance of some of the global political and economic actors – the major states, IMF, World Bank, WTO, and TNCs – about the biases of globalization. Although its proposals for an alternative regulation of globalization concerning global taxation, cancellation of the poor countries' debts and the protection of public services are not taken into account in global decision-making, they have gained legitimacy and are no longer easily brushed off as radical nonsense. In certain cases, such as the production of low-cost medical drugs by developing countries, the TPS together with national public opinion have been able to modify the global agendas and policies. Amongst other positive developments, in which the pressures exercised by TPS agents played a role, are the decisions adopted by the G-8 to cancel the multilateral debts of the Highly Indebted Poor Countries and to double, by 2010, the public development aid to African countries.

The limits of reformism: global governance as enhanced multilateralism

There are two possible paths towards a renovated and upgraded governance of globalization: (a) re-enforcing multilateralism through a reformist approach, which is considered in this section, and (b) aiming at shaping and, in some respects, inventing the patterns of an alternative global governance through a transformative process, which will be discussed in the next section.

These two options are not contradictory, and under certain conditions they can be cumulative as the progress towards the second would need advances in the first. However, the continuity between the two cannot be linear; at some point in the process certain radical changes would have to be introduced to move from reform to transformation.

The reformist approach has been focusing on rendering the current architecture of multilateral institutions a more effective instrument of global governance. "Traditional" multilateralism is exclusively state-centric, top-down, and still very much at the centre of interstate cooperation through the major IGOs. Recently, reference has been made in the literature to "bottom-up" or "cosmopolitan" multilateralism, as well as a move from international governance to global governance (Schechter and Zierler, 2005; Ritterberg, 2002). But traditional multilateralism does not seem to be ready to abandon its supremacy. The argument in this chapter is that since multilateral cooperation remains almost exclusively within the interstate space (see the previous section), it will hardly progress towards global governance. Serious global reforms through a multilateralism in which the states are the only agents would be either impossible or extremely limited.

Numerous ideas and proposals have been forwarded for reform towards more effective multilateral global governance and its institutions – that is, the UN and its specialized agencies, as well as the international financial institutions. A lot of work was done on the subject by individual experts and independent and/or international commissions (Thakur and Cooper, 2004). They range from specific proposals – such as creating a "Peoples Assembly" at the UN in addition to the intergovernmental General Assembly, changing the weighted voting system and accountability in the IMF and World Bank, increasing the number of the permanent members of the Security Council, and establishing a Council for Economic and Social Security – to the radical proposition of closing down the UN system and redesigning an entirely new institutional architecture for global governance (Bertrand, 1986). Almost all have been quietly shelved. Formulated by experts, they had no political support and public visibility. A rare exception was the Bruntland Commission's report on sustainable development, which had a policy impact.

The latest reform plan for enhancing the multilateral system was presented by the Secretary-General, on the basis of the proposals of an International Panel, the UN Summit, which met in September 2005 (United Nations, 2004). It seemed to have more political support and visibility through the strong personal engagement of Kofi Annan. However, the outcome was disappointing and confirmed the limits of "top-down multilateralism". The most important proposal was aimed at enlarging the Security Council with new permanent members without a veto power, particularly countries such as Brazil, India, Nigeria, South Africa, as well as Germany and Japan, so that it would become truly representative of the current global power configuration, but this failed for lack of consensus between and within the North and the South. The few decisions taken were to replace the UN Human Rights Commission by a council with more powers, establish a commission to consolidate peace and oversee the reconstruction operations in societies suffering from armed conflict, and certain measures aimed at improving the management of the organization. They are certainly useful, but far from the expectations raised by the UN Secretary-General's initiative.

Multilateral approaches to reform the global governance architecture and arrangements are confronted with the conservatism of dominant states, starting with the five permanent members of the Security Council, but also that of others, particularly the regional powers, which compete with each other. They are also handicapped by the fact that the non-state agents, influential on the transnational public space are not allowed, or only marginally, to participate. Furthermore, the USA under the Bush administration has been displaying an active hostility towards multilateralism and disdain for the primacy of international law over the national law, refusing to accept whatever positive outcomes have been obtained by multilateralism, such as the Kyoto Protocol on climate warming, the interdiction of anti-personnel mines, or the International Criminal Court. Worse still, it is actively trying to escape previous commitments taken under the existing multilateral legal instruments – for example, the withdrawal from the protocol of the Vienna Convention concerning the rights of foreigners convicted in the USA to seek the assistance of their consulates, or efforts to by-pass the rules of the WTO trade regimes by signing bilateral trade agreements with as many countries (especially the poorer and vulnerable ones) as possible. The USA is of course far from being alone in breaching the rules of multilateralism, but, being the most powerful country and claiming global leadership, its actions are more damaging than in the case of others.

If efforts to enhance global governance through multilateralism encounter such difficulties, which is after all a familiar concept and a rather
well-charted area since the creation of the United Nations, it is easy to
imagine that obstacles and resistance against a more democratic global
governance would be much stronger.

The way to legitimate global governance: a multi–level and participatory transformative process

How, then, to advance from the global norm-setting and regulation that
are apolitical, non-accountable, technocratic and driven by private interests, to legitimate global governance. Sovereign states which support or
accept the neo-liberal direction of globalization and its regulation, rather
than fostering public interest and common good, as well as the transnational corporations (TNC), which yield enormous resources and power,
are the central agents in global governance. The involvement of NGOs,
as networks of experts and reliance on them for monitoring and enforce-
ments of norms do not change the technocratic character and private
biases of global governance. They merely add to it a network governance
dimension. The logic of efficient output prevails, while the issue of legitimate democratic input is neglected. Global governance tends to become
dysfunctional in terms of equity, as well as in coping with other major
global challenges, linked in many ways to socio-economic issues, such as
environmental degradation and climate change (Florini, 2003) (see Ariffin, Chapter 9, this volume).

The configuration of a global governance possessing democratic features is, to a large extent, terra incognita, somewhat as democratic institutions were in the eighteenth century to their early promoters in the
USA and Europe. National democratic systems were not pre-established
blueprints. Their practical conditions and institutions had to be invented
and developed through agency and progress. This is also the case for
global governance, and, needless to say, beyond the national level, the
challenge is even more complex. National democratic institutions, developed on a territorial basis, can hardly be replicated mechanically at the
transnational level.

Beyond the borders of the state, the foundational elements of democracy, structured around the principle of sovereignty, such as a centralized
political authority, political community, citizenship, civil society, social
contract and the regulation of the economic and social spheres through
the freely expressed will of citizens, do not exist. There is no global community of states sharing similar values and worldviews, either. Under

such conditions, transnational representative institutions cannot be established. Yet, such principles should somehow inspire efforts towards a legitimate global governance, displaying the following characteristics: representation of populations, participation, accountability and effectiveness. In this respect, statehood – that is, the concern with democratic political processes and public good – is a central element. And statehood at the transnational level requires that the sovereign state plays its role as a political agent and not as a promoter of private interests in global governance.

Without the agency of the sovereign states, non-state agents alone cannot change significantly the course of events. The reverse is also true: reform efforts need the participation of non-state agents. As discussed earlier, the sovereign states' approach to multilateralism is by definition top-down and conservative. Reform initiatives at the global level concerning international institutions, in order to increase the capacity to solve international problems, fail more often than not as long as they remain a strictly interstate affair. They are needed, for the IGOs, as instruments of the common interest and will of the states, are important actors of global governance. However, piecemeal improvements of an already fragmented cluster of multilateral bodies fall very much short of seriously renewing the system. These IGOs are to change, but as part of a more comprehensive and ambitious approach. Partial technical improvements aimed at avoiding or mitigating political, financial and commercial failures, thus securing the continuation of the same global institutional architecture, will not serve the goal of a redistribution of power and resources, or a reduction of systemic inequities.

The case of the European Union, an unprecedented and probably non-replicable regional integration process, is quite symptomatic of the difficulties involved in establishing a democratic governance beyond the territorial state. Even the availability of enabling factors – such as a community of states sharing the same democratic system of values, striving towards an integrated regional entity through negotiated voluntary transfer of sovereignty prerogatives to common institutions; the creation of a European citizenship and common electoral procedures, including voting rights in local elections given to citizens of EU member states residing in other states of the Union; a single market and currency – could not lead, after decades of efforts, to a real democratization of European governance. The separation of powers that characterize democracy does not exist at the European Union level. The European Parliament is much weaker than national parliaments, despite the recent increases in its prerogatives in controlling the European executive and budget. The executive is powerful, but is split between the Commission – the members of which are not elected but appointed and thus it has no democratic legitimacy – and the Council of Ministers, which is an intergovernmental body.

In addition to the deficiencies regarding representative institutions, the European Union's governance was always deficient in terms of participation. Stakeholders' arrangements, introduced early in the process, have long remained rather weak, although they have become more systematic and broader since 2000. The judiciary is split between the European Human Rights Court, dealing with political and civil rights, and the European Court of Justice, which operates in the realm of private law, corporate law and socio-economic rights. The EU Constitutional Treaty, ratification of which was refused in 2005 by the French and Dutch states, contained further elements of democratization, but, even if it were adopted, the European Union would still have a long way to go to become a true transnational democracy. Rejection of the Treaty shows how difficult it is to achieve transnational democracy even amongst political systems and societies sharing similar principles and patterns.

Unique as it is, the European experience may still offer certain institutional tools and practices to the architects of a democratized global governance, with the caveat that, at the latter level, the aim can only be the introduction of a number of democratic principles and practices, but not integration and federalism. The most obvious governance tool would be the principle of subsidiarity, which guides the repartition of powers between the Union and its member states. At the global level, subsidiarity would involve regional bodies, or ad hoc coalitions of states under a UN mandate. In fact, the UN has already started to implement the subsidiarity principle. For example, the UN entrusted peacekeeping functions in the Balkans, particularly in Kosovo, first to NATO and more recently to the European Union. Subsidiarity would also be useful in global governance areas other than collective security.

Institutional innovation and invention in global governance can only happen through a transformational approach. A basic element to take into account here is the multilevel characteristics of global governance, ranging from sub-state, state and regional levels, to global levels. Any blueprint for a relevant global governance must integrate the importance of the interactions between such levels.

Thus the structures and rules of a democratized global governance cannot be built at the global level only, since what happens there is related to other levels. Furthermore, if the design and implementation are kept behind closed doors, confined to diplomatic and economic interests, and their agents and experts, an alternative global governance will never come into being. Unless the top-down process is accompanied and balanced through bottom–up processes, rooted in local, national and regional interests and their agents, non-accountable, non-participatory, technocratic governance cannot be replaced by a more democratic and legitimate one.

The way forward would be to implement broad participatory strategies, which, in addition to the states, involve in the process of deliberation and decision, IGOs, TNCs and other transnational non-state agents, national representatives and other bodies, such as the parliaments, elected local authorities, grass-root NGOs, social movements, trade unions, business and professional organizations. These bodies should be able to participate in the reform process and, subsequently, in decision-making at various levels, from local to global, via regional.

The regional level has a strategic role in a democratized multilevel global governance (see Fawcett, Chapter 7, and Berthelot, Chapter 8, this volume). Two interrelated arguments, among others, would justify the important role of regionalism. The first one is that regional integration efforts and intergovernmental regional organizations are instruments for articulating and defending the interests and policies of the governments concerned at the global level. Secondly, they offer a solution to the perennial dilemma of the transnational system and global governance: the rule of one state, one vote – at once unavoidable as a fundamental expression of sovereignty (which is, as argued above, a *conditio sine qua non* of political community, citizenship, democracy and civil society) and an obstacle to a smoothly operating and equitable global governance. Indeed, political relations at any level of action cannot ignore power differentials between actors, but only regulate them so as to keep the system together through a mediation between the stronger and smaller states. In this way, allowing regional organizations to participate as actors in global governance would realistically help counter-balance the weight of the larger states, such as the USA or China, while, at the same time, protecting the interests of the smaller states, such as Luxemburg or Vanuatu. This, in fact, already happens in the case of Luxemburg, through the EU. Regional integration in the Asia-Pacific area involving Australia, New Zealand and the smaller island-states would offer similar advantages to Vanuatu.

An inclusive multilevel approach would require that national democratic systems, citizens and civil societies be connected to regional and global governance. Indeed, rooting the transformative process in national debates and provoking local ownership of global issues by citizens are crucial elements for starting and developing it. Organized and sustained pressures of electorates on their governments would be one of the more powerful incentives to encourage states to change their behaviour and policies at the global level and support efforts towards better global governance.

The UN, its specialized agencies, the Bretton Woods institutions, and the WTO would have to be reorganized so as to have multipartite, multi-layer structures to involve a variety of actors and constituencies. Statehood would have a central place in such structures and processes through governmental representatives, but the latter's power would be counter-balanced with representation from non-state actors. These principles and guidelines would also apply in regional organizations. Another crucial element would be a balanced representation from the northern and southern hemispheres in each of these state/non-state categories, the participation of a multiplicity of interests, values and world views being essential for a legitimate and effective global governance. Special measures would be taken to help small and failed states participate in the process.

In addition to such institutional innovations, fora for transnational dialogues and debates would be created, and issue-based, goal-oriented transnational networks promoted. Such fora and networks would be developed particularly at regional and sub-regional levels, linked to the UN at the global level, and their output integrated into the higher level decision-making processes as sources of innovative ideas and antidote to the technocratic tropism of national and international bureaucracies. One advantage of such arrangements would be to offer to civil society agents, autonomous transnational political spaces, free from the direct interferences of public and private powers (Väyrynen, 2003).

Admittedly, such suggested arrangements and processes for institution-building are complex and expensive, but the task itself is immensely complex. It cannot be dealt with through technocratic solutions in the name of efficiency, but through a process based on the principles of democratic politics adjusted to the conditions of the transnational scene.

Substantive issues would be addressed from the early stages of the process. The process itself is a key factor in ensuring not only a renewed form of global governance, but also providing a means towards substantive ends – namely, the conditions for an equitable world order and globalization. Such goals are of a political nature. The adverse effects of current globalization, and the political, economic and social failures of privatized and technocratic global governance, stem, to a great extent, from the priority accorded to the requirements of the economic and financial system and free trade over political and social concerns (Dervis 2005). This is reflected in the dissociation of political and civil human rights from the socio-economic rights, the latter being almost completely ignored.

Such a normative distortion is observed in the institutional architecture of global governance, as well as in policy priorities. The financial and commercial IGOs – the IMF, World Bank and WTO – get adequate political support and budgetary resources from the rich countries, and participate actively in the technocratic governance of globalization. By contrast, the socio-economic wing of the UN, dealing with developmental, social and environmental issues – the Economic and Social Council, and the specialized agencies, programmes and funds under its supervision – get limited political support and are weaker. The new institutional architecture should terminate the current dissociation between the financial/commercial IGOs and those dealing with social development, and aim at a regulation of globalization which accords equal priorities to economic efficiency, social equity and environmental protection.

In this respect, an important task would be to provide a greater substantive, functional and operational coherence to the United Nations. A possible solution would be to broaden the mandate of the current Security Council and to rename it the "United Nations Council". This new body would encompass all the areas of activity of the UN – that is, not only peace and collective security, but also human rights, as well as socio–economic, financial, commercial, developmental and environmental issues. Existing sectoral bodies, such as the specialized agencies, Bretton-Woods institutions, funds and programmes would become the UN Council's subsidiary bodies, reporting directly to the UN Council. The Economic and Social Council would be abolished, since its functions would be transferred to the UN Council. The five permanent members would keep their veto power, but the overall membership of the Council would be enlarged, with a number of permanent members without veto power, as well as seats reserved for the states representing the regions, on a rotationary basis. The UN Council would have sessions meeting with specialized representatives of its member states, as per the issues on its agenda.

G-8, the vehicle through which just eight powerful states are steering the world order, must be enlarged to include at least China, India, Brazil and South Africa. Otherwise, its already questionable legitimacy, due to its inadequate membership, will become even weaker.

Conclusion

A legitimate global governance and its institutional architecture can only emerge through a bold transformative approach, rather than a reformist one. As regards the process, both the northern and southern states, which are to be the leading agents, would not readily agree to such a transformative approach without strong pressure from non-state agents of the transnational public space, as well as from national democratic forces and public opinions. The World Social Forum, and Regional Social Fora in Europe, Africa and Asia, were useful in helping to set up global debates in local contexts and linking them to regional and national public opinions. Similarly, the holding in January 2004 of the World Social Forum in Mumbai, India – for the first time away from Porto Alegre, and again in January 2006, and in successive sessions, in Bamako, Mali and Caracas, Venezuela – was instrumental in fostering the diffusion of critical debates on globalization and its governance to other contexts. A combination of constructive and imaginative dialogue involving state and non-state agents, and democratically expressed pressures on the TPS, including massive street demonstrations, have played a central role in articulating a worldwide demand in favour of a democratized global governance and its institutions.

Statehood is central to the process. The state and the principles of sovereignty would no doubt be considerably transformed to become a more shared one through interaction with non-state agents. However, the ultimate decision-making would still rest in the realm of statehood, with strong inputs and influence coming from the transnational public space.

Concerning substance, a sustainable and legitimate global governance would need to focus on democratization and development strategies. States in different parts of the world will always be remarkable for their different interests, cultures and world views. In addition, the diversity in their size, power and wealth will be there to stay. However, it should be possible to set up a global community of democratic and prosperous states and civil societies which is a sine qua non for a peaceful world. Since the end of World War II, there has not been a single armed conflict amongst the democratic states. A central aim of a renewed global governance should be to achieve such a sustainable world order and peaceful relations between all states, north and south, east and west.

A crucial question is the financing of such encompassing, complex procedures and processes of democratic global governance. The solution lies, of course, in the establishment of a global taxation system to fund such processes as well as aid the development of poor countries. The global tax would be managed through an accountable and transparent transnational mechanism in which the state as well as non-state agents would participate. This idea has long been rejected on the argument that it is not feasible, both technically and because it would be impossible to have all states agree to it. In fact the argument is strictly ideological, as it runs against the neo-liberal dogma. Global taxation is perfectly possible – on two conditions: (1) that the major economic powers, such as the USA, the EU, Japan, China, Australia, India, Brazil, Canada, reach a consensus to introduce it; and (2) that fiscal paradises are abolished. All other countries would then readily agree to it. An encouraging development in 2004 has been the advocacy in favour of a global taxation by Brazil and France, supported by another 110 states. The introduction by France, in 2005, of a small tax on air travel, supported by other countries such as the UK and Canada, is a first step in this direction.

Such a global taxation system would also foster global democracy in conformity with the principle: "No taxation without representation". It would be a good leverage towards the invention of specific representative, participatory and accountable institutions for legitimate global governance, giving priority to a global social contract, as well as to public interest and public good, over private interests and market forces (Patomaki, 2001).

Notes

1. Patrick Artus (2002), a mainstream French economist, by no means a Marxist but using Karl Marx's concepts, explains such crises through the problems of capitalist accumulation. Taking the example of the US economy in the 1990s, he demonstrates with convincing data that in situations of high capital accumulation over a relatively long period, the capital stock grows, while profits as a percentage of GDP diminish. This is the process which Marx described as capitalism's trend towards the falling rates of profit. Such a decline in the profitability of capital due to diminishing returns hampers the capitalist accumulation. To recover higher rates of profit, it is necessary that the growth of wages is lower than the growth in labour productivity. In order to obtain such an outcome, the negotiation capacities of the wage-earners should be weakened, thanks to higher unemployment rates, creating what Marx called "the reserve army" of workers. In the USA, there was a considerable accumulation of capital between 1992 and 2000. As of 1997, with a low unemployment rate of 5 per cent, the "reserve army" disappeared, and the share of wages in the GDP increased. On average, the annual productivity growth was 1 per cent, while wages increased by 1.4 per cent. In 1998–2000, wages grew annually 1.5 per cent higher than productivity. Artus calculated that a 7 per cent unemployment rate would have been necessary to restore the profitability of capital, concluding that resorting periodically to recession in order to increase unemployment and render capital profitable is inefficient and socially problematic. Beyond this particular example of *fin de siècle* USA, the longer-term structural problems of capital accumulation appear to be a factor that has induced all major states at the centre of the world system to foster deregulated economic and financial globalization as of the mid-1970s. The trend towards falling rates of profit is a recurrent systemic problem over the long term, with cyclical ups and downs that do not modify the trend. The requirements of democratic regimes, however, rendered policies to keep the increased labour costs lower than the increased labour productivity more difficult. The ecological crisis, which forced firms to internalize costs for environmental protection, increased production costs further. The rapid decline of peasantry in industrial countries restricted the availability in the market of cheap labour from rural areas. Hence the "reserve army" tended to shrink structurally. To compensate for this, the hopes put in new technologies to replace workers in the production processes fell short of expectations, while the likelihood of resorting to the use of immigrant workers was constrained by various cultural and social problems. It remained difficult to achieve control of wage increases and input costs, or to mitigate the decline in profit rates in many sectors of the economy. Hence, in order to foster labour-market "flexibility", there were continuous efforts to cut tax rates and keep wage increases at low levels through

dismantling labour legislation and the transfer of industrial activities to low-wage countries. This was done in the face of the strong resistance of market forces and the competitive state against regulation towards redistributive justice.
2. www.afnor.fr; www.iso.org; www.cepaa.org; www.accountability.org.uk; www.globalreporting.org; www.unglobalcompact.org

REFERENCES

Aron, Raymond (1962) *Paix et Guerre entre les nations*, Paris: Calmann-Levy.

Artus, Patrick (2002) "Karl Marx is back", CDC Ixis – Capital Markets, Flash, 4 January.

Artus, Patrick and Marie-Paule Virard (2005) *Le capitalisme est en train de s'autodétruire*, Paris: La Découverte.

Badie, Bertrand (2000) "La régulation sociale au-delà de la souveraineté des Etats", in Pierre de Senarclens (ed.) *Maîtriser la mondialisation*, Paris, Presses de Sciences-Po.

Bayard, Jean-François (2004) *Le gouvernement du monde: une critique politique de la mondialisation*, Paris: Fayard.

Berr, Eric and François Combarnous (2005) "Vingt ans d'application du Consensus de Washington à l'épreuve des faits", *Economie Appliquée*, 58(2) June.

Bertrand, Maurice (1986) *Refaire l'ONU: un programme pour la paix*, Genève: Ed. Zoe.

Bobbio, Norberto (1998) *L'Etat et la démocratie internationale*, Brussels: Ed. Complex.

Dervis, Kemal (2005) *A Better Globalization: Legitimacy, Governance and Reform*, Washington DC: Centre for Global Development, Brookings Institution Press.

Deutsch, Karl (1968) *The Analysis of International Relations*, Englewood Cliffs, NJ: Prentice Hall.

Florini, Ann (2003) *The Coming Democracy: New Rules for Running a New World*, Washington/London: Island Press.

Fukuyama, Francis (2004) *State-Building: Governance and World Order in the 21st Century*, Ithaca, NY: Cornell University Press.

Geertz, Clifford (2004) "What is a state if it is not a sovereign?", Sydney W. Mintz Lecture for 2003, *Current Anthropology* 45(5) December.

Gerschenkorn, A. (1966) *Economic Backwardness in Historical Perspective*, Cambridge, Mass: Belknap Press.

Ha-Joon, Chang (2003) *Globalization, Economic Development and the Role of the State*, London/New York: Zed Books and Penang, Malaysia: Third World Network.

Hausmann, Ricardo and Dani Rodrik (2003) "Economic development as self-discovery", Harvard University, J.F. Kennedy School of Government, RWP02–023, March.

Held, David (1995) *Democracy and the Global Order*, Cambridge UK: Polity.

Held, David and Mathias Koenig-Archibugi (eds.) (2003) *Taming Globalization: Frontiers of Governance*, Cambridge UK: Polity.

Hibou, Béatrice (1999) *La privatisation des Etats*, Paris: Karthala.

Hoang-Ngoc, Liêm and Bruno Tinel (2005) "La régulation du 'nouveau capitalisme': analyses positives et recommandations normatives comparées", *Economie Appliquée* 58(1) March.

Kazancigil, Ali (2003) "Apprivoiser la mondialisation: vers une régulation sociale et une gouvernance démocratique", in Carlos Milani, Carlos Arturi and German Solinis (eds.) *Démocratie et gouvernance mondiale: quelle régulation pour le XXIè siècle?*, Paris: UNESCO and Khartala.

Keohane, Robert and Joseph Nye (1971) *Transnational Relations and World Politics*, Cambridge MA: Harvard University Press.

—— (1977) *Power and Interdependence: World Politics in Transition*, Boston: Little and Brown.

Mazower, Mark (1998) *Dark Continent: Europe's Twentieth Century*, New York: Knopf.

Ocampo, José Antonio (2005) "Globalization, development and democracy", Social Science Research Council, *Items* 5(3).

Patomaki, Heikki (2001) *Democratizing Globalization: The Leverage of the Tobin Tax*, London: Zed Books.

Peyrelevade, Jean (2005) *Le capitalisme total*, Paris: Seuil.

Pogge, Thomas (2002) *World Poverty and Human Rights: Cosmopolitan Responsibilities and Reforms*, Cambridge UK: Polity Press.

—— (2003) "Interview", Social and Human Sciences Newsletter, UNESCO, October–December, pp. 4–8.

Polanyi, Karl (1957) *The Great Transformation: The Political and Economic Origins of Our Time*, Boston: Beacon Press.

Putzel, James (2005) "Globalization, liberalization and prospects for the state", *International Political Science Review* 26(1) January.

Ritterberg, Volker (ed.) (2004) *Global Governance and the UN System*, Tokyo: United Nations University Press.

Rosenau, James (1991) *Turbulences in World Politics: A Theory of Change and Continuity*, Princeton NJ: Princeton University Press.

Rosenau, James and Ernst-Otto Czempiel (1992) *Governance Without Government: Order and Change in World Politics*, Cambridge UK: Cambridge University Press.

Sen, Jai, Anita Anand, Arturo Escobar and Peter Waterman (2004) *World Social Forum, Challenging Empires*, New Delhi: Viveka Foundation.

Senarclens, Pierre de (2005) *Mondialisation: théories, enjeux et débat*, Paris: Armand Colin (4th edn).

Schechter, Mickeal G. and Matthew C. Zierler (2005) "Multilateralism: Does it still matter?", Academic Council on the United Nations System (ACUNS), Informational Memorandum 64, Fall.

Stiglitz, Joseph (2002) *Globalization and its Discontents*, New York, W.W. Norton.

Strange, Susan (1996) *The Retreat of the State. The Diffusion of Power in World Economy*, Cambridge UK: Cambridge University Press.

Thakur, Ramesh and Andrew F. Cooper (eds.) (2004) *International Commissions and the Power of Ideas*, Tokyo, United Nations University Press.

Thakur, Ramesh and Peter Malcontent (eds.) (2004) *From Sovereign Impunity to International Accountability: Search for Justice in a World of States*, Tokyo: United Nations University Press.

United Nations High-Level Panel on Threats, Challenges, and Change (2004) *A More Secure World: Our Shared Responsibilities*, UN Doc. A/54/565, 2 December.

Wade, Robert Hunter (2003) "The disturbing rise in poverty and inequality: Is it all a 'big lie'?", in David Held and Mathias Koenig-Archibugi (eds), *Taming Globalization: Frontiers of Governance*, Cambridge UK: Polity.

Wallerstein, Immanuel (1979) *The Capitalist World Economy*, Cambridge UK: Cambridge University Press.

Wallerstein, Immanuel (1986) "The states in the institutional vortex of the capitalist world economy", in Ali Kazancigil (ed.) *The State in Global Perspective*, Aldershot UK: Gower/UNESO.

Väyrynen, Raimo (2003) "Institutions and ideas of global governance", Report of the Helsinki Conference 2002: Searching for Global Partnerships, Helsinki, Finnish Ministry for Foreign Affairs, January.

Weiss, Linda (1998) *The Myth of the Powerless State: Governing the Economy in a Global Era*, Oxford: Polity Press.

Weiss, Linda (2005) "The state-augmenting effects of globalization", *New Political Economy* 10(3) September.

World Commission on the Social Dimension of Globalization (2004) *A Fair Globalization: Creating Opportunities for All*, Geneva: International Labour Organization.

Zammit, An (2003) *Development at Risk: Rethinking UN–Business Partnerships*, Geneva: South Centre and UNRISD.

4

Financial globalization, "global governance" and the erosion of democracy

Virgile Perret

Introduction

The international monetary and financial order established by the Bretton Woods agreement (1944) was based on the assumption that public control of monetary and financial policy was the key to the fulfilment of newly embedded democratic aspirations, most notably high employment and economic welfare, and the condition to prevent the return of the currency disorders that had undermined the political legitimacy of states during the interwar period. Since then, one of the most significant trends in international finance has been the emergence of private or quasi-private authorities in global markets, which has prompted the call for the "governance" of global finance. This dynamic has, however, brought about an *erosion of democracy*. In effect, by giving rise to private, unaccountable authorities, financial globalization has weakened the regulatory capacities of states and reconfigured state–citizen relations along the lines of a more restrictive notion of the public good.

The main contention of this chapter is that the erosion of democracy is actually being concealed by the discourse on "global governance" that permeates the rhetoric of international organizations and that is very much in fashion in international relations. By claiming the obsolescence of the public/private divide in favour of a structural–functionalist approach of globalization, advocates of global governance tend to ignore the effects of the processes they study in terms of their democratic significance. While it is true that the absence of a global political community

Regulating globalization: Critical approaches to global governance, de Senarclens and Kazancigil (eds), United Nations University Press, 2007, ISBN 978-92-808-1136-0

makes democratic procedures partially irrelevant to the study of global issues like finance, the entanglement of the financial system in monetary policies and its overall socio-economic impact make it part of those issues of such collective importance that they may be placed at the centre of the public domain (Underhill, 2001: 281). Thus, the regulation of global finance has a crucial importance for democracy. More specifically, my argument is divided into three sections. The first one looks at financial globalization and examines how this dynamic has unleashed processes of privatization of authority that have led to the erosion the regulatory capacity of democratic states. The second section aims at shedding light on the incapacity of the governance approach to account for this erosion of democracy. More precisely, it seeks to demonstrate how its proclaimed insensitivity to the public–private divide makes this approach indifferent to the democratic significance of shifts in the balance of power between public and private authority. In contrast, a political reading of regulation theory offers a more cogent analysis by highlighting the political impact of global finance on the regulatory capacities of states and on the structuration of state–citizen relations. The last section proposes a more thorough inquiry into the political economy of international finance in order to refine this argument. In contradistinction to the "external constraints view" which states that it is the *structural* dominance of international finance that undermines social democracy, I contend that the erosion of democracy proceeds also from a political rationality, in that it follows from a struggle for comparative advantage between states. Proposals for the reform of the international financial architecture are examined in conclusion.

Financial globalization and the erosion of democracy

Bretton Woods (1944): The "first publicly managed international monetary order"

According to Spero, "The Anglo-American plan, approved at Bretton Woods, became the first publicly managed international monetary order" (1977: 32). The management of the international monetary cooperation was indeed essentially in public hands, relying on consultation between central bank governors, finance ministers and IMF officials. One of the key principles of the system was compartmentalization – the separation of the financial system into different segments or compartments. It was central to various regulatory mechanisms that were established around the world in reaction to the crisis of 1929–1933, most notably the US

Glass–Steagall Act (1933) which formally separated banking from securities business, in the sense that it prevented commercial banks from setting up securities affiliates (Dale, 1992: 2). The essential aim of compartmentalization is risk segregation, by preventing external shocks from creating domestic chain reactions.

In addition, a restrictive stance was adopted towards capital flights. Indeed, given the high significance of short-term capital movements in the economic debacle of the 1930s, flows of "hot money" were regarded as a "nuisance" in the post-war international financial system. This is evident in the IMF Articles of Agreement, especially in Article IV which specified that these flows ought to be controlled if governments want to use the Fund's resources (de Cecco, 1979: 49). Capital controls together with fixed but adjustable exchange rates were designed to serve another central aim of the Bretton Woods negotiators, namely, national macroeconomic autonomy. More precisely, domestic monetary policy had to be immune from (external) pressures of international finance so that it could be activated according to (internal) objectives like economic growth and full employment (Mackinnon, 1993: 11–15). This reflected the domestic interventionism inherent to the "embedded liberalism compromise" (Ruggie, 1982: 393). The philosophy of this "compromise" profoundly modified the definition of what is public and what is private. Indeed, the Keynesian–Beveridge revolution implied the establishment of a public sphere that would create solidarity relations through redistribution and a large role for the state in the economy (Drache, 2001: 52).

However, the public foundation of the international monetary system was rapidly going to be put under stress by the growth of international capital markets which is generally held to have involved three interconnected processes: decompartmentalization; deregulation; and disintermediation through securitization (Bourguinat, 1992: 91–100). The next sections examine how these processes have shifted the balance of power between public and private authority in the international system and eroded the regulatory capacity of democratic states. More precisely, it looks at how they have led to the strengthening or the emergence of a multitude of private or quasi-private actors forming "a complex web of governance, working through multiple, often unaccountable layers of market, hierarchy and network, mixing public and private in ways which increasingly privilege the latter at the expense of the former" (Cerny, 2000: 60–61). In turn, and in a dialectical fashion, these newly arisen actors have exercised "structural power" (see Strange, 1988: 24–25) on states for the adoption of policies amounting to embedded austerity in the neo-liberal mode.

The internationalization of banking and the privatization of balance of payments financing

The growing volume of international trade in the late 1950s and early 1960s generated an increase in demand for commercial credit in foreign currencies, in particular, in the dollar. However, the US adoption of banking regulations and capital controls in order to stem the outflow of dollars was rendering such credit expensive and difficult to get. This restrictive regulatory context shifted the foreign operations of US banks to their foreign branches and the demand for international finance to the eurocurrency market in the 1960s. The spectacular growth of these markets stimulated the international mobility of capital and the emergence of an unregulated financial environment, offering favourable conditions to the development of speculation against official exchange parities (Strange, 1988: 105). Together with the adoption of a passive payments policy by the Nixon administration (benign neglect) and the intrinsic ambiguities of the Bretton Woods system in terms of responsibilities for payment positions adjustment, it eventually led to the closing of the gold window in 1971 and the abandonment of the system of fixed rates in 1973 (Williamson, 1977: 51). Global corporations played a significant role in the intensification of movements of short-term capital. Their impact on the international monetary system was magnified by their dominance on world trade, their globally coordinated financial management, and the increased speed of their operations. As a UN study noted in 1973, their massive use of unrecorded transactions – via the eurodollar market – for shifting liquid assets in anticipation of devaluation affected international monetary stability, by undermining the capacity of central banks to defend their currencies. The development of intra-company transfers[1] also frustrated the attempts of governments to control their own money supply (Barnet and Müller, 1974: 284–285).

The oil shock of 1973 further boosted the growth of off-shore capital markets. The eurodollar market attracted the oil-exporting states, which had succeeded in quadrupling the price of oil and thus had massive earnings to deposit. For oil-importing states, the picture was reversed: faced with severe balance-of-payments problems, they decided to finance their deficits in the lowest-cost credit markets. Commercial banks operating in the euromarkets were thus in an ideal position to play a role of international intermediary: they could "recycle" petrodollar surpluses by accepting short-term deposits (many from oil producers) and making medium-term loans (many to oil consumers) (Lipson, 1981: 605). Euromarkets were bound to perform a similar function when oil prices doubled again in 1979. In a few years, they expanded massively and came to represent "a gigantic pool of quasi-stateless mobile capital, not subject to political authority or accountability" (Gill, 1992: 274). By the same token, private banks had become major creditors of sovereign states. This privatization of balance of payments financing shows that during the 1970s "the private international banking sector became an integral part of the international monetary system and came to adopt roles previously regarded as within the province of the official sector" (Llewellyn, 1985: 203).

Disintermediation, securitization and the rise of private institutional channels of credit

During the 1980s, the composition of financial flows changed radically, with the relative decline of foreign direct investments (FDI) and the sharp increase of portfolio investment (Germain, 1997: 124). This reflected the transition from a "credit-based financial system", in which banks play an intermediation role between deposits from households and loans to companies, to a "capital-market based system", in which credit for large enterprises is accessible directly on capital markets via security offerings (Zysman, 1983: 18). This transition was underpinned by a twin process of disintermediation and securitization which developed in reaction to the economic insecurity following the debt crisis, characterized by high rates of inflation and volatile interest and exchange rates. In this context, banks needed to reduce their exposure to bad loans. They decided to cut back on loans in general (disintermediation) and to look for new sources of funds (securities).

Disintermediation refers to the decline of the traditional role of banks as intermediaries between borrowers and lenders, whereas securitization broadly describes the process by which financial intermediation has been moving from banks to capital markets. More precisely, securitization implies the transformation of traditional bank assets like mortgages into marketable instruments. This twin process has led to the progressive privatization of the international credit system, as complex networks of private, unaccountable institutions have gained authority and increased their influence in the system – a process referred to as "decentralized globalization" (Germain, 1997: 104). In particular, securities firms, merchant banks, institutional investors (pension funds, mutual funds, insurance companies, hedge funds), and rating agencies have emerged as prominent actors within networks of credit.

Most illustrative to our discussion is perhaps the rise of rating agencies. The twin processes of disintermediation and securitization have produced information problems for supplier and user of funds. It has created an environment in which no institution stands to evaluate the risk of lending money to borrowers. Given the high cost of gathering this information, this vacuum has stimulated the development of debt security rating

agencies. Bond raters make judgements on the capacity of an issuer to
pay in due time principal and interests on a security. Ratings are produced on corporations, financial institutions, municipalities and sovereign
governments. This market is dominated by two American agencies –
Moody's Investors Service (Moody's) and Standard and Poor's Ratings
Group (S&P) – that have expanded considerably since the mid-1980s.[2]
Bond rating agencies derive epistemic authority from their expertise and
local knowledge. They operate as coordination services firms (CSFs) by
establishing standards for the behaviour of agents and by generating
(narrow) consensus upon them, especially in terms of information coordination, risk coordination and strategic coordination. The democratic
significance of this trend can best be seen in rating decisions about municipalities in the US. For instance, Philadelphia was downgraded by the
major rating agencies in 1990 and 1991 and consequently cut from access
to lower cost financing. A new mayor was elected in November 1991,
who decided to implement a five-year fiscal plan calling for massive sav-
ings through cutting labour costs, management efficiencies and stricter
tax collection. The city's credit rating increased rapidly and the deficit
was eradicated in 1992/1993. This episode illustrates the pressures that
rating agencies can exert on the macroeconomic management of public
authorities. In general, rating agencies adhere to an orthodox financial
agenda based on the need to reduce social policy, essentially by recon-
necting remuneration and productivity in the public sector, and on the
privatization of services (Sinclair, 1994a, 1994b, 1999).

Overall, the process of "decentralized globalization" tends to make the
channels of credit more complex and more difficult to regulate for public
authorities. Traditional mechanisms of state regulation "are no longer as
effective simply because the main institutional objects of state regulation
– banks – no longer play the same kind of role within the financial system" (Germain, 1997: 168–170). Indeed, although banks are private
institutions, they traditionally perform public functions in the regulation
of financial markets by controlling risks and reducing uncertainties. By
reducing the role of banks as intermediaries between borrowers and
lenders, the disintermediation trend forces banks to give up their public
regulatory role within channels of credit. In addition, the process of securitization erodes the efficacy of traditional means of monetary policy
such as the determination of interest rates, the setting of reserve requirements and the selective use of open market operations (ibid.: 104).

*Free capital mobility and the "structural power" of private
authorities*

By the 1990s, financial globalization led towards "the consecration of free
capital mobility as a universal norm" (Cohen, 2003: 63). This process has

generated pressures in favour of convergence in regulatory practices and economic development models that tend to conflict with the imperatives of local and national political legitimacy (Underhill, 1999). The greatest pressures originate from growing financial interdependence and have affected the effectiveness of national stabilization policies because of the incompatibility of exchange-rate stability, capital mobility and national policy autonomy – what Cohen labelled the "unholy trinity". This theorem points to a trade-off policy-makers have to face in the context of rising international capital mobility:

> The problem is that in an environment of formally or informally pegged rates and effective integration of financial markets, any attempt to pursue independent monetary objectives is almost certain, sooner or later, to result in significant balance-of-payments disequilibrium, and hence provoke potentially destabilizing flows of speculative capital. (Cohen, 1993: 147)

In this context, interest rates that differ from the rest of the world will be contravened by financial flows. In particular, an expansionary monetary policy engenders a financial outflow as investors sell the currency (Frieden, 1991: 431). Mitterrand's U-turn of 1982 is a classic example of the constraint such financial outflow can exert on macroeconomic policies. Thus, the degree of capital mobility is regarded as a *structural* feature of the international system that "can swiftly force governments which deviate from policies seen as suitable by the 'market' to change course" (Gill and Law, 1989: 486). In particular, it is held to exert structural power on states by generating "pressure for monetary convergence" (Goodman, 1992: 217). This idea has been epitomized by Andrews with the "capital mobility hypothesis" which states that "as national capital markets become more integrated, the foreign exchange pressures associated with the pursuit of independently chosen monetary objectives increase" (1994: 204). In other words, the cost of monetary independence increases with financial integration.

Thus, free capital mobility provides incentives for governments to conform to the expectations of private holders of funds. This is particularly the case in the context of processes of disintermediation and securitization that have increased the power of the players active in the debt security market – referred to as "bond vigilantes" – over public authorities. As governments have increasingly financed their deficits with foreign debt in the 1980s, they have become dependent on "bond vigilantes" that are likely to react swiftly if they feel that inflation may threaten their interests. This dependence provides public officials with incentives to incorporate international credit ratings into the planning of their policy agenda (Sinclair, 1994b: 142). Thus, securitized finance allows private interests to exert indirect leverage on public financing and, thereby, to interfere within domestic policy commitments. More precisely, governments are incited to pursue national macroeconomic strategies seeking low and stable rates of inflation through budgetary discipline and a tight monetary policy. Such a cautious strategy allows governments to secure the approval of financial markets. In this context, "bond vigilantes" are associated to "private makers of public policy" and investors tend to acquire structural power on states for the redefinition of the public good along the lines of a system of embedded financial orthodoxy (Sinclair, 1994a: 448).

The role of institutional investors is particularly significant in this context. Indeed, the process of disintermediation has led to the reinforcement of the investors' delegation of the management of their portfolios to professional fund managers. Contrary to the neoclassical view that suggests that disintermediation has contributed to the decentralization of the capital allocation process, it has in fact been accompanied by the (re)centralization of investment decision-making among institutional investors.[3] This concentration of decision-making and the herd-like behaviour of fund managers increase the risk of "price overshooting" – a situation where prices fail to reflect the true value of assets. According to Harmes, "the political result of price overshooting has been a dramatic shift in the balance of power between investors on the one hand and governments, corporations and workers on the other". While it may actually be sound that financial actors have the possibility to impose some discipline on governments that pursue unsustainable economic policies, for instance, by trying to "buy votes by stimulating the economy through overly inflationary policies and excessive spending" (2001: 43), market overreaction and price overshooting tend to "transform the discipline of investors into a form of punishment" (ibid.: 45). A well-known example of "punishment" imposed on governments by institutional investors was George Soros's speculative attack on the British pound in 1992. He borrowed about $10 billion and was able to force a devaluation of the British pound. As a result, Britain was obliged to abandon its fixed exchange rate and Soros became famous for making over $1 billion on his bets. This shows that the capacity of hedge funds to raise huge sums of money and to act as market leaders enables them to generate self-fulfilling attacks and to fuel currency crises (ibid.: 132).

More broadly, it can be concluded that in a context of free capital mobility, welfare state functions become problematic, as "opening the economy to unrestricted inflows of capital may magnify the welfare cost of existing distortions" (Agenor and Aizenman, 1998: 26) and as "the mobility of capital and of employers ... render it more difficult to generate the public resources needed to finance social insurance schemes" (Rodrik, 1997: 73). Cerny notes that financial globalization has increased pressures on "cost-cutting in the welfare state" and has tended to privilege entitle-ment programmes to the detriment of public and social services (1996: 96). In the same perspective, Kurzer demonstrates in her comparative analysis of Austria, Belgium, the Netherlands and Sweden that financial globalization has empowered firms and financial actors but has weakened the power resources of labour, which has led to the erosion of social con-sultation and of the ability of governments to purchase national economic strategies (1993: 5). Frieden also notes that the politics of international capital mobility have differential distributional implications on socio-economic groups. In the long run, capital mobility tends to favour capital over labour, in particular in industrialized countries, whereas, in the short run, it favours economic agents with mobile or diversified assets and tends to penalize those with assets related to specific locations like man-ufacturing or farming (1991: 426). Eventually, as Moses concludes, there is a "crisis of social democracy", in the sense that the rapid development of international short-term capital movements has created an environ-ment in which traditional social democratic instruments are no longer ef-fective (1994: 133).

The next section examines how the erosion of democracy is actually being masked by the discourse on global governance. In contrast, it pro-poses a political reading of regulation theory in order to highlight the po-litical impact of global finance on the regulatory capacities of states and on the restructuring of state–citizen relations.

"Global governance" and the neglect of democracy

Democracy in a floating world: Who governs in the era of global governance?

The rise of non-state actors in "global governance" and the transformation of authority

The notion of governance appeared at the World Bank in the 1980s. It was intended to depict the evolution of the Bank's policies towards developing states. Indeed, the Bank's discourse on "good governance" reflected a supposedly wider (including institutions) conception of devel-opment putting at its core the reform of the political structures of devel-oping states, the enhancement of civil society and of its capacity to exert pressure on public authorities to render them more accountable. There-after, the notion of governance rapidly permeated the discourse of other international organizations, in particular of the OECD (Organisation for Economic Co-operation and Development), certain UN agencies like the

UNDP (United Nations Development Programme), and the European Commission.

In the 1990s, it emerged as a "key vantage point" on the question of global change, its causes and consequences. It has been used most prominently within the debates on economic globalization, "in a critical relationship to the 'states and markets' theme which dominated the latter" (Hewson and Sinclair, 1999: 5). Concerns with the consequences of an unregulated world stimulated arguments for strengthened global-level governance. Pioneering works use this concept to explain that globalization implies the diffusion of authority away from states towards multiple networks of public and private actors. This shift was epitomized as a transition from government to "governance without governments" (Rosenau, 1992: 5). According to the Commission on Global Governance:

> Governance is the sum of the many ways individuals and institutions, public and private, manage their common affairs.... At the global level, governance has been viewed primarily as intergovernmental relationships, but it must now be understood as also involving non-governmental organizations (NGOs), citizens' movements, multinational corporations, and the global capital market. 1995: 4)

What is fundamentally new about global governance is the development of "global-level 'private' authorities that regulate both states and much of transnational economic and social life" (Murphy, 2000: 794). Private governance contributions are supposed to emerge from a vast array of actors, including business associations or multinational corporations (Sell, 1999; Spar, 1999). The mere emergence of private actors on the international scene is generally seen as a necessary and sufficient condition for these actors to be considered as *legitimate* authorities. Indeed, according to Hurd, as long as their newly acquired power is not challenged, these non-state actors are implicitly legitimated as authoritative: "To the extent that a state accepts some international rule or body as legitimate, that rule or body becomes an 'authority'". In this context, the legitimacy of a rule is purely subjective, in that it refers to "the normative belief by an actor that a rule or institution ought to be obeyed" (1999: 381). Thus, the concept of private authority is intended to shed light on the exercise of (legitimate) authority by newly arisen private actors. In this perspective, global governists proclaim the very obsolescence of the public–private dichotomy (Cutler, 1997: 277), and, more broadly, of the legal formalism inherent to the "liberal art of separation" (Cutler, 2002: 24), on the ground that "there is a growing asymmetry between the theory and the practice of international relations: the theory makes an impossibility of private authority and private international regimes, while the activities of non-state actors grow increasingly authoritative" (ibid.: 33).

Global governists are right to emphasize the growing regulatory role performed by private actors. The main methodological virtue of the concept of private authority is to widen the analysis of political agency beyond traditional (Weberian) conceptions of the state. In addition, this widening proceeds from a valuable effort not to reify the distinction between the private and public spheres that is part of the analytical foundation of the bourgeois state. However, by claiming the obsolescence of the public/private divide, global governists tend to ignore the constitutive role of this dichotomy within channels of democratic legitimation. In contrast, I contend that all claims of authority may not be worthy of acceptance in a democratic system and that the public/private distinction retains a high *heuristic utility* in order to shed light on the democratic significance of shifts in the patterns of regulatory authorities.

Ambiguities with global governance: democracy turned upside down?

The definition of governance provided by the Commission on Global Governance strikes by its openness and seduces by the way it proposes to transcend the rigidities of the "domestic/foreign" dichotomy. In this respect, it is in full accord with its Parsonian structural-functionalist logic, according to which governance turns out to be always effective and ultimately good (Latham, 1999: 37–39). However, the problem with it lies in its fuzziness and its intrinsic ambiguity. It not only offers "little basis for identifying structures of domination" (ibid.: 34), but it creates a confusion between what *is* and what *should be*, as Latham underlines: "global governance is a too comfortable vessel for both analysis and advocacy" (ibid.: 25). It is indeed one thing to *describe* the increasing involvement of private actors within regulatory arrangements, but it is quite another to actually *prescribe* their incorporation in global governance. This ambiguity subsumes a more fundamental one regarding authority. Indeed, the question of authority can be envisaged from two different perspectives, analytical and normative. From an analytical point of view, it is focused on the "criteria by which we may recognize the possession, exercise, and acceptance of authority". From a normative point of view, it is interested in analysing what renders authority legitimate, "what justifies the claims of authority as being worthy of acceptance?" (Lukes, 1990: 203). I argue that these two dimensions of the question of authority should be distinguished – that is, "that we can elucidate the concept of authority and as separate matter ask when, if ever, submission to it is justified" (ibid.). This means that a private actor that has gained power and influence in the international system may be considered as a private authority, but not necessarily as an authority to which submission is justified.

The confusion of these two dimensions of authority in the global governance discourse reflects a form of hybrid and informal pluralism that confers as much voice to market agents as to elected officials. By mixing indifferently public and private actors in a single fabric of global governance, the governance discourse conceals the democratic significance of the public/private dichotomy within changing patterns of authority. Indeed, this indifference is problematic because the nature (public/private) of authority raises crucial issues of both accountability and equity. The argument outlined in the previous section relating to financial globalization illustrates this friction between the rise of private authorities and the democratic exercise of politics. It can be extended to question the main assumptions of the global governance approach, especially with regard to the involvement of non-state actors in the securities industry regime. Indeed, as Haufler recalls, "The existence of private regimes must raise questions about the legitimacy of their goals, the accountability of their decision-making processes, and the distributional effects of the regime itself" (2000: 133). In the financial sector, this warning is particularly applicable to the International Organization of Securities Commissions (IOSCO) policy process, wherein non-state bodies outside the traditional legislative process take part in important decisions concerning the structure of international capital markets. Indeed, these decisions affect the ability of governments to regulate their societies in accordance with preferences democratically expressed (Underhill, 1995: 253). The argument I am making here is not to be confused with a nostalgic, state-centrist vision of the world, but it is to be taken as a warning against a concept (global governance) whose ambiguity and fuzziness may threaten the very democratic foundation of regulatory arrangements. For this reason, the next section proposes to replace the concept of governance by a political reading of regulation theory that is sensitive to the democratic significance of shifts in the balance of power between public and private authorities.

The process of regulation and the legitimation of state–citizens relations

The concept of regulation was introduced into economics to explain how capitalist accumulation endures despite its internal contradictions. It emphasizes the capacity of social norms and institutions to impose convergence to antagonistic forces. In contradistinction to global governance discourse, the state is assigned a central role within the ensemble of regulatory institutions (Vercellone, 1994: 13–14). This centrality of the state is underpinned by the conviction, common to most critical accounts of neoclassical models, that economic action cannot be considered autonomous insofar as it is necessarily "embedded" in a social order that allows for its functioning.[4] As Palan underlines:

> The "market" cannot be seen as an equivalent and alternative mode of social organization to politics. On the contrary, relationship between politics and economics is of a different order, encapsulated by, or more appropriately hinted at, the notion of "embeddedness" – the market is embedded in social and political practice. (1998: 110)

Regulation theory clearly reflects the *political embeddedness* of the economy by stressing how economic action is shaped by power struggles that involve non-market institutions, especially the state and social classes (Caillé, 1995: 29). Thus, a mode of regulation is "an ensemble of mediations that maintain the distortions produced by the accumulation of capital in limits compatible with social cohesion within nations" (Aglietta, 1997: 412). This definition shows that the concept of regulation is somehow vulnerable to the same criticism as the notion of governance, as it endorses a prescriptive bias regarding the limits (i.e. social cohesion) capitalist accumulation should not overtake. However, in contradistinction to global governists who equate globalization with the supposedly salutary decentralization of state authority, regulationists remain committed to the *primacy of political agency* and thus to the primary regulatory role of public authorities. Such ontological commitments are fundamental prerequisites of representative democracy.

More specifically, a political reading of regulation theory allows increasing its sensitivity to the democratic significance of transfers of authority. Indeed, according to Purcell, the process of regulation occurs not only in response to economic imperatives (the promotion of competitiveness and accumulation), but also in response to the state's concern to maintain its political legitimacy in the eyes of its citizenry. He states that "Just as capitalism evolves dialectically through the twin processes of crisis and resolution, so we can think of the agreement between state and citizens as remaking itself in a dialectical fashion" (Purcell, 2002: 300). Such a holistic conception of regulation allows us to bridge the gap between the analysis of the (global) dynamic of financial globalization and the (domestic) process of state–citizen relations. In this perspective, the democratic significance of shifts in the balance of power between public and private authority can only be acknowledged insofar as the dialectical remaking of the agreement between state and citizens is explicitly taken into account. But is it possible to refine the analysis of the *democratic* significance of the rise of private authorities in global markets? Democracy is a concept that defies precise definition. However, it can be argued that the emergence of private authorities may affect state–citizen relations in two interrelated manners, referring to both formal (procedural) and substantive (normative) dimensions of democracy.[5] On the formal side, the emergence of private authorities tends to reduce means of controlling power, as these actors stand removed from traditional procedures of democracy (at the national level) and mechanisms of accountability (at the international level). On the substantive side, newly arisen private authorities can potentially exert influence on the capacity of governments to define and provide public goods. Applied to financial globalization, this framework aims at demonstrating that the rise of private, unaccountable authorities in global markets has eroded the regulatory grip of states and reconfigured state–citizen relations along the lines of a more restrictive notion of the public good – a process that fuels the erosion of democracy. The next section proposes a more thorough inquiry into the political economy of international finance in order to refine this argument.

Reflections on the political economy of international finance

Most explanations of how financial integration compromises social democracy tend to fit the "external constraints" view that "holds that macroeconomic policies in principle can be effective in durably influencing the economy, but that national governments have lost control over economic policy instruments" (Notermans, 1997: 202). However, this view neglects the fact that much of these "external constraints" has actually been generated by the active support of national monetary authorities to the development of international financial markets. In other words, the problem with this account lies in its determinism, in that international finance appears as an exogenous factor constraining states autonomy and leaving very little room for collective action and social change. Thus, some reflections on the political economy of international finance may be useful in order to refine this argument with respect to the differential role of states.

Financial globalization has certainly been a source of challenges for states, but it has also fulfilled the national interest of major powers. Indeed, the United States and Britain had strong economic and political interests in promoting a more open international financial order. By unilaterally providing financial actors with a location free of regulation, these states unleashed competitive pressures that "forced" other states to follow the lead by liberalizing and deregulating their own financial systems (Helleiner; 1994: 12). In other words, the transnationalization of financial markets is underpinned by a dynamic of "competitive deregulation", which provides the state with incentives to impose "upon market actors – and upon itself – *new market-oriented rules*" (Cerny, 1993b: 52). The pursuit of international competitiveness leads to the "competition state", that is, the "commodification" or the "marketization" of the state policy and structure (Cerny, 1993a: 17). This transformation process is based on a political rationality of "struggle for comparative advantage" in terms of jobs, prosperity, and prestige, which focuses on states" systems of regulation:

> The struggle for comparative advantage is the dominant fact of life in financial markets; systems of regulation are themselves powerful sources of comparative advantage; the single most important feature of a system of regulation is the form and extent of state power in that system. (Moran, 1991: 6–7)

This political rationality of financial globalization (the struggle for comparative advantage) testifies to the fact that state agencies (most notably those of major powers) have been actively involved in the internationalization of financial markets. What is the significance of this political logic with respect to the erosion of democracy? Does it amount to say, in direct opposition to the "external constraints" view, that financial globalization does not hamper the running of democracy as it follows from political decisions taken by democratically elected governments? Such an argument is dubious for at least three reasons. The first and most evident one relates to the asymmetric consequences of financial globalization on developing and developed states. The process of financial globalization has transnational repercussions which undermine the political legitimacy essentially of developing states, as it unleashes powerful competitive pressures on these states for the "marketization" of their state policy and structure. Indeed, the pressures for liberalization of the capital account are stronger in countries where dependence on foreign finance is high and with balance-of-payments difficulties (Haggard and Maxfield, 1996: 37). In this context, Mosley points out that the financial market influence is limited to inflation and government budget deficit levels in OECD countries (macroeconomic indicators), whereas it "extends to cover both macro- and micro-policy areas" in developing nations (2003: 17).

Second, the argument according to which policies adopted by democratically elected governments can only be "democratic" may also be relativized on the ground that it is based on a formalist conception of democracy that neglects its substantive (normative) dimension. Indeed, recall from above that democracy cannot be reduced to its formal aspect because elected governments in democracies might adopt policies which tend to erode rather than maintain or strengthen democracy – for instance, by modifying social equity systems in a way that enhances international competitiveness but increases social disparities. This is all the more relevant to representatives who are imbued with a form of market (neo-liberal) ideology that is "inherently antithetical to democratic principles", since it tends to "paralyse or delegitimate political thinking as a gateway to democratic action" (Birchfield, 1999: 30). Thus, both aspects of democracy (formal and substantive) should be taken into account in the study of state restructuring within the process of financial globalization.

Finally, it has to be emphasized that if the political elites of industrialized states have played a pro-active role in financial globalization, they might not have fully appreciated the consequences of their decisions for themselves. As Goodman and Pauly astutely observe with respect to the diminishing utility of capital controls, "unintended consequences" may result from previous policy choices:

> governments encouraged or at least acquiesced in both the growth of offshore money markets and the international expansion of firms. Yet ... governments continued to impose capital controls long after such developments became salient. In this sense, the diminishing utility of capital controls can be considered the *unintended consequence* of other and earlier policy decisions. (1993: 79, my emphasis)

The overall erosion of democracy in OECD states proceeds in part from a similar dialectical logic. Indeed, financial globalization is a political dynamic of struggle for comparative advantage which provides states with incentives to adopt market-oriented reforms of their systems of regulation, thereby creating a propitious, transnational environment for the emergence of private or quasi-private actors. In turn, and in a dialectical fashion, private actors progressively acquire "structural power" and authority in the international system and succeed in influencing the definition of the public interest in the policy formulation process. In other words, the politics of financial globalization have generated transnationalized economic structures and private pressures that eventually alter the nature of democracy itself, by eroding the regulatory grip of states and (re)defining state–citizen relations along the lines of a more restrictive definition of the public good. This does not mean to say that policymakers from major powers have deliberately sought to compromise the working of social democracy, but rather that their prior aim has been competitiveness, and that the erosion of democracy has resulted partially as an "unintended consequence". This reflects the existence of a trade-off between the quest of competitiveness of states – and the "commodification" of systems of regulation that it implies – and the necessity for governments to maintain their democratic legitimacy.

Conclusion

Financial globalization has stimulated the rise of private, unaccountable authorities which have eroded the regulatory capacity of democratic states and reconfigured state–citizens' relations along the lines of a more restrictive notion of the public good. The democratic significance of this process is neglected by the discourse on global governance which claims the obsolescence of the public/private divide in International Relations in favour of a structural-functionalist conception of globalization. In contrast, a more political reading of regulation theory allows us to emphasize the potential influence of these shifts on the regulatory capacities of states and on the structuration of state–citizen relations. However, this is not to say that international finance represents an exogenous factor constraining states autonomy and leaving no room for collective action and social change. Indeed, the political struggle for comparative advantage of major powers has greatly contributed to the creation of a propitious environment for the emergence and the consolidation of the "structural power" of private or quasi-private authorities. In turn, this privatization of structural power has made increasingly problematic the fulfilment of internal democratic aspirations such as the maintenance and enhancement of an elaborate welfare state. This points to the centrality of political decisions in the erosion of democracy.

The risk that financial globalization further undermines the political legitimacy of states raises the issue of the reform of the international financial architecture. One way of increasing the autonomy of states in formulating monetary and macro-economic policy would be to "throw some sand into the wheels of international moncy markets" with the introduction of a currency transaction tax, as proposed by Nobel laureate James Tobin in his address to the Eastern Economic Association in 1978. Such a tax has raised contentions about its technical and political feasibility. However, on the technical side, subsequent refinements have shown how it could be reconciled with new financial instruments like forwards, swaps, futures and options involving foreign currency transactions. On the political side, advocates of the tax sustain that it could be effective even without universal application – that is, through an international agreement including the major economies and financial centres of the world: G7 countries, all other European Union states that are not members of the G7, plus Singapore, Switzerland, Hong Kong and Australia (Kennen, 1996; Griffith-Jones, 1996). But the problem remains of how to generate enough political will to set the tax into motion. Non-state actors may well play a functional role in this respect. Indeed, by opening a new space of contestation and public deliberation at the transnational level, they can revive the normative issues of democracy and social justice, and create a favourable ideological context to the idea of taxing financial transactions. This will be all the more so because the failure of the OECD to establish the Multilateral Agreement on Investment, the financial crises that hit Asia (1997), Russia (1998), Brazil (1999) and Argentina (2002), the failures of the third and fifth Ministerial Meetings of the World Trade Organization (WTO) in Seattle (1999) and Cancun (2003), and the growing perception that globalization increases inequalities show that the orthodoxy of the "Washington Consensus" is being increasingly contested.

Meanwhile, a more politically realist agenda would be to reform international financial institutions, most notably the International Monetary Fund (IMF) and the World Bank. The last two decades have seen the role of these two institutions expanding far beyond their original mandate. Indeed, they have been increasingly intruding into the domestic political processes of developing states by making the grant of new loans conditional to the adoption of stabilization and structural adjustment programmes involving orthodox policies and market-oriented reforms (fiscal austerity, monetary tightening and trade liberalization). In the 1990s, the number of conditions included in loans increased dramatically so as to cover issues of "good governance", such as the rule of law, judicial reform and corporate governance. This expansion of activities has created overlaps between the two institutions and magnified problems of accountability. These two deficiencies need to be addressed if the erosion of democracy is to be limited or reversed. To begin with the problem of accountability of the IMF and the World Bank, measures should be taken in order to (1) increase the *transparency* of these institutions through the publication of voting records, executive board minutes and performance evaluations; (2) strengthen the evaluation and the *monitoring* of their work and make the findings accessible to the public; and (3) enhance mechanisms of *enforcement* so that policies continue to conform to the rules for which the institutions can be held to account (see Woods, this volume, Chapter 5).

In addition, both institutions should be better separated in their functions and activities. To start with the IMF, the Meltzer report[6] suggests that it should stop engaging in poverty reduction programmes and defer this function to the World Bank. More precisely, the IMF should stop lending to countries for long-term assistance (as in sub-Saharan Africa) and for long-term structural transformation (as in the post-Communist transition economies). Instead, it should renew with its original (more modest) mandate, that is, the provision of liquidity (short-term resources) to members with balance of payments deficits. The Bank, for its part, should cut lending to middle-income countries and provide more funds to low-income countries (more precisely the 80 to 90 poorest nations without access to private-sector resources) in the form of grants rather than loans. In addition, the report assigns the IMF a role of lender of last resort in international financial crises and urges it, together with the Bank, to write off in entirety their claims against all heavily indebted poor countries (HIPCs) (IFIAC, 2000: 6–15).

This more specific definition and attribution of tasks to the Fund and the Bank may contribute to improve their accountability. However, the proposed modalities for implementation may actually not serve the objective of re-giving some macroeconomic autonomy to developing countries. For instance, while the report recognizes the "overuse of conditional lending and the imposition of multiple conditions" (ibid.: 20), it suggests that IMF short-term liquidity loans should be accessible only to countries that have met *pre-conditions* of financial soundness. Among these pre-conditions, an eligible member country would have to agree to open its banking system to foreign banks. Under such a regime, Brazil would be ineligible for future IMF funding, since this country intends to impose limitations upon foreign ownership of domestic banks. Such requirement illustrates a technocratic approach that tends to neglect national interests (ibid.: 125). In addition, the access to loans should depend on a fiscal requirement established by the IMF to assure that resources would not be used to sustain "irresponsible budget policies" (ibid.: 43). The problem with this recommendation is that it leaves full leeway to the IMF to define "irresponsible budget policies". Thus, pre-qualification for assistance reintroduces conditionality by the back door and would be even more constraining on governments. In addition, the risk with imposing preconditions of financial soundness may be to deprive countries most in need of funding (for example, after a crisis) from IMF assistance (ibid.: 125–126). Therefore, the IMF should not only return to its original mandate, but it should also be restricted to imposing only macroeconomic (not structural) conditions and required to provide a forecast of the programme's impact, not only on growth and inflation, but also on poverty, unemployment, and wages (Stiglitz, 2003: 131).

With respect to the World Bank, the proposal to cut lending to middle-income countries is based on the argument that these countries already have access to international capital markets and that these markets work well enough to provide such financing. However, not only do private markets not work perfectly, they moreover have been highly volatile since 1990. Thus, they cannot be considered as a reliable source of long-term finance for development, especially for projects which are not attractive to private investors. This means that the Bank is still needed to provide middle-income emerging markets with better access to international capital markets. Regarding the idea of providing more funds to low-income countries in the form of grants rather than loans, it may actually result in a considerable loss of development resources for these countries given the political climate, especially "the historic difficulty in obtaining Congressional appropriations for IDA financing" (IFIAC, 2000: 43). Finally, in the aftermath of the Asian financial crisis, international financial institutions should be much more tolerant towards capital controls which may be useful to preserve national autonomy in the face of global markets, in particular, for developing countries that are more vulnerable to speculative flows.

Notes

1. Intra-company transfers enable global companies to buy from and sell to their own subsidiaries, that is, at prices ("transfer prices") that often have little connection to the market price. This deviation from market price aims at maximizing the global profits of the parent corporation (see Barnet and Müller, 1974: 157).
2. S&P propose four categories of investment grade, from AAA to BBB, and seven of speculative grade, from BB to D. Moody's rank from Aaa to Baa, and Ba to C respectively.
3. Of particular significance has been the rise of mutual and hedge funds and the concentration within each of these industries. The total assets of US mutual funds rose from $241 billion in 1980 to $3.39 trillion in 1996. The largest mutual fund company is Fidelity Investments which, in 1997, managed $175 billion worth of 401 (k) assets – about 19 per cent of the total 401 (k) market. With its retail mutual funds added, Fidelity controlled almost $1 trillion in 1999. Hedge fund assets rose from $21 billion in 1990 to over $70 billion in 1995 with the ten largest funds ("macro" hedge funds) controlling 45 per cent of these assets. In 1995, the three largest macro hedge funds – Quantum Fund, Tiger Management and Steinhard Partners – controlled 25 per cent of the industry total (Harmes, 2001: 33).
4. Sociologists distinguish four kinds of "embeddedness": cognitive, cultural, social and political (Zukin and Dimaggio, 1990: 15–23).
5. The distinction between formal and substantive democracy is based on Tocqueville's analysis of the two meanings of democracy: "one was a political regime defined by the rule of the people, with all the institutional and procedural mechanisms that had been specified by earlier theorists of democracy; the other was as a condition of society characterized by its tendency towards equality. This social, societal condition, the Tocquevillian 'habits of the [democratic] heart' meant that democracy could not be reduced to its formal, institutional aspect" (see Kaldor and Vejvoda, 1997: 62–63).
6. In November 1998, the International Financial Institution Advisory Commission was established by the US Congress in order to consider the future roles of international financial institutions. The Commission included, among others, Allan Meltzer, a well-known orthodox economist, after whom the Commission's report has come to be known. The report was released in March 2000.

REFERENCES

IFIAC (2000) Report to US Congress on reform of the development banks and the international finance regime (Meltzer Report), International Financial

Institution Advisory Commission, WWW site: http://www.house.gov/jec/imf/meltzer.pdf.

Agenor, P.-R. and Aizenman, J. (1998) "Volatility and the welfare costs of financial market integration", Working Paper 6782, National Bureau of Economic Research (NBER), Cambridge.

Aglietta, M. (1997) *Régulation et crises du capitalisme*, Paris: Odile Jacob.

Andrews, D.M. (1994) "Capital mobility and state autonomy: Toward a structural theory of international monetary relations", *International Studies Quarterly* 38: 193–218.

Barnet, R.J. and Müller, R. (1974) *Global reach: the power of the multinational corporations*, New York: Simon and Schuster.

Birchfield, V. (1999) "Contesting the hegemony of market ideology: Gramsci's 'good sense' and Polanyi's 'double movement' ", *Review of International Political Economy* 6: 27–54.

Bourguinat, H. (1992) *Finance internationale*, Paris: Presses Universitaires de France.

Caillé, A. (1995) "Embeddedness, ordres et contextes", in A. Jacob and H. Vérin (eds) *L'inscription sociale du marché*, Paris: L'Harmattan.

Cecco, M. de (1979) "Origins of the post-war payments system", *Cambridge Journal of Economics* 3: 49–61.

Cerny, P.G. (1993a) "The political economy of international finance", in P. G. Cerny (ed) *Finance and World Politics: Markets, Regimes and States in the Post-Hegemonic Era*, Cambridge: Edward Elgar.

—— (1993b) "The deregulation and re-regulation of financial markets in a more open world", in P. G. Cerny (ed) *Finance and World Politics: Markets, Regimes and States in the Post-Hegemonic Era*, Cambridge: Edward Elgar.

—— (1996) "international finance and the erosion of state policy capacity", in P. Gummett (ed) *Globalization and Public Policy*, Cheltenham (UK) and Brookfield (US): Edward Elgar.

—— (2000) "Embedding global financial markets: securitization and the emerging web of governance", in K. Ronit and V. Schneider (eds.) *Private Organizations in Global Politics*, London and New York: Routledge.

Cohen, B. (1993) "The triad and the unholy trinity: Lessons for the Pacific region", in R. Higgott, R. Leaver, and J. Ravenhill (eds) *Pacific Economic Relations in the 1990s: Co-operation of conflict?*, Boulder, Colo.: Lynne Rienner.

—— (2003) "Capital controls: the neglected option", in G.R.D. Underhill (ed) *International Financial Governance under Stress*, Cambridge: Cambridge University Press.

Commission on Global Governance (1995) *Our Global Neighbourhood*, http://www.itcilo.it/actrav/actrav-english/telearn/global/ilo/globe/gove.htm.

Cutler, C.A. (1997) "Artifice, ideology and paradox: the public/private distinction in international law", *Review of International Political Economy* 4: 261–285.

—— (2002) "Private international regimes and interfirm cooperation", in R.B. Hall and T.J. Biersteker (eds) *The Emergence of Private Authority in Global Governance*, Cambridge: Cambridge University Press.

Dale, R. (1992) *International Banking Deregulation. The Great Banking Experiment*, Oxford: Blackwell.

Drache, D. (ed.) (2001) *The Market or the Public Domain? Global Governance and the Asymmetry of Power*, London and New York: Routledge.

Frieden, J.A. (1991) "Invested interests: the politics of national economic policies in a world of global finance", *International Organization* 45: 425–451.

Germain, R. (1997) *The International Organization of Credit*, Cambridge: Cambridge University Press.

Gill, S. (1992) "Economic Globalization and the Internationalization of Authority: Limits and Contradictions", *Geoforum* 23: 269–283.

Gill, S. and Law, D. (1989) "Global hegemony and the structural power of capital", *International Studies Quarterly* 33: 475–499.

Goodman, J.B. (1992) *Monetary Sovereignty: The Politics of Central Banking in Western Europe*, Ithaca: Cornell University Press.

Goodman, J.B. and Pauly, L.W. (1993) "The obsolescence of capital controls? Economic management in an age of global markets", *World Politics* 46: 50–82.

Griffith-Jones, S. (1996) "Institutional arrangements for a tax on international currency transactions", in U.M. Haq, I. Kaul and I. Grunberg (eds) *The Tobin Tax: Coping with Financial Volatility*, Oxford: Oxford University Press.

Haggard, Stephen and Maxfield, Sylvia (1996) "The political economy of financial internationalization in the developing world", *International Organization* 50: 35–68.

Harmes, A. (2001) *Unseen Power: How Mutual Funds Threaten the Political and Economic Wealth of Nations*, Toronto and New York: Stoddart.

Haufler, V. (2000) "Private sector international regimes", in R.A. Higgott, G.R.D. Underhill and A. Bieler (eds) *Non-State Actors and Authority in the Global System*, London and New York: Routledge.

Helleiner, E. (1994) *States and the Reemergence of Global Finance: From Bretton Woods to the 1990s*, Ithaca and London: Cornell University Press.

Hewson, M. and Sinclair, T.J. (1999) "The emergence of global governance theory", in M. Hewson and T.J. Sinclair (eds) *Approaches to Global Governance Theory*, New York: State University of New York Press.

Hurd, I. (1999) "Legitimacy and authority in international politics", *International Organization* 53: 379–408.

Kaldor, M. and Vejvoda, I. (1997) "Democratization in central and east European countries", *International Affairs* 73: 59–82.

Kennen, P.B. (1996) "The feasibility of taxing foreign exchange transactions", in U.M. Haq, I. Kaul and I. Grunberg (eds) *The Tobin Tax: Coping with Financial Volatility*, Oxford: Oxford University Press.

Kurzer, P. (1993) *Business and Banking: Political Change and Economic Integration in Western Europe*, New York: Cornell University Press.

Latham, R. (1999) "Politics in a floating world: Toward a critique of global governance", in M. Hewson and T.J. Sinclair (eds) *Approaches to Global Governance Theory*, New York: State University of New York Press.

Lipson, C. (1981) "The international organization of Third World debt", *International Organization* 35: 603–631.

Llewellyn, D.T. (1985) "The role of international banking", in L. Tsoukalis (ed.) *The Political Economy of International Money. In Search of a New Order*, London: Sage.

Lukes, S. (1990) "Perspectives on authority", in J. Raz (ed.) *Authority*, New York: New York University Press.

MacKinnon, R. (1993) "The rules of the game: International money in historical perspective", *Journal of Economic Literature* 31: 1–44.

Moran, M. (1991) *The Politics of the Financial Services Revolution*, Houndmill and New York: Palgrave Macmillan.

Moses, J.W. (1994) "Abdication from national policy autonomy: What's left to leave?", *Politics and Society* 22: 125–148.

Mosley, Layna (2003) *Global Capital and National Governments*, Cambridge: Cambridge University Press.

Murphy, C.N. (2000) "Global governance: poorly done and poorly understood", *International Affairs* 76: 787–803.

Notermans, T. (1997) "Social democracy and external constraints", in K. Cox (ed.) *Spaces of Globalization: Reasserting the Power of the Local*, New York: Guilford Press.

Palan, R. (1998) "Ontological consternation and the future of international political economy", *Economies et Sociétés* 34: 101–115.

Purcell, M. (2002) "The state, regulation, and global restructuring: reasserting the political in political economy", *Review of International Political Economy* 9: 284–318.

Rodrik, D. (1997) *Has Globalization Gone Too Far?*, Washington DC: Institute for International Economics.

Rosenau, J. (1992) "Governance, order, and change in world politics", in J. Rosenau and E.O. Czempiel (eds) *Governance without Government: Order and Change in World Politics*, Cambridge: Cambridge University Press.

Ruggie, J.G. (1982) "International regimes, transactions, and change: embedded liberalism in the postwar economic order", *International Organization* 36: 379–415.

Sell, S.K. (1999) "Multinational corporations as agents of change: The globalization of intellectual property rights", in C.A. Cutler, V. Haufler and T. Porter (eds) *Private Authority and International Affairs*, New York: State University New York Press.

Sinclair, T.J. (1994a) "Between state and market: Hegemony and institutions of collective action under conditions of international capital mobility", *Policy Sciences* 27: 447–466.

—— (1994b) "Passing judgement: credit rating processes as regulatory mechanisms of governance in the emerging world order", *Review of International Political Economy* 1: 133–159.

—— (1999) "Bond-rating agencies and coordination in the global political economy", in C.A. Cutler, V. Haufler and T. Porter (eds) *Private Authority and International Affairs*, New York: State University New York Press.

Spar, D.L. (1999) "Lost in (Cyber)space: The private rules of online commerce", in C.A. Cutler, V. Haufler and T. Porter (eds) *Private Authority and International Affairs*, New York: State University New York Press.

Spero, J.E. (1977) *The Politics of International Economic Relations*, London: George Allen & Unwin.

Stephens, J.D., Huber, E. and Ray, L. (1999) "The welfare state in hard times", in H. Kitschelt, Peter Lange, Gary Marks and John D. Stephens (eds) *Continuity and Change in Contemporary Capitalism*, Cambridge: Cambridge University Press.

Stiglitz, J.E. (2003) "Democratizing the International Monetary Fund and the World Bank: Governance and accountability", *Governance* 16: 111–139.

Strange, S. (1988) *States and Markets*, London: Pinter.

Underhill, G.R.D. (1995) "Keeping governments out of politics: transnational securities markets, regulatory cooperation, and political legitimacy", *Review of International Studies* 21: 251–278.

—— (1999) "Transnational Financial Markets and National Economic Development Models: Global Structures versus Domestic Imperatives", *Economies et Sociétés*, série ME: 37–68.

—— (2001) "The public good versus private interests and the global financial and monetary system", in D. Drache (ed.) *The Market or the Public Domain? Global Governance and the Asymmetry of Power*, London and New York: Routledge.

Vercellone, C. (1994) "L'approche en termes de régulation: richesse et difficultés", in C. Vercellone and F. Sebaï (eds) *Ecole de la régulation et critique de la raison économique*, Paris: L'Harmattan.

Williamson, J. (1977) *The Failure of World Monetary Reform, 1972–1974*, New York: New York University Press.

Zukin, S. and Dimaggio, P. (1990) "Introduction", in S. Zukin and P. Dimaggio (eds) *Structures of capital: the social organization of the economy*, Cambridge: Cambridge University Press.

Zysman, J. (1983) *Governments, Markets, and Growth: Financial Systems and the Politics of Industrial Change*, Ithaca: Cornell University Press.

5

Trends in global economic governance and the emerging accountability gap

Ngaire Woods

Introduction

Globalization has created pressures for better governance at the global level. This means that international organizations such as the UN, the IMF, the World Bank and the WTO need to take on broader, deeper roles in ensuring stability, growth and security *within* as well as among states. So, too, other actors are playing a growing role in global governance. Large corporations are organizing not just their commercial activities but also their lobbying and self-regulation at a global level so as better to protect their transnational activities and opportunities. Non-governmental organizations are spreading further afield and delving deeper within fields to monitor and publicize the activities of other global actors. In brief, the twenty-first century brings us more global actors, processes and issues, and a growing public anxiety about who is governing and at whose behest at the global level?

The implications for democracy are profound. Within the boundaries of the state people have at least enjoyed a *potential* to hold their governments to account, as described above through elections, impartial courts, ombudsmen, the media and such like. Yet increasingly, governments are delegating or ceding control over such decisions to international organizations, networks or other actors. This means that even in democracies, governments cannot be held to account for a widening range of decisions. A serious democratic deficit or accountability gap is emerging.

Regulating globalization: Critical approaches to global governance, de Senarclens and Kazancigil (eds), United Nations University Press, 2007, ISBN 978-92-808-1136-0

In some areas the accountability gap is being partially plugged by an ever-expanding number of NGOs and active investigative media attention, not only on domestic issues but increasingly targeted at international actors. Government agencies, international organizations, and large corporations such as BP, Shell and De Beers have all found themselves the targets of uncomfortable scrutiny. In the public sector, consumers, parents and patients are being offered more information and choice about products, schools and hospitals. Indeed, on some public sector issues in industrialized countries there is even an emerging debate about the downside of "too much accountability" by people wearied by what seems an excess of monitoring, reporting and measuring outputs in public services, and concerned about the diversion of resources into those areas.

The largest accountability gap at the global level affects developing countries. In international organizations, developing country governments have little power and influence to wield in holding these agencies to account. Furthermore, their actions in these organizations are less monitored by their own national media and NGOs. In the global private sector, in new public–private expert networks and in "global civil society", developing countries have even less capacity to hold global actors to account. For these reasons, accountability in global governance and particularly its implications for developing countries needs rethinking.

This chapter examines emerging models of regulation in the world economy and considers their implications for global governance and accountability. Although, traditionally, global governance has been concerned with formal multilateral organizations, a more accurate contemporary description includes a burgeoning array of institutions, networks, coalitions and informal arrangements many of which lie a little further beyond the public gaze and the direct control of governments. Three trends in particular are worth highlighting. The first is the rise of more global private sector forms of self-regulation and governance. The second is the growth and activities of non-governmental organizations. The third is a fashion towards more "expert" or "independent" institutions of governance. Each of these deserves some attention as it highlights gaps in accountability which are emerging beyond the better publicized and more familiar territory problems of the accountability of international organizations (Woods 2001).

The accountability gap in global governance

Accountability, as discussed in this chapter, refers to the liability of public and private officials to answer for their actions in discharge of their duties. It involves duties to report, to stay within specified rules, and some degree of enforcement of these requirements. The requirements might be laid out as legal or constitutional duties, and enforced by investigators or regulators. In public institutions, varying measures of accountability are provided by elections, constitutional limits on power, and checks and balances exercised through ombudsmen, courts and parliaments.

It is worth highlighting that accountability is a limited concept. It is closely linked to notions of legitimacy and justice, but it does not encompass them. Enhanced accountability may mitigate some forms of injustice, but does not substitute for decision-making. Often accountability is focused on procedural requirements designed to ensure that "policies" decided elsewhere are properly implemented. Furthermore, some forms of formal accountability result in distortions in performance where officials focus their capacities and resources on meeting specified indicators to the detriment of other broader goals.

At the international level there are three kinds of accountability discussed in this chapter which potentially constrain the exercise of public or private power. These are worth elaborating briefly in order to give a structure to the subsequent discussion of the accountability gap and emerging trends in global governance.

First, there are formal legal and constitutional forms of accountability. In international relations these are elaborated in treaties and public international law. The system relies upon states to uphold the laws with the International Court of Justice playing an adjudicatory role. There is little, if any, international legal redress against organizations acting outside of international legal commitments, in part because of the paucity of enforcement at the international level. There is no international judicial oversight of the activities of international private or public institutions. Individuals or groups seldom enjoy legal standing to bring any action against them, except in cases for which special panels or tribunals have been established – as we will see below. Furthermore, legal or constitutional forms of accountability will only be constraining where the actions being so regulated are clearly definable and enforceable.

A second form of accountability – mainly relevant just to international public institutions – is political. To some extent this is limited in international relations. There is an obvious (but easily overestimated) democratic deficit which occurs because people do not directly elect, or throw out, their representatives in international organizations or in public–private partnerships on which sit representatives. At most, people participate in elections for national politicians who, in turn, appoint represen tatives to international organizations. Yet the resulting accountability gap is easy to overestimate. For even at the national level, the literature on electoral accountability demonstrates that voters seldom use elections to reward or punish poor performance. Rather, voting tends to be dictated by partisan allegiance, ideology, group identity, or specific issues. Even at the national level, accountable governance relies heavily on supervision, oversight and control by peer agencies rather than by direct political representation. That said, however, representation is a means of institutionalizing particular voices and interests in a decision-making process. Without appropriate representation, political decision-making is much more likely to be perceived as incapable of balancing competing interests and priorities.

A third kind of accountability is provided by markets and consumers. This requires as a prerequisite a degree of public information and scrutiny. Journalists, commentators, academics, non-governmental organizations and civil society play a key role in investigating, confirming and publicizing information which is then fed to the public. In turn, members of the public (or business competitors or partisan supporters or detractors) can use the information in decisions to purchase (or not) from particular companies, to vote for particular politicians, or to protest (or not) against organizations.

Taken together, these three forms of accountability – legal restraint, voice and participation, and purchasing or voting power – offer ways for citizens and their governments to hold global agencies and companies to account. But how effective are these forms of accountability when we consider emerging trends in global governance?

The rise of "self-regulation" in the global economy

Global private sector governance is much quieter and less visible than multilateralism and inter-state institutions. Yet it is a powerful and unbalanced system of regulation. On the one hand, international agreements entrench the rights and freedoms of corporations and invest, globalize and shift capital in an enforceable way (see WTO, TRIPS, TRIMS, bond and other debt instruments). On the other hand, the correlate responsibilities and duties of corporations *in their international activities* mostly take the form of light self-regulation which permits of very little accountability or redress (Zammit, 2003).

There is a growing trend for the private sector itself to undertake voluntary codes of self-restraint and self-regulation. For example, the International Chamber of Commerce declares that it enjoys "unrivalled authority" in making rules that govern the conduct of business across borders. Although these rules are voluntary, they are observed in countless thousands of transactions every day and have become part of the fabric of international trade" (ICC, 2001). Along with its private rule-setting function, the ICC provides the International Court of Arbitration, the world's leading arbitral institution. Like other private sector organizations, the ICC has close links to governments and multilateral organizations. Indeed, within a year of the creation of the United Nations, the ICC was granted consultative status at the highest level with the UN and its specialized agencies. This is but one small part of private sector global governance.

The trend towards private sector (sometimes referred to as private network) governance in part reflects the needs of companies who have become more global in their operations, productions networks and commodity chains (Gereffi and Korzeniewicz, 1994). Where possible, such transnational corporations avoid state or inter-state regulation. Instead they create their own tier of private-sector "governance", "standard setting", "codes of best practice" or self-regulation. For example, from 1973 onwards the International Accounting Standards Committee successfully edged out intergovernmental efforts to promulgate regulation and the setting of accountancy standards, taking up a central role now recognized by the G-7, the IMF and the World Bank in 1998 (Martinez, 2001). Similarly in the financial sector there is the Washington DC-based Institute for International Finance with its role lobbying and proposing self-regulation for financial sector actors, major private credit-rating agencies such as Moody's and Standard and Poor's, and US cyberspace companies who have crafted codes on privacy, property rights and copyright laws (Lessig, 1999).

The US private sector plays a powerful role at the centre of this kind of governance. In the international chemistry industry, for example, it is the American Chemistry Council representing all major US chemical companies that launched a "Responsible Care" code in 1988 in response to public concerns about the manufacture and use of chemicals. The code requires members continually to improve their health, safety and environmental performance; to listen and respond to public concerns; to assist each other to achieve optimum performance; and to report their goals and progress to the public. The code is now being adopted in some 46 countries, representing over 85 per cent of the world's chemical production (ACC, 2001). It has become a leader in emerging private sector self-regulation. However, independent researchers argue that at best the impact of the code is insignificant. More damagingly, some of their findings suggest that members of Responsible Care "are improving their relative environmental performance more slowly than non-members" (King and Lenox, 2002). Without explicit sanctions for non-performance, the King and Lenox study reveals the risk that self-regulation in some sectors can amount to little more than a public relations exercise.

In large part, these private sector governance bodies have been created to obviate the need for government or intergovernmental regulation and, in some cases, as a response to growing NGO and media pressure in their own home countries. These kinds of private sector self-governance regimes leave major private sector actors based in the world's largest economies in the driving seat. That said, however, this does not spell an involuntary shift in power and authority away from governments and states and towards private actors. On the whole, private sector governance emerges where powerful states choose not to regulate, or indeed where states actively support private sector actors in generating their own regime and then cooperate closely with that regime.

For example, the United States government helped to create the Internet Corporation for Assigned Names and Numbers (ICANN), a non-profit corporation formed to assume responsibility for the governance of various aspects of the Internet such as the IP address space allocation, protocol parameter assignment, domain name system management, and root server system management functions previously performed under US Government contract by IANA and other entities (ICANN, 2001). In this instance, the US turned to a non-governmental form of governance because it feared that a formal intergovernmental organization would be too slow and cumbersome in dealing with rapidly developing issues (Keohane and Nye, 2000: 24).

The problem for people within developing countries is that private sector governance and standard-setting emanates almost without exception from within the most powerful industrialized countries. This creates private arrangements which affect life in the developing world even more than in the industrialized world, where the activities of large corporations tend to be quite heavily government-regulated. In much of the world, the main task of monitoring and publicizing the activities of these companies and their codes is undertaken by non-governmental organizations.

One advance in the accountability of the global private sector has been the emergence of "multi-stakeholder processes", meaning networks and commissions which bring together NGOs, transnational corporations and governments in order to provide ad hoc monitoring and reporting units (Hemmati et al., 2001). For example, the World Commission on Dams began work in 1998 with four commissioners from governments, four from private industry and four from NGOs. It was set up to review the developmental effectiveness of large dams and to develop internationally acceptable criteria, guidelines and standards for the planning, design, appraisal, construction, operation, monitoring and decommissioning of dams (World Commission on Dams, 2000; see also Dubash et al., 2001). This network highlights a growing sensitivity by private corporations and governments to criticism and monitoring by transnational NGOs whom they are now including within networks of governance.

A yet more ambitious example of public–private-NGO partnership in governance is the UN's Global Compact. The objective of the Compact is to bring together governments, companies, workers, civil society organizations and the United Nations organization itself to advocate and promulgate nine core principles drawn from the Universal Declaration of Human Rights, the ILO's Fundamental Principles on Rights at Work and the Rio Principles on Environment and Development. In signing up to the Compact, companies are asked to commit themselves to act on these principles in their own corporate domains. Since the formal launch of the Compact on 26 July 2000, it has grown to encompass several hundred participating companies as well as international labour groups and more than a dozen international civil society organizations.

It bears highlighting that the Global Compact is neither a regulatory regime nor even a code of conduct. The UN describes it as "a value-based platform designed to promote institutional learning. It utilizes the power of transparency and dialogue to identify and disseminate good practices based on universal principles" (UN Global Compact, 2001). Nevertheless, the Compact reflects the degree to which international organizations and large multinational private actors today perceive a need to respond not just to global markets but to global social and political pressures: "as markets have gone global, so, too, must the idea of corporate citizenship and the practice of corporate social responsibility. In this new global economy, it makes good business sense for firms to internalize these principles as integral elements of corporate strategies and practices" (UN Global Compact, 2001).

In large part, the new awareness of multinational companies has been achieved by the actions of NGOs and the media, especially in industrialized countries. Many companies are now wary of the power of consumers in their largest markets to boycott or respond negatively to bad press. For example, large oil companies such as BP and Royal Dutch/Shell have been publicly accused of colluding in human rights violations in countries such as Colombia and Chad-Cameroon. Both companies have adopted human rights policies strongly endorsing the UN Universal Declaration on Human Rights. Both companies are also offering to work more closely and openly with NGOs (BP, 2001; Royal Dutch/Shell, 2001).

On a sceptical view, like other actors in global governance companies are simply learning to invest more in their public relations (Zammit, 2003). Nevertheless, some critics believe that corporations have a potential power to effect change, even in areas such as human rights. As Human Rights Watch notes "a well-implemented policy [by BP] could have far-reaching effects, since BP merged with the U.S. oil major, Amoco, to form the third-largest oil company in the world (behind Shell and Exxon), with operations in countries with poor human rights records such as Algeria and Colombia, and operating in alliance with Statoil – which also has a human rights policy – in Angola and Azerbaijan" (Human Rights Watch, 1999).

In a similar vein, diamond companies such as De Beers have attracted bad publicity about their role in mining "blood" and "conflict" diamonds in countries where the industry funds and perpetuates brutal civil wars such as Sierra Leone. In their Annual Report 2000, De Beers write of the "threat to the entire legitimate diamond industry" posed by the "effect of conflict diamonds on consumer confidence" (De Beers, 2000). To ward off this threat, the diamond industry has created a World Diamond Council based in New York to develop, implement and oversee a tracking system for the export and import of rough diamonds to "prevent the exploitation of diamonds for illicit purposes such as war and inhumane acts" (World Diamond Council, 2001). As with the oil companies above, the extent to which diamond companies implement effective policies in this area will depend not on governments or intergovernmental institutions but on NGOs who monitor and publicize infractions and thereby create the link between consumers in the North and corporate operations in the South.

Private sector initiatives to improve the environment, human rights, workers' rights, and such like, reflect a response to the growing capacity of consumers and shareholders in large industrialized countries to hold companies to account. They also reflect companies' fears that not only consumers but also employees (both present and future) may turn away from companies branded pariahs by transnational NGOs or that governments might intervene and regulate at the behest of their voters. The result is a web of private sector generated and monitored "standards", "principles" and policies, sometimes in cooperation with governments or intergovernmental institutions, which form an important element of global governance. The accountability in these new networks is patchy. Often the world is relying on transnational NGOs as agencies of accountability without which many global corporate activities would remain almost entirely unmonitored.

The new role of non-governmental organizations in global governance

Highlighted in the discussion so far has been the increasing role of non-governmental organizations in monitoring and drawing attention to issues of global governance. Often a small group of large and well organized NGOs are mistakenly referred to as "global civil society". As Jan Aart Scholte has persuasively argued, the two are not the same. "Global civil society" involves the many different ways societies organize – not just advocacy movements, but established trade unions, social organizations and religious groupings are all part of civil society and have counter-parts at the global level (Scholte, 1999). It has been estimated that transnational non-governmental organizations have grown from about one hundred groups at the turn of the century to over 5,000 at the end of the 1990s (Held et al., 1999: 54). More recently, two different kinds of non-governmental organizations have not only increased in number, but have become important parts of global governance.

The most visible and vocal NGOs are large transnational non-governmental organizations based in industrialized countries, who lobby for particular principles or issues such as debt relief, environmental protection and human rights, such as Amnesty International, the World Wildlife Fund or Oxfam. These groups do not claim to represent countries or geographical groups, nor do they represent particular commercial interests (although they are accountable to their donors and members and many are also in the business of delivering aid or similar goods). Their stake in the arena of global governance is more of a deliberative one. They bring principles and values to the attention of the policy-makers and firms. They also play a role in monitoring global governance, analysing and reporting on issues as diverse as the Chemical Weapons Treaty, negotiations on global climate change, world trade, and the actions of the IMF, World Bank, and transnational corporations. In so doing, transnational NGOs provide information, debate and criticism which is fundamental to holding both private and governmental sectors to account.

A rather different community of NGOs is now also becoming increasingly involved in the debate and implementation of global governance. More "locally-based" NGOs, predominantly in developing countries, are being drawn into the fray. These groups claim to represent local constituencies. Many operate to plug gaps in their own country's government. Some try to make up for the fact that their governments fail to represent a certain section of the population. Others attempt to make up for a government's lack of capacity to deliver certain kinds of assistance or services. Some are opposed and repressed by their governments. Others work closely with their government.

Increasingly, these groups are being included in discussions with international aid donors, international organizations, and other arenas of global governance. Their entry has been catalysed by a number of shifts in thinking about both aid and governance. Already in the 1980s, non-governmental organizations, private charities and voluntary services were applauded by new conservatives, especially in the Thatcher and Reagan governments in the UK and USA, as alternatives to government involvement in welfare, aid and social policy. This thinking spilled over into aid policies which sought to channel aid through non-governmental groups in both the industrialized and developing countries. That trend changed in the 1990s with the rise of international support for democratization and a wave of development thinking focused on strengthening and modernizing the state. It is now recognized that good policies and outcomes require good politics. That means effective government, not effective NGOs competing with a weak government.

A different logic now drives the inclusion of locally based NGOs in international fora. Aid institutions and donor governments have recognized that wider participation and "ownership" on the ground is necessary for development policies to be successfully implemented. This has been reiterated in numerous World Bank and IMF publications (World Bank 1989, 1992, 1994, 1996, 1999 and IMF 1997, 2000). Getting wider ownership and participation is difficult, especially in countries where governments have few networks for consultation or representation and where wide gaps exist in terms of who they represent and how. For these reasons, agencies such as the UN, the IMF, the World Bank and the UNDP are encouraging both their own local representatives and government officials to develop consultative links and closer relations with local NGOs. This brings new tensions and problems to both local and international politics.

A key issue raised by the emergence of NGOs in global governance is who chooses which NGOs to include or consult in national or international negotiations? At the national level, if the government plays a key role, critics allege that genuine consultation is not taking place. Where outsiders play a role, governments argue that their sovereignty and their own processes of democracy are being subverted. Where the local representatives of international organizations are involved, they risk becoming powerful gate-keepers who use their power to favour some groups over others to cement and further their own position. At the international level, all these problems are replicated. For these reasons, the increasing reliance at the global level on NGOs to provide some modicum of accountability in itself poses important new challenges to the legitimacy and accountability of global governance.

The rise of technocratic governance

A growing trend in global governance is the temptation by governments to use "technical" or "expert" groups or networks as a flexible and efficient way to manage globalization. The approach eschews old-fashioned representative institutions in which politics and power among states are central. Rather, the emerging pattern of governance replaces state-based institutions of governance with networks of experts so as "to preserve national democratic processes and embedded liberal compromises while allowing the benefits of economic integration" (Keohane and Nye, 2000: 37).

The presumptions underpinning this model are institutionalist and functionalist. The focus is on cooperation rather than power. The goal is to "get the job done" rather than to waste undue energy on process. Networks comprise participants with special technical expertise and material stakes in an issue, such as the chemicals, accountancy and financial stability networks mentioned above. Because they are selective, these networks are cohesive, technically sophisticated and efficient. Their legitimacy derives from their efficiency or the quality of the outcomes they produce, that is, *results not process* matter most, or to express it in the language of some political scientists, the quality of the outputs matters more than the democratic inputs.

An example of expert or network governance is the Financial Stability Forum (FSF) which was convened at the behest of the G-7 in April 1999 to promote international financial stability through information exchange and international cooperation in financial supervision and surveillance. The new network was self-consciously selective, bringing together experts from the most important players in the international financial system including national authorities responsible for financial stability in significant international financial centres, international financial institutions, sector-specific international groupings of regulators and supervisors, and committees of central bank experts. There was no sense that the FSF should represent all countries or regions of the world. Rather its goal was to coordinate the efforts of various bodies in order to promote international financial stability, improve the functioning of markets, and reduce systemic risk (FSF, 2001). The legitimacy of the FSF rests on its efficiency in achieving its stated goals. That said, however, interestingly the G7 have found it necessary to expand its membership to include representatives from Hong Kong, Singapore, Australia and the Netherlands (ibid.).

The "efficiency" or output rationale for governance is enjoying a growing appeal among scholars and policy-makers alike. Indeed, we find it being applied to a number of other intergovernmental bodies. Three examples come to mind: the IMF, the European Union, and the WTO. In each case arguments have been made for more independent and expert-oriented governance so as to avoid the problems, vested interests and contradictions which arise from domestically-rooted intergovernmentalism.

Part of the argument has been elegantly expressed by Ernst-Ulrich Petersmann in the following terms: "governments risk to become prisoners of the sirene-like pressures of organized interest groups unless they follow the wisdom of Ulysses (when his boat approached the island of the Sirenes) and tie their hands to the mast of international guarantees" (Petersmann, 1995: 5). Away from the hurly-burly of domestic politics, policy-makers (we are led to believe) can come to more rational and selfless conclusions.

In respect of the IMF, it has been argued that it "should be made truly independent and accountable" so as "to permit it to focus more efficiently on surveillance and conditionality" (De Gregorio et al., 1999). These authors proposed that the IMF's executive directors should be discouraged from taking advice from their governments. Like a central bank, the IMF should be permitted to work in a more technical, independent way with its accountability ensured through transparency and a different kind of oversight by member governments. The rationale is that just as independent central banks have proven better at fighting inflation, so too an independent world authority would better protect international financial stability.

The proposal for a more independent IMF does also provide for more accountability. Three discrete measures are proposed to ensure this: (1) increased transparency with the publication of voting records, executive board minutes and performance evaluations; (2) the strengthening and bolstering of an oversight committee comprising finance ministers; and (3) a requirement that executive directors justify their actions in terms of an explicit mandate such as "to advance economic and financial stability" and face dismissal by the oversight committee if they failed. In and of themselves these measures would doubtless improve the accountability of the IMF (Woods, 2001).

The problem with the proposal for a more independent IMF is that it underplays the extent to which the IMF makes political rather than technical decisions and the extent of disagreement even on so-called "technical" issues about what policies undertaken in which order and in which country will best advance economic and financial stability. At the very least, considerations of "for whom?", and "at whose cost?" will weight the answers. This is why the process of decision-making in the IMF is unavoidably political. In the end, it involves ranking and prioritizing the rights and obligations of different groups of people. Protesters on the streets argue that the IMF always resolves such questions in favour of creditors, both government and private sector. Developing countries argue that they are marginalized not just by the formal rules but equally, if not more, by the informal mechanisms of influence and decision-making within the institutions. It is not clear that making the IMF more independent would alter either of these perceptions.

In the European Union a similar output-oriented rationale for governance is emerging. Put simply it is that: "At the end of the day, what interests them [i.e. people living in the EU] is not *who* solves these problems, but the fact that they are being tackled" (Prodi, 1999). This output-oriented rationale is strongest in arguments for European Monetary Union (EMU) and more specifically in the nature and structure of the European Central Bank (ECB) which lies at the heart of EMU. The ECB is an independent and unaccountable body (e.g. compared to its counterparts in the UK, USA and Japan all of which publish formal voting records of their decisions), whose legitimacy rests on its technical and expert nature rather than a potential representativeness or democratic accountability.

More recently efficiency or output arguments have been extended beyond the European Central Bank. They are emerging in wider and more political initiatives such as institutional reform and enlargement where questions of legitimacy and democracy, it has been argued by one scholar, are increasingly being left to be dealt with as issues for public relations not institutional reform (Kohler-Koch, 1999). European Commissioner Michel Barnier underscored this view in his very recent call for European policy-makers to go beyond negotiating the "necessary technical adaptations" to institutions and to consider how to reinforce the democratic legitimacy of the European Union (Barnier, 2001).

The World Trade Organization (WTO) is a final example of an organization we are told should be more independent. In order to minimize the rent-seeking producer interests who have so much power at the national level, it has been argued that the global trading system should be "constitutionalized" where a written constitution is understood as "a contractual means by which citizens secured their freedom through long-term basic rules of a higher legal rank" (Petersmann, 1995). Similar arguments are made by quite a wide range of scholars pressing for the WTO to become a vehicle for enforcing core values in human rights, environmental protection and labour standards.

In constitutionalizing the WTO it is assumed that the "long-term basic rules" on which trade should proceed are relatively incontestable and should not be shipwrecked on the ragged shores of national politics. Yet many would argue that these rules belong in the national realm, encroaching as they do into issues of welfare, the environment, labour rights and intellectual property protection. They reflect not some higher legal truth but deeply political priorities and choices over which citizens should have some say. This is not a simple contest between economists who favour liberalization versus NGOs pushing human rights and other values. The outcomes involve subtle adjudications over priorities, means and ends. Should one form of environmental protection be privileged over another? Should one species of dolphin be protected more than another? Most importantly of all, who should decide and to whom should they be accountable?

One response to the political problems of constitutionalizing the WTO has been to argue that the institution should be more "inclusive" (Howse and Nicolaidis, 2001). By including NGOs and other interested or expert parties, for example, we can improve the quality of deliberations and decisions on trade issues. To quote one enthusiast: "the right way to defeat bad ideas is with better ideas. Just as national democracy entails participation and debate at the domestic level, so too does democratic global governance entail participation by transnational NGOs" (Charnovitz, 2000). There are a couple of problems embedded in this argument.

In the first place, the inclusion of NGOs will not necessarily redress the failure of the WTO adequately to represent some countries and groups while it over-represents others. Indeed, inclusion might exacerbate rather than redress the lack of voice and influence suffered by developing countries. For instance, of the 738 NGOs accredited to the Ministerial Conference of the WTO in Seattle, 87 per cent were based in industrialized countries. Enthusiasts of inclusion need to consider more carefully how NGOs might be included without further distorting the under-representation of developing countries and peoples in the WTO.

A second problem arises with the broader argument that we might consider the WTO as a deliberative space within which the best ideas win. In this argument for "network governance" the focus shifts from procedures and "inputs" (i.e. elections and representative government) to the quality of debate and the "outputs" of the system. The inclusion of NGOs and experts is said to ensure high-quality deliberation which improves outputs. This is because the process of deliberation is one in which the best ideas can be aired and genuinely expert participants can partake without the limitations of a representative system. Participants "learn" and change their minds, coming to understand alternatives better and to modify their own starting positions.

The missing element in the deliberative network model is politics. The kinds of vested interests which "distort" trade policy at the national level are assumed to disappear at the international level. Yet even a cursory examination of private sector participation in existing WTO negotiations reveals their powerful influence. Groups such as the US Coalition of Services Industries (USCSI, 2001) and International Financial Services, London (IFSL, 2001) were deeply involved in negotiations on the General Agreement on Trade in Services and the WTO Basic Telecommunications and Financial Services Agreements. The Financial Leaders Group, a private sector group of North American, European, Japanese, Canadian and Hong Kong financial leaders, publicizes its role as "a key player in securing the 1997 Financial Services Agreement and continues its work in the current WTO services negotiations" (FLG, 2001). Naturally, representatives of private sector organizations bring a high level of expertise and ideas to the negotiating table. However, they represent, indeed they have a duty to represent, the narrow sectoral and material interests of their members. It distorts reality to propose that they should ensure that the "best" or "better" ideas win. The reason they exist and have come to the negotiating table is to represent the interests of their members.

The debate about deliberative networks highlights the need to pay attention in global governance to who defines the rules and outcomes of deliberation. Those who focus on "outputs" pay too little attention to inputs and decisions about who participates, who sets the agenda, and within what parameters the acceptable outcomes must fall. In so doing, the network governance enthusiasts overlook deep problems of legitimacy and accountability which arise from these processes.

For developing countries the question of who controls networks, their agendas and powers is vital. Take the example of the FSF mentioned above which has three issues on its agenda: capital flows, off-shore financial centres and highly-leveraged institutions (FSF, 2001). All three have a direct impact on developing countries who are vulnerable to the systemic risks and issues involved, and some of whom will be directly affected by regulation in this area which could reduce offshore financial activities upon which they rely. Governance in these areas – be it regulation or standards – will benefit some countries and cause significant costs to others. What will justify these choices?

For output-oriented governance specialists the answer is the quality of the results and their contribution to international financial stability. Critics, on the other hand, argue that the results are very subjective. There are many competing models of international financial stability. Some focus on regulation, others on liberalization. Some emphasize capital controls, others on universal openness of capital accounts. The vigorous debate about which measures best achieve international financial stability underscores the need for a legitimate process of goal-setting and policy-making and the need for that process to be an accountable one.

The new trend towards more independent, technocratic governance neither responds to anxieties about illegitimate and unaccountable governance at the global level, nor does it extinguish the political pressures and vested interests which distort rule-making – even though it might hide them from view. For this reason the rise of technocratic governance does not provide a solution to calls for greater accountability in global economic governance.

States and international organizations in accountable global governance

Accountable government – at a number of levels – is a cornerstone of any effective and legitimate system of global governance. Accountable governance requires information, monitoring and the enforcement of limits and rules in the use of power. It must offer ways to dissatisfied or disenfranchised groups who are deeply affected by global governance to call those who exercise power to account, whether in the public or private sector.

Within democratic political systems accountable governance is achieved through elections, ombudsmen, court actions, non-governmental agencies and the media. In global governance, no actor can claim to have been elected by voters. Nor are many institutions subject to the normal restraints or checks and balances of public office. Multilateral organizations grapple with an unwieldy structure of government representation which makes accountability complex and difficult. Private corporations face even fewer, mostly self-imposed, restraints. Non-governmental organizations set standards for other actors and play a vital role in monitoring performance, yet critics argue that NGOs themselves are not adequately held to account.

It is easy to imagine that if all governments in the world were both democratically elected and equally represented in international organizations, there would be far less of a problem of accountability in global governance. However, it is worth noting immediately that even in such an ideal world, the capacity of people to hold international institutions to account would still be very limited.

In the first place, there is an unavoidable "democratic deficit" in international organizations because people do not get to elect (or to throw out) their representatives on the WTO, IMF, World Bank or UNSC directly. Instead, those who live in democracies get to elect politicians some of whom form a government which appoints ministers who represent and choose delegations to represent a country. For this reason, even in an ideal, universally democratic world, international economic governance is removed from representative government. Even if they so wished, citizens could not use their votes effectively to influence, restrain or hold to account their government in its actions in an international organization. In countries with highly developed systems of parliamentary accountability such as the United Kingdom, the oversight by parliament of international institutions is weak. In most developing countries it is yet weaker.

However, the "democratic deficit" does not rule out improving the accountability of international organizations. In fact, looking a little harder at the argument for democratizing international institutions, it is sometimes used wrongly to suggest that in directly elected democracies, voting and representation are the principal means by which governments are held to account. In theory, citizens could use elections to reward or punish politicians. In reality, votes are rarely used this way. Political scientists have shown that voters do not tend to use their votes to sanction officials for abuse, neglect or incompetence (or indeed to reward the opposite). Voters often use elections to express party loyalty or enthusiasm for a future set of policies (Przeworkski, Stokes and Manin, 1999). Very often voters face "problems of information, monitoring, and commitment" (Maravall, 2003). For these reasons, elections are not the principal form of accountability within national political systems. And if they are not in national politics, it is inconceivable that the same elections might hold a government to account for its actions in an international economic organization.

Governments are held to account through a variety of different social, political and legal institutions. These same institutions also hold other actors to account. And it is to these institutions that we must turn to find ways in which to make global governance more accountable. The fundamental elements include ensuring that:

(1) actors exercising power are transparent about what they are doing and why;
(2) actors are monitored in their work, policies and operations and that the results are reported;
(3) enforcement takes place to make certain that actions stay within jurisdictional bounds and conform to relevant rules, norms and policies.

In respect of global governance, we need to examine whether such steps are being taken so as to increase the accountability of international organizations.

Enhancing accountability in global governance

This chapter has discussed the growing role of the private sector, nongovernmental organizations and technocrats in global governance. It has argued that to ensure accountability close attention must also be paid to the workings of governments and intergovernmental institutions.

In recent years a revolution has occurred in many international organizations such as the IMF, the World Bank and, to a less extent, the WTO. In the IMF, where information was previously inaccessible to anyone outside the walls of the institution, most research is now published on the website along with a substantial amount of documentation regarding its work with individual countries. Furthermore, the IMF is pressing governments to permit greater disclosure and publication of policies and agreements made with the IMF (these must be kept confidential if a government so wishes).

The most noticeable gap in the transparency of both the IMF and the World Bank regards decisions taken by their executive boards – a point recognized in the earlier mentioned proposal for a more independent and accountable IMF. The minutes of board meetings are not published. Votes are not taken and therefore cannot be recorded or publicized. This is a significant omission for institutions which purport to be representative and whose member governments claim to be accountable to their own people. Indeed, recall from above that transparency at this level was called for in the argument for a more independent IMF. It is extremely difficult to hold one's government to account for a collective decision if their role in that decision is not known.

Transparency is but one necessary element of accountability. Equally important are evaluation and monitoring of the uses (or abuses) of power by decision-makers. As discussed earlier in this chapter, both private and public sector agencies are under increasing pressure from shareholders and members as well as outside NGOs and critics, to evaluate their operations and effectiveness in a more through, effective and public way. The new expectation was highlighted by the UN's publication of a very critical independent examination of UN policy in Rwanda, commissioned by the Secretary General in May 1999 (UN, 1999). Similarly the Executive Board of the IMF has undertaken and published three independent evaluations of the work of the Fund: the Enhanced Structural Adjustment Facility, IMF surveillance, and the research role of the institution. More recently, an Independent Evaluation Office has been created within the IMF and has published a critical report on the prolonged use of IMF resources (IMF/IEO, 2002). Within the World Bank the Operations Evaluation Department (OED) is one of the oldest independent evaluation offices in an international organization. It rates the development impact and performance of all the Bank's completed lending operations, the Bank's policies and processes.

The weakness of monitoring and evaluation is that too often reports and reviews are ignored and not followed up. This was highlighted by the specially formed Evaluation Group of Executive Directors in the IMF who noted the lack of follow-up and monitoring of changes and reform subsequent to their first independent reviews (IMF, 2001). Indeed, the very first listed goal of the IMF's new Independent Evaluation Office (IEO) reads: "Enhancing the learning culture of the IMF and enabling it to better absorb lessons for improvements in its future work" (IEO/IMF 2001).

Many, both within and outside of international organizations, believe that publishing critical evaluations of an organization is one way to ensure that findings get some public attention and external pressure for change which can help to overcome inertia or vested interests within the organization. As yet, however, the IMF does not publish all evaluations of its work. For example, the work of the Office of Internal Audit and Inspection (OIA) is not published, nor are all internal evaluations undertaken by operational staff. More importantly, the institution has yet to announce any mechanism by which it will monitor the adherence of its staff to its new Guidelines on Conditionality (IMF, 2002).

Equally, in the World Bank, not all the work of the OED is published even though since 1993 its "Annual Review of Evaluation Results" (ARDE) has been published along with summaries of evaluation reports for selected projects. Without publication not just of activities but of independent assessments of what organizations are doing, it is difficult for the public to judge how well or poorly an organization is undertaking its responsibilities and equally difficult for outsiders to offer support to insiders who recognize the need for change. For this reason, monitoring and transparency are intertwined in both public and private sector organizations.

Turning to members who wish to hold institutions to account, two specific issues arise in the debate about improving and enhancing transparency and monitoring. The first is whether increased information and monitoring in and of themselves can help – say people in developing countries – hold global institutions or corporations adequately to account? Here accountability depends on the capacity within and among developing countries to absorb, publicize and act on information. When information is released into the public domain, it needs to be picked up and publicized by NGOs, the media, politicians and others at the national level and subsequently translated into governmental and nongovernmental pressures on the international organization. The problem for developing countries is that they see this occurring much more in industrialized countries. The result is to increase the influence of industrialized countries through informal channels and thereby further marginalize the influence of developing countries. Unsurprising then that developing countries have often opposed increased transparency and monitoring.

However, blanket opposition cuts off an important longer-term goal of holding these institutions better and more equitably to account.

A second issue which arises in respect of transparency and monitoring concerns choices about what kinds of information (collected by whom and how) will most benefit those by whom institutions should be held accountable. Too often arguments for transparency ignore the costs and opportunity costs of choices about what to monitor and what to publicize. In practice, transparency requires making some difficult trade-offs. For example, at the national level consider the choice between collecting elaborate forms of data which might assist in economic modelling, and simpler forms of data which might be adequate for development planning. The choice has implications both for cost and for the capacity of local agencies to aggregate the information. At the international level the same trade-offs apply but the question of who pays for transparency is often less clear. In the IMF and World Bank, for example, it is borrowing members who bear the cost of increased transparency and monitoring through increased loan charges. Across the wider spectrum of international agencies, budgets spent on transparency and monitoring not only might otherwise be spent directly on development, but also represent choices about what to monitor and at whose behest.

Along with transparency and monitoring, the third element of accountability is enforcement. Mechanisms of enforcement are deeply lacking across global governance, whether in private sector self-regulation regimes or in international organizations in respect of their operational rules and conduct guidelines. In national systems of governance, several forms of enforcement are familiar. These include both formal means such as the use of courts, tribunals, ombudsmen, or elections, as well as informal means of redress such as adverse publicity, consumer boycotts, and so forth. In global governance there are some limited parallels to these mechanisms of enforcement which are worth building upon.

At the informal level, as already discussed, global campaigns and other activities of a variety of non-governmental organizations, consumer groups and such like are using traditional media and the Internet to hold international private and public sector actors to account in the court of public opinion (UNHDR, 2002).

Formal mechanisms of enforcement also exist at the global level. An example of the formal enforcement of rules lies in the Inspection Panel created by the Executive Board of the World Bank in 1993 to service the IBRD and IDA. The Inspection Panel is a forum which can adjudicate complaints from groups within countries who believe that the failure of bank staff to follow the institution's own policies and procedures has led to them being adversely affected by a bank project. The final outcome of any inspection depends upon a decision of the Executive Board of the World Bank to whom the independent inspection panel reports. A less formal procedure has subsequently been created to service the International Finance Corporation (IFC) and the Multilateral Investment Guarantee Agency (MIGA) within the World Bank Group. The Compliance Adviser/Ombudsman's office (CAO) is directed to mediate and conciliate among parties with powers to make recommendations to the President of the World Bank but not to act as "a judge, court or policeman". Within the IMF there is as yet no such complaints procedure.

One positive effect of this kind of formal enforcement mechanism is that it forces institutions to develop and publish detailed operating principles and procedures for which they can subsequently be held to account. However, there are several important limits to this kind of enforcement. First, not everyone is in an equal position to use the procedures available, not just in bringing formal complaints but in ensuring that the threat of such actions keeps officials of an institution within their powers and rules. In many cases, people in developing countries have relied on northern NGOs to assist in funding and presenting their case. Indeed, critics allege that the role of NGOs risks skewing the work of accountability tribunals in favour of issues and areas of most concern to people within industrialized countries, as expressed through northern NGOs, leaving unserviced those people in the developing world who have not attracted the attention of such NGOs.

A second limitation on enforcement by a formal tribunal is that the process can be used to attack good decisions which suffer minor technical flaws in respect of the rules. It can also be long, costly and time-consuming, diverting resources away from the central purposes of the institution. For this reason the threshold or cause for complaint which can spark a full inspection or action is crucial.

A final important limitation in formal enforcement is that the process examines whether an institution has adhered to its existing policies and operational rules. It does not examine or adjudicate the quality or purposes of those policies or rules. It cannot prevent or call to account bad decisions being made within the rules. This means that accountability for the quality of the rules themselves has to be achieved through some other means.

Conclusions

Increasing interdependence in the world economy has produced an expectation on the part of citizens that governments should better manage globalization and, at the same time, a strident criticism of their failure so to do. Yet much of the emerging governance in the world economy lies beyond the reach of governments. This chapter has described a web of arrangements which extends beyond governments and multilateral institutions to private sector initiatives, non-governmental organizations and networks of public and private actors. It portrays a system in which the underlying power and hierarchy of states permeates and structures relations among non-governmental and private sector actors perhaps even more strongly than it does in the public sector.

For some, the solution is to rely more heavily on global technical and expert networks to whom governments can delegate decision-making. Subsequently, these technocratic governors can be held to account for their performance measured against a narrow range of desired outputs. The problem with this vision is that it ignores the core contemporary problem of accountability in global governance: who sets the outputs, who picks the experts, and who is held to account for these decisions?

Democratizing global governance either from the bottom-up or from the top-down offers a range of solutions. A restructured Economic and Social Security Council has been proposed as a way to hold existing institutions to account for the wider range of issues that they now deal with (Dawes and Stewart, 2000). This does not offer a solution for the huge area of governance beyond governmental reach. That said, however, such an agency could play a crucial role in monitoring the coordination (or lack thereof) among existing intergovernmental institutions.

A different proposal argues that a global people's congress could be constituted to provide a non-governmental forum which would broaden and deepen the means by which actors are held to account in world affairs (Falk, 2001). To some extent, this function is already played by the emergence of "Porto Alegre" or global summits of non-governmental actors which raise awareness of different points of view and critiques of the present structures of global governance.

A complementary, if less dramatic, way to improve global governance is to ensure that powerful actors in the world economy are held to account. This requires addressing gaps in information, bolstering capacities for monitoring information and strengthening and reinforcing formal legal, political and market mechanisms of enforcement. A combination of legal restraints, political accountability, and market and public pressure are required for accountability to work in global governance. Yet emerging trends in governance do not suggest a growing degree of such accountability.

REFERENCES

American Chemistry Council (ACC) (2001) "Responsible care", at www.cmahq. com.

Barnier, Michel (2001) "L'urgence europeene", Note personelle (Brussels: European Commission, 17 October 2001) and at europa.eu.int/comm/commissioners/ barnier/document/171001_fr.pdf.

British Petroleum (BP) (2001) "Human Rights Policy", at www.bp.org.

Charnovitz, Steve (2000) "On constitutionalizing the WTO: A comment on Howse and Nicolaidis", at www.ksg.harvard.edu/cbg/trade/charnovitz.htm.

Dawes, Sam and Frances Stewart (2000) *Global challenges: an Economic and Social Security Council at the United Nations*, London: Christian Aid.

De Beers (2000) *De Beers Annual Report 2000*, London: De Beers.

De Gregorio, Jose, Barry Eichengreen, Takatoshi Ito and Charles Wyplosz (1999) *An Independent and Accountable IMF*, Geneva: ICMB, CEPR.

Dubash, Navroz K., Mairi Dupar, Smitu Kothari and Tundu Lissu (2001) "A watershed in global governance?: An independent assessment of the World Commission on Dams", Lokayan: World Resources Institute.

Falk, Richard (2001) *A Global People's Congress*, manuscript, Princeton University.

Financial Leaders Group (FLG) (2001): documentation, membership and description at www.uscsi.org/groups/finLeader.htm.

Financial Stability Forum (FSF) (2001): documentation at www.fsforum.org.

Gereffi, Gary and Miguel Korzeniewicz (eds) (1994) *Commodity Chains and Global Capitalism*, Westport CT; Greenwood Press.

Held, David, Anthony MacGrew, David Goldblatt and Jonathan Perraton (1999) *Global Transformations: Politics, Economics and Culture*, Palo Alto CA: Stanford University Press.

Hemmati, Minu and Felix Dodds (2001) "Multi-stakeholder processes: A methodological framework", UNED Forum, see www.earthsummit2002.org/msp/ report/draft_framework.htm.

Howse, Robert Lloyd and Nicolaidis, Kalypso (2001) "Legitimacy and global governance: Why constitutionalizing the WTO is a step too far", in R. Porter, Pierre Sauve, Arvind Subramanian and Americo Beviglia Zampetti (eds) *Efficiency, Equity, and Legitimacy: The Multilateral Trading System at the Millennium*, Washington DC: Brookings Institution.

Human Rights Watch (1999) *Human Rights Watch World Report 1999* at www.hrw.org.

International Chamber of Commerce (ICC) (2001): description and documentation at www.iccwbo.org/home/intro_icc/introducing_icc.asp.

International Financial Services London (IFSL) (2001): documentation at www. bi.org.uk.

International Monetary Fund (IMF) (1997) *Good Governance: The IMF's Role*, Washington DC: IMF.

——— (2000) *A Guide to Progress in Strengthening the Architecture of the International Financial System*, Washington DC: IMF.

———— (2001) Report of the Working Group on Evaluation (www.imf.org)

———— (2002) Guidelines on Conditionality (www.imf.org).

IMF/IEO (2002) Report on Prolonged Use of IMF Resources (www.imf.org/ieo).

Internet Corporation for Assigned Names and Numbers (ICANN) (2001) at www.icann.org.

Keohane, Robert O. and Joseph S. Nye (2000) "Introduction", in Joseph S. Nye and John D. Donahue (eds) *Governance in a Globalizing World*, Washington DC: Brookings Institution.

King, Andrew and Michael Lenox (2002) "Industry self-regulation without sanctions: The chemical industry's responsible care program", *Academy of Management Journal.*

Kohler-Koch, Beate (1999) "Europe in Search of Legitimate Governance", *ARENA Working Papers WP 99/27* (www.arena.uio.no/publications).

Lessig, Lawrence (1999) *Code and Other Laws of Cyberspace*, New York NY: Basic Books.

Maravall, José María (2003) "The rule of law as a political weapon", in Adam Przeworski andJosé María Maravall *Democracy and the Rule of Law*, Cambridge, UK/New York, NY: Cambridge University Press.

Martinez, Leonardo (2001) *Setting the Rules for Global Business: The Political Economy of Accounting Standards*, Oxford University, M. Phil Thesis.

Petersmann, Ernst-Ulrich (1995) "The transformation of the world trading system through the 1994 agreement establishing the World Trade Organization", *European Journal of International Law* 6(2): 161–221.

Prodi, Romano (1999): speech to the European Parliament as President-Designate of the European Commission, 21 July 1999.

Royal Dutch/Shell (2001) "Human rights policy", at www.shell.org.

Stewart and Daws (1996) *Global Challenges: The Case for a United Nations Economic and Social Security Council*, London: Christian Aid.

Scholte, Jan Aart (1999) "Global civil society: Changing the world?", CSGR Working Paper No. 31/99, Warwick University, UK (May 1999).

United Nations (UN) (1999) "Report of the independent inquiry into the actions of the United Nations during the 1994 genocide in Rwanda", 15 December 1999, New York: UN, and at http://www.un.org/News/dh/latest/rwanda.htm.

United Nations Human Development Report (UNHDR) (2002) *Deepening Democracy in a Fragmented World*, New York: UNDP.

United Nations Global Compact (2001) "Updates", at www.unglobalcompact. org.

US Coalition of Services Industries (CSI) (2001), documentation at www.uscsi. org.

———— (2001) "Making the IMF and the World Bank more accountable", *International Affairs* 77(1): 83–100.

World Bank (1989) *Sub-Saharan Africa: From Crisis to Sustainable Growth*, Washington DC: World Bank.

———— (1992) *Governance and Development*, Washington DC: World Bank.

———— (1994) *Governance: The World Bank's Experience*, Washington DC: World Bank.

———— (1996) *The World Bank Participation Source Book*, Washington DC: World Bank.

———— (1999) *Annual Review of Development Effectiveness*, Washington DC: World Bank.

World Commission on Dams (2000) *Dams and Development: A New Framework for Decision-Making*, World Commission on Dams, 16 November 2000, www. dams.org.

World Diamond Council (2001) "About WDC" at www.worlddiamondcouncil. com.

Zammit, Ann (2003) *Development at Risk: Rethinking UN–Business Partnerships*, Geneva: UNRISD.

6

Rule-making in global trade: The developmental challenge*

Miguel F. Lengyel

Introduction

As in the 1950s and 1980s, the birth of the twenty-first century shows many developing countries struggling again to find a sustainable path to development. The sequence of events is already well known: decreasing returns from, even fatigue with, the state-led, inward-looking model of industrialization – embraced with almost blind faith in the knowledge of public sector bureaucrats to drive the process – paved the way in the 1980s for an across-the-board U-turn. Either out of pragmatism or conviction, but with similar determination, countries adopted development policy prescriptions coined by international organizations stressing the role of markets and deeper integration in the world economy. Privatization of public assets, deregulation and greater exposure to international competition became the thrust of the standard policy package.

Although contrasting in terms of policy scripts, both experiences share some striking weaknesses. First, they rely on development views that, on the one hand, assume that the road to progress has clear and predefined contours so that it mainly involves adapting policies and institutions to a given series of blueprints; and, on the other, they endorse what some authors have called *dirigisme*, i.e.

> the assumption that ... there is an expert agent that already sees the future of development and can, therefore, issue instructions for arriving there. Whether through celebration of the developmental state or by adulation of a cosmopoli-

Regulating globalization: Critical approaches to global governance, de Senarclens and Kazancigil (eds), United Nations University Press, 2007, ISBN 978-92-808-1136-0

tan, technical elite, this dirigisme has led to unholy alliances with the powerful and the exclusion of the weak. (Reddy and Sabel, 2002: 1)

Second, both experiences ended in deep financial crises – with their corresponding episodes of debt default – that in turn underscored serious macroeconomic imbalances and fiscal accounts on the verge of collapse. What gives tragic dimensions to the experience of the past two decades are the unprecedented rates of unemployment, poverty and immiseration.

Trade policy was an essential component of the package of policy reform in many parts of the developing world.[1] First through unilateral liberalization of trade regimes and later by anchoring and expanding it through the full-fledged commitments made at the Uruguay Round (UR), many developing countries clearly showed their willingness to come out of the fringes and play by the new rules.[2] Hopes that such a move would contribute to bringing tangible benefits in terms of market access for their products and of development as well were as large as disenchantment is today. It is not surprising therefore that increasingly critical appraisals of those reforms started to emerge in many developing countries by the late 1990s. Moreover, the very organization that epitomizes the drive towards trade liberalization the world over, the World Trade Organization (WTO), has also come under fire.

This chapter examines the main results of the UR for developing countries to put forward some ideas that dovetail with the redesign of trade institutions at the global, regional and national levels. More specifically, the chapter seeks to use those results as a platform to present an argument, still incipient and exploratory, on how the rules and practices governing trade could become more supportive of development – a matter that became the subject of a heated debate after the fiasco of Seattle. It ranks high in Doha's discourse and underlies the collapse of the Cancun ministerial meeting in September 2003, as well as the meagre concrete progress reached at the Hong Kong ministerial meeting.[3] In line with the previous critical comments on standard views, this argument will draw from an alternative development approach that focuses on individual and collective learning, and stresses institutional diversity and innovation instead of convergence and adaptation or outright "clonation".[4]

In keeping with this goal, the chapter is organized as follows. The first section looks at the existing evidence on the gains and losses of the Uruguay Round agreements (URAs), linking them to the processes of rule making at the WTO. The next section moves from the multilateral to the national level, discussing the public-private dynamics prevailing in many developing settings regarding trade policy and underlying some flawed institutional traits. The final section three addresses the main problems identified in the previous sections. It does so by discussing first some changes in the configuration and functions of the WTO whose rationale is to relax the constraints they place on developing countries to devise their own solutions to major development bottlenecks. It then moves on to discuss some novel institutional arrangements and mechanisms that may foster local knowledge for crafting development-promoting policies in a wide range of (in the WTO's jargon) "trade-related" policy fields; and, finally, it suggests a new role for sub-regional integration initiatives as intermediate-level instances of coordination where national solutions could be rendered compatible and linked, in turn, to the global trade regime. The protection of intellectual property rights will be given particular attention to ground this exploratory exercise empirically.

The outcome of the Uruguay Round: some critical issues at stake

Following the conclusion of the Uruguay Round (UR), and as countries gradually got into the implementation of commitments, scholars and policy-makers increasingly agreed that the net gains accruing to developing countries were extremely lean, if not negligible. Moreover, such a consensus still holds, no matter whether the yardstick for assessment is market access payoffs (the traditional GATT's purview) or the suitability of the domestic regulatory/institutional reforms unleashed by the URAs in several "trade-related" policy fields now under the reach of the WTO (intellectual property rights, investments, sanitary and phytosanitary measures and technical barriers to trade) (Hoekman, 2002; Rodrik, 2001; Finger and Nogués, 2002). Complaints of an unbalanced or asymmetrical exchange of concessions and claims to redress it were thus voiced by a growing number of developing countries in the run-up to both the 1999 ministerial meeting in Seattle and the 2001 ministerial conference at Doha (World Bank, 2001). These perceptions pervaded talks at the Cancun ministerial conference, fuelling the emergence of various groupings of developing countries (the G-20, least-developed groups and the ACP countries) that opposed, for different reasons, any kind of substantive compromise, hitting once more the credibility of the WTO (Tubiana, 2003; Jonquières, 2003).

To be sure, it is well known today that developing countries did not leave the UR negotiation table with their pockets empty. The inclusion of agriculture, the commitment to phase out the restrictions on textiles and the strengthening of the dispute settlement system can be deemed as important returns. In exchange, however, those countries made concessions that largely compensated for such gains, including a more restrictive special and differential treatment (S&D) approach, the binding of all tariffs on goods and more stringent disciplines on subsidies and custom valuation. The expansion of the multilateral agenda in areas such as intellectual property and services further loaded their package of concessions.

Furthermore, a more careful assessment of the outcome underscores that many of the alleged gains have yet to materialize or have been largely diluted during the implementation of the agreements.[5] Just to illustrate, let us consider the cases of two agreements – Agriculture (AA) and Textiles and Clothing (ATC) – that particularly matter to developing countries. Although the AA contemplates several provisions aimed at increasing market access (reduction of tariffs, export subsidies and domestic supports, replacement of non-tariff measures with tariffs), it has not inhibited the proliferation of tariff peaks (well over 100 per cent in some cases) in many OECD countries that affect export products particularly sensitive for developing countries (Josling, Tangermann and Warley, 1996; Olarreaga and Ng, 2002). Similarly, the progressive phasing out of quotas committed in the ATC did not mean that significant trade liberalization was to be achieved before the end of the 10-year transition period in 2005 (Panagariya, 2001; Kheir-El-Din, 2002). Equally relevant, while the new dispute settlement mechanism is an asset, the need it imposes on developing countries to generate new expertise on international trade law to take full advantage of it has called for caution regarding their capacity to bring cases efficiently as complainants and to protect their interests as defendants (Weston and Delich, 2003). Last, but not least, full adherence to some WTO agreements (e.g. SPS, TRIPS, custom valuation) required domestic institution building, which has proved not only costly due to the investments at stake but also not always fully consistent with the development needs and priorities of many developing countries (Finger and Schuler, 2000).[6]

Within this general picture, a more disaggregated analysis is necessary to better grasp the mix of costs and benefits resulting from the agreements, its complexities and nuances. In particular, two aspects are worth discussing in some detail – namely, the interplay between unilateral reforms and multilateral disciplines, on the one hand, and the distributional game the agreements entailed, on the other.

As for the first aspect, a quite common reading made in the aftermath of the Uruguay Round emphasized that the WTO agreements were economically and politically functional to the processes of trade reform many developing countries had already chosen to adopt. To put it shortly, they greatly helped to "lock-in" those reforms by both anchoring the policy move towards more open trade regimes through enforceable commitments and helping to contain domestic pressures to roll back or mitigate trade liberalization. The agreements should thus be deemed as largely beneficial by their contribution to endowing trade policy regimes with greater transparency and predictability, and by undermining the rent-seeking practices that plagued the period of import substitution industrialization.

While these assessments are right when taken at a broad level of generalization, they fall short of capturing the full picture; therefore, some refinements and qualifications are in order. First, by the closing phase of the Uruguay Round, neither the stage nor scope of the process of unilateral trade reform across developing countries was uniform. That is, in terms of granting access to their own markets, most countries had already made considerable progress by the early 1990s,[7] and cemented it into the UR by binding a large proportion of their tariff lines.

Yet, the situation is not as straightforward in other policy areas such as export promotion and investments. In those areas, rather than just "locking in" ongoing reforms, the UR catalysed deeper policy changes than the ones many countries were ready to make. In Latin America, for instance, with the only exception being Mexico – which had revamped its export promotion regime within the framework of NAFTA (Ortiz Mena, 2004) – the Agreement on Subsidies and Countervailing Measures (ASCM) implied the redefinition or abandonment of policy instruments untouched by unilateral reform. Even Chile, a front-runner within the region regarding trade reform, faced the need to dismantle or reconvert some of its programmes to make them fully consistent with multilateral disciplines (Agosin, 2001; Silva, 2004). The picture in the field of investments policies is quite similar, with the caveat that countries such as Mexico, Brazil and Argentina (under the umbrella of the Mercosur Automotive Regime), and Colombia and Venezuela (within the framework of the Andean Common Automotive Policy) resorted to the waivers allowed in the Trade-Related Investment Measures (TRIMs) Agreement to postpone the adjustment of domestic legislation to multilateral disciplines (Ortiz Mena, 2004; Tussie et al., 2004; da Motta Veiga and Ventura-Dias, 2004; Echavarría and Gamboa, 2004). In East Asia, in turn, Malaysia, the Philippines and Thailand were able to obtain extensions to bring their laws into conformity with the TRIMs Agreement on grounds of the financial crisis that had hit the region (Abrenica, 2000; Tyndall, 2000).

Second, even in those policy areas in which unilateral reform was well under way, the actual impact of the "lock-in" effect should not be overestimated, as countries attempted and were able to keep some margin of manoeuvre to deal with the new rules. The case of tariffs stands out, as all countries bound tariffs at the WTO well above the applied levels (Laird, 2002; Francois and Martin, 2002). Actually, some countries have taken further advantage of this remaining manoeuvring room. Mexico, for instance, raised tariffs by 3 and 10 per cent in 2001, moving the average applied rate from 14 to 16.5 per cent. Similarly, Brazil managed to keep higher levels of protection to industrial sectors such as motor cars, electric and electronic goods, and capital goods, which had been the major targets of former decades' industrial and export promotion policies. A similar argument may be extended to other policy areas such as trade relief measures (Tórtora and Tussie, 2003) and export subsidies (Tussie and Lengyel, 1998). Against this backdrop, it is fair to say that the lock-in effect of URAs was not to reduce developing countries to bare role-players, since it craftily left some room for them to use loopholes or interstices in the rules.

However, the picture is quite different when the analysis moves from the above policy areas to several of the so-called "new issues" of the UR agenda. These issues involve "non-border" policies and domestic regulatory regimes that were beyond the boundaries of many developing countries' unilateral reform programmes but on which they had, nonetheless, to undertake significant commitments.[8] Moreover, the outcome in these cases was the adoption of specific rules that usually reflected "best practices" as defined by developed countries or plainly transplanted standards prevalent there. The case of TRIPs is paradigmatic of this kind of UR "induced" reform. This agreement's commitments can easily be singled out as a key demand of the United States for a successful conclusion to the negotiation round. Except for a few cases, such as Mexico – which by the early 1990s had already brought its intellectual property regime in line with the standards prevailing in high income economies – developing countries had to pass new laws and set up new institutions in order to fulfil those commitments (Maskus, 2000; Watal, 2002). The case of the agreements on SPS, TBT and Custom Valuation closely mirrors developments in TRIPs.

The former discussion about the impact of UR agreements for developing countries raises concerns about the manner in which the WTO works as a platform for the integration of developing countries in the world trading system. Some of these concerns, such as the challenges those countries face to manage the increasingly complex WTO agenda, and how they may enhance the effectiveness of their participation in multilateral negotiations, has been largely addressed elsewhere (see, for instance, Tussie and Glover, 1993; UNCTAD, 2000; Tussie and Lengyel, 2002; Oyejide, 2002). Yet, the discussion also raises concerns over the rule-making process of the WTO, particularly when the issue is addressed from a development rather than just an integration perspective. To put it neatly, the rationale of that process was, on the one hand, the expansion of market access and, on the other, the harmonization of a broad range of developing countries' "behind-the-border" regulatory policies and institutions with the practices existing in their developed counterparts. In this last sense, there was an inherent bias in the WTO process of rule-making towards a particular set of institutional arrangements, with disregard for any careful pondering of the actual development needs in different national settings (Rodrik, 2001; Hoekman, 2002). Of course, the other side of the coin is that developing countries were left with minimal, is any, policy autonomy in many "trade-related" areas to search for and devise home-grown rules and institutions to address those needs. These are fundamental concerns that link developing nations, cutting across regional particularities and concretely expressing themselves, as in Cancun, as a stubborn resistance to deal with development-relevant issues under the usual logic of negotiations.[9] Not by coincidence, the impasse over the Singapore issues (investment, competition policy, transparency in government procurement and trade facilitation) was crucial to bring negotiations to a halt, largely reflecting the fact that "standard" Northern rules for those policy areas were not perceived as development-friendly at all.[10]

This trait of the WTO rule-making process may be challenged on conceptual grounds as it relies on various highly questionable assumptions. The first, which might be called the "monopoly of knowledge" assumption, is that knowledge about the best policies in critical areas for the working of market economies lies in only a few countries, the developed ones, out of the 145 that are members of the WTO. The second, "universal fitness" assumption is that the policy prescriptions therein established are deemed to work appropriately and efficiently in every context, regardless of local economic, political and social peculiarities. The third assumption, which logically derives from the former two, is that a division of labour exists between countries that are "thinkers", and are thus in charge of coining the policy solutions, and those that are merely "doers", whose task is to apply the scripts crafted elsewhere. Yet, as the following paragraphs highlight, the WTO rule-making may be also challenged on grounds of the distribution of tangible gains and losses it has brought about.

Considering developing countries as a whole, a continuum may be identified in which the Agreement on Agriculture (AA) leans towards the positive side, TRIPS clearly falls on the extreme of costs, and a more mixed picture prevails in the rest of the agreements. The AA had gathered the greatest expectations regarding gains in market access, although these were only partially realized.[11] To be sure, the relative success achieved in tariffication of non-tariff barriers and identification of export subsidies is an asset in that it lays the ground for further reform of international trade on agricultural goods. This particularly holds for highly competitive countries in world markets for several farm products, such as those involved in the Cairns Group.[12] Yet, actual gains in market access shrank during the implementation of the agreement as the flexibility and "dirty tariffication" it allowed enabled countries to get away with minimal tariff reductions (Finger and Schuknecht, 1999; Geithner and Nankani, 2002). Moreover, because tariff and subsidy reductions sharply varied across products, benefits were uneven among countries depending largely on their specific export profile. For instance, while market access gains for some of Mexico's largest agricultural exports (e.g. fruits, vegetables and tropical products) were overshadowed by export subsidies, some agricultural products (honey, fresh flowers, avocados, mangoes, lemons, coffee, oranges, papayas, onions and cantaloupes) benefited from the AA (Ortiz Mena, 2004).

On the side of costs, nearly absolute consensus exists that the TRIPs agreement left developing countries empty-handed.[13] To begin with, gains to be reaped through the overhaul of the domestic normative and institutional architecture governing IPRs – i.e. greater technology transfer and local innovation and increased inflows of FDI – never materialized.[14] Further, anecdotal evidence indicates that post-reform prices rose substantially, particularly in the case of the pharmaceutical sector. This had largely to do with the fact that the new legislation endowed pa tent rights holders with an overly dominant position in particular market segments while developing countries lacked strong competition laws or enforcement capacity. Of course, this also meant that a significant transfer of rents occurred from royalty payers (domestic firms) to patent right holders (international companies).[15] Finally, the TRIPs Agreement has not lessened pressures from the United States over IPRs' protection and enforcement. Under different allegations (broad compulsory licence provisions, omission of data protection requirements, weak enforcement against piracy and counterfeiting of copy right laws, etc.) the United States Trade Representative (USTR), following Special 301, has put nine developing countries in the Priority Watch List and 32 more in the Watch List (USTR, 2003). Given these results, it is hard not to agree with *The Economist* when in 1851 it stated that "The public will learn that patents are artificial stimuli to improvident exertions; that they cheat people by promising what they cannot perform; that they rarely give security to really good inventions, and elevate into importance a number of trifles ... no possible good can ever come of a Patent Law, however admirably it may be framed" (*The Economist*, 12 September 2002, p. 13). The Agreement on Subsidies and Countervailing Duties is also deemed costly, even for countries where export promotion policies and instruments were more attune with WTO disciplines. In the case of Chile, to mention just one example, the impact of the policy changes required by the agreement should not be underestimated in that "the few instruments that had to be revised were deemed vital for export development, such as the Simplified Export Drawback System [and] the Deferred Payment System for Imports of Capital Goods" (Silva, 2004).

The balance of gains and losses in other policy areas is much more complex. In this sense, for instance, although small and medium-size firms can be usually placed as "losers" from URAs in many sectors, it is quite difficult to identify clear-cut patterns not only across countries but also across sectors within countries and even across products within the same sector.

The distinction between "export-oriented" vis-à-vis "import-competing" activities provides a fair proxy to individualize the distribution of costs and benefits at the sectoral level. For instance, commitments on market access for manufactured goods benefited, even if modestly, some outward oriented sectors (e.g. beer and spirits, pharmaceuticals and chemicals, computers, furniture and glass in Mexico, orange juice in Brazil, and footwear in some East Asian economies). At the same time, they brought huge adjustment costs to many other sectors formerly sheltered from international competition. On the other hand, the meagre improvements resulting from the Antidumping Agreement (AD) to restrict the discretionary use of contingent protection by large importers is a liability for exporting sectors (e.g. steel and orange juice in Brazil, steel, lemons and honey in Argentina, salmon in Chile, cut flowers in Colombia, bed linen in India, steel rebar in Turkey, etc.), while an asset for those exposed to heightened competition at home (industrial goods producers, in general).[16] In other cases, however, it is necessary to go beyond the exporter–importer axis to disentangle the actual distribution of gains and losses better. In several production chains – say, manufactured leather products – the so-called "tariff escalation" resulting from commitments on market access skews gains against final products and in favour of raw materials or low-processed goods (UNCTAD, 2002). Similarly, as is the case in automobile production chains, losses for one segment of the production chain (auto parts producers) stemming from tariff reductions or lower local content requirements may be an asset for the following segment (car makers) bidding to have access to inputs at lower international prices. Analysis at a product or production chain-level, which due to space constraints cannot be undertaken here, is thus required to get a more accurate and refined picture of the UR gains and losses in these policy areas.

In any case, the former discussion strongly suggests, as many authors stress for developing countries in general (Hoekman, 2002; Finger 2001; Rodrik, 2001; Panagariya, 2001), that the UR exchange of concessions short-changed Latin American countries. This is particularly so when results are opened up into market access and "trade-related" issues (or non-border policies), the two grand negotiation areas addressed in that round. Paraphrasing one author, on their a priori *gain* dimension, market access – where multilateral disciplines essentially accompany domestic reforms already in course – Latin American countries did not achieve a mercantilist surplus;[17] on the other hand, their concessions in most of the new areas – where domestic reforms were not their choice – have been unrequited (Finger, 2001). Moreover, it should be borne in mind that what they gave in these new areas is qualitatively different, as WTO disciplines on IPRs and standards are concerned with the structure of the economy and its institutional underpinnings, and influence social choices in depth. These facts make concerns over the rationale of WTO rule-making even stronger, helping to explain why such a dimension has become under stiffer scrutiny and calls for some sort of redefinition.

At the same time, the discussion also underscores the fact that an intricate and not necessarily equitable distributive game of gains and losses took place within each country in which the interests of many actors were at stake. In this sense,

> trade policy is inherently a re-distributive instrument whereby interests among sectors and between winners and losers within a sector will be at odds. The trade-offs must be clarified and negotiated so that compromises are allowed to emerge during rather than after the process when compliance is socially and politically costly and lack of compliance leads to international disputes which bear financial as well as credibility costs. (Tussie, 2003b: 9)

This squarely places the spotlight on the domestic process through which commitments are decided, particularly its fairness in terms of interest representation and its capacity to device development-sensitive negotiating proposals.

The public–private framework of trade policy decisions: feeble bridges and institutional lags

The interaction between the public sector and socio-economic actors in Latin American countries around multilateral trade negotiations shows common trends with some national peculiarities.[18] A first striking trait of that interaction is its rather low level of institutionalization. That is, no particular formal instances of exchange and collaboration have been created either through legal means or under the initiative of public authorities or private actors. Some mild exceptions to this trend are, for instance, the cases of Chile, Colombia and Mauritius, where permanent channels of public–private exchange of information and discussion or formal coordination mechanisms on multilateral trade issues were created (Silva, 2004; Echavarría and Gamboa, 2004). These cases, however, lacked clear-cut working principles and rules of engagement and fell short of fuelling an effective involvement of socio-economic actors and generating an institutional space for meaningful deliberation.

It is noteworthy that this poor record of formal institutional innovations contrasts to a large extent with the experience around other recent international trade negotiations, particularly the Free Trade Agreement of the Americas (FTAA). Indeed, these negotiations have triggered several institutional experiments at the national level, more strikingly in Peru and Brazil. In the former, the Chamber of Commerce created the FTAA–Peru Commission as an open forum gathering businessmen, academics and the most important unions. Its structure mirrors the FTAA, being thus organized along similar working groups (Fairlie, 2004). In Brazil, the Brazilian Business Coalition was born, bringing together business associations from manufacturing, resource based and services industries (Motta Veiga and Ventura-Dias, 2004). These novel institutional spaces have been quite successful in coordinating and consolidating business positions on different issues of the FTAA agenda, and in generating a quite effective avenue for economic actors to voice their interests and opinions. In any case, two caveats are in order regarding these experiences. On the one hand, those institutional channels of participation were not the result of any concrete opening of domestic avenues by governments, but a by-product of the incorporation of "civil society" into the hemispheric forum.[19] On the other hand, none of these experiments were born with the specific aim of developing new, more fruitful, institutional channels of public–private interaction but of articulating private sector interests and priorities. Therefore, the fact that they actually helped to open those channels has occurred rather by default than by design.

Now, the paucity of institutionalized patterns of participation does not mean the absence of interaction at all. To the contrary, the active engagement of many developing countries in the UR spurred the emergence of informal channels for civil society involvement in the process to define negotiating positions. Of course, the particular configuration, scope and dynamics of those channels in each national setting varied. Just to mention two examples in the same region, in Colombia the government adopted in 1991 a "working system" or "linking strategy" with business sectors that focused on the establishment of permanent communications and coordination on multilateral trade issues. The system provided a discussion ground for the crafting of negotiating positions that even included the treatment of technical aspects (Echavarría and Gamboa,

2004). In contrast with this quasi-formal mechanism of interaction, informal channels of involvement in Argentina rarely went beyond discontinued and case-by-case exchanges fuelled to some extent by interpersonal knowledge. Further, those exchanges fluctuated depending on the phase (presentation of proposals, elaboration of lists of commitments, etc.) of the negotiation process (Tussie et al., 2004). Outside Latin America, Hong Kong provides another interesting example as quite strong, though "sectorialized" links developed there between a coalition of service industries and the trade department and the WTO mission.

Yet, even in the cases in which informal mechanisms were stronger and more systematic, they were not an appropriate substitute for institutionalized modes of interaction. Their usual lack of principles of ample participation, clear rules of engagement and effective procedural criteria was a fertile ground for the development of quite opaque, biased and discretion-prone patterns of interaction. Indeed, in virtually all developing countries, the strongest business associations – i.e. those more resourceful, better organized and endowed with professional cadres – became the preferential, if not exclusive, interlocutor of government authorities. In other words, access to informal channels was to a greater or lesser extent contingent on the lobbying capacity of business interest representatives. It is not surprising, therefore, that the lack of, or feeble participation of other stakeholders, such as unions, consumers and the Congress, has usually been the rule.

A complex blend of factors, both institutional and conjunctional, has underlain the above picture. There are, to begin with, organizational and functional traits of the public sector that create disincentives for the development of thicker and more stable public-private links; among these, the excessive rotation of bureaucratic cadres, the lack of coordination among public agencies and even jurisdictional struggles among them over the control of the negotiating process have been highly consequential. On the other side, the lower priority many sectors of the business community gave to the WTO vis-à-vis other negotiation fora (e.g. subregional or bilateral agreements), different evaluation across sectors of the issues at stake, the atomization of interest representation and the growing number of foreign actors on scene (particularly multinational companies in public services and manufacturing) have also had a significant weight.[20] Finally, well-entrenched habits and rules of the game in the domestic political-institutional context have conspired against the emergence of more open and transparent patterns of participation in that they only tend to integrate that part of society structured along corporatist lines or patronage webs, condemning the rest to exclusion (Prats, 2000).

At least two critical and intertwined consequences for the fairness and efficacy of the decision-making process on multilateral trade issues stem from the above "institutional deficits". First, biased and opaque institutional arrangements for the involvement of socio-economic agents mean that both the entitlement and actual capacity to participate are at stake. Those agreements therefore run against the sense of "ownership" stakeholders may achieve over the policy options there devised, obviously hampering the building of a minimally appropriate degree of consensus on decisions and undermining their legitimacy. This is particularly relevant in view of the fact that the weaving of negotiating positions has become a daunting political task, as decisions imply an important distributive game. That is, negotiating positions involve international trade-offs across a mounting number of trade issues as well as domestic trade-offs across and within sectors. From the standpoint of private sector interests, who gets what is thus inseparable from engagement and leverage. In turn, from the standpoint of the public sector, the challenge of outlining the "national interest" is enormous, as decision-making needs to aggregate a myriad of divergent interests. In this sense, prevailing patterns of public–private interaction in many developing countries seem ill-suited to build common ground out of different, even antagonistic, concerns. In other words, the national interest is now a contested term as domestic actors have distinct preferences, and fashioning some single national preference is conditioned by the resources the actors posses, their strategic interactions and the institutions in which they operate (Milner, 1998).[21]

Second, the dilemmas for national decision-making on multilateral trade issues are compounded by an increasingly complex and dynamic agenda, which turns the configuration of trade-offs fuzzy and highly volatile. In other words, decision-making has to deliver in the face of, to use a telling phrase, "an open ended series of moments of choice which demand agile responses, less adept to the strategic planning world in which most policy-makers have been trained" (Tussie, 2003a: 7). This casts additional doubts on the capability of prevailing patterns of public–private interaction in developing countries to help to produce adequate and timely responses. Indeed, as in many other macro- and micro-level domains where similar challenges and needs for problem-solving exist, those dilemmas put a premium on institutional arrangements suited to generate and stock knowledge on workable solutions (see, for instance, Sabel, 1994; Lengyel, 2000). In essence, as the existing evidence teaches and will be further discussed below, those arrangements build upon principles of democratic participation and operative rules (on information exchange, knowledge-sharing, etc.), a scarce asset in many areas of the developing world. They rest, in turn, on the assumption that the knowledge of actors is necessarily limited but, at the same time, can be substantially enriched through an open and sustained collective discussion.

As in the case of rule-making in the WTO, the pattern of private–public interaction in most developing countries also calls for improvement. In the spirit of avoiding preordained and "magic-bullet" solutions, moves in that direction will surely need to be sensitive to the institutional and political specificities of each country. To address these critical questions is the concern of the closing section.

Looking ahead: It is about rules!

The analysis conducted in this chapter has so far underscored some fundamental shortcomings in the WTO process of building the rules that govern the exchange of trade concessions at the multilateral level, as well as in the national-level institutional practices through which negotiating positions are built in developing countries. In this section, both aspects are considered not in isolation but as integral parts of the multi-level institutional architecture governing trade relations. Moreover, the argument to be sketched here advances some ideas to reform that architecture by which changes in the multilateral and national dimensions are logically connected and bridged in practice by further institutional renewal in regional or sub-regional trade agreements.

By and large, this section aims to address some key questions that forcefully underscore the nature of the issues at stake in the debate about WTO reform. On the one hand, should there now be a serious push for a more consciously development-oriented and less harmonization-oriented rule system for global markets, and a reoriented WTO, such as has been suggested by the UNDP among others? What would such a system look like? Rather than merely "waivers", delayed obligations and increased "technical assistance" within an unchanged and rigid system, can one instead imagine a looser and more "rolling" rule system in which the emphasis is upon development, monitoring, evaluation and learning? On the other hand, is there still under-exploited opportunity for renewed regional agreements, in which common approaches and policies may be agreed without the pressure of more powerful external actors with interests of their own to protect?[22] This section will address these questions by focusing on the thorny issue of a development-consistent trade–IPRs link.

Reform at the top

Arguments stressing the need to introduce changes in the WTO rule-making system are driven by the same concern, namely, how to make that system more development-consistent. Yet, the agreement barely goes beyond that, as positions about means diverge considerably.

On the one hand, sophisticated free traders propose what might be called a "horizontal decoupling". This essentially involves refocusing the WTO purview onto a traditional market-access agenda that includes all products – goods and services – while transferring the crafting of "behind-the-border" regulatory policies to other international bodies (e.g. the International Organization for Standardization (ISO), the Codex Alimentarius Commission (CAC), the World Intellectual Property Organization (WIPO), the International Labour Organization (ILO), and so on). Developing countries would obtain a twofold gain from this move: a greater likelihood that "good practices" are defined out of the high specialization of the agencies involved as well as, unlike in the WTO, the lack of enforcement to comply with the rules arrived at.[23] The scheme is complemented by increased technical assistance to developing countries in order to reduce the resource and knowledge gaps impinging on their ability to meet the standards and norms agreed upon (Hoeckman, 2002; Henson et al., 2001; Wilson, 2001).[24] Countries' self-interest would be the driving force moving forward this cooperative process.

Developmentalists propose, on the other hand, a "vertical decoupling". The central idea here is also to remove the discussion of "trade-related" policies from the ambit of the WTO through mechanisms allowing developing countries to opt out of multilateral disciplines whenever their developmental needs require it and provided that such a move is a social choice, i.e. that broad support exists among all concerned parties after due deliberation.[25] The strengthening of the WTO monitoring and surveying role would ensure, in turn, that opt-outs are made for the right reasons and in compliance with established procedures. The WTO would also carry out the fundamental task of rendering the resulting policy alternatives compatible. This reform would benefit developing countries by expanding their policy autonomy while providing enough reinsurance that the opt-out option is not abusively employed (Rodrik, 2001; Amsdem, 2000).

Both arguments go a long way towards helping developing countries to break the logjam in which the WTO grand bargain placed them, i.e. to give up policy autonomy in several pivotal development areas in exchange for increased market access in developed countries. They thus lay the ground for a greater institutional diversity that challenges the "one size fits all",[26] or harmonization assumption informing the WTO rules. Yet, for different reasons, these arguments go only halfway. The former still sees the task of consensus building about rules as internationally centralized, even when moving it outside the boundaries of the WTO. Additionally, it may also be questioned whether the lack of enforcement in the process and top-down technical assistance are more relevant than domestic learning-enhancing institutional innovations for developing countries to take full advantage of the more cooperative and permissive spirit. The developmentalist account, in turn, while stressing decentralization, only marginally addresses the issue of how the capacity of those countries to generate relevant indigenous knowledge may be harnessed. The unwanted result could be what Hirschman (1973) labelled a "low equilibrium trap" – quite common in different policy fields – that aborts any attempt of reform favouring greater flexibility and manoeuvring room for developing countries on "trade-related" issues. To put it briefly, those countries are unable to develop strong proposals of their own vintage – in the sense of addressing both their development needs and a deeper integration in the world trading system – as the existing rule-making system severely constrains their ability to search for and experiment with new alternatives; developed countries, on the other hand, are reluctant to acquiesce to looser rules as they find that developing countries generally fail to advance such proposals. Therefore, in order to enhance its prospects to prosper, such a reform needs to overcome simultaneously the rigidities of the multilateral rule-making process and the domestic institutional barriers to knowledge accumulation and application.

A reform scheme along these lines could start where developmentalists do, but would also redefine some of their operational criteria. It would advocate a delegation "downstream" to developing countries of the responsibility for devising proposals in the "trade-related" fields now handled through the centralized and astringent rule-making process of the WTO. This could adopt the concrete form of a "standstill" on new issues (such as environment), or on issues in which commitments have not still been made (e.g. the Singapore Agenda), or a "roll-back" of some of the existing agreements deemed more detrimental for developing countries' interests (e.g. TRIPS and SCM Agreements). Of course, to become credible and thus more feasible, this relaxation of constraints at the top cannot be so lax as to give a carte blanche to those countries. Rather, it needs to be balanced with procedural reassurances that their enlarged policy autonomy will be geared to produce proposals in which development needs are given priority status without obliterating integration concerns. This means that the enlarged room for experimentation it allows – which turns the "monopoly of knowledge" and "universal fitness" assumptions of existing rules upside down – needs to be somehow fenced by a new set of rules that includes both inducements and enforcement. In practice, this can be done by requiring, first, that decisions on stand-stills and roll-backs be duly notified in terms of both the potential and/or the actual damage of the issue at stake for developing countries; second, that assessments to that end be subject to public discussion at the domestic level with the mandatory participation of all stakeholders, to avoid deliberation being captured by sectoral interests, in particular those that would benefit from the decision in question; third, that developing countries establish a cooperative, workable mechanism of self-monitoring in which progress can be compared and considered on the basis of both procedural and substantive benchmarks; finally, that a sunset clause be established by which the return to the status quo is automatic if developing countries fail to deliver the proposals in question after a given time frame – say, ten years.[27]

It could surely be argued that advanced countries would not be ready to accept a rule-based arrangement like this. To be sure, it means for them to move away from the largely beneficial traditional approach making rules and nailing commitments, and to accept a qualitatively different negotiation logic in which they have to concede today while eventual rewards are far in the future. Seen from this standpoint, the situation for developing countries would be just the opposite, i.e. they suspend disciplines that have been costly while committing themselves to distant and uncertain concessions. However, in the international mood surrounding current multilateral trade negotiations, such an arrangement could be deemed as a win-win option. In this sense, the Cancun and Hong Kong episodes plainly show that negotiations launched at Doha are facing significant obstacles to move forward, in particular, because so far it has been cumbersome to give concrete meaning to the discursive appeal of the name of the development round.[28] The fears about the prospects of fulfilling the 2005 deadline to conclude the round have become a crude reality. At the same time, this arrangement would be not only an opportunity, but also a challenge, for developing countries to build credit-deserving negotiating proposals that allow for divergent institutional practices, more suited to disentangle their development problems, without returning to past positions of detachment. Finally, from the perspective of the multilateral trading system as a whole, this provisory arrangement might lay the ground for a more enduring reform of the WTO rule-making by proving itself on the road to being able to deliver a more balanced and widespread distribution of benefits.

In any case, as noted before, this reform at the top is not going to have sustainable pay-off for developing countries if it does not go hand-in-hand with substantial institutional re-engineering at home. The key and challenging task in this sense is to introduce reforms in the decision-making process on multilateral trade issues that enhance its capacity to learn and to apply the new knowledge to the crafting of negotiating proposals that meet the development/integration yardstick.

Reform at the bottom

As shown earlier, the record of institutional innovations in developing countries geared to make decision-making on multilateral trade negotiations participatorier is rather poor. On the other hand, the existing evidence strongly suggests that when they occurred, as in Peru and Brazil, results were largely positive, in that communications among private actors improved and new channels enabling them to voice their opinions emerged. Equally relevant, it should not be overlooked that these experiences worked to some extent as institutional learning spaces. As noted in the case of Brazil, "although at the beginning [the business position] was convergent with the defensive position of the Brazilian bureaucracy, it has gradually been evolving towards a more strategic position in which both defensive as well as assertive areas are identified" (Motta Veiga and Ventura-Dias, 2004).

This outcome should not be surprising at all, as evidence from many other policy fields (*World Development*, 1996; Sabel, 1996; Tendler, 1997; McDermott, 2000; Sen, 2001) highlights the strong potential of those types of arrangements to generate synergies across the public–private divide that enhance the conditions for learning and improved performance. Scholarly analysis has also discussed at length the multiplicity of factors (economic, social, political, institutional) favouring or hindering their emergence and long-term sustainability (Evans, 1996 and 1997). In any case, a key lesson from this analysis is that, even in contexts that are hostile to those arrangements, the rules governing public- private interactions are usually crucial to draw the line between success and failure.

As in the case of reform at the top, how such an arrangement would look can only be addressed here in a sketchy way. The central idea in this regard is the construction of rule-based participatory instances for decision-making that bring together relevant public officials and socio-economic actors with the aim of enabling interactive and iterative learning and, therefore, nurturing the capacities for collective problem-solving. Rules of engagement and deliberation are an obvious building block in this task in that they structure the participation of actors, set the tone of their relations and define criteria for assessment and redefinition of positions.

In developing countries, as already noted, more than one state agency is usually involved in decisions on multilateral trade issues, and civic participation is narrow and biased in favour of the more resourceful. Therefore, the rules of engagement would need to ensure, to begin with, that the involvement of public officials cut across functional boundaries and that both the sectoral and geographical representation of private actors' interests is as encompassing as possible. Yet, as entitlement cannot be equated with actual participation, additional aspects may influence the effectiveness of those rules. In this sense, motivation need not to be a crucial obstacle, even when WTO negotiations are in general a more remote concern for private actors than negotiations in other fora. This is so because the interest of an increasing number of economic agents (particularly those normally excluded from decisions) in those negotiations is on the rise as they are feeling the brunt of commitments made there and know that they have to learn more about the issues at stake. Further, as the experience in the FTAA teaches, when business calls for greater participation, other actors such as unions and non-governmental organizations (NGOs) readily follow suit (Botto, 2003). Motivation, however, might not be enough, as engagement could entail significant opportunity costs for some actors – especially those heavily burdened by the day-to-day management of their specific affairs. The government could thus help to level the playing field by making access to the relevant information more transparent and easier.

Public initiatives could, however, do more to stimulate active engagement and the disposition of actors to share their partial and complementary knowledge, to enable the mutual and incremental learning and collective tackling of problems. Subsidization of participation and for the acquisition of skills that are lacking (through, for instance, training and support from external consultants) may be important, provided that it is tied – through adjustable rules of mutual oversight and assessment – to the disposition of actors to learn and make the new knowledge public. In such a way, the risk that those incentives lack transparency or are diverted to other ends, providing thus fertile ground for clientelism or capture by special interests, is substantially minimized (Reddy and Sabel, 2002).[29] Needless to say, this structure, well endowed to become the locus of a network of formerly scattered public and private actors, would be a masquerade if the principles and rules governing participation and interactions stop at the gate of final decisions. That is, whatever the specific mechanism adopted to make them (say, consensus or majority vote), those decisions have to be informed by open debate and meticulous review by all interested parties.

Ideally, the upshot of this process would be a negotiation proposal in a given area (e.g. TRIPS or SPS) that contains the main elements (even at the level of standards of behaviour, criteria for performance assessment, etc.) to fill a domestic policy vacuum or to improve existing policy regimes. Indeed, the embeddedness of the process in a network of relevant state and social actors, and its reliance on a open and systematic exchange of information and ideas, substantially increases the likelihood that the resulting option both gives due attention to local circumstances and embodies the better alternatives discovered.

Again, sceptics may contend that institutional innovations of this sort are an uphill task in many developing countries, where practices of patronage and even corruption are rampant and people suffer the lack of accountability of both public and private actions. In this context, the question is how much room exists for participatory governance structures that seek to tape on existing resources for more socially-valuable uses by re-defining patterns of public–private relations and allowing the "disfran-chised" a strong voice in the construction of policy proposals? After all, that kind of structures does not abound in any of the developing regions. Some reasons for optimism, however, exist if those changes are seen against the backdrop of the reform of the WTO rule-making system pro-posed above. Indeed, such reform would require that developing coun-tries carry out domestic institutional changes which expand stakeholders' participation in trade policy decisions in order to benefit from the greater latitude for policy-making it affords. In other words, even if the prospects of getting better results are not a powerful enough incentive to trigger those institutional innovations, the "conditionality" included in the new multilateral rules could be a good substitute to get the task in motion. At the same time, such conditionality is "soft" enough in that it is not so intrusive and constraining as to require local institutional innovations to follow a given specific design beyond basic principles of participation, let alone confine the content of debate to preordained parameters.

Regional agreements through new lenses

By the mid-1980s, analysis of the relationship between multilateralism and regionalism in academic and policy circles revolved around whether the latter would be a building or a stumbling block for the former. The key question was if regional agreements would foster trade liberalization or would become the fortress's walls, as many claim it was the case in the "first generation" of integration efforts in Latin America during the 1960s and 1970s. The question was settled a decade later, when it became clear that "open regionalism", in the sense of an outwardly oriented model of integration, was the dominant trend throughout the region (ECLAC, 1994).

A second, equally relevant, question about that relationship was whether open regionalism would serve, as aimed and envisaged by most of its mentors, as a learning platform that allowed its members greater participation in the "major league", the multilateral trade game. The an-swer in this case is that, at best, there is still a long road ahead, particu-larly when the assessment is narrowed down to the generation of policy alternatives in the trade-related areas that are thorny under WTO rules. This does not mean that some learning has not occurred, as Ventura-Dias (2004) rightly points out. Yet, this learning was piecemeal and rarely crystallized in consistent home-grown initiatives in those areas. The ex-amples of Mercosur and the Andean Community of Nations (ACN) serve to illustrate the point, as they share this pitfall even when adopting different institutional designs – NAFTA-like in the case of Mercosur and EU-like in the case of the ACN. In Mercosur, for instance, decisions on export subsidies, SPS and trade in services, and the protocols on IPRs, until recently virtually duplicated the templates established in the UR, while in the ACN the same thing happened in IPRs, SPS and support policies. In this sense, the enactment of the WTO agreements in those fields as domestic laws in the member countries largely defined the boundaries for debate and negotiations within the regional spaces during the 1990s.[30]

Within the framework of the former ideas to reform the WTO rule-making, regional trade agreements would not only have an opportunity to remedy this situation but their commitment to do so would be called for.[31] On the one hand, the new set of multilateral rules would require that countries establish mechanisms to monitor the proposals they craft as a result of their enlarged freedom of initiative. On the other hand, in order to work properly, the new rule-based system needs to avoid being paralysed or subverted by an overload of proposals. Some sort of inter-mediate instance of coordination and aggregation of national initiatives is, therefore, almost an imperative. Regional trade agreements could well be fertile ground for that provided they are willing to undertake learning-encouraging institutional reforms.

How could this be made operative? Drawing from forceful arguments made with regard to particular policy fields (Sabel et al., 1999; Charny, 2000), the first step would be to constitute independent entities within the regional institutional structure as coordinating and convening in-stances of the proposals devised in the member countries in each of the policy areas subject to stand-stills or roll-backs at the multilateral level. Independent experts from those countries, as well as from regional and international organizations (for instance, ECLAC, IADB, regional spe-cialized networks, UNCTAD, the World Bank in the case of Latin America, or similar international agencies, plus ESCAP and the ADB in the case of ASEAN) would integrate those agencies. Their programmatic criterion would be to foster development in the region and their mission would be to become the focal point of a process of collaborative and structured competition among national positions whose final result would be a collective proposal that brings consistency among, and improves, the individual ones. As in reform at the top and at the bottom, the rules gov-erning this process would be essential for it to be workable and bring tan-gible achievements.

The starting point in that sense would be the development by the con-vening entity of a set of benchmarking criteria for the comparison and evaluation of national proposals along substantial and procedural perfor-mance dimensions. This benchmarking would provide initial standards by which participants could contrast and ponder local norms and practices without attempting to impose a unique formula on national institutional arrangements. If, for instance, TRIPs were the issue at stake, those benchmarking criteria could include dimensions such as medicine prices, market competition, technological transfer as well as mechanisms of monitoring of results and enforcement. Transparency would be, of course, a key precondition for the fairness of the process but, equally important, to turn it in a source of useful information and ideas for the improvement of national proposals. The convening entity should be thus in charge of building a data base on criteria for assessment, proposals submitted and results as well as of making that information fully accessible for the public.

The goal is that, over a certain span of time, several rounds of assessment and redefinition are set in motion in which countries use the new knowledge acquired to enhance local arrangements and the proposals devised therein. In practice, this would imply that in each step of the process, a new phase of debate takes place at the national level – under the rules already set through reform at the bottom. This learning-encouraging local exchange could be reinforced by regional instances of exchange among national authorities, in which the role of already existing institutional ambits (e.g. the *Grupo Mercado Común* in Mercosur, the General Secretariat in the ACN and the Secretariat in ASEAN) could be fine-tuned to that end. In this sense, the risk that debates at this level are captured by special interest is no smaller than at national level. Therefore, the public disclosure of discussions should, at least, be established to avoid or minimize that risk.

It is crucial to note that assessment and redefinition not only takes place with regard to national proposals. If the wish is really for the process to elicit incremental but continuous improvement, the benchmarking criteria cannot be fixed targets. Rather, they would also have to be upgraded *pari passu* with changes in the national proposals so that they push for further improvements. This means that learning in this process is a two-way road: countries have at their disposal clear (supranational) regional yardsticks to assess where they stand, and a stock of new knowledge to strengthen their standing; the convening entity, in turn, may draw on national proposals to gradually adjust criteria and standards. The expected final result is a collectively constructed set of rules and procedures that all member countries can make, to a large extent, their own.

Last, but not least, if this arrangement looks workable, there is nothing in principle why it should be confined to one area rather than progressively involve a whole region or even other regions. This would imply the setting of similar processes of collaborative and structured competition at the intraregional or interregional level to compare, improve and eventually harmonize rules and policies highly crucial for their development aspirations.

The inevitable question is, again, whether the conditions for these institutional innovations are present or not within the space of the regional trade agreements. In keeping with the optimistic position so far adopted, the answer is that some incentives exist to give them a shot. First, there is a feeling across some developing regions (i.e. Latin America, the APEC area, etc.) that sub-regional agreements need to achieve a new impulse if they are to play a more decisive role in the development of the region. This is particularly so in view of the fact that, among other challenges, considerable uncertainties continue to stem from both ongoing multilateral trade negotiations and bilateral initiatives within the region. The "more-of-the-same-approach" on these fronts is not likely to bring about different results to what it has so far done. In addition, inasmuch as they sound workable, those innovations might also contribute to a nurturing of the political meaning of regional integration initiatives for their participants. As emphasized, for instance, by da Motta Veiga (2002) in the case of MERCOSUR, the value of the regional integration initiative for Brazil is political and strategic as much as economic in that, if the bloc can organize itself to negotiate collectively in trade negotiations, its members stand a better chance of achieving more favourable terms, such as flexible scheduling for tariff reduction, regulatory leniency, and support for social and economic programmes that assist less competitive industries and groups affected by economic transition. In other words, countries may realize that the challenges of being exposed to the push and pull of competition may be worth facing vis-à-vis the risks of forfeiting new sources for improvement and acting individually. Finally, the institutional innovations here proposed could well provide a way out to overcome the highly sensitive dilemma of reconciling national sovereignty with supranational instances of decision-making. Indeed, they would entail that the partial sacrifices of sovereignty implied by regional convening might prevent deeper erosion – at least in certain policy fields – resulting from the lack of any coordination at all.

Actually, recent developments on IPRs involving Mercosur, particularly Argentina and Brazil, could be fertile ground for testing the value of the above "learning-oriented" approach. The first case concerns the effort initiated by a group of developing countries – the so-called Group of Friends of Development – with the impulse of both Argentina and Brazil to refurbish the discussion of intellectual property issues at the WIPO. The effort consists so far of a document presented at the WIPO calling for the incorporation of the development dimension in the organization. To that end, the proposal focuses on a development-oriented agenda (still with fuzzy contours) seeking to promote a critical assessment of the social, economic and technological consequences of the adoption of IP norms. The cornerstone of the argument is that, even when the TRIPs flexibilities allow some room for development-oriented policies, gross disparities in human, economic and technological development across countries still persist; therefore, they should be given due consideration when dealing with IP protection if the needs of different countries are a matter of genuine concern. The challenge ahead is to give operational meaning to this claim – a task that will require comparison, refinement and consolidation of different initiatives through a process nurtured by mutual exchanges and learning.

The second development has been taking place within Mercosur through the work of the Commission on Intellectual Property (as a constitutive section of the Working Sub-group No. 7, known as "Industry") geared to harmonize the legislation and procedures on intellectual property issues among member countries. The most dynamic areas of work are those related to the harmonization of trademarks and geographical indications. Issues related to patentability and transfer of technology remain as very sensitive matters with rigid positions from all the actors that leave a narrow space for negotiation. During 2004, a preliminary agreement was reached about a trademark protocol and the states are closing the gap on geographical indication issues in order to reach a new protocol, but there is still a considerable way to go. Even more significant, a general protocol on IP that covers almost every aspect related to this area is under negotiation with different positions from each country on several matters that need to be bridged. Even though it will not totally modify the IP map within Mercosur, the general protocol constitutes a key piece for negotiations in other fora, such as the WTO, the FTAA or the FTA with the EU.

Notes

* This chapter builds upon Lengyel (2004).
1. For encompassing analyses on this process, see, for instance, Rodrik (1997), Dean et al. (1994), Tussie (1993a), Martin and Winters (1996).
2. This was a sea change with regard to previous positions; indeed, in former rounds, countries that had already joined the General Agreement on Trade and Tariffs (GATT) had either remained as by-standers or concentrated their efforts in expanding their rights to free themselves from prevailing rules (Tussie and Lengyel, 2002).
3. For an interesting account of the ambiguities concerning the Doha Declaration, see "The Doha Declaration's Meaning Depends on the Reader", *Bridges* 5(9) (November/December), 2001. For some interesting inputs concerning the failure of Cancun, see *Bridges* 7(7) (September/October), 2003.
4. For extremely stimulating ideas about a learning-centred approach to development, see Reddy and Sabel (2002). For an account that places institutional diversity and innova-

tion as crucial elements of a novel global trade regime, see Rodrik (2001). See also Evans (2002) for the role of institutional alternatives in development.

5. For a very interesting assessment of the UR gains and losses for developing countries from a welfare perspective, see Weisbrot and Barker (2002).

6. For a very interesting account that looks at the shortcomings of some of the WTO "trade-related" agreements through the lenses of the Dispute Settlement Body Reports, see Drache and Froese (2002). The analysis of implementation costs of URAs is being carried out in Latin America by the Latin American Trade Network (LATN) with support of the World Bank, through the case studies of Argentina, Costa Rica and Peru.

7. The process included large reductions of both tariffs and non-tariff barriers, as well as reductions of tariff dispersion and escalation. Of course the "deepness" of this process varies across countries, particularly in terms of granting access to their own markets. While, for instance, virtually all Latin American countries bound all their tariff lines, countries such as Hong Kong and Singapore, where applied tariff rates are low, have bound 38 and 66 per cent of their tariff schedule. The proportion is even lower in other countries such as India, Pakistan and Nigeria (Michalopoulos, 1999a).

8. Some authors have argued that in fact the grand bargain between developed and developing countries at the UR was that the latter would take substantial commitments in the "new areas" while the former, in exchange, would open up in areas of particular export interest to developing countries, such as agriculture and textiles/clothing (see, for instance, Finger and Nogués (2000) and Rodrik (2001)).

9. This obviously raises the issue of the hierarchy between trade and development in that by putting development in the driver's seat, as the Doha Declaration claimed was the goal of negotiations, means that trade liberalization or integration in the world economy is essentially the means to achieve that goal. As one author has put it, "[It] means evaluating each agreement and every progress from the point of view of its impact on sustainable development [and] to open the debate on economic development perspectives and the best policies to reach development goals" (Tubiana, 2003).

10. Facing the impasse, Korea and Japan insisted on an immediate launch of negotiations on all four topics, while the European Union, the chief *demandeur* of negotiations on these issues, offered to drop the most controversial topics, investment and competition policy. The offer was, however, rejected by most developing countries led by a coalition formed in Cancun between three groups of the poorest African WTO members.

11. Obviously, these gains should be viewed as opportunities for a broader insertion which, in practice, have to be seized. This depends, in turn, on a mix of complex factors relating to both the working of markets (e.g. consumer preferences, distribution channels) and macro- and micro-level factors shaping the competitive standing of goods (e.g. exchange rate, support policies, firm strategies, and so on).

12. The Cairns Group is a coalition formed in the UR by agricultural exporters to bring the sector under GATT disciplines and includes, from the developing world, Argentina, Bolivia, Brazil, Chile, Colombia, Costa Rica, Guatemala, Indonesia, Malaysia, Paraguay, the Philippines, South Africa, Thailand and Uruguay. The group proposed "lines of negotiation" (for instance, over subsidies or export credits) that pushed for liberalization of agricultural trade while accommodating the key particular interests of its members.

13. This holds even when the relevance of TRIPs matters differs across these countries. For instance, while the protection of pharmaceutical patent rights is a common concern, the traditional knowledge debate is particularly significant for the Andean countries (see Fairlie, 2004). For developing countries, in more general terms, see Maskus (2000).

14. As for FDI, the evidence so far suggests that the opposite could be the case. In Chile, for example, most foreign subsidiaries in the pharmaceutical industry opted to leave the

country and source from abroad after an "upgraded" IPRs legislation was passed (Finger and Nogués, 2000).

15. Estimates for Argentina (Finger and Nogués, 2000) suggest that such transfer amounted to an eighth of the total expenditure on pharmaceuticals in 1999, i.e. about US$425 millions in a market the size of which amounted to about US$4 billions that year.

16. Actually, countries such as Mexico, Argentina, Brazil, India and Turkey have become heavy users of trade relief measures, and particularly AD, to protect producers operating in their domestic markets. Further, this question goes far beyond the North–South dimension, as many of those measures have been applied against neighbours who, because of geographical proximity, are able to benefit most from trade liberalization (see, for instance, Durling (2003)).

17. With regard to the terms of trade, for instance, the net effect after the URAs was to lower the prices that some of the poorest countries received relative to what they paid for the imports. In other words, the result was that some of the poorest countries in the world were actually worse off. The West has driven the globalization agenda, ensuring a disproportionate share of the benefits at the expense of the developing world. Furthermore, it should be borne in mind that an assessment made from a bare mercantilist viewpoint makes sense because the world is mercantilist and hence unilateral liberalization in such a world may be deleterious for most countries.

18. The focus of the analysis in this section refers to the public–private interaction in the process of the national agenda setting and definition of the negotiating strategy. It does not address the involvement of socio-economic actors during the implementation of the UR agreements as a result of provisions contained there making such participation legally necessary. This is mainly the case in the field of trade relief measures, where the URAs set up requirements concerning the representativeness of the applicants seeking protection or directly mandate the participation of some stakeholders in the mandatory process of investigation that precedes the application of one of those measures (e.g. representatives of consumer organizations in cases in which the product under investigation is sold at the retail level).

19. Particularly in the case of FTAA negotiations, entrepreneurs have formed the nucleus of the American Business Forum, which was created in 1995 and meets two or three days before ministers do to voice their opinion on every item under negotiation.

20. For interesting and comprehensive analyses of these issues in Latin America, see Jordana and Ramió (2002) and Aggarwal, Espach and Tulchin (2004).

21. It should not be overlooked that patterns of participation in trade negotiations are not alien to the political economy of former protection and of trade liberalization that followed it. In other words, who gets to have a voice and the forms participation take are to a certain extent shaped by the previous policy record and the ideology from which the policy shift was promoted.

22. Both questions were recently posed by Professor Gerry Helleiner in a presentation made at the Fifth Plenary Meeting of the Latin American Trade Network (LATN) in Mexico City on 13 November 2003.

23. As one author has put it, "cooperation is driven by the self-interest of countries, and implementation is gradual, depending on national circumstances and capacity ... There is generally no binding dispute settlement mechanism or threat of sanctions for non-implementation" (Hoekmam, 2002: 14). For an interesting discussion on enforcement vs. cooperation as mechanisms to get compliance, see Talberg (2002). Actually, a proposal along these lines is under discussion in the eight-member Consultative Board of eminent persons set up by WTO Director-General Supachai Panitchpadki to "institutionally strengthen and equip the WTO to respond effectively to future systemic challenges brought about by an increasingly integrated global economy".

24. Perhaps the most important initiative to this end is the adoption of an Integrated Framework (IF) by the High Level Meeting on an Integrated Initiative for Least Developed Countries' Trade Development for trade-related technical assistance to support those countries. It is anchored on the assessment of needs by the countries themselves, which are then examined by the participating international agencies (IMF, UNCTAED, World Bank, ITC, UNDP and WTO) in order to design a comprehensive programme of technical assistance. The WTO itself provides support, focused on training and the dissemination of information.
25. Rodrik (2001), for instance, proposes an expanded "safeguard clause" enabling an "opt-out" possibility.
26. See Hoekman (2002).
27. This time limit may look excessive and could, of course, be subject to discussion. It looks short, however, when compared with the one for the year 2020, proposed by some free traders, to get a Jubilee that eliminates protection on agricultural products. See, for instance, Bhagwati (2002).
28. To a large extent, these obstacles devolve around how to redefine Special and Differential Treatment in a way that goes beyond the different time frame to fulfil commitments granted to developed and developing countries in the UR. This, in turn, has to do with the rigidity of the WTO rules that are discussed in this chapter (see Tórtora, 2002; Botto et al., 2003).
29. The availability of funds for these incentives should not be highly problematic, even in national economies plagued with severe budget constraints. Current soft loans from international organizations (such as the Inter-American Development Bank (IADB)) to many Latin American countries, directed to the institutional strengthening of their external trade policy, may be redirected at least in part to those ends.
30. The WTO rules had also a more subtle but equally relevant impact, namely, they set up the discursive parameters to conduct trade conversations in those spaces as GATT language (world trade's lingua franca) became the language to use on trade matters.
31. Actually, they could serve to counteract the trend observed mainly in the bilateral trade agreements being currently pushed by the US within the hemisphere, in which (again, the case of TRIPs is paradigmatic) the flexibilities existing in multilateral agreements are being used to craft stricter, more stringent and rigid disciplines (Lengyel and Bottino, 2005).

REFERENCES

Abrenica, Joy (2000) "The Philippine Automotive Industry", paper prepared for the PECC-ASEAN Auto Project, School of Advanced Technology Management, Manila.
Aggarwal, V.K., R.H. Espach and J.S. Tulchin (2004) *The Strategic Dynamics of Latin American Trade*, Washington DC: Woodrow Wilson Center Press/ Stanford University Press.
Agosin, Manuel (2001) "Export performance in Chile: Lessons for Africa," in G. Helleiner (ed.) *Non-Traditional Exports and Development in Sub-Saharan Africa: Experience and Issues*, Basingstoke, UK: Palgrave.
Amsden, Alice (2000) "Industrialization under new WTO Law," paper presented at the High-Level Round Table on Trade and Development, UNCTAD, Bangkok, 12 February 2000.

Bhagwati, Jagdis (2002) "The Poor's Best Hope", *The Economist*, 22 June 2002.

Botto, Mercedes (2003) "Conclusiones: La Internacionalización del Proceso de Decisiones y el Impacto en la Agenda Nacional", in D. Tussie and M. Botto (eds.), *La Nueva Agenda Hemisférica: Patrones Nacionales y Tendencias Regionales de Participación*, Buenos Aires: FLACSO/Temas.

Botto, Mercedes, Valentina Delich and Diana Tussie (2003) "La lógica política de las negociaciones multilaterales: implicaciones para la Argentina", in C. Bruno (ed.) *Argentina. Un Lugar en el Mundo*, Buenos Aires: Fondo de Cultura Económica.

Charny, David (2000) "Regulatory competition and the global coordination of labor standards", *Journal of International Economic Law* 3(2).

Dean, Judith, Seema Desai and Jane Riedel (1994) "Trade policy reform in developing countries since 1985: A review of the evidence", *World Bank Discussion Paper* 267, Washington, DC.

Drache, Daniel and Marc Froese (2002) "One World, One System? The diversity deficits in standard setting, development and sovereignty at the WTO. A report card on trade and the social deficit", Robarts Centre Research Papers, Toronto: York University.

Durling, James P. (2003) "Deference, but only when due: WTO review of antidumping measures", *Journal of International Economic Law* 6(1).

Echavarría, Juan J. and Cristina Gamboa (2004) "Colombia and Venezuela: Trade Policy Reforms and Institutional Adjustments", in M. Lengyel and V. Ventura-Dias (eds.) *Trade Policy Reform in Latin America*, Basingstoke, UK: Palgrave McMillan.

ECLAC (1994) *Open Regionalism in Latin America and the Caribbean: Economic Integration As a Contribution to Changing Production Patterns with Social Equity*, Santiago de Chile: ECLAC.

Evans, Peter (1996) "Government Action, Social Capital and Development: Reviewing the Evidence on Synergy", *World Development* 24(6).

——— (1997) "Introduction: Development strategies across the public–private divide", in P. Evans (ed.) *State-Society Synergy: Government and Social Capital in Development*, Los Angeles: University of California Press.

——— (2002) "Beyond 'institutional monocropping': Institutions, capabilities and deliberative development", Berkeley CA: University of California, mimeo.

Fairlie Reynoso, Alan (2004) "Peru: Trade policy and international negotiations", in M. Lengyel and V. Ventura-Dias (eds.), *Trade Policy Reform in Latin America*, Basingstoke UK: Palgrave McMillan.

Finger, J. Michael (2001) "Implementing the Uruguay Round Agreements: Problems for developing countries", *World Economy* 24(9) September.

——— (2002) "The unbalanced Uruguay Round outcome: The new areas in future WTO negotiations", *World Economy* 25(3) March.

Finger, J. Michael and Julio Nogués (2000) "WTO negotiations and the domestic politics of protection and reform", presented at CEPR/ECARES/World Bank Conference on The World Trading System Post-Seattle: Institutional Design, Governance and Ownership, Brussels, 14/15 July 2000.

Finger, J. Michael and Ludger Schuknecht (1999) "Market Access Advances and Retreats since the Uruguay Round Agreement", presented at Annual World

Bank Conference on Development Economics, Washington DC, 29/30 April 1999.

Finger, J. Michael and Philip Schuler (2000) "Implementation of Uruguay Round commitments: The development challenge", *World Economy* 23(4) April.

Francois, Joseph and Will Martin (2002) "Binding tariffs: Why do it?", in B. Hoekman, A. Mattoo and P. English (eds.), *Development, Trade and the WTO. A Handbook*, Washington DC: World Bank.

Geithner, Timothy and Gobind Nankani (2002) *Market Access for Developing Country Exports: Selected Issues*, Washington DC: International Monetary Fund/World Bank.

Henson, S., K. Preibisch and O. Masakure (2001) "Review of developing countries needs and involvement in international standards-setting bodies", www.dfid.gov.uk.

Hirschman, Albert (1973) *Desarrollo y América Latina: obstinación por la esperanza*, México: Fondo de Cultura Económica.

Hoekman, Bernard (2002) "Strengthening the global architecture for development", Santiago de Chile: ECLAC/World Bank.

IMF/World Bank (2002) "Market access for developing country exports: Selected issues", Washington DC, mimeo.

Jonquières, Guy de (2003) "Crushed at Cancun", *Financial Times*, 15 September 2003.

Jordana, Jacint and Carles Ramió (2002) "Diseños institucionales y gestión de la política comercial exterior en América Latina", *INTAL-ITD-STA, Documento de Divulgación* 15 (June 2002).

Josling, Thimoty, Stefan Tangermann and T. Warley (1996) *Agriculture in the GATT*, New York: St. Martin's Press.

Kheir-El-Din, Hanaa (2002) "Implementing the Agreement on Textiles and Clothing", in B. Hoekman, A. Mattoo and P. English (eds.) *Development, Trade and the WTO*, Washington DC: World Bank.

Laird, Sam (2002) "Market access issues and the WTO: An overview", in B. Hoekman, A. Mattoo and P. English (eds.) *Development, Trade and the WTO*, Washington DC: World Bank.

Lengyel, Miguel F. (2000) *La Organización Moderna. Más Allá del Fordismo*, Buenos Aires: Mercado/Editorial Coyuntura.

——— (2004) "The Latin American countries and the world trading system: Addressing institutional barriers to development", in M. Lengyel and V. Ventura-Dias (eds.) *Trade Policy Reform in Latin America*, Basingstoke, UK: Palgrave MacMillan.

Lengyel, Miguel F. and Gabriel Bottino (2005) "The Latin American Countries, the World Trading System and Development: The Case of Intellectual Property", presented at "The TRIPS Agreement 10 years on: European and Latin American Perspectives, International Association of Economic Law" workshop, Buenos Aires, 1–2 November 2005.

Lengyel, Miguel F. and Vivianne Ventura-Dias (2004) *Trade Policy Reform in Latin America. Multilateral Rules and Domestic Institutions*, Basingstoke, UK: Palgrave McMillan.

McDermott, Gerald (2000) "Reinventing federalism: Governing decentralized institutional experiments in Latin America", policy paper for the Finance, Private Sector and Infrastructure Division, World Bank.

Martin, Will and Alan Winters (eds.) (1996) *The Uruguay Round and the Developing Countries*, Cambridge, UK: Cambridge University Press.

Maskus, K. (2000) *Intellectual Property Rights in the Global Economy*, Washington DC: Institute for International Economics.

Michalopoulos, Constantine (1999a) "Trade policy and market access issues for developing countries", World Bank, mimeo.

———— (1999b) "The developing countries in the WTO", *World Economy* 22(1) January.

Milner, Helen (1998) "Rationalizing politics: The emerging synthesis of international, American, and comparative politics", *International Organization* 52 (Autumn).

Motta Veiga, Pedro da and Vivianne Ventura-Dias (2004) "Brazil: The fine-tuning of trade liberalization", in M. Lengyel and V. Ventura-Dias (eds.) *Trade Policy Reform in Latin America. Multilateral Rules and Domestic Institutions*, Basingstoke, UK: Palgrave McMillan.

Olarreaga, Marcelo and Francis Ng (2002) "Tariff peaks and preferences", in B. Hoekman, A. Mattoo and P. English (eds.) *Development, Trade and the WTO*, Washington DC: World Bank.

Ortiz Mena, Antonio (2004) "Mexico: A regional player in multilateral trade negotiations", in M. Lengyel and V. Ventura-Dias (eds.) *Trade Policy Reform in Latin America*, Basingstoke, UK: Palgrave MacMillan.

Oyejide, Ademola (2002) "Special and differential treatment", in B. Hoekman, A. Mattoo and P. English (eds.) *Development, Trade and the WTO*, Washington DC: World Bank.

Panagariya, Arvind (2001) "Developing countries at Doha: A political economy analysis", University of Maryland, mimeo.

Prats, J. (2000) "Reforma del Estado y Desarrollo Humano en América Latina", *Quórum. Revista de Pensamiento Iberoamericano*, 2000.

Reddy, Sanjay and Charles F. Sabel (2002) "Learning to learn: Undoing the Gordian knot of development today", mimeo.

Rodrick, Dani (1997) "Trade Reform and Economic Performance in Sub-Saharan Africa", Harvard University, Cambridge, Massachusetts, November 1997.

———— (2001) "The global governance of trade as if development really mattered", Geneva: UNDP.

Sabel, Charles (1994) "Learning by monitoring: The institutions of economic development", in J. Smelser and R. Swedberg (eds.) *The Handbook of Economic Sociology*, Princeton: Princeton University Press.

———— (1996) *Local Partnerships and Social Innovation: Ireland*, Dublin: OECD.

Sabel, Charles, Dara O'Rourke and Archon Fung (1999) "Open Labor Standards: Towards a System of Rolling Rule Regulation of Labor Practices", presented at Annual Meeting of World Bank Seminars on Labor Standards, Washington DC, 28 September 1999.

Sen, Amartya (2001) "What development is about", in G. Meier and J. Stiglitz (eds.) *Frontiers of Development Economics*, New York: Oxford University Press.

Silva, Verónica (2004) "Chile: A multi-track market access strategy", in M. Lengyel and V. Ventura-Dias (eds.) *Trade Policy Reform in Latin America*, Basingstoke, UK: Palgrave McMillan.

Talberg, Jonas (2002) "Paths to compliance: Enforcement, management, and the European Union", *International Organization* 56(3) Summer.

Tendler, Judith (1997) *Good Governance in the Tropics*, Baltimore: John Hopkins University.

Tórtora, Manuela (2002) "Special and Differential Treatment in the Multilateral Trade Negotiations: The skeleton in the closet", presented at the Fourth Plenary Meeting of the Latin American Trade Network (LATN), Santiago de Chile, 12–13 December 2002.

Tórtora, Manuela and Diana Tussie (2003) "Commercial defense policy: Issues at stake", in D. Tussie (ed.) *Trade Negotiations in Latin America: Problems and Prospects*, New York: Palgrave.

Tubiana, Laurence (2003) "Post-Cancun WTO: Focus on the objectives, not the means", *Bridges* 7(7) September/October 2003.

Tussie, Diana (ed.) (2003a) *Trade Negotiations in Latin America: Problems and Prospects*, New York: Palgrave.

——— (2003b) "Introduction: On Shifting Ground – the Crossroads of Regional and Sectoral Associations", in D. Tussie (ed.) *Trade Negotiations in Latin America: Problems and Prospects*, New York: Palgrave.

Tussie, Diana and David Glover (1993) *The Developing Countries in World Trade: Policies and Bargaining Strategies*, Boulder CO: Lynne Rienner.

Tussie, Diana and Miguel F. Lengyel (1998) "WTO commitments on export promotion", *Latin American Trade Network (LATN) Working Paper* 1, Buenos Aires: LATN, November.

——— (2002) "Developing countries: Turning participation into influence", in B. Hoekman, A. Mattoo and P. English (eds.) *Development, Trade and the WTO*, Washington DC: World Bank.

Tussie, Diana, Gabriel Casaburi and Cintia Quiliconi (2004) "Argentina: In a logic of nested games", in M. Lengyel and V. Ventura-Dias (eds.) *Trade Policy Reform in Latin America*, Basingstoke, UK: Palgrave McMillan.

Tyndal, Paramjit (2000) "The Malasian Automotive Industry", paper prepared for PECC-ASEAN Auto Project, School of Advanced Management Technology, Manila.

UNCTAD (2000) *Positive Agenda and Future Trade Negotiations*, New York: UNCTAD.

——— (2002) *Back to Basics: Market Access Issues in the Doha Agenda*, New York: UNCTAD.

United States Trade Representative (USTR) (2003) *2003 Special 301 Report*, available at http://www.ustr.gov/reports/2003/special301.htm.

Ventura-Dias, Vivianne (2004) "Juggling with WTO rules in Latin America", in M. Lengyel and V. Ventura-Dias (eds.) *Trade Policy Reform in Latin America*, Basingstoke, UK: Palgrave McMillan.

Watal, Jayashree (2002) "Implementing the TRIPs Agreement", in B. Hoekman, A. Mattoo and P. English (eds.) *Development, Trade and the WTO*, Washington DC: World Bank.

Weisbrot, Mark and Dean Baker (2002) "The Relative Impact of Trade Liberalization on Developing Countries", CEPR, June 2002.

Weston, Ann and Valentina Delich (2003) "Settling disputes", in Diana Tussie (ed.) *Trade Negotiations in Latin America: Problems and Prospects*, New York: Palgrave.

Wilson, J.S. (2001) "Bridging the standards divide: Recommendations for reform from a development perspective", World Bank, mimeo.

World Bank (2001) *Global Economic Prospects and the Developing Countries: Making Trade Work for the World's Poor*, Washington DC: World Bank.

World Development (1996) Special Issue 24(6).

7

Regionalism and global governance: An appraisal

Louise Fawcett

This chapter looks at the ways in which the practice of regionalism inter-acts with and influences the architecture of global governance. It analyses the origins and development of regionalism and its relationship with states, multilateral and other institutions, locating the place of region-based movements, institutions and actors in the existing framework of global governance. While acknowledging that regionalism is part of the very fabric of global governance, it argues that as such it contains within it the possibility to condition its structure, parameters and development, and in this sense may be seen as a useful force in managing globalization. In assessing regionalism's potential, it shows how regionalism has greatly increased in scope and importance since the end of the Cold War, repre-senting a significant if underutilized tool for promoting security and development, and for mitigating inequalities between states. Critics over-state regionalism's weaknesses and undervalue its possible roles, compar-ing it to some ideal type or seeing it as a mere adjunct of globalization and therefore complicit in its processes. It is argued here that regionalism can both help strengthen weak states and influence the terms of the de-bate about globalization. A case is made for the further promotion and development of regional structures as key elements in the management of the international order.

Introduction

There exist diverse views of regionalism, and its place in world politics, and these views have changed over time. Some have long regarded re-

Regulating globalization: Critical approaches to global governance, de Senarclens and Kazancigil (eds), United Nations University Press, 2007, ISBN 978-92-808-1136-0

gions and regionalism as an important and positive ordering principle in international relations. Here there are many different perspectives among practitioners and scholars: from Winston Churchill to Jean Monnet; or from Ernest Haas to Joseph Nye. Though few advocates of regionalism could claim to be satisfied with the success of their project, all can point to real and potential achievements; their thinking and ideas feed current debates about the trajectory of regionalism.

A significant body of opinion remains sceptical of the theory and practice of regionalism and its ability to regulate international relations. Proponents of universalism have argued that any dilution of global goals is undesirable and undermining of order. This point, made by the founding fathers of the League of Nations and the United Nations, is still reflected in contemporary literature (Goulding, 2002: 218). The essence of these views is picked up in the chapter by Pierre de Senarclens. Cosmopolitan theorists, like advocates of globalization also highlight the advance of global structures, norms and values and the relative decline in salience of units like states or regions. Early accounts of globalization in turn saw regionalism as a competitor. And still, in current approaches to international problem-solving, the global level remains the first port of call.

Mainstream approaches to International Relations, characterized by the realist school, have also influenced the debate, holding that regionalism, as a form of international cooperation, can be no more than a limited and transitory phenomenon, bounded by state interest. In a classic early statement, Gunnar Myrdal wrote of international organizations as "nothing else than instruments for the policies of individual governments" (Myrdal, 1955). Stanley Hoffman would later declare that such institutions could render only "modest services" (Hoffman: 1987: 75). Modern critiques focus on regions and regionalisms as reflections of current power balances: strong regions depend ultimately on strong states who may be global as well as regional leaders, there is hence little independent regulatory regional role. Critical theorists take a different perspective, suggesting that since regions and regionalism are embedded in the dominant discourse and practices of International Relations, they cannot contribute to any fundamental reshaping of the prevailing international system, only reinforce its existing structure (Pugh, 2003: 31–46).

This essay dissents from the above views in arguing that regionalism can have a positive, regulatory and even transformative role. The universalist position is flawed in many respects, contributing to false expectations of order, similar to those of the 1930s in which hopes placed in the League of Nations contributed to an "illusion of peace" (Marks: 1976). The attractions of universality like globalization overlie a reality that is today neither universal nor global, one characterized by inequality of influence, opportunity and resources. In such an order regional contexts can play useful roles, whether in plugging gaps in global structures, strengthening weak states or contesting the existing hierarchy of power and influence, both through collective action and by the diffusion of regional ideas.

The realist perspective similarly underrates the importance and, in particular, the durability and adaptability of the regional domain, neglecting how shared experiences and common concerns, the consequences of growing interdependence and improved communications, and the cooperative potential of institutions and networks, can modify and even shift the nature and parameters of state power, as the most important example of regionalism, that of the European Union, has shown. The period since the Second World War has seen both sustained cooperation and institution building at the regional level, both inter- and non-governmental. In the rapidly changing international landscape regional processes have increased in salience and demonstrated flexibility, showing that state power is no longer the only common currency.

This regional momentum has proved resilient and diverse. In extending its reach to peacekeeping and peacemaking, disaster relief, distributing aid and development funds; dismantling trade barriers; fighting terror; or building democracy, regional initiatives – whether by governments, civil society or non-governmental organizations (NGOs), play out roles that daily impact on peoples and states and their decisions. Regionalism, broadly conceived, is part of an increasingly complex global governance network and, as such, has considerable potential in shaping the emerging contours of international relations.

Much focus on regionalism has been locked into the European example, with progressive moves toward economic integration and resultant functional and political spillovers as the yardstick by which it has been judged (Haas, 1958). Recent focus on the phenomenon of "interregionalism" – for example, the Asia-Europe Meeting (ASEM) – also draws on the European experience in highlighting and promoting interregional connections. The European Union (EU) does offer a useful starting point for thinking about the potential of regionalism while also acting as its promoter, but it also has limitations, particularly as a constant yardstick for comparisons. Firstly, the European experience is very different from elsewhere – an advanced case of regionalism – and one which is often complementary to the processes of globalization. Non-European experiments are relatively weak, and are frequently designed as attempts to facilitate or level the field as regards globalization. Europe's power of attraction has perhaps encouraged neglect of the diverse possibilities presented by extra-European regional initiatives, and the fresh perspectives they offer on global governance. One important aspect of European regionalism that is highly relevant to our discussion of global governance is its potential to create and embed regional norms, which in turn can influence global norms, whether on issues of security, democracy, human rights or economic development.

This is not to ignore the limitations of regionalism, whether as a means of alternatively mitigating, or bolstering, state power, or contesting the dominant trends in globalization. Indeed, for some, globalization itself has represented little more than a "little dance" between the three regional triads: Europe, North America and East Asia (Thompson, 2005: 54). This chapter concludes there is no room for complacency. Strong states, the engines of globalization, are often inclined to disregard even those institutions and mechanisms they have played a part in creating, as is evident in the current unilateralist turn in US foreign policy. Weak and poor states, lacking both capacity and relevant expertise, have little individual or collective bargaining power whether inside or outside institutions. Non-state actors remain relatively marginalized, and those with influence are mainly concentrated in strong northern states. Regionalism cannot be seen as an *alternative* to governance by states or global institutions, but as a both a complementary and regulatory structure.

Regions and regional actors do perform some tasks well however. They are suited – geographically, culturally and functionally – to dealing with certain aspects of regional governance, demonstrating comparative advantage, a fact that is increasingly recognized by the wider international community. They can also demand voice and representation in global fora, in looking for ways to change the existing balance of power both normatively and materially. States also *like* regionalism, and may regard home-grown regional institutions as a source of legitimacy. Today, there are more regional institutions than ever before, and their numbers and memberships continue to grow. With a multiplicity of states and other actors engaged in a growing number of regional institutions and networks, it is difficult to conceive of regionalism as merely serving a single global project. Rather they contribute to "multilayered" or "hybrid" forms of governance whether in the economic, political or security sphere (Sholte, 2000).

Regionalism is thus not merely the servant of globalization or strong states. It can help address the sources of state weakness and provide an entry point and a bargaining counter for states to participate in and engage with global processes. That regionalism has served a growing range of needs and demands is borne out both in its rich history, as discussed below, but increasingly in the contemporary era. This point is highlighted by a growing consensus among international actors and institutions – particularly the United Nations, as the 2004 High Panel Report showed (UN, 2004) – that not only is there room for creative regional thinking and action in the global marketplace, but also that these are worthy of support.

This chapter draws on a wide range of examples to consider the different arenas in which regionalism can play regulatory roles in contesting or influencing globalization. There is a particular focus on security, based on the now widely accepted premise that without security there can be no development, and without development is little chance for many states to engage effectively with global processes. If regions can serve to promote security and foster development, even in small ways, they are contributing to their greater inclusion in such processes. A underlying concern explored in the conclusion is how regional institutions and actors in developing countries may be further empowered to consolidate their collective identities and purposes and achieve better global representation.

Regions, regionalisms and regional governance

Making a case for regional governance, requires a brief consideration of existing definitions and parameters of regionalism. Regions, regionalism and regionalization, like globalization, are ambiguous and contested concepts (see the chapter by Yves Berthelot, this volume). All relate in different ways to interactions, be they formal or informal, deliberate or spontaneous, at the regional level. But what then *is* this regional level that matters in the debate about the containment of globalization? The perspective adopted here is that understanding regions and regionalism requires definitional flexibility, to include the newer and expanded domains of regional action (Fawcett, 2004a).

Most definitions of *regions* focus on geographical reality, a cluster of proximate states or territorial units. Certainly we cannot escape geography – or states – but a simple territorial definition does not take us very far in describing merely a regional system but not a regional society. We need to refine regions to incorporate commonalities and cooperative possibilities – whether on issues of trade, security or the environment – and display identifiable patterns of behaviour, generated by local needs, systemic constraints, or by culture or historical experience. A central feature of such regions or "zones" (Holsti, 1996: 142–3) is that they are smaller than the international system of states, but larger than any individual state or territorial unit. On this reading, regions and regionalisms run the gamut from macro to micro, international to transnational – from large continental blocks to small "sub-regions", from groups of countries to growth triangles to civil society networks (Soderbaum and Shaw, 2003). Such units may be permanent or temporary, institutionalized or not.

Regionalism (unlike regionalization) is what animates regions, or rather their members: where different actors consciously articulate and coordinate ideas and strategies.[1] It moves from the promotion of a sense of belonging or consensus building to the realm of action: from simple functional cooperation to the consolidation of formal organizations performing a wide range of tasks.

Depending on the regional unit in question, regionalism thus conceived can operate both above and below the level of states – from the policies of the Organization of American States to the actions of regional networks like Via Campesina.[2] And sub- or supra-state regional activity can inform state level activity, and so on. Indeed, any successful regionalist project today presumes complex linkages between state and non-state actors: an interlocking network of regional governance structures – the EU is the obvious example here, but the Americas and Africa offer others. One only has to look at the role that civil society networks have played in shaping debates about hemispheric free trade in the Americas, their contribution to peacemaking in Africa, or NGO activism in trade, environmental and human rights fora to understand their potential. As different scholars have shown, such transnational social movements are contributing to a redefinition of norms and practices at global and regional governance levels (Keck and Sikkink, 1998). Because, however, their membership is necessarily of individuals, or private organizations, and their functions very diverse, the principal focus of studies on regionalism remains the more measurable, and institutionally-based forms of interstate cooperation. In other words, the state is still typically regarded as the region's gatekeeper, and plays the predominant role in most regional arrangements (Russet and Oneal: 2001).

The flexibility and openness of the terms involved are important to understanding and locating the place of regions and regionalism in the global governance debate. Territory, alongside shared histories, cultures, ideas and interests, provide the foundations of regionalism, generating new norms and practices and, in turn, new layers of governance. Yet the mixture is fluid and volatile. Above all, regions and regionalisms are what states or other actors make of them. Regionness, like identity is "not given once and for all: it is built up and changes" (Maalouf, 2003: 23). There is no "ideal" region, or any single agenda to which all regions and regionalisms aspire. Indeed many regionalisms have evolved from an initial focus on economics, to politics and security, with institutional structures adapting accordingly. This is a significant point, often neglected in answering the question which kind of regional arrangement is best. On a practical level, the United Nations Charter, in its definition of regional agencies is imprecise and all encompassing (Sarooshi: 1999).

Implicit in the discussion so far is the notion that regionalism is a global phenomenon. Early successes in Western Europe have given way to a growing variety of different practices. The story of regional power is also about civil society networks in the Americas – recall the origins of the World Social Forum; *soft* security cooperation on the ASEAN model; election monitoring in the broader Europe; peacekeeping in Africa, and so on. International regionalism presents many possible models. Since regions are quite different in their make up and experience – not least their experience with globalization – we would expect their needs to differ also. From an institutional and normative perspective, the African, Latin American, Southeast Asian, or Central Asian experiences offer sometimes different insights and expectations – about shared identities, self-sufficiency, or balancing power – of what regional governance can offer.

In contemplating the regional phenomenon therefore, we must recognize that the make-up and history of the region under discussion are vital to understanding its prospects and possibilities in terms of engaging with globalization. In particular, the nature of states and regimes are central, though it would be unwise to discount regions or regional activity because of regime type or state instability. Certainly, regionalism may thrive better in a democratic environment, where civil society is relatively advanced, but it is not only the preserve of stable democracies, as examples from Southeast Asia and Africa show. Democracy and trade proved a strong combination in the creation of a Southern Cone common market (MERCOSUR) – indeed the very existence of the institution may have helped to consolidate and protect democratic practice and norms in the region. Their relative absence has helped prevent the development of an Arab one, despite continuing plans to initiate a Greater Arab Free Trade Area. Similarly security regionalism has worked better for some areas than others (contrast the West Africa case with that of the Persian Gulf), and so on.

The point here is to discover and develop those functions which particular regional groups are most adept at performing at any given time (and these functions can change). It is also appropriate to think of ways to build regional capacity, to make regions more effective actors in systems of global regulation, whether in the area of development, peacekeeping or good government, and here there is an important role for the United Nations and other multilateral institutions. In the words of the Report of the International Commission on Intervention and State Sovereignty, *The Responsibility to Protect*: "Those states which can call upon strong regional alliances, internal peace, and a strong and independent civil society, seem clearly best placed to benefit from globalization" (ICISS, 2001: 1–34). These are aims to which all regional institutions can contribute.

In spending some time on regionalism's history and development the intention is first to remind ourselves that regionalism has always had a role to play in mitigating global policies and trends and, second, to high-

light its evolving position within the dominant trends in global governance. It is also salutary to remember that, while for some parts of the
world regionalism is still a recent and quite shallow phenomena, there
are important precedents which help in terms of revealing the limitations
and prospects of current practice. Learning by doing, the practice of regionalism over time, may well be an important determinant in its relative
success, as the European case shows. ASEAN, for example has developed a particular style of normatively based consensus building; the second ECOWAS-led intervention (in Sierra Leone) benefited from the experiences, both positive and negative of the first (in Liberia). This does
not support the neat logic of neo-functionalist theorists with their predic-
tions of spillover and progressive integration, but it does suggest a continuing a dynamic and momentum to regionalism that is absent in many
accounts.

Regionalism: a long view[3]

Regionalism and globalization have long been with us. Historians of
globalization identify "waves of interconnectedness" going back at least
500 years (Robertson, 2003: 4), while regions – as empires, spheres of influence, or powerful unions of states – have long dominated in different
international systems. Indeed, one might say that in different regional
systems lie the origins of globalization. Still, in asking if regionalism can
help to manage globalization, we need to look more to an understanding
of regionalism as a global project that transcends state power and its projection onto a regional frame.

It is only really in the twentieth century that we can start thinking of
regionalism in this way – as having some role in balancing, mitigating or
complementing both state strength and global order. When we consider
the multiple actors operating at the global, regional and local levels
today, it is worth remembering that the growth, complexity and interdependence of the structures of international governance is a rather recent
affair. Until the end of the Second World War, apart from states, there
were still relatively few actors on the world stage.

Regionalism as a force distinct from wider global processes starts to
emerge, albeit imprecisely, in the international system after World War
I. The League of Nations system accorded (in Article 21 of its Covenant)
legitimacy to regional groups or "understandings" (Zimmern, 1945: 522),
and the period started to witness debates about the desirability of universal versus regional arrangements. Regionalism gained little *positive*
momentum however, as the experience of the 1930s shows. Beyond the
growth of functional cooperation, reflected in the expansion of interna-

tional agencies, formal institutions were few (one exception was the Inter-American System). Civil society movements – women's pacifist or humanitarian groups – all featured on the international scene, but were still rather dispersed and few in number. As regards the League itself, the idea that any formal interstate institution could deliver collective goods was novel, and one that failed the test of the 1930s. Security was still sought unilaterally or through ententes and alliances, often of an ad hoc nature. One lesson later reaffirmed by the United Nations is that, Charter pronouncements notwithstanding, no single institution can act as a global security provider, particularly when great powers reserve enforcement for themselves.

Economic interdependencies between states were deep in many instances, as Norman Angell famously demonstrated in the period even before World War I, but these were not institutionalized in any systematic way. The balance of power remained the major ordering mechanism of international politics. But the League and related institutions, like the United Nations later, encouraged states and peoples to think differently about issues of peace, security, equality and development, contributing to a new definition of international relations, and a changed normative architecture. In similar fashion, the experience of the Depression and subsequent inflation of the 1930s informed cooperative and preventative efforts in the early European economic institutions post-World War II.

Once embedded, such ideas persisted, to be refurbished in the UN era, which, in turn, came to embrace more squarely the idea and practice of regionalism. If the United Nations project was intended to be global, like the agendas of the newly formed Bretton Woods institutions and GATT, the UN Charter legitimized regional agencies, offering them, in Chapter VIII, Articles 52–4, a formal if somewhat undefined role in conflict resolution. This followed lobbying from both Arab, American and Commonwealth states. The principle of regional action and cooperation was firmly established. And the Charter link is important here for the endorsement it supplied and the accountability it demanded. As regards the GATT, although the spirit of a multilateral trading system enshrined in its agreement contradicted regional trade arrangements, its own Article 24 did make provision for them, provided they did not discriminate against non-members. And within both the UN and GATT/WTO frameworks we can see today how regional actors, whose presence is legitimized by these respective institutions, are capable of asserting independent agendas.

Take the regional economic commissions – an early and integral part of UN activity, drawing in different sets of actors (see the chapter by Yves Berthelot, this volume). These commissions, covering the five major world regions, were evidently designed to deal with problems at the local level within the broader UN framework, but they also, notably the Economic Commission for Latin America (ECLA), were responsible for introducing a new set of ideas which contested the dominant international economic order. Similarly, the newly founded intergovernmental organizations which started to participate as observers at UN General Assembly sessions were not all willing to follow the dominant themes of the day as expressed by the great powers – non-alignment, for example, became a powerful motif.

Non-governmental organizations, which had proliferated since the UN's early days, were referred to in Article 71 of the UN charter, which authorized ECOSOC consultation with NGOs, a reflection of their growing significance. Regionalism, in a variety of early forms, was set to take off. And, in this way the UN was extremely important in developing the idea and practice, but also the legitimacy of regional agency, both at the state, and also at the non-state level.

The possibility of globally-sanctioned regional action, or of meaningful relations evolving with the United Nations and regional agency, was necessarily curtailed by the Cold War and the composition of the Security Council which reflected the East–West divide. But the region as a unit of analysis was elevated by the Cold War, a regional system par excellence. With the evident constraints on the United Nations, peace and security were delivered unilaterally or regionally through the Warsaw Pact, the North Atlantic Treaty Organization (NATO), and related institutions. At another level, the European Community project, built around the idea of economic integration, but with security and democratic consolidation as key priorities, became a powerful model.

This empowerment of regional actors, despite their superpower dependence in the early days and the relative quiescence of the United Nations, was to create a powerful and enduring precedent. Regional organizations proliferated in the post-war period, from the Organization of African Unity (OAU) and Organization of American States (OAS), to NATO-inspired security pacts like the South East Asian Treaty Organization (SEATO), or the Central Treaty Organization (CENTO). Many spawned, like the UN, a set of related organizations – development banks and the like: huge bureaucracies drawing on regional (as well as external) funds and expertise. Their records were necessarily mixed; some reached an early plateau and failed to thrive, in the manner described by Karl Deutsch (1978: 226), others survived and expanded. The triple challenges of decolonization, modernization and the Cold War made coherence difficult, enabling institutions to be hijacked by powerful members or outside actors. But these were key years for regionalism with lessons, not only in economic integration and institutional development, but balancing, non-alignment, and the development of security communities. Transnational and non-governmental actors, multinational corporations, aid agencies, and the like, many also with a regional- (often Northern-) based focus also started to encroach more fully on the international scene, helping to shift the normative frame of regional operations.

For many countries, the prospect of regional integration had wide appeal, partly in response to European successes. This was the age of EFTA and NAFTA, but also PAFTA and LAFTA (Bhagwati, 1991: 70–71). For the developing world regionalism – then of the closed variety – incorporated the idea of independence and self-sufficiency. So did the wave of reformist Third Worldism, represented by the activities of the Non-Aligned Movement, or the Group of 77, with its demands for a New International Economic Order. In groupings, like that of the Organization of Arab Petroleum Exporting Countries (OAPEC) – with its successful drive to increase oil prices in the 1970s – regionalism became a *Southern* issue, a way of pushing developing country concerns on to the global agenda (Mayall, 1990; Morphet, 1996). Much of this activity can be mapped on to what is happening today in representations by developing countries at the WTO – the Southern Coalition at the Cancun Summit in 2003, for example, and other multilateral fora. In some ways the dilution of the South, and the continuing weakness of many southern states, has only increased the importance of regional alternatives as developments in the reformed African Union demonstrate. Then, as now, these were not mere exercises to consolidate or adapt to the dominant order, but attempts, albeit often clumsy, to change it or at least to introduce new terms to the debate.

The later Cold War period saw a further round of regional activity, with regional actors in more assertive, post-independence seeking new roles for themselves in shaping the local economic and security environment. Changing economic orthodoxy and the powerful example of European renewal in the 1980s, as well as a desire to manage their own security environment, helped to push states into new cooperative projects. Some now familiar examples include the Association of South East Asian Nations (ASEAN), the Economic Community of West African States (ECOWAS), the South Asian Association for Regional Cooperation (SAARC), or the Gulf Cooperation Council (GCC); somewhat different in their geographical reach and orientation are the Conference of Security and Cooperation in Europe (CSCE, now OSCE) and the Islamic Conference Organization (ICO). These institutions, founded between the years 1967–1986, were responses by regional governments to the challenges of the prevailing global order. They all still feature today – some still have only limited capacities – but many have continued the attempt to flesh out the contours of a system of regional governance by adjusting their agendas to the new economic and security architecture that has emerged since the end of the Cold War.

The post-Cold War climate

If the Cold War proved to be an arena for selective but cumulative regional growth and projects, a partial attempt to supplement the prevailing international order, the post-Cold War period presented new opportunities. Although in retrospect it might appear that many of the older limitations of regional activity – like resources and capacity – had scarcely been removed, expectations rose that the end of the Cold War would offer new incentives to states to cooperate in a variety of international institutions. Alongside, the process of globalization, regionalization and regionalism increased in salience. Both the number and membership of formal regional organizations, as well as interest in what was dubbed the "new regionalism", grew exponentially, and this process has continued, as have the non-state-based elements of regional and global governance in the form of civil society or transnational actors. At the present time, we see ever new impulses to regionalism complementing and, at times, competing with older patterns and trends. Some areas like Eastern Europe and Central Asia are experiencing and articulating the regional phenomenon for the first time; others are involved in revived or renewed efforts, drawing in an increasing network of actors. Conditions have changed, but the lessons of the past remain highly relevant.

For those who see only the tightening grip of globalization since the end of the Cold War, it may seem paradoxical that the regionalism of the 1990s was also promoted by the decentralization of the international system and the removal of superpower competition. There was also a trickle-down effect from the United Nations and the European Union as far as the empowerment and perceived capability of international institutions was concerned. The example of the EU generated competitive region building in both the Americas and the Asia-Pacific region. The OAU Summit in 1991 made also regional integration a priority, a response to the region's widely perceived marginalization. Economic regionalism generally was spurred on by doubts and fears as to the nature and direction of the multilateral trading order. Despite the new WTO regime, and the reform of the Bretton Woods institutions, their agendas and prescriptions remain challenging to all but the more robust developing economies.

As regards security, further challenges, and growing pressure on the United Nations, promoted in turn task-sharing with regional organizations, with terms like sub-contracting creeping into the UN vocabulary

(Weiss, 1998). Different UN secretary-generals have been instrumental in this process, notably Boutros-Ghali in his *Agenda for Peace* (1992), which highlighted both the need and the opportunity for regional action. Later, in his "Agenda for Democratization", he spoke of the "new regionalism" not as a "resurgent spheres of influence, but as a complement to healthy internationalism". Boutros-Ghali also established the precedent of convening regular meetings with the heads of regional organizations to discuss ways to enhance cooperation. And again, regional action was not only state-directed, NGOs were further empowered (Boutros-Ghali, 2000: 110–113). So the post-Cold War environment invited a greater regional awareness and involvement and was actively promoted by international actors. The larger space that has thus been opened up for regionalism is important both to the more competent regional groups, but also to those regions which lack viable structures, or whose own institutions are weak.

If regionalism has expanded to meet new demands and needs, it has also prospered in a more supportive international environment where regions have been relatively freer to assert their own identity and purpose. There is little doubt that regional actors and groups welcome this development and the opportunity it has brought to increase their influence. After the turbulent and regionally active decade of the 1990s, the "Brahimi Report" of 2000, with its only limited references to non-European regional contributions to UN peace operations, elicited disappointment, particularly among developing countries (UN, 2000). This, in turn, gave rise to the more explicit recommendations of the High Level Panel in 2004 which paid particular attention to the needs of southern states and institutions.

For such states, regionalism, like coalition-building within multilateral institutions, has helped to promote a greater degree of autonomy and representation, providing both a door into, and an alternative to, a Western-dominated "globalizing" order in which their interests are sidelined, as well as a forum where interaction, debate and agenda-setting are possible. It may simply guarantee a seat at negotiating tables. These impulses are necessarily poorly developed in "peripheral" regions where organizations are weak or new, or where the requisite technical expertise is in short supply (Hettne: 2001, 4–5). But there is widespread awareness of the possibility of regional groups influencing developments within their own space and contributing to norm creation over time, as the experience of, first, Europe, and now the Americas, Africa and Southeast Asia, show.

In part, engaging in regionalism may be just doing what others do. In a world where established states are regionally organized, none wish to remain outside current trends. Like democratization, it may attract aid and development funds. A lesson for emerging states is that they cannot afford to ignore the potential of regionalism. Indeed, as a recent UN-sponsored research centre shows, there are very few states today that remain outside the remit of any regional organization and many have multiple memberships (UNU-CRIS, 2005). Consider the recent efforts of China, Iran or the Central Asian states at region-building. What is interesting is that where states have options, they will chose the regional route time and again: they like to adopt the language and practices of regionalism. Both civil society actors and multilateral institutions have also come to recognize its importance. To construct viable programmes of aid, development and democracy assistance, or to promote human rights and environmental protection, often require a region-friendly approach and instruments of delivery at the regional level. The role of regional development banks after the respective financial crises in Asia and the Americas provide a useful illustration of how such institutions may be more sensitive and therefore attractive to local actors (Boas and McNeill, 2003). The contemporary instruments of global governance have revealed their inadequacy, displaying the need for complementary structures: any global approach security and development requires a wide variety of multilateral instruments, including regional agency.

A balance sheet

Speaking about the expansion of regional activity, of regional empowerment, challenges to multilateral and global fora, or burden sharing with the United Nations as characteristics of the post-Cold War era demands further precision. What has changed in existing institutions and what new institutions and actors have evolved? How has regionalism contributed to the evolving structures of global governance? Evidence of the impact of "new regionalism", an expression coined in the early 1990s (Fawcett and Hurrell, 1995: 3), can be found in three areas: first, numerical expansion as well as increased membership of existing institutions; second, increased capacity and range of tasks undertaken; and, third, "constitutional" reform, meaning sometimes quite radical adjustment to existing charter provisions. Singly, none of the factors can sustain the argument that regionalism constitutes a major element within existing global governance structures; taken together they suggest that it is an increasingly important force which has to be reckoned with.

New organizations, new members

The growth in numbers, as well as membership, of different types of regional, state-based organizations is well documented for both the first and second regional waves (Taylor, 1993: 24–26). Every year new organizations are formed, and new members accede to existing ones. These developments are tracked both by the UN and the WTO to whom different regional arrangements are notified. Non-governmental organizations have also grown exponentially, with overall numbers reaching over 40,000 by the year 2000. Less well documented is the growth of non-state-based entities of a regional nature, though understanding of their role in global governance is improving (Drainville, 2004: 121–130).

Simple membership expansion has been a characteristic of numerous institutions, from ASEAN's growth in the 1990s or the EU accessions of 2004, to the Economic Cooperation Organization (ECO), which in 1992 took in the six former Soviet (Muslim) republics and Afghanistan. Association or partnership agreements are also common from the NATO Partnership for Peace (PfP) arrangement to ASEAN's "Plus Three" (APT+3) formula. The related phenomenon of "inter-regionalism", examples of which are ASEM or the EU-MERCOSUR and EU-ACP relationship, has similarly grown in importance.

In terms of *brand new* organization, the former Soviet and Central Asian space stands out for a range of projects, including the Central Asian Cooperation Organization, the Collective Security Treaty Organization, the Shanghai Cooperation Organization and the Eurasian Economic Community, all products of the 1990s (*International Affairs*, 2004). Outside this area, new projects have taken root in the Asia-Pacific region: the ASEAN Regional Forum and Asia Pacific Economic Conference, and, in South America, MERCOSUR. Regions that lack viable or effective groupings are party to continuing discussions both about their creation and about which type of regionalism is most appropriate. The Middle East–Gulf area is a good example of a region where many proposals have been mooted – mainly by external powers – including a security condominium along the lines of the former CSCE, a Middle Eastern NATO, or an enhanced partnership with Europe. None of these options looks particularly promising in the short term (recall the 6–2 framework incorporating the Gulf States and two outsiders that was proposed after the Gulf War of 1991), but they do suggest that no state or international agency imagines a peaceful Gulf region without a meaningful regional security regime (Fawcett, 2004b).

New tasks

Both new and old organizations and groups have made commitments to upgrade and expand their range of activities. This, as discussed above, has been in response to new economic and security challenges, prompting by external actors, and general desire to enhance the profile of regionalism in the belief that it can address the problems caused by globalization. If we look at the activities of the WEU, ASEAN, ICO, ECOWAS and MERCOSUR, or the OAS and AU we can identify renewed expressions of unity among members, and expansion of tasks and services. Alone, declarations of intent may have little meaning, but set alongside a commitment to expand the range of activities and services provided by regional organizations, and the charter changes outlined below, they look more robust.

Different areas of growth can be identified. First, economic cooperation, directed towards the goals of regional free trade and market integration, has been given priority by a wide range of institutions including MERCOSUR, ASEAN or the Arab League, though with varying degrees of success. Also embraced is a developmental agenda, most notably in the New Economic Partnership for African Development (NEPAD). Second, as regards security cooperation, a number of institutions have made commitments to upgrade and expand their capacity into new areas – drugs trafficking and terrorism, for example – and increasingly to act as regional security providers, often in cooperation with the United Nations. They have already been active in conflicts in Africa (OAU/ECOWAS/ SADC), Central America and South America (OAS/CARICOM), the former Yugoslavia, and the Soviet space (NATO/CIS/OSCE) (Pugh and Sidhu, 2003). Of the 18 peacekeeping operations in existence at the end of 2005, nine had strong regional involvement, and discussions in the UN about further strengthening the role of regional organizations continue – most recently in the September 2005 World Summit. Finally, political cooperation has been particularly prominent in relation both to human rights issues and the promotion and consolidation of democracy as examples from the Americas but also the Commonwealth show.

Of growing importance in all these areas is the role of regional agency expressed sub-nationally and transnationally by networks of regionally based groups – "activists beyond borders" – who lobby inside and outside the formal institutional remit for better deals for the regions, groups and peoples they represent (Keck and Sikkink, 1998). An increasing amount of region-based activity relevant to our discussion of contesting globalization is of such civil society origin. Today over 1,500 NGOs enjoy consultative status within ECOSOC. In the Global Compact Initiative (1991), the UN has coordinated a bold project to promote public–private-NGO partnership further. Increasingly, as Ngaire Woods demonstrates in her chapter, such global civil society actors are entering into different arenas of global governance. Here, also, human rights remain a prominent area of activity along with labour, gender, environmental, developmental and humanitarian concerns. Consider the role of different regional NGO and other civil society lobbies at global summits. Just as important, however, is their growing security role in post-conflict peace-building as deliverers of aid, relief and related services (Barnes, 2003: 7–24).

Constitutional change

The range of activities described above has intimately affected the work-ing of regional organizations, putting some of them on the map for the first time. Charter change, or reinterpretation, has been an important and innovative feature of many international organizations since the end of the Cold War. One might start here with the changed UN stance over issues of humanitarian intervention, or the continuing discussions over the EU constitution. Real changes are not restricted to these two orga-nizations, however, as a few examples show. In the Americas, the com-mitment to political coordination was evident in the OAS Declaration on the Collective Defense of Democracy (1991) – applied in the cases of Haiti, Peru, Guatemala and Paraguay – and followed up with the Inter-American Democratic Charter in 2001. In Africa, the (then) OAU estab-lished a Mechanism for Conflict Prevention, Management and Resolution in 1993. SADC, ECOWAS and the OSCE also developed similar mecha-nisms. Perhaps most ambitious reform of all is the Constitutive Act of the African Union (May 2001), which lays down the framework for an African Parliament, Court of Justice and Peer Review Mechanism.

The picture painted above is necessarily diverse, but in regionalism today we already have a wide selection of responses to the perceived challenges of the post-Cold War order, whether through new mecha-nisms, agents or practices. If, in the European case, moves towards deeper integration and constitutional design, as well as membership ex-pansion, stand out, changes in doctrine and institutional capacity have been a characteristic of both African and American institutions, which have moved firmly into the field of democratization, human rights, as well as upgrading security capacity and provision for peacekeeping.

In describing and examining these processes and their global if differ-ential reach, it is hard to escape the conclusion that overall this is a pic-ture of greater regional empowerment. Despite the continuing obstacles it faces, not least in adapting to the post-9/11 US-driven security agenda, regionalism has an important role to play in contributing to, complement-ing and challenging global trends. It is becoming an increasingly impor-tant tool for many countries, first, because it facilitates a more stable regional environment, and, second, in providing both the muscle and le-gitimacy that individual states may lack and with this collective bargain-ing power the ability to interact more effectively with multilateral institu-tions. Regions without effective institutions, and the accompanying

network of civil society actors, are especially disadvantaged by the consequences of globalization and prone to external intervention. States without them – those of the Middle East, for example – are particularly vulnerable.

Obstacles to regional governance

In ascribing positive roles to regional governance, expectations often exceed evidence. It may be true that regional organization and activity have
expanded, as described above, but what is its real significance? Writers
and policy-makers are frequently accused of wishful thinking, or engage
in fulsome rhetoric rarely matched by action. A glance at the lofty ideals
articulated in the AU's *Strategic Plan* for the years 2004–2007 suggest
how wide this gap can be.

Lack of measurable and durable success, particularly in contrast with
other tools of global governance is clearly one major objection to regionalism. States and major multilateral institutions, with few exceptions, still
dominate in the power stakes with regionalism taking a weak third place.
There is also a North–South divide as regards strong and weak regions
and regionalisms, with the latter still mainly located in the South. This
hegemony among regionalisms is reflected in the Northern agenda of
many non-governmental and civil society organizations, well illustrated
in issues relating to the environment (see the chapter by Yohan Ariffin,
this volume). Further, in terms of "civilizational" inputs, writes Scholte,
"supraterritorial civic activity has on the whole drawn much more from
Western Judeo-Christian traditions" (Scholte, 2000: 195).

Potentially more serious, is the critique that regions are not always
sources of good or enlightened policies. They may, as in the past, become
"enclaves of reaction" (Falk, 2002: 177), or provide the source of transnational terrorism, conflict and crime in areas like human trafficking and
the arms or drugs trade. Such negative regionalisms feed on and benefit
from globalization, but hardly represent desirable sites of contestation.
For some writers, globalization is seen as promoting a form of negative
regionalism or transborder activities which merely serve to increase insecurity (Duffield, 2000). Certainly, as has been argued for the case of democratization, regionalization and regionalism do not always contribute
to a stable or positive outcomes in the short term.

Regionalism, like globalization is a work in progress. One need only
consider the obstacles that the European project has faced, and the difficulties the EU has encountered in placing its imprimatur on the globalization agenda. Outside Europe, the hurdles are much higher. In this
final section, I address some of the common problems associated with

regionalism under the three broad headings of capacity and performance, sovereignty and hegemony in response to those critiques which suggest that regionalism remains peripheral and unimportant, or even obstructive to better global governance.

Capacity and performance

The limited resources of many regional actors represent a major stumbling block to improved performance, and this raises real questions about their potential to influence global governance. The ability of any group to impact on a given regional space depends on the capabilities and willingness of its members and the existence of core issues over which cooperation is desirable and possible. The mere creation of a regional grouping, often the result of multilateral treaties and agreements, may have no more than rhetorical consequences if members are unable or unwilling to proceed to further stages of cooperation. This was the case with a number of attempts to copy the early European Community-style institutions in developing countries. A not unfair critique of a number of groupings, from APEC to CASCO, is that they have failed to progress beyond the debate and discussion stage.

Outside the advanced industrialized countries, limited capacity is clearly an obstacle to action, whether in the military, economic or political sphere. Economic integration has made slow progress in regions where internal trade levels, and hence incentives to cooperate, are low. Where suspicion, rivalry and competition are persistent, the prospects for political and security coordination are similarly reduced. In addition, the resources required to initiate and sustain such coordination are limited, whether human or material. Southern institutions and actors remain chronically weak when it comes to influence in dominant multilateral fora like UN or WTO; their coalition successes (like those of the G-77 or G-22) are still few and far between (Narlikar, 2003).

The capacity of member states is an impediment to cooperation, and will, along with the nature of the regional and international environment, crucially affect the success or failure of any regional project, and its ability to engage effectively with multilateral fora. The relative newness or fragility of states is an important factor here: in an unstable system cooperation is likely to be sporadic and superficial, limited to one or two functions, and driven by powerful insiders and outsiders. However, from unpromising beginnings, a stable system can emerge, showing how an appreciation of the time frame is important in judging regionalism's prospects: conditions change and with them the prospects for further cooperation. Economic regionalism of the "open" variety has achieved more in the second wave than the "closed" variety in the first. ECOWAS is said to have performed better overall in its later intervention in Sierra Leone than in its earlier one in Liberia. The NGO/transnational landscape is also changing, as demonstrated in the increasingly diverse origins of anti-global movements in recent years and in the "thicker" layers of regional civil society. This is particularly evident in a region like South America.

Regionalism can also help to strengthen weaker states – providing support and example – making them more effective regional and global players. Further, if the capacity of regional institutions is limited in some areas, it may actually be superior in others. Regional actors may be better placed to engage quickly and effectively, say in the area of conflict prevention. They may have improved understanding and information of the local situation, commanding greater acceptance. Southern transnational actors and NGOS may be few in number, and lack the power of their Northern counterparts, but their attunement to the needs of a given region and their local acceptability make them attractive. Regionalism can thus escape some of the well-rehearsed critiques of globalization and of multilateral institutions regarding accountability, legitimacy and representation (see the chapter by Jean Marc Coicaud, this volume).

Not all the new or revived post-Cold War institutions will endure or produce significant results. There have been many institutional disappointments. But some have endured and will continue to do so, and the reasons for this will relate to state capacity, domestic as well as external pressures and influences, existing commonalities, and the growth and development of shared interests. Since none of these conditions are fixed, groups, whose roles are currently limited, could assume new functions – a belief that underlies the new project embraced by the African Union. MERCOSUR in South America is a further example of a grouping which built upon the experience of the 1960s to re-emerge more forcefully as an organization with not only a viable economic dimension, but also a political and security agenda. Improving capacity and performance is not an idle dream; it is becoming a reality of a growing number of regional institutions.

Sovereignty and hegemony

The issues of sovereignty and hegemony can complicate and weaken the capacity of regional initiatives. Critiques of cooperation have long focused on the anarchical nature of the international system and the self-interested nature of states, one in which the prizes of sovereignty and hegemony are too valuable to sacrifice to any cooperative project. New states are particularly sensitive to encroachments on their sovereignty: sovereignty is fragile where it has only recently been obtained. The limitations that sovereignty imposes are augmented by constitutional constraints – charters which place high priority on principles like non-intervention and non-interference, well illustrated in the early Latin American, and now in Asia-based, institutions.

Though much cited, the sovereignty argument fails to constitute a convincing case against regionalism. Boutros Ghali famously remarked that "the time of absolute sovereignty has passed" (Boutros Ghali, 1992: 17) a comment reiterated in 2004 by South Africa's Finance Minister, Trevor Manuel, in reference to developments in the newly reformed African Union. Certainly the principle has become more porous in respect of the UN Charter where a new norm of intervention for humanitarian purposes is emerging; the same could be said for regional institutions – both inside and outside Europe. As noted, significant changes have been introduced into the Charters of the AU and OAS, while smaller groups like ECOWAS and MERCOSUR have sidestepped the sovereignty principle under prescribed conditions. Others adhere fervently to the principle. Still, for the purposes of our debate, respecting sovereignty does not however preclude a successful regional action. The Southeast Asian states, in their proactive response to the Cambodian crisis, offer some lessons here. Despite ASEAN's subsequent failure to provide regional leadership over the East Timor question, its experience shows that confidence-building measures, the politics of consensus and cooperation, can contribute to a more secure regional environment, while commanding local legitimacy and acceptance.

Hegemony is also a recurrent issue in discussing regionalism, where institutions are often seen as merely providing a power platform for a strong state. It is true that one major actor may set the agenda in any regional initiative, an argument that can also be applied to multilateral institutions. That actor may have been instrumental in its creation and maintenance, or the dominant role may pass from one state to another – the role of the United States in the creation and maintenance of the EC is just one example. In contrast, all regional activity in the Americas following the now extinct Monroe Doctrine is predicated on the predominance of United States. And it is easy to see how in an emerging region like Central Asia, institution-building has much to do with balancing or band-wagoning with the local strong power – often Russia, but also countries like Iran, Turkey, even China. Outside these areas we can see how the achievements of ECOWAS depended on Nigerian muscle; how the Southern African Development Community was conceived of as a response to a (then apartheid) powerful South Africa, or how the Saudis regard the Organization of the Islamic Conference as *their* project.

Seen at its most negative, regionalism can, of course, be viewed as an instrument for the assertion of hegemonic control, part of a strong state's toolbox (Hettne: 2001). Hegemony can undermine the legitimacy of any regional project. This maps on to the view of multilateral organizations as also dominated by core states, of globalization as "Westernization" – a process driven by the exigencies of US politics in a unipolar world. One might further argue that hegemons, by their very nature, eschew deep commitment to institutions which will limit their freedom of action, and some recent parallels are pertinent here: the USA's sidestepping of both NATO (over Afghanistan in 2003) and the UN (over Iraq in 2004), for example. But hegemony is a poor reason for decrying regional action: it is an argument for setting standards and guidelines; for promoting institutional democratization. Hegemons can be contained by regional institutions and practices: the EC project was partly about containing a resurgence of German power; the CSCE acted as a constraint on the USSR; new and old Middle Eastern schemes have focused (hitherto unsuccessfully) on containment of dangerously powerful or rogue states. Latin Americans tend to view inter-American institutions in this light – as a way of enhancing their bargaining position vis-à-vis the United States.

Hegemons play a vital and positive roles in promoting regional peace, security and development – often acting where others are unable or unwilling to do so. In this regard, parallel cooperation with UN structures and guidelines can help modify behaviour, mitigating hegemony and increasing accountability. Institutions can promote greater transparency, but, importantly, also supply legitimacy that may be lacking from unilateral efforts. States may choose to ignore international law and institutions, but such actions have costs both at the level of domestic and international public opinion. Ultimately, even hegemons need friends, and no state can afford permanently to ignore the cooperation of like-minded nations: sharing common interests and values is vital (Nye, 2002). This gives allies some leverage. Despite heated debates about the nature and direction of US policy, it is naive to believe that any state – particularly a democratically elected one – has either the ability or willingness to act unilaterally all of the time. Cooperation with others is not a choice, but a necessity (Patrick and Forman: 2002, 2).

Conclusions and recommendations

An appreciation of both the potential and the limitations of contemporary regionalism requires a historical and comparative perspective. Regionalism and multilateralism have evolved and coexisted, sometimes competitively, sometimes comfortably, since at least the end of the Second World War. Regions have witnessed a variety of experiments with different regional types, from those which have a broad reach, to narrower sub-regional projects. All this activity does not, in itself, necessarily indicate cooperation or integration in any deep sense or the creation of regional orders to contest or replace existing global structures. What it does indicate is that participation in, and accountability to, international institutions may have an importance that transcends the agenda of powerful states and global institutions, and hence can influence and modify patterns of behaviour. Often it provides a safe "friendly" environment in which regional actors can state freely their ambitions and goals – something that may not be possible in a broader multilateral forum – one in which regional as well as global norms can operate. Despite the continuing critiques of regionalism, there is a growing consensus that the overall balance sheet is favourable, that regionalism can contribute positively to stability, security and autonomy, particularly in an order where one state attempts to frame the terms about globalization.

In particular, regionalism can protect, respect and nurture identity and culture in a way that global institutions cannot. It can help reduce the fear of what Edward Said has called "global homogenization" (Said, 2002). One hard lesson of 9/11 and subsequent events was that international society is contested and fragile: global norms and practices cannot be imposed from above. In this respect, a historically constructed account of regionalism can be helpful in understanding the evolution of not one, but a series of – at times overlapping, at times conflicting – international societies. Asian, European, African and Latin American states may thus conduct regional affairs *their* way. A regional approach may then soften the hard edges of globalization, alongside the more flexible, democratized and transparent institutions demanded by the critics of multilateralism.

Regionalism cannot reasonably be presented as an *alternative* to a global or state-driven order. This chapter has highlighted its many limitations in this regard. Exploring regional processes reveals how much more could be done. For some, like Falk, most regional communities have simply not evolved to a point where they can counter what he calls "negative globalism" (Falk, 1999: 72). Functional cooperation is likely to continue where there are obvious functions that states and non-state actors can agree on and can share, and here functionalist theory has much to teach us. Sustained high-level cooperation in many areas remains unlikely, requiring a more stable and durable system to emerge – where state power is consolidated, where regional rivalries are mitigated, where shared interests can be identified and fostered. A secure regional system is not a sufficient condition for regionalism, but it helps. Once established however, regionalism, like democracy, can help stabilize a new order or compact between states, as the cases of Europe or Mercosur, and perhaps NAFTA also, have already shown. It can help to embed new norms and values, to consolidate processes of democratization.

In this respect, international cooperation and support are increasingly important and suggest ways forward for regional projects: states can benefit and learn from the aid and experience of others. Even if successful regionalism, like the democracy which helps to foster it, must come from below, there is a role for the international community. One of the most encouraging aspects of regionalism, which opens up possibilities for further reform, is the widespread support and acknowledgement it has received. Both the UN, the EU and individual states have been party to strengthening regional structures, with the UN High Level Panel in 2004 looking at ways to improve regional representation and performance – through the training and exchange of peacekeeping personnel, for example. For the case of African regional organizations specifically, donor countries were asked to commit to a 10-year process of capacity building within the AU framework. There was even a call to amend the rules for the UN peacekeeping budget to allow the UN the option to finance regional operations authorized by the Security Council (UN, 2004: 112). Such developments suggest important avenues for the further strengthening of regional actors, to increase their capacity and weight in multilateral fora and enhance their cooperation with other structures.

Providing assistance to regional actors – whether in support of peacekeeping or development or trade-related activities – or the promotion of interregional arrangements – are all ways forward in making them more effective partners in any system of global governance. Regional institutions and actors can complement, but not replace, the roles that other actors – states, civil society and multilateral institutions – play in setting the rules that regulate globalization (see the chapters by Kazancigil, Woods and Senarclens for contrast). If the role of the state – and the strong state, in particular – has proved remarkably robust, this chapter has argued that other fora and structures are constantly shaping and remaking global order. Even in the current era of US unilateralism, the structures of global governance are simply too complex to be managed by any single actor or uniform set of ideas. Evidence points squarely in the direction of multilayered governance, rather than any system in which states, or regions, or global structures dominate. While still neglected theoretically, the regional level of analysis has surprising power.

In trying to make sense of regional inputs, we are not talking about the regionalization of the world, as some brave theorists once suggested (Kothari, 1974), but coexistence between different levels of governance. Regionalism is going on around us all the time, responding to global and state, and civil society pressures. There is no single international issue, whether war, trade, drugs, justice, environment, refugees, terrorism or weapons of mass destruction that is not now addressed by regional actors. Regionalism has become part of "everyday global governance";

often uncoordinated, but revealing ever new "rhythms of regulation" (Slaughter, 2003). The challenge for regional governance is to extend its reach into new domains, and further extend its representation in multilateral fora, and to demand greater accountability.

The years since the end of the Cold War have seen increasingly bold attempts at regional governance, first in Europe, then Africa, Asia and Latin America. Despite the scepticism that accompanied the birth and development of many regional structures, they have endured and developed. Regionalism – in a multiplicity of forms – has come to assume an increasingly important role in the management of international relations and the shaping of international order – a significant pillar and regulator in any global governance regime, and one that is deemed worthy of support. If, as is claimed in the 2005 Human Security Report, the world has become a somewhat safer place since the "explosion of international activism" that followed the end of the Cold War, regionalism has had a part to play in making it so (Human Security Centre, 2005). The responsibility of the international community – whether states, multilateral institutions or civil society – is to continue to provide it with the necessary tools and support.

Notes

1. Here I distinguish between *regionalism* as policy or project and *regionalization* as the process of interaction and creation of regional spaces.
2. An international movement which coordinates peasant organizations of small- and middle-scale producers, agricultural workers, rural women and indigenous communities from Asia, Africa, America and Europe.
3. This section draws on Fawcett and Hurrell (1995).

REFERENCES

Baghwati, Jagdish (1991) *The World Trading System at Risk*, Princeton: Princeton University Press.
Barnes, Catherine (2003) "Weaving the web: Civil-society roles in working with conflict and building Peace", in Paul van Tongeren, Malin Brenk, Marta Hellema and Juliette Verhoeven (eds.) *People Building Peace II*, London: ECCP.
Boas, Morten and Desmond McNeill (2003) *Multilateral Institutions*, London: Pluto Press.
Boulden, Jane and Thomas G. Weiss (eds.) (2004) *Terrorism and the UN: Before and After September 11*, Bloomington: Indiana University Press.
Boutros Ghali, Boutros (1992) *Agenda for Peace*, New York: United Nations.

———— (2000) "An agenda for democratization", in Barry Holden (ed.) *Global Democracy: Key Debates*, London: Routledge.

Deutsch, Karl W. (1978) *The Analysis of International Relations*, Englewood Cliffs NJ: Prentice Hall.

Drainville, Andre (2004) *Contesting Globalization*, London: Routledge.

Duffield, Mark (2000) "Globalization, transborder trade, and war economies", in Mats Berdal and David Malone (eds.) *Greed and Grievance. Economic Agendas in Civil Wars*, Boulder: Lynne Reinner/IPA.

Falk, Richard (1999) *Predatory Globalization*, Cambridge: Polity Press.

Fawcett, Louise (2004a) "Exploring regional domains: A comparative history of regionalism", *International Affairs* 80(2, May): 429–446.

———— (2004b) "Alliances, cooperation and regionalism in the Middle East", in Louise Fawcett (ed.) *The International Politics of the Middle East*, Oxford: OUP.

Fawcett, Louise and Hurrell Andrew (eds.) (1995) *Regionalism in World Politics*, Oxford: OUP.

Haas, Ernst B. (1958) *The Uniting of Europe*, London: Stevens.

Held, David (2005) *Debating Globalization*, London: Polity Press.

Hettne, Bjorn, Andreas Inotai and Osvaldo Sunkel (eds.) (2001) *Comparing Regionalisms: Implications for Global Development*, London: Palgrave.

Human Security Centre (2005) *The Human Security Report, 2005*, Oxford: OUP.

International Affairs (2004) "Regionalism and the changing international order in Central Asia", Special Issues 80(3).

International Commission on Intervention and State Sovereignty (2001) *The Responsibility to Protect*, www.iciss-cisse.gc.ca/Report-English.asp.

Keck, Margaret and Kathryn Sikkink (1998) *Activists Beyond Borders: Advocacy Networks in International Politics*, Cornell: Cornell University Press.

Kothari, Rajni (1974) *Footsteps into the Future*, New Delhi: Longman.

Maalouf, Amin (2003) *In the Name of Identity*, London: Penguin.

Marks, Sally (1976) *The Illusion of Peace. International Relations in Europe 1918–1933. International Relations in Europe 1918–1933*, London: Macmillan.

Mayall, James (1990) *Nationalism and International Society*, Cambridge: Cambridge University Press.

Morphet, Sally (1996) "The Non-Aligned and their 11th Summit at Cartagena, October 1995", *The Round Table* 340: 455–463.

Myrdal, Gunnar (1955) "Realities and illusions in regard to inter-governmental organizations", L.T. Hobhouse Memorial Trust Lecture, London: OUP.

Narlikar, Amrita (2003) *International Trade and Developing Countries: Bargaining Coalitions in the GATT and WTO*, London: Routledge.

Nye, Joseph (1968) *International Regionalism*, Boston: Little, Brown.

———— (2002) *The Paradox of American Power*, Oxford: Oxford University Press.

Pugh, Michael (2003) "The world order politics of regionalization", in M. Pugh and W.P.S. Sidhu (eds.) *The United Nations and Regional Security: Europe and Beyond*, New York: Lynne Reinner.

Russett, Bruce and John Oneal (2001) *Triangulating Peace*, New York: Norton.

Said, Edward and Bamenboim, Daniel (2003) *Parallels and Paradoxes*, London: Bloomsbury.

Sarooshi, D. (1999) *The United Nations and the Development of Collective Security: The Delegation by the UN Security Council of its Chapter VII Powers*, Oxford: Oxford University Press.

Shepard, Stewart and Patrick Foreman (2002) *Multilateralism and US Foreign Policy*, Boulder: Lynne Reinner.

Sholte, Jan Aart (2000) "Global civil society", in Ngaire Woods (ed.) *The Political Economy of Globalization*, London: Macmillan.

Slaughter, Anne Marie (2003) "Everyday global governance", *Daedalus* 132(1) Winter.

Taylor, Paul (1993) *International Organization in the Modern World: The Regional and Global Process*, London: Pinter.

Soderbaum, Fredrik and Timothy M. Shaw (2003) *Theories of New Regionalism*, London: Palgrave.

United Nations (2000) "Report of the Panel on United Nations Peacekeeping Operations", New York.

——— (2004) *A More Secure World: Our Shared Responsibility*, Report of the High-level Panel on Threats, Challenges and Change, New York.

UNU-CRIS (2005) see www.cris.unu.edu.

Weiss, Thomas G. (1998) *Beyond UN Subcontracting: Task Sharing with Regional Security Arrangements and Service-Providing NGOs*, London: Macmillan.

Zimmern, Alfred (1945) *The League of Nations and the Rule of Law*, London: Macmillan.

8

Regionalization and globalization: Two concomitant dynamics in need of coherent institutions

Yves Berthelot

Regionalization and globalization are developing simultaneously as a result of spontaneous forces and deliberate political decisions. These two trends interact in many ways and can raise tension or ease problems depending on how regional and global institutions are articulated and used.

After a definition of regionalization and some statistical proof of its dynamism, the chapter will review examples that illustrate some aspects of the theoretical debate. Then, it will take up a few cases where regionalization could help to address intractable global problems. The dynamism of regionalization and its capacity to respond to difficult problems leads one to wonder under which conditions regional institutions could become effective instruments of global governance and how the United Nations, with its global and regional structure, could be an active player.

Regionalization: definition and statistical evidence

Regionalization results from a mix of political will, pragmatism and spontaneous economic forces. Yet, before looking for confirmation of this assertion by reviewing some experience and statistical data, it is useful to recall the definition of "region" and to define regionalization.

Definitions

The dictionary gives the following definition of a region: "Region: a relatively large territory, possessing physical and human characteristics that

Regulating globalization: Critical approaches to global governance, de Senarclens and Kazancigil (eds), United Nations University Press, 2007, ISBN 978-92-808-1136-0

make it a unity distinct from neighbouring regions or within a whole that includes it". Indeed, this definition fits with the practice of using the word "region" to designate a part of a country as well as a group of countries, small or large, depending on the unifying characteristics retained. It also suggests that the boundaries of any region depend upon the geography and history and the choice of those who belong or wish to belong to it. The case of Switzerland, whose people refused to join the European Union (EU) that surrounds them and the examples of the countries at the periphery of the EU that, with the exception of Norway, struggle to join in illustrate this point. This element of choice renders the governments and inhabitants of a region willing to develop common behaviours and accept common rules in the domains that unite them.

Regionalization, a word that, like globalization, has not found a place in the dictionary, is the process through which a region acquires common objectives, rules and practices. The states of the region, noting their interdependency in some economic and social domains, decide to institute a political mechanism aiming at developing common rules and practices in order to strengthen their mutual relations in these domains and, possibly, exercise collectively some influence outside the region. As in the concept of region, the concept of regionalization covers a variety of cases depending on the domains retained for cooperation, the competencies transferred and authority delegated to the regional institution by the national states. And, moreover, for each case, these characteristics evolve over time depending on success or failure.

The concept of regionalism, as used by Louise Fawcett in her chapter, contrasts with the relatively narrow definition of regionalization used in this chapter, a definition that assumes that a region has a geographical continuity and that this is important.

Regionalization or globalization: a statistical perspective

Trade flows and capital movements offer a first illustration of the fact that geography matters. Their liberalization over the last twenty-five years was expected to be a powerful instrument of globalization and mark "the end of geography". This should have been demonstrated by statistics.

Trade flows

The ratio of intra-trade flows of the countries of a region to their total external trade is an indicator of the integration of the region. The evolution of this ratio is given in Table 1 for a series of regional groupings over the period 1960–2002. Contrary to what could be expected, given the

Table 8.1 Intra-trade of Regional Trade Groups as percentage of total exports of each group

	1960	1970	1980	1990	2000	2002
EC (6)	34.6	48.9				
EC/EU (15)			60.8	65.9	62.1	61.0
EU (25)			60.9	67.1	67.2	66.8
CMEA	62.3	60.5	51.1	38.2	–	–
CIS				28.6	20.2	18.9
NAFTA			33.6	41.4	55.7	56.0
FTAA			43.4	46.6	60.7	60.7
APEC			57.9	68.4	73.1	73.5
Andean Group	0.7	2.3	3.8	4.1	8.4	10.6
CACM	7.5	26.8	24.4	15.3	14.8	11.5
MERCOSUR		9.4	11.6	8.9	20.9	17.7
CARICOM	4.5	5.3	5.3	8.1	14.6	13.5
ECOWAS	1.2	2.9	9.6	8.0	9.7	11.1
SADC			0.4	3.1	11.7	8.8
ASEAN	21.7	21.1	17.4	19.0	23.0	22.8

Sources: UNCTAD Statistical Yearbook, 1983, 1993 and 2003

relentless publicity about the "global village" and global markets, the external trade of these groupings evolved, with few exceptions, towards a much closer integration rather than towards a global engagement. It is a strong indication that geography matters.

Table 8.1 shows that, generally, the constitution of a regional grouping stimulates intra-trade. This may be due to the political signal given to the market, to the simplification of cross-border operations, or/and to the reduction of custom duties. The regional trade concentration increased rapidly in Western Europe during the 1960s to 1970s, and in the NAFTA region in the 1980s and the first half of the 1990s. Then it stagnated at a high level. In the groups involving only developing countries, intra-trade progressed in most cases but remained at relatively modest levels. This leads to a second conclusion: the more a region is industrialized, the more important is its intra-regional trade. For Asia as a whole, including China and Japan, intra-regional trade in the 1990s grew and it represents now 40 per cent of total external trade of the countries of the region. For Latin America, the ratio is 19 per cent. For Africa and the Middle East, the very low level of regional integration reflects those countries' continuing dependence on a few commodities exported throughout the world and their low level of industrialization.

In all regions, the share of manufactured goods in total exports of goods has grown continuously over the last two decades. It is now 81 per cent for industrialized countries, 78 per cent for Asia, 58 per cent for Latin America and 31 per cent for Africa. The concentration of industrial trade is compounded by technical progress, which lowers the material content of GDP and reduces the share of primary commodities in external trade. Trade in manufacture is increasingly intra-industry as opposed to inter-industry and consists largely of intermediate and capital goods. An explanation for this pattern is that, as the extent of the market increases, economies of scale and coordination allow the intermediate parts and processes required in the production of manufactured goods to be separated and entrusted to specialist producers external to the enterprise. This dynamic division of labour could in principle be extended on a global basis, given the decline in transport costs, the reduction of tariffs and other trade barriers, and the cheaper business travel and telecommunications. But, in practice, it is likely to proceed more rapidly among neighbouring countries with similar industrial structures. As increased interdependence resulting from increased specialization has a cost – the risk of disruption in the supply of intermediate inputs – enterprises will attempt to minimize this risk by keeping their supply lines as short as possible, both in geographic and economic terms.

Capital movement

With the liberalization of capital movements, it was expected that capital flows would globalize. It may be true for short-term capital flows, but, foreign direct investments, for which data are available, replicate, if slightly less sharply, the pattern of regional trade concentration. Even if FDI data by provenance and destination are not among the most reliable of economic statistics, they suggest indeed that, for Western Europe and North America, FDI is positively, and not negatively, correlated with the structure of trade by partner country. The evolution in Asia and Latin America goes in the same direction. For Europe, in a longer historical perspective, the change in concentration is especially marked. According to Angus Maddison, in 1914, at the end of what could be called the previous phase of "globalization", just under 19 per cent of the gross value of Western European capital invested abroad went to other parts of Western Europe, 40 per cent was invested in Latin America, Asia and Africa, 14 per cent in eastern Europe, against 58.7, 12.6 and 3.7 per cent respectively for the period 1990–1997 (Maddison, 1995). The UNCTAD Foreign Direct Investment Report confirms the concentration of FDI in industrialized countries despite strong variation from one year to another.

Despite the reality of deregulation and technical factors, which should have accelerated globalization, regional integration as measured by trade flows and foreign direct investments is growing and positively correlated to the level of industrialization. In addition, trade and direct investments flows are closely linked: "both are at least partly affected by factors related to distance, location and size of the economy and at the same time, they appear to exert a significant reciprocal influence" (OECD, 2003). This does not support the view that liberalization will reduce the income gap between countries, but it confirms that geography matters and, therefore, the rationale for regional agreements.

Factors underlying regionalization

Since time immemorial, human groups – enlarged families, clans, states – have concluded alliances between themselves to increase their security or, eventually, attack others who threatened them. With the emergence of nation states and the expectation of the citizens that policies would improve their welfare, states have entered into regional economic arrangements to secure stability and to facilitate trade and economic development. At the heart of these arrangements are perceived common interests or needs, strong enough to overcome actual political tensions, nationalist sensitivities or competition.

Examples of regionalization

The examples of the United Nations Economic Commission for Europe, the European Union and the regional groupings in the Third World will illustrate successively four factors of regionalization: the need for regional instruments, the political will, the institutional capacity and the external pressure.

The UN Economic Commission for Europe (UNECE)

The UNECE was created in 1947 to facilitate the reconstruction of the European countries devastated by World War II and to stimulate cooperation among them.[1] Just after its creation, the Cold War started. UNECE was maintained because of the political cost of dismantling an institution created in the aftermath of the war. Yet, there was no political will to do much with an institution that united two incompatible economic and social systems: UNECE, for instance, was not asked to manage the Marshall Plan, as initially envisaged by some in the State Department and the Foreign Office (Kostelecky, 1989). Despite this poor political environment, Gunnar Myrdal initiated dialogue on technical issues of common interest. Progressively, useful agreements were negotiated in UNECE covering domains such as security of motor vehicles and safety of road transport, transport of dangerous goods, trans-boundary air and water pollution, border crossing, facilitation of trade and custom operations, use of riparian waters for the production of electricity, and so forth. These agreements constituted many bridges between East and West. The number of agreements signed – more than 300 – is impressive. But, they remained technical and sectoral; they were neither guided by, nor articulated in, a strategic vision for an integrated development of Europe. Nor did they ever provoke the need for closer political cooperation (Berthelot and Rayment, 2004).

After the fall of the Berlin Wall, the fact that these agreements were part of the *acquis communautaire* renewed the interest of all countries seeking to join the Union in the work of the UNECE. To the contrary, the CMEA, which was created by the sole will of the USSR and which failed to develop mutually beneficial instruments, fell apart when the economic and social system imposed upon central Europe collapsed and none of its accomplishments survived. The case of UNECE provides a good example of how a regional framework can promote cooperation when its members consider it advantageous, but at the same time shows its limits when the political will and a common vision of the world are absent.

The European Union

The case of the European Union is quite different. At the beginning, the European Coal and Steel Community was created to manage investments in these two sectors and to avoid over-capacity when the demand for steel, generated by the reconstruction of housing and infrastructure in the immediate after-war, decreased. The European Coal and Steel Community (which, *en passant*, was based on a study made by the UNECE) was to become the first step towards the European Union, each step corresponding to a newly perceived need by member countries.[2] Contrary to what happened in the UNECE, the several sectoral and technical instruments were developed as instruments of common policies (trade and agriculture, in particular) or because the efficient functioning of one instrument called for the development of a new one. The difference between the evolution of the UNECE and the successive institutions that ended in the European Union lies in the political will to use them and the power delegated to them.

The firm will of all the European political leaders could be progressively concretized in economic and political institutions because countries of the region shared common values and had compatible views on desirable economic and social organization, and because their people could attribute progress to the work of the European Economic Community.

Regular meetings of heads of states and ministers also stimulated this will. In particular, the French–German leadership, sealed by the Elysée Treaty in 1963, continued over decades independently of the personalities of the French president and the German chancellor. Its institutionalized regular summits were key to maintaining the process when the two leaders had little in common or when the agenda per se did not require they should meet.

Brussels was granted means and powers that no other regional group ever enjoyed. Thanks to significant financial resources, an established set of meetings at ministerial level, and the welcome initiatives of some commissioners and the secretariat, the Commission was able to assume the responsibilities of common European policies, play the role of scapegoat for unpopular decisions, overrule national decisions contrary to European rules, maintain the line despite difficulties encountered in member states, and take initiatives giving life to the most innovative ideas of some of its members despite the reluctance of others – such as the Euro, for instance.

The common goal to build a strong Europe that would improve the welfare of its citizens was sustained, first, by the common fear of a new war between the member countries, which slowly vanished, and, second, by the fear of the USSR and the communist regime. After the fall of the Berlin Wall and the dismantling of the USSR, this second fear disappeared as well. The achievement of the single European market and the launching of the single European currency maintained for a while the dynamism of the European construction. The failure of the European Constitution broke the dynamic, but at the same time highlighted the strength of accumulated rules and practices: without clear goals since the 2005 summer, the European Union continues thanks to its institutions.

The regional groupings in the developing world

In developing countries, regionalization objectives were broader and more ambitious at the outset than in Western Europe, and in fact too broad and too ambitious. Inspired by the first success of the European Economic Community (EEC) and of the European Free Trade Association (EFTA), free trade associations and common markets blossomed throughout the world in the 1960s and 1970s. Leaders expressed their visions and hopes to secure peace, stability and development and to prepare the economies of their countries for global competition through regional agreements. The same message with local nuances is conveyed, more or less explicitly, in all the conventions or treaties that establish the diverse regional entities. Some examples are: "to fulfil within the shortest possible time the hopes and aspirations of their peoples" (Caribbean Community and Common Market (CARICOM));[3] "to ensure, through common action, the progress and well being of the people of Southern Africa" (South African Development Committee (SADC));[4] "to accelerate the economic growth, social progress and cultural development in the region through joint endeavours in the spirit of equality and partnership in order to strengthen the foundation for a prosperous and peaceful community of Southeast Asian nations" (Association of South East Asian Nations (ASEAN));[5] to secure "their countries a proper place in the international economy" (Southern Cone Common Market (MERCOSUR)).[6]

As for the economic dimension, in addition to dispositions aiming at the free circulation of goods, and, later, services between member countries, provisions for joint development policies were often made, particularly in the industrial sector. The rationale for industrial cooperation was indeed twofold. First, national markets were often too small for some industrial activities to be economically viable, and the regional arrangement was expected to enlarge the market while, at the same time, protecting infant industries from outside competition of foreign enterprises. Second, active industrial cooperation within the region would help, it was hoped, to organize a fair division of labour among member countries and to avoid ruinous competition between enterprises producing the same type of goods.

For diverse reasons, regionalization failed to facilitate the emergence of a diversified industrial fabric and to create markets broad and strong enough to encourage the creation of economically viable enterprises. Countries, whose main fiscal revenue came from custom duties, continued to levy them at their borders, which did not stimulate regional trade. Enterprises, even when offered incentives, rarely settled where encouraged. They preferred to locate where other industries had already settled as they could expect to find an industrial culture, skilled labour, good transport and communication systems, and opportunity to sub-contract part of the production process.[7] Foreign enterprises attracted by cheap labour and fiscal exemption did not contribute either to the development of the local industrial fabric if they had no compelling reasons to call on local suppliers and could easily import spare parts, equipment and services.

The experience of the 1960s and the following decades confirms what Robert W. Gregg had already noted in 1966: that regional integration is more the result than the cause of development. "If recent experiences with integration yield any lesson, it is that urban-industrial societies with a relatively high level of economic diversification are better candidates for more rapid progress towards union than underdeveloped, monocultural societies. Ironically, the integration movements in Europe ... are probably an important factor in spurring experimentation with economic unions in areas which otherwise fail to meet some criteria for integration" (Gregg, 1966).

In addition to this behaviour of enterprises that explains the failure of regional groupings in developing industries, governments of a same region did not take time to learn how to work together on technical well-delimited issues. In most cases, the institutions created were weak without delegation of authority and financial autonomy; they were able to make reports and to organize meetings, but not to take initiative and substitute for political leadership when necessary. Therefore, enthusiasm for regionalization faded away in the 1980s, but took off again in mid-1990s with the fear of globalization.

External influences

External factors can either stimulate or hamper the political will to create a regional entity. Two factors come to mind: the fear of a common threat and the policy of big powers. In the West, the Soviet threat helped all along the development of the European Economic Community (EEC), in the East, the Council for Mutual Economic Assistance (CMEA) was a response to the creation of the EEC. The Communist regime in Vietnam was a determinant reason behind the creation of ASEAN and its survival over the years despite the little progress made in achieving economic integration (see Table 8.1). Eventually Vietnam joined ASEAN when China was flexing its imperialistic muscles. South Africa was the cause of the creation of the concerted action of the "Frontline states" against apartheid.[8]

A constant goal of the United States' foreign and trade policy is to defend the interest of American farmers and industries, i.e. market access and safety for investments. It had a pragmatic rather than a doctrinal approach to regionalization. The USA was one of the strong supporters for the creation of the UNECE in 1947 and it conceived and financed the Marshall Plan, of which one important component was to impose the review of the projects of one country by the other beneficiaries of the Plan. When the EEC and the European Free Trade Association (EFTA) were about to be created, the United States expressed cautious support. It recalled its consistent support to "the political and economic strength and cohesion of Western Europe", but warned that the European market was important for agricultural exports from the United States and that it "will wish therefore to study carefully the possible impact of common-market arrangements" (State Department Bulletin). From that point until the WTO ministerial meeting in Cancun, the main debates in GATT and the WTO were between the USA and the EC and, in particular, on the trade of agricultural products. The American press saw the euro as a threat to the dollar and campaigned against its creation. But the US government did not oppose it. In the Third World, and particularly in Latin America, the United States did not encourage the creation of regional groupings. Rather, it has preferred bilateral relations with countries or, when groupings have developed in a direction that could hurt its commercial interest, it has tended to include them in a broader grouping that has included the US. This will be discussed in the final section of this chapter.

France and the United Kingdom in the 1960s encouraged cooperation among groups of their former colonies. The cement of the CDEAO (Communauté des Etats d'Afrique de l'Ouest) and UDEAC (Union des Etats d'Afrique Centrale) was a common official language, French, and a common currency, the CFA franc linked to the French franc. But, custom agreements among the members of each group were hardly respected. When the French franc melted into the euro, the UMOA (Union Monétaire Ouest Africaine) was created and trade agreements in this zone are progressively implemented. The countries of the East African Common Market (Kenya, Tanzania and Uganda) inherited common postal, telecommunication and railways services. But these technical links did not survive the political tension that opposed the member countries.

Later, the success of the European Common Market exercised, as already mentioned, a strong influence on the creation of several regional groupings throughout the world. But, in the absence of a common foreign policy, Europe did not aim at the creation of any regional group. The Asian, Caribbean and Pacific (ACP) countries, partners of the EU, have never constituted a regional group. Rather, they are countries, essentially former colonies, that benefit from financial and technical assistance, special trade agreements, and mechanisms to mitigate the damages caused to their economies by the instability of commodity prices. The EU set aside funds to support projects of interest to existing regional groups within ACP countries, but it faced difficulties in spending them for at least two reasons. Most of the regional groupings have no delegation of authority to receive and spend funds for infrastructure or other investments of common interest, and their member governments prefer to receive financial support for their own projects rather than for regional ones. Moreover, Europe did not use its leverage in favour of regional projects.

The theoretical background

The examples of regional integration, sketched above, illustrate different aspects of the theories of international integration developed over the past decades and that benefit from a renewed interest in the concomitant development of regionalization and globalization.

"Functionalism" assumes that societies, like living organisms, have to meet functional needs and that institutions are conceived as mechanisms that respond to specific social needs. Applied to international relations, it means that societies have developed needs that cannot be satisfied at the national level and require inter-state coordination in the framework of international organizations designed to this end. These functional organizations would realize concrete tasks of common interest to member states. Progressively, further coordination in one sector would require coordination in another sector. Over time, the multiplication of technical coordination would require a political dimension. This approach, proposed by Mitrany in *A Working Peace System*, influenced the structure of the UN family and inspired the founders of the European Community. It also guided Gunnar Myrdal in the UNECE. But, as mentioned above, UNECE remained a technical institution and even the move from sectoral to cross sectoral issues, such as studying the interaction between transport and environment, while technically logical, was not automatic and required a political decision of member states. At each step of the construction of the European Community and the European Union, governments had to decide to move forward, even on technical matters. "Contrary to what Mitrany alleged, the technique has no "capacity of self-determination" by itself. It is the policy that occasionally confers it a right to self-determination" (Senarclens and Ariffin, 2006).

At the other extreme, Andrew Moravcsik and other authors of realist inspiration underline the decisive role of national governments in each step of the process of economic integration. Integration is a rational decision of governments in order to manage the interdependency of their economies, each of them pursuing the economic interests of its country and not the development of common public goods. The supranational mechanisms are created and used to service national economic, strategic and political interests of interdependent countries. This vision begs the question: Are the supranational institutions shaped in the interest of the major powers of the region? In Europe, France benefited more than other members of the Common Agricultural Policy and Mrs. Thatcher obtained "her money back". But, on average, it is recognized that all members took advantage of the integration and that the income gap between countries was reduced. It may be different when there is a single major power in a regional group. The NAFTA has benefited the US more than Mexico and Canada, while the FTAA seems designed to transfer to a regional institution the responsibility of achieving the commercial interests of the United States that previously had been obtained through bilateral arrangements.

The neo-functionalists attempt to nuance the idea that governments have the sole power and are guided entirely by national interests. They argue that the common institutions influence the analyses and the preferences of member governments through their studies and the frequent meetings they organize. It is certainly true that complicity is created that facilitates agreements and that supranational institutions develop a certain autonomy that makes them actors on the international stage. The President of the European Commission attends the G8 and the World Bank IMF meetings. The European Court of Justice and the European Parliament have gained an independence that tempers the absolute sovereignty of the national states. It remains that, on politically sensitive issues, governments are guided by what they perceive as the national interest. In the same vein, the fact that, in the developing world, governments have not created strong intergovernmental institutions, even less supranational ones, can be explained either by the low level of the interdependence of the countries of a region or by the fear of governments to see their sovereignty reduced. It will be interesting to see how this evolves with the growing interdependence within regional groups in Asia and Latin America.

The rejection of the European Constitution approved by the governments obliges one to reflect on the role of the people in regional integration. Certainly, the fact that in France, as in several other countries, successive governments did not lean on the people to move Europe forward, but on Europe to move the people, played a role in the rejection of the Constitution. But, the rejection is more than a movement of feeling against the government and some European irritating decisions; it is a claim of the people to discuss the finality of the Union. The people do not want to discuss the feasible, which the elite does, but the desirable. "The people want, in 2005, to preserve the democracy and the power of the politics, when these are obsolete in the eyes of the elite that see nothing but the markets and the open sea" (Rozes, 2005). It is clear that the technical dynamic of the functionalists finds its limits in the politics. The question is whether a supranational institution has to find its legitimacy through consultations organized by national governments or directly from the people of the region.

Political considerations are essential in the decision to build any regional agreement. Sustained political will is necessary for its success and for overcoming unavoidable tensions. Equally important in this perspective are the institutions created to implement and monitor the agreement. If well staffed, managed and financed, they rapidly acquire their own dynamic and are instrumental not only in maintaining the will of the members but also in supplementing that will by taking initiatives and making proposals. As regions multiply in the world, the issue of their interrelations and the coherence between regional and global institutions arises. This will be addressed in the fourth part of the chapter, but first the importance of a regional approach will be illustrated in reviewing a few protracted global issues that more easily find solutions at the regional level (Senarclens and Ariffin, 2006: ch 6, pp. 165–188).

Relevance of regional approaches for global concerns

The previous sections have highlighted the dynamism of the regionalization process. Three issues of concern for all the countries of the world – the right to food, corporate governance and prevention of financial crises – illustrate the relevance of regional approaches.

Hunger and regional agricultural policy

If regional agreements based on trade preferences for manufactured goods did not succeed in accelerating the industrial development of non-diversified economies, one may wonder if it would not have been wiser to build regional arrangements on agricultural development, which was a pillar of the construction of the European Union. Food products in any region are both diversified and similar. Exchanges could have developed based on differences in quality and prices, and availability when the irregularity of rainfalls would have created shortages in one country and excess in another. This potential was not exploited and more often than not food aid has not been used to stimulate regional trade but rather to dispose of stocks from Europe or the United States. But, the scandal of hunger that hurts mainly poor peasant families – according to FAO, IFAD, and the World Bank, more than 70 per cent of those suffering hunger today are peasants – points to the limits of global trade liberalization in agriculture. This view is obviously controversial as the common battle of the developed and developing countries in WTO is not protection but "access to market".

The desire of governments to feed urban citizens at low cost, bilateral pressures of food exporting countries, conditions imposed by international financial institutions in the framework of structural adjustment programmes or debt alleviation mechanisms, and WTO rules, led progressively to food trade liberalization in most developing countries and countries with economies in transition. This put the small farmers of these countries in direct competition with farmers from developed countries who have benefited from state support for decades and whose exports are directly or indirectly subsidized. Confronted with declining prices and obliged to meet compulsory expenditures such as housing, health care, education and food, peasants are forced to sell an increasing share of their production. This leaves their families without enough to eat and themselves, and without the resources to buy the equipment and inputs necessary to increase yields. Markets do not automatically adjust production when prices are low. On the contrary, peasants, who cannot shift to other productions and who are not ready to migrate to cities, tend to increase their production to compensate the reduction of prices, which creates over-supply and accelerates the fall of prices. In most of the OECD countries subsidies permit peasants to survive; such a remedy is not possible in developing countries that need to recover the necessary policy space to conduct their agricultural policies and fight against hunger.

Over-supply and subsidies decrease the value of food products on international markets of economic significance: they do not even reflect the production costs of the most productive agricultural systems. These prices should not, therefore, be taken as reference when deciding on agricultural development policies and should not be allowed to determine prices on domestic markets. Developing countries should have the right to impose duties on food imports as part of a strategy to increase food security and formalize the right to adequate food for both small farmers and vulnerable urban dwellers. Import duties are not contrary to the principles and good functioning of a market economy. Many advanced countries have, at a certain moment of their development process, protected their agriculture to increase the income of peasants and to provide a market for emerging industries and services.

Countries would derive an advantage from pursuing such policies at an appropriate regional level for at least two reasons. The first is that contrary to industry, agriculture is diversified, even in poor developing countries. Operating on a regional basis could help overcome climatic hazards, induce regional trade, promote the harmonization of food norms and facilitate further integration in other sectors. Second, a group of countries carries more weight in international negotiations or vis-à-vis financial institutions for obtaining in international forums the margin of manoeuvre they feel is necessary to fight against hunger.

Put in provocative terms, it is not the end of the CAP that is advocated here, but the multiplication of CAPs in the developing world – of course, not CAPs with subsidies creating over-supply, but CAPs aiming at the survival of small family farms, the most direct way to reduce hunger.

Rules for global corporations

In the case of global corporations, the issue is more whether the rules to which they have to comply have to be global or regional. Enterprises attach great importance to predictability and transparency of the rules to which they have to comply. This does not mean that these rules have to be global, only that they have to be known and stable. Global intergovernmental organizations, like the WTO, promote rules related to trade, investments, national competition and intellectual property rights. But there are two important issues where the absence of international rules is damaging: competition and accounting.

While on the agenda of the WTO, little progress has been made on international competition rules. The EU, for its part, has developed regional ones that could inspire the endlessly postponed debate at the global level. But, the existence of competition rules in the EU, or in any other regional group, may have unexpected consequences in the absence of global ones. Two regional enterprises may be prevented to merge in order to avoid a regional monopoly and then be acquired by an enterprise foreign to the region, which, at the same time, deprives it of two enterprises and makes it dependent on an external monopoly. Here, there is a need for broad global principles that are translated into rules at the regional level.

Recent scandals have shown that existing accounting and reporting mechanisms can be manipulated and provide misleading information to stakeholders who, therefore, lose confidence, which may undermine growth and employment. Existing accounting systems permit the practice of certain multinational corporations to manipulate the internal transfer prices of services or goods in order to make losses or benefits appear where more advantageous. This may lead to organizing the bankruptcy of a sound subsidiary, leaving creditors and employees without recourse, and eventually retirees with under-financed pension liabilities. The liberal answer is that the market will eventually sanction wrong behaviour. It is not convincing, but attempting to negotiate a unique detailed accounting system may not be the answer, as a good lawyer can demonstrate that a company did not infringe the precise rules. Moreover, it would not be easy because of differences in legal systems and habits and, in addition, it may prove difficult "in a political climate in which corporate insiders get pretty much what they want" and the politicians who do their bidding are likely to pay any price (Krugman, 2004). What is needed is an agreement on guiding principles at the global level, the spirit of which should be respected independently of the regional accounting system.

The international debate on guiding principles on competition and accounting should address the responsibilities of the enterprises vis-à-vis customers, employees, shareholders and the environment. In the private sector, it is encouraging that some investment funds privilege enterprises with good social and environmental records. Even if still marginal, it is a signal that long-term and ethical considerations can balance the search of immediate return. At the international level, the United Nations Secretary-General, Kofi Annan, had these long-term and ethical issues in mind when he proposed the "Global Compact" to the heads of large companies gathered in Davos. It is regrettable that the UN has not been able to follow up with debates gathering governments, enterprises and unions and leading to global principles.

Competition and accounting systems are cases where principles should be discussed at the global level and detailed at the national or regional levels depending on the degree of integration of the regional grouping.

The case for regional approach in global finance

In the aftermath of the crises of the 1990s, particularly those of Asia and the Russian Federation, renewed attention was given to the prevention of financial crises and contagion. The dynamism of intra-regional trade and financial flows, which increases macroeconomic linkages among countries of the same region, gives a permanent actuality to these two issues and strengthens the argument that regional institutions could play a central role (Ocampo, 1999).

The prevention of financial crises requires the improvement of prudential regulation, macroeconomic surveillance and supervision of national financial systems. Immediately after the crises of the 1990s, there was an attempt to design global prudential norms. But it soon appeared that differences in legal traditions would make it difficult to establish such norms, and that it would be preferable to leave responsibility in the hands of existing regional institutions. Indeed, mechanisms for setting prudential norms already exist in America, Europe and Asia and could be established for Africa and the Middle East.

Traditionally, the IMF exercises surveillance. Nevertheless, during the turmoil of the Asian crisis, Japan went as far as proposing an Asian Monetary Fund (AMF), a regional IMF for regional surveillance and crisis management. Later, Africa, in the framework of its New Partnership for African Development (NEPAD), decided to exercise regional surveillance, and the Economic Commission for Africa has since proposed some preliminary guidelines for peer reviews. Surveillance can certainly be exercised at the regional level, but if the IMF keeps responsibility for crisis management and does not recognize the validity of regional surveillance, countries are likely to be reviewed twice, which is time-consuming and could be confusing if norms differ. This calls either for regional IMFs or for an agreement between the IMF and regional surveillance institutions. The issue of articulation between regional and global, which will be addressed later, surfaces here about a sectoral matter.

The risk of international contagion in the case of major balance of payments crises could, *a priori*, justify management of these crises by a world institution, such as the IMF. But, in fact, during the Asian crisis, it was not the measures taken by the IMF that prevented a world extension of the crisis, but the injection of liquidity by the Federal Reserve. From an Asian point of view, the crisis itself was not appropriately managed: contagion in the region was not avoided, conditionality delayed the transfer of funds that were immediately needed to prevent the deepening of the crisis, and policies imposed on the countries pushed them into a long recession, with the exception of Malaysia that ignored IMF strategies (Berthelot, 2001). Macroeconomic consultation and surveillance under the auspices of the IMF are necessary to guarantee policy coherence among major industrialized countries (meeting of the G7 ministers of finance); but it is inefficient to try to manage the externalities generated by macroeconomic policies on neighbouring countries, regional effects of potential debt standstills and workout procedures globally. Regional arrangements offer a far more adequate framework and, in particular, may react more rapidly and adequately than the global international financial institutions.

Beyond crisis management, a regional institution could play a role in resource allocation. There is a precedent with the European Regional Development Fund that allocates resources to less advanced regions of the EU countries. It played a key role in the development of Ireland, Greece and Portugal, and was an element of EU attractiveness for Eastern European countries. The creation of similar funds for Africa, Asia, Latin America and Western Asia would require resources, allocation criteria and institutions for managing them. Resources should come from each region as a mark of regional solidarity and could be based on import duties. They should be supplemented by international public aid. Allocation criteria should be established on a regional basis to fit country needs better and facilitate regional integration. The UN Regional Commissions have the capacity to host the necessary negotiations and to monitor implementation of the criteria. For managing the funds, regional banks exist in each region with the exception of Eastern Asia. They have the expertise and the credibility. That said, the failure of establishing a fund for the diversification of African commodities under the auspices of the African Development Bank illustrates the reluctance of developed countries for funding they do not control. The poor achievements in development and surveillance by global financial institutions remains a justification at least for exploring other avenues, including the regional ones.

Strong regional financial institutions could serve as buffers in crisis management, provide a better-informed and appropriate service and finance to small countries. The idea of regional monetary funds, brushed aside by the US Treasury, should be reconsidered, and the role and means of Regional Development Banks enlarged. Indeed, "for smaller countries, access to a broad menu of alternatives to manage a crisis or to finance development is relatively more important than 'the global public goods' that the largest international organizations provide" (Ocampo, 1999). Due to their small size, their negotiating power vis-à-vis large organizations is very limited, and regional organizations are more likely to address their needs better. And, the regional institutions can avoid the "one fits all policies" more easily than the global ones.

These three cases illustrate the different roles that a region can play in addressing global problems. It can cushion the brutal impact of globalization, translate global principles into operational rules adapted to the regional circumstances and prepare member countries to a global negotiation, be an instrument of solidarity and complement the action of global institutions.

The regions as instruments of global governance

The dynamism of regional integration, its manifestation in trade and foreign investment statistics and the mushrooming of regional political and economic, sectoral and general institutions invite one to consider the regions as structuring elements of the world scene and their institutions as indispensable instruments of global governance.

General principles

For regional institutions to play a role in global governance, there are two basic conditions. First, the division of labour between global and regional institutions should be complementary and coherent. Second, regions have to enter into regular dialogue and negotiations.

Complementarity and coherence between global and regional institutions

When recommending policies, designing rules and adopting conventions, global institutions have a tendency to enter into too many details and to consider that the provisions they take should be applied universally. The idea of "special and differential treatment" that was conceived to address differences in economic development levels has lost ground in favour of a single vision of how the economy works. In universities, development economics has disappeared. In the WTO, delays can be granted to the least developed countries, but for a limited time. Many norms are universal that simply cannot be applied in poor countries or by poor people. This is where well-articulated, global and regional institutions addressing the same issue could help. Indeed, an issue of global concern should not necessarily be given the same answer throughout the world. Air pollution, river management and waste management are three issues of global concern: the first, because wind scatters toxic particles throughout the world, requires a global approach; the second, with trans-boundary and riparian rivers, is typically a regional problem; and the third issue for most products is addressed nationally or locally.

When deciding to address an issue internationally, two considerations should guide the choice between global or regional institutions: the possible diseconomy of scale and the principle of subsidiarity. In most cases, the global institutions will be well placed for agreeing on general principles that give an objective and secure a minimum of coherence between the measures taken at the regional level. At the regional level, these principles should be translated into policies, rules and instruments that integrate cultural and economic specificity of the region.

Interregional relationships

The European Commission was first to establish relations with other regional arrangements. The EEC and ASEAN established informal relations in 1972; they were formalized in 1977 and consist mainly of dialogue on, and reviews of, political, security and commercial issues. Progress is slow and, despite the dynamism of the region, the ASEAN-EU dialogue is still to envisage a Trans-Regional EU-ASEAN Trade Initiative (TREATI) that could lead to a preferential trading agreement in the future. With Latin America, initiatives of cooperation focused on cultural and political matters and were more directed to individual countries than to regional groupings until the 1980s. Major changes occurred in the 1980s and 1990s: Europe became aware that its natural cultural links were no longer sufficient to maintain its presence and influence in a region that was becoming less Latin and more American. In addition, Spain and Portugal had joined the community. Europe helped to restore peace and democracy in Central America through the San José dialogue in 1984. In the 1990s, the emergence of an outward-oriented regionalism in Latin America, which ECLAC labelled open regionalism, incited the EU to shift its attention from bilateral relations with countries to relations with regional groupings. Today, the ongoing negotiation with MERCOSUR aims, in principle, at establishing a free trade agreement between the two regions and is the occasion to discuss the organization of the institutions of this region. The EU and MERCOSUR have exchanged information on tariff barriers and have clarified tariff offers, but doubts linger about the intentions of the EU to finalize a comprehensive agreement on market access which is at the very heart of objectives of the MERCOSUR countries.[9]

The United States, as with the European Union, had long favoured bi-lateral agreements with selected countries, but the renewal of regional groupings in Latin America and the development of direct relations between them and the EU could not leave it indifferent. Not only was the Union playing a political role in Latin America, but it was also exploring with MERCOSUR new forms of relations between regional entities that could set a precedent. The USA did not choose to intensify relations with the regional groupings in Latin America and the Caribbean, but preferred to include their member countries in a broad arrangement, the Free Trade Area of the Americas (FTAA). The FTAA, still in a phase of difficult negotiations, is interested in both the traditional pursuit of US interests and also a response to the role that the European Union wants to play, as illustrated by the two following quotations.

> The United States is committed to completing the Free Trade Area of the Americas (FTAA) process by 2005 in order to expand markets for the U.S. goods and services and help insure safe destination for U.S. foreign investments.[10]

> One reason behind the U.S. push to implement the FTAA earlier is the fact that MERCOSUR is set to clinch a free-trade deal with the European Community within the next two years. The United States would like to firm up the FTAA before that happens.... MERCOSUR's turn to Europe has to do with more than just trade and investment. There is also talk for a "little Maastricht" for countries of the Southern Cone, and European know-how and experience is being sought in this regard. (Reich 2003)

Interestingly, the North American Free Trade Alliance (NAFTA) – that came into force on 1 January 1994 and the dynamism of which appears in the rapidly growing intensity of intra-trade (see Table 8.1) – might be for the USA the model to which the FTAA should aspire. NAFTA was indeed seen by the Americans as a "catalyst for broader international co-operation".

In the same spirit, the United States launched the APEC with riparian countries of the Pacific Ocean, disregarding Kurt M. Campbell's advice that in Asia "leadership on multilateral initiatives should arise from within the region and then gain support from Washington, rather than the other way around" (Campbell, 2001). This view expressed about security issues is also valid for economic matters and echoes some Japanese voices calling for a sweeping reconsideration of the fundamental "Follow the US" mindset that dominates the Ministry of Foreign Affairs. Makoto Taniguchi notes that Japan has more in common with China than with the USA because of history and geography, remembering that the USA opposed a plan for an Asian Monetary Fund that could have prevented the Asian crisis from spreading and also interfered in many Asian economic issues. He therefore welcomes the participation of Japan in ASEAN + 3 (China, Japan and South Korea) and calls for "regional cooperation in East Asia through the establishment of economic zone [which could] be one of the ways to bring peace and political stability in this region" (Taniguchi, 2002). Following suit, regional entities in the developing world, traditionally attached to develop intraregional activities, are enlarging their ambitions to the development of interregional relations.

Toward interregionalism

The development of interregional relations described above are first steps toward an organized system of global and regional institutions cooperating and negotiating, which would reconcile the diversity and governance of a globalized world.

For this to gain momentum, there are at least two conditions. First, bilateral relations between regional groups should be institutionalized, which means that they take place regularly with an agenda prepared by the secretariats. So far, only a few regions have established bilateral mechanisms for regular consultations and eventually negotiations of binding agreements. This is evolving, but the encounters are too infrequent and lack focus. Second, the secretariats of the regional groupings should have delegation of authority and clear mandates to take initiatives and explore possible interregional agreements. This is hardly the case. But without delegation of authority, negotiations will be hampered by immediate national interests, as illustrated in an encounter between the EU and ASEAN, where Pascal Lamy, then the European Commissioner, found himself alone vis-à-vis ministers from each ASEAN country who had divergence among themselves on what to achieve and how. Third, regional groupings should acquire legitimacy. Today their legitimacy depends on the will of member governments; it would be reinforced if regional parliaments could approve the agreements they conclude in interregional negotiations.

Interregional relations are still in need of proper practices, clear goals and concrete results. They have to transform dialogues into the negotiation of agreements, prove that they have a positive impact on global negotiations, solve pending issues, give a voice to the weakest nations and contribute to global equity. If they succeed, they will have a decisive influence on the management of globalization; if not, they will remain another layer of discussion, useful but time-consuming.

The case of the United Nations

If the United Nations wants to influence global governance actively, it has to make better use of its global and regional entities that have now coexisted for decades. While there have been many positive examples of successful regional global interactions, they have not been part of a deliberate strategy. This is needed.

The regional dimension in the UN

The Economic Commissions for Europe, Asia and the Far East, Latin America, Africa and, finally, Western Asia were created over a period of 26 years. The five regions were in varying degrees confronted with unity, growth and development, and, later, globalization. The fact that they found different answers to similar problems legitimizes regional approaches.

Within the UN System, developing an idea to meet some regional need or adapting a global idea to the specificity of a region is not exclusive to the regional commissions (RCs); most UN specialized agencies, funds and programmes have established regional offices. The crucial difference, however, is that, contrary to regional commissions, these offices do not respond to regional intergovernmental machinery, but to global. The general mindset developed between governmental representatives and the staffs of the commissions through a multitude of meetings and negotiations permits the latter to interact constructively with its "customers" (Berthelot, 2004).

Global and regional interactions

After more than fifty years it is clear that the regional commissions contributed to the UN ideas and instruments: the deterioration of the terms of trade inspired UNCTAD's work; the import substitution strategy influenced the Second Development Decade. The pioneering work of the Economic Commission for Asia and the Far East (ECAFE) on population prompted UN entities and specialized agencies to integrate the population dimension into their activities. Several of the conventions and norms or standards adopted in the Economic Commission for Europe (ECE) became global. The ECE convention on the transport of dangerous goods, for instance, is now global and followed by the ECOSOC while the ECE secretariat continues to service it. The protocol on the emission of heavy metals to the ECE convention on air pollution served as a reference in the preparation of a global convention by UNEP on the same issue. Regional commissions contribute to the main global reports and conferences bringing in the diversity of the regional concerns and proposals.

Conversely, the regional commissions received encouragement from UN Headquarters for adapting global principles to their region and following up on recommendations agreed at the global conferences of the 1970s and the 1990s or at the Millennium Summit. They were then recognized as being the regional arms of the UN. Even if some commissions had pioneering roles – for example, in population (ECAFE), environment (ECE), women (ECA), or poverty (ECLAC) – the direction received at the global level stimulated the commissions that had not yet addressed the issues. Moreover, as the regional arms of the UN, implementing global agreements, the secretariats of the commissions were able to table issues that otherwise would not have been addressed due to their sensitivity – for example, women and population in the ESCWA region.

The relations between Regional Commissions are gradually developing, despite an earlier reluctance on the part of governments to undertake joint analytical studies on a given theme. On the other hand, governments appreciate that the work of one commission can benefit others. For example, policy proposals, conventions or norms developed by one commission have been taken up by others as they meet some of their needs. The International Road Transport (TIR) convention of the ECE was adopted in the Mediterranean region and in Asia; ECE, ESCAP and ECWA secretariats discussed harmonization of road networks and road safety measures. In addition, the commissions increasingly work together on joint projects funded by the UN Regular Budget in areas that concern more than one commission, such as trade facilitation or transport linkages.

The above demonstrates that, within the UN system, the interaction between the global and regional levels is a reality. However, the potential benefits of this interaction have not been fully realized. Indeed, there is no recognition of the value of the potential of the regional entities within the United Nations as illustrated by the conclusion of Willy Brandt's report *Our Global Neighbourhood*. The report recommended that the United Nations prepare itself for the time "when regionalism becomes ascendant world-wide, and even helps the process along". But, to reach this objective, it did not call on the regional commissions. To the contrary, after a formal acknowledgement of the work of the commissions, "notably ECE and ECLAC", it considered that: "The continuing utility of the [Regional] Commissions now needs to be closely examined and their future determined in consultation with governments in their region". Finally, it concluded that the objective of strengthening regional groupings and developing links with them "could be helped if resources now spent on the Regional Commissions were diverted to the support of these [regional and sub-regional] organizations and their activities" (UN Commission on Global Governance).

A strategy for the United Nations

The recommendation of the Brandt report to abandon the regional dimension in the United Nations was not implemented. But it stimulated reflections on a UN strategy for a world confronted simultaneously with the forces of globalization and regionalization. "Indeed, we believe that the United Nations should become the forum in which the world regions can enter into dialogue with one another.... In the long run, multiregionalism is about autonomous regions that meet in a global forum such as the UN" (Langenhove et al., 2004). In this perspective, the UN offers a forum for dialogue and global rules. Here, an approach is proposed that aims to improve the mission of the United Nations to build upon the existence of global and regional entities within its system.

A first mission of the UN is to set principles, norms and rules. If systematically exploited, the interaction between the global and regional levels would permit the organization to distinguish better between what has to be global and what should remain at the regional level. The regional commissions, as regional arms of the United Nations are well placed to give strength to global principles while respecting the diversity of the regions. They have also demonstrated their ability to bring regional responses to intractable global problems as some of those evoked in the third section of this chapter. These responses could circulate easily within the UN System and eventually become global when appropriate.

Another mission of the UN is to provide information and analyses not biased by particular interests. So far, the opportunity to build on the wealth of experience accumulated in the regional commissions and the regional or national offices of UN agencies or programmes has not been used to forge new development paradigms. The UN, mobilizing all its entities should take such an initiative. Persisting poverty and inequity, the non-sustainable consumption model, the inappropriate dissemination and use of scientific progress, poor articulation of global, regional and local institutions, all call for this.

A third mission of the United Nations is to provide technical assistance to countries that require it. This is often done by cooperating with regional groupings of countries. In an effort to accompany the movement of regionalization, the United Nations could ask the regional commissions to strengthen their cooperation with regional groupings. More generally, the regional commissions should be the intermediary between the UN and the regional groupings in the economic and social field. It would certainly be simpler and more efficient for the UN headquarters to deal with this blossoming nebula of regional organizations through the commissions rather than directly with them, as suggested in the Brandt's report. In the domain of peacekeeping and security, the situation is different as the decision to use a regional body that has the capacity to accomplish peacekeeping operations or even exercise coercive measures has to be taken by the Security Council.[11]

Civil society organizations (CSOs) are also actors of global governance. The United Nations has involved them in its work for many years. But, because of the multiplicity of the CSOs and their divisions, the relationship between the UN and civil society risks becoming unmanageable, unless they organize themselves. Representatives of civil society met in Geneva in June 2003 at the invitation of the United Nations Non-Governmental Liaison Service (NGLS) to discuss the matter. Interestingly, they recommended refraining from participating massively in fashionable global meetings and regionalizing their relations with the organization.[12]

The elements of the strategy outlined above rely heavily on the regional commissions. They have, therefore, to be better recognized and utilized. Their size and the common history of their members facilitate dialogue among members and agreements on issues of common interest. Their secretariats, closer to governments' concerns than those of a global entity, can develop a common mindset with country representatives that permit them to elaborate jointly new ideas. Their domain of competence includes all aspects of economic and social life and they can address complex multisectoral issues, which the sectoral global UN entities cannot do (see the chapter by Pierre de Senarclens). Moreover, as part of the United Nations, the regional commissions have the added advantage of benefiting from its moral authority. Their neutrality on divisive issues reassures the weakest countries, which gives them the possibility to voice their concerns and to receive attention. They are therefore an asset to the United Nations for playing its role in global governance.

Concluding remarks

Regionalization demonstrates its dynamism through the construction of multiple regional entities. These entities will progressively enter into organized relations and will contribute to the management of globalization to the extent that nation states delegate them more responsibilities. It is hoped that nations – that are exclusively today at the base of international legitimacy – will progressively share this character with the regions. This would give more weight to small countries in international debates than the "one country one voice" fiction.

Regional economic arrangements, whatever form they take, recall the necessity of understanding the historical context of the socio-economic problems for which they are seeking effective policies and strategies. Automatically, they go against the neo-classical approach embedded in the normative dimension of globalization that, in its tendency to prescribe "one-size-fits-all" policies, plays down the importance of the socio-economic processes they present as a constraint on policy-makers' freedom of action.

The conditions of a successful and sustainable regional arrangement are sustained political will, common values, compatible economic and social systems, the gradual construction of common useful instruments, and strong regional institutions with regular meetings of the secretariat and the delegation of authority. It takes time to build a regional entity and it is wise to do it progressively. In this process, the role of the secretariat is essential and the first sign of common will is to give it means and capable staff.

By giving the example of how to translate global principles into regional practices and find regional solutions to intractable global problems, the United Nations could take a lead in the building of a world where the complementary forces of globalization and regionalization, of unity and diversity, would be utilized to the benefit of all the people.

Notes

1. The ECE region covers all European countries, including former-USSR countries, as well as USA, Canada and Israel.
2. UN-ECE (1949) *European Steel Trends in the Setting of the World Market*, New York. See *ECE, The First ten Years, 1947–1957*, Geneva 1957, footnote (1) pages XIV–10: "M. Jean MONNET, when ... he set out to draft a practical plan for cooperation in the coal and steel field, needed independent expert advice and, at the request of the French Government, the Director of the ECE Steel Division and his assistants were instructed to give whatever help they could ... The first draft of possible technical clauses for the creation of a European Coal and Steel Community was worked out in ECE by the then Director of the Steel Division, though naturally without our taking sides on the political issues involved."
3. Treaty establishing the Caribbean Community and Common Market (CARICOM), 4 July 1973.
4. Declaration on the establishment of an international organization to be known as the Southern African Development Community (SADC), August 1992.
5. Treaty establishing the Association of Southeast Asian Nations, 8 August 1967.
6. Southern Common Market (MERCOSUR) Agreement, 26 March 1991.
7. The difficulty in planning the geographical distribution of industries was already exemplified in the 1950s by the relative failure of the Italian government to attract perma-

nently in the Mezzogiorno enterprises that were gathering in the Milan and Turin areas.
8. Between 1975 and 1993, the Frontline states – Angola, Botswana, Mozambique, Tanzania, Zambia and Zimbabwe – regrouped.
9. "Global positioning of the European Union and MERCOSUR: Towards a New Model of Inter-regional Cooperation", Annual Lecture of the Chair, MERCOSUR, Institut d'Etudes Politiques, Paris, 4 April 2002.
10. US-AID, Caribbean Regional Program.
11. The UN charter foresees that the UN can pass agreements with regional bodies provided the agreements are compatible with the principles and objectives of the United Nations. After the fall of the Berlin Wall, Boutros Boutros Ghali underlined in the *Agenda for Peace* the advantages and conditions of involving regional bodies in the peace process. Since then, NATO intervened in the Balkans, the CIS in the Caucasus, ECOWAS in Liberia and Ivory Coast, and the African Union in Darfur exercised such missions under UN mandates.
12. Report of the Consultation with Civil Society on "The Crisis in Global Governance: Challenges for the United Nations and Global Society", Geneva, 4–6 June 2003.

REFERENCES

Berthelot, Yves (2001) "The international financial architecture: plan for reform", *International Social Science Journal* 170(December): 585–596.

――― (2004) "Unity and diversity of development: the regional commissions' experience", in Yves Berthelot (ed.) *Unity and Diversity of Development Ideas: Perspective from the UN Regional Commissions*, Bloomington IND: Indiana University Press, Chapter 1.

Berthelot Yves and Rayment Paul (2004) "ECE: a bridge between East and West", in Yves Berthelot (ed.) *Unity and Diversity of Development Ideas: Perspective from the UN Regional Commissions*, Bloomington IND: Indiana University Press, Chapter 2.

Campbell, Kurt M. (2001) "The Challenges Ahead for US Policy in Asia", condensed version of a presentation to FPRI's Inter University Study Group on the US and Asia, 30 March.

Gregg, Robert W. (1966) "The UN Regional Economic Commissions and Integration in the Underdeveloped Regions", *International Organization* 20(2) (Spring): 213.

Kostelecky, Vaclav (1989) *The United Nations Economic Commission for Europe: The Beginning of a History*, Göteborg: Geographic Systems AB. (Kostelecky gives a detail account of the negotiations related to the choice of a secretariat for the implementation of the Marshall Plan.)

Krugman, Paul (2004) "The US corporate system still needs fixing", *International Herald Tribune*, Saturday/Sunday, 10–11 January.

Langenhove, Luk van, Costea, Ana-Cristina and Gavin, Brigid (2004) "From multilateralism to multiregionalism: What role for regional integration in global governance?", UNU-CRIS Occasional Papers, 0–2004/5.

Maddisson, Angus (1995) *Monitoring the World Economy 1820–1992*, Paris: OECD (Table 3–3, p. 63).

Ocampo, Jose Antonio (1999) "Recasting the International Financial Agenda", paper drawing on the work of the author as coordinator of the Task Force of the United Nations Executive Committee on Economic and Social Affairs, as well as joint work with Stephany Griffith-Jones, supported by the Swedish Ministry of Foreign Affairs.

OECD (2003) "Trends in Foreign Direct Investment in OECD countries", *Economic Outlook* 73: 163, Paris: OECD (ch. V).

Reich, Otto J. (2003) *U.S. Policy in the Americas and the Role of Free trade*, usinfo.state.gov/journals (Internet access 28.08.2003).

Rozes, Stéphane (2005) "La renationalisation du débat européen", *Quark*, August, p. 42.

Senarclens Pierre de and Ariffin Yohan (2006) "La politique internationale: Theories et enjeux contemporains", 5th edn, Paris: A. Colin, ch 6, p. 170.

Taniguchi, Makoto (2002) "Without an independent and multilateral foreign policy, there is no future for Japan, in *Sekai*, July 2002.

UN Commission on Global Governance (1995) *Our Global Neighborhood*, Oxford: Oxford University Press, pp. 286–291.

UN-ECE (1949) *European Steel Trends in the Setting of the World Market*, New York: UN-ECE. (See also ECE (1957) *The First ten Years, 1947–1957*, Geneva: United Nations, II-3.)

US Department of State Bulletin, XXXVI, 919, 4 February 1957, p. 182.

www.fordham.edu/HALSALL/MOD/1957-ecc-efta-us.html

www.usinfo.state.gov/journals/

9

Developmental and environmental policies: Past trends, present issues, future prospects

Yohan Ariffin

Introduction

The relation between development and environment has become a hotly debated issue. In the views of some observers – particularly in the industrialized world – environment protection should take precedence over development considerations on the grounds that *grow now, clean up later* strategies are self-defeating if adverse effects on ecosystems eventually prove to be irreversible. In the views of others – particularly in southern hemisphere countries – development problems, on the contrary, should be given precedence over environmental ones on account that the former, notably mass destitution, overpopulation and landlessness, are often direct causes of the latter. The concept of "sustainable development",[1] devised by the World Commission on Environment and Development in its 1987 report, sought to bridge the gap between these two visions by declaring that development and environment were mutually dependent and limiting objectives. It restricted the sovereign right of states to exploit their own resources to those activities that would not prejudice future livelihood prospects. But it continued to stress the overriding importance of development and predicated its achievement on the pursuit of economic growth. By reflecting two seemingly irreconcilable goals in a neat formula that merely blunted their respective edges, the notion gained widespread acceptance by policy-makers and academics in the northern and southern hemispheres alike.

Regulating globalization: Critical approaches to global governance, de Senarclens and Kazancigil (eds), United Nations University Press, 2007, ISBN 978-92-808-1136-0

For all its fuzziness, "sustainable development" has now become an umbrella term under which systemic transformations appear to be at work. It has justified and informed the negotiation of global treaties, conventions and protocols which aim at mitigating various kinds of environmental damage or resource depletion while incorporating in their preambles promises to "bear in mind the developmental needs of developing countries". In a context when industrialized countries are reducing their overall contributions to concessional loan facilities, environmental projects seem to attract a growing volume of whatever little hot money is left for so-called development purposes.

This chapter does not attempt to provide a comprehensive catalogue of the multifarious ills that plague southern hemisphere countries. Its problematique is to examine from a historical perspective the main legalistic processes that have been designed for purposes related to the exploitation and conservation of resources in less developed countries (LDCs). In so doing, the present chapter addresses itself to a specific topic, namely, the ambiguities and contradictions underlying the creation and functioning of those international regimes that seek to link environment and development issues. The central question here is whether such regulatory frameworks are likely to constitute banes or boons for LDCs. To anticipate, it is the opinion of the present writer that past and present trends do not allow us to be particularly sanguine in this regard.

The discussion falls into three parts. Section two provides a brief history of the twin pressures at work – developmentalism and environmentalism – the roots of which can be traced back to colonial times. Indeed, as will be made clear, concern about "sustainable development" represents but the latest twist of a debate that has resurfaced during the nineteenth and twentieth centuries in what seems to be a never-settled academic and policy debate. We need this historical understanding for the light it can throw upon the judiciousness of some of the strategies that are currently being devised, particularly the ones based on the notion of *public trust* in nature conservation which are often but reminders of how close recent trends in living resource management are getting to former colonial practices predicated on the *dual mandate* or *trusteeship* ideology. There is much truth in the famous dictum of George Santayana engraved over the US Archives building in Washington DC: "Those who do not remember the past are condemned to repeat it".

The third section proposes an analysis of the ways in which multilateral environmental agreements are currently shaping expectations related to, prescribing roles pertaining to, and constraining activities in relation to, development practices. Consideration of this point requires a careful analysis of the genesis of the two most important agreements from the perspective of North–South relations: the Conventions on Biological Diversity (CBD) and Climate Change (FCCC), their Protocols, and the

Global Environment Facility (GEF) as their principal mechanism for funding.

The fourth section examines a general trend the author believes should cause a great measure of concern, namely, the extent to which the dominant forces shaping patterns of environmental governance appear to be overwhelmingly associated with northern hemisphere corporate interests. The subject of "sustainable development" has been so much obscured by its very vagueness which verges on the commonsensical – who indeed would be in favour of "unsustainable development"? – and the judgement of the public has been so industriously worked upon by interested groups that cool and serious reflection is required in order to arrive at safer conclusions.

Critics of development fall into two categories. The "reformist" views development practices as flawed but nevertheless necessary from an ethical standpoint and improvable from a practical one. The "radical" considers that official development assistance has so often misused the ethos of responsibility to serve the interests of the powerful that it has often aggravated or created new forms of what it was supposed to remedy or reduce, namely, the equity gap between rich and poor and resource depletion. In many respects, the author of this chapter is inclined to favour the latter perspective. But a common objection to the radical argument is that by both voicing dissent and opting for "exit" – that is, by refusing to propose any means, however theoretical, to solve the problems raised – it contributes little or nothing to changing the much maligned status quo. One of the attendant paradoxes of radicalism of this kind is that its end effect is somewhat akin to that of a particular brand of reactionary rhetoric which Albert Hirschman (1991) labelled the "futility claim" – that is, the claim that social engineering is absolutely powerless to change the order of things. This is why the discussion will conclude on some reflections on how it *may* be possible to resist dominant trends, though it must be stressed at the outset that the overall aim of this chapter is more to identify problems than to make concrete policy statements.

The ideology of southern hemisphere resources management from colonial times to decolonization: A brief sketch

The dual common heritage ideology of colonial development: Rational exploitation and conservation as a sacred trust of civilization

This is not the place to sketch a systematic history of developmental and nature conservancy practices that have been carried out in the colonies and, latterly, within decolonized countries. For the purposes of our argument it will be enough to set in contrast and comment on a series of passages from famous texts which have left a durable imprint on such practices.

The first quotation is from Lord Lugard's *Dual Mandate in British Tropic Africa*. The book was published in 1922 when Lugard was the British member on the Permanent Mandates Commission of the League of Nations after having served as Governor of Nigeria. He was a key figure in the colonial question and an indefatigable propagandist. It is no exaggeration to say that his views exerted immense influence not only in Britain but more generally in imperial Europe. When discussing the legitimacy of the scramble for Africa, Lugard laid down the following proposition which summarizes admirably his views on the *dual mandate* of colonialism:

> The tropics are the heritage of mankind, and neither, on the one hand, has the suzerain Power a right to their exclusive exploitation, nor, on the other hand, have the races which inhabit them a right to deny their bounties to those who need them. (Lugard, 1965 [1922]: 61)

There are two threads of arguments that need to be disentangled here. One consists of a negative claim: it denies sovereign rights over natural resources to those peoples who happen to inhabit territories with raw materials and foodstuffs which they are *incapable of exploiting* despite demand from civilized countries. The other part of the argument is positive: it defines a colony as a *public trust* over which the colonial power should exercise its rights for the benefit of "mankind", that is, for the benefit not only of its own citizens but also of those from other civilized countries (it cannot deny them commercial access to the resources over which it has custody) and for the benefit of the natives (by providing them with sanitary and educational services).[2] In Lugard's perspective, imperial powers had a mandate to exploit the natural resources of the colonies and to acculturate the native peoples into civilization. Such views were neither novel nor exceptional. They were very much in accord with the enlightened spirit of the time and can be found espoused in French writings and even in American official documents.[3] Lugard should be merely regarded as the most vocal representative of this particular school of thought.

A modern reader might well be expected to note a striking similarity with the attitude of the 1990s regarding the "global commons". We will return to this aspect later, but it must be noted at this stage that the right to interfere and impose a public trust was grounded on the *lack of productivity* on the part of the natives and on the capacity of the mandatory to correct this situation by exploiting the land in a manner deemed profitable, capital-intensive and export-oriented.

This is not to say that there were no conservancy practices seeking to *restrict* exploitation of resources so as to allow their natural reproduction. Such schemes were introduced in British and French colonial forestry as far back as the second decade of the nineteenth century and were nurtured by a concern that reckless felling was diminishing timber supply at a rate that would not allow replenishment. The need for conservancy was moreover fuelled by broader environmental fears voiced by natural scientists and medical surgeons that deforestation might have devastating impacts on rainfall, water flow, soil preservation and animal life – and these holistic speculations provided the very first scientific insights on the relationship between human activity, climate change and biodiversity (Grove, 1995).

However, what is of interest here is that the various restrictive regimes set up by empire forestry were initiated in the first place by the massive drain on forest resources wrought by the "civilizing process" with its concomitant acccleration in shipbuilding and demand for railway sleepers. As Roderick Nash (1967: 343) aptly remarked: "The civilizing process which imperils wild nature is precisely that which creates the need for it". A second point to note is that environmentalism of this sort was founded on a utilitarian logic of long-term resource management which suited the priorities of the colonial state and its entrepreneurs. New rules created various classes of forests – reserved, protected, open – the aim of which was, on the one hand, to restrict forest use by shifting cultivators on the grounds that such practices induced reckless depletion of valuable essences, and, on the other hand, to promote large-scale "rational" timber trade so as to secure higher revenues for the colonial government by way of royalties and tolls (Guha, 1989; Guha and Gadgil, 1989; Grove, 1990; Sivaramkrishnan, 1997; Thomas, 2003). This alone explains why, by the beginning of the twentieth century, forest conservancy in the British colonies alone could encompass a land mass ten times as big as Great Britain (Barton, 2001: 529).

Nor was conservancy restricted to forestry. As early as 1900, seven colonial powers – Great Britain, Germany, Spain, Belgian Congo, France, Italy and Portugal – signed a draft convention to regulate the conservation of wildlife. Though the "London Convention Designed to Ensure the Conservation of Various Species of Wild Animals in Africa which are Useful to Man or Inoffensive" never entered into force for lack of ratification by all signatories, it constituted a first attempt to establish sustainable exploitation of game animals by means of harmonized international regulations on hunting licences and closed seasons.[4] Finally, in 1933, the "London Convention Relative to the Preservation of Fauna

and Flora in their Natural State was implemented. Its object was to preserve colonial big-game hunting grounds and revenues "(i) by the constitution of national parks, strict natural reserves, and other reserves within
which the hunting, killing or capturing of fauna, and the collection or destruction of flora shall be limited or prohibited, (ii) by the institution of
regulations concerning the hunting, killing and capturing of fauna outside
such areas, (iii) by the regulation of the traffic in trophies, and (iv) by the
prohibition of certain methods of and weapons for the hunting, killing
and capturing of fauna".[5] This is another illustration of how institutionalized conservation – in effect, an amalgamation of restrictive trade regimes and "wilderness containers" such as parks and reserves – was set
up so that wildlife could be enjoyed by people from Europe and America
while securing revenues for the colonial governments. The consequences
on the native population included various restrictions on grazing and
farming as well as on hunting and trading game. Whatever negative social
impact these measures may have had was in some cases brought to the attention of the colonial rulers but was seldom taken seriously into account.

The ideology of post-colonial development: National sovereignty, growth, aid, and the ethics of catching up

The next two passages to be set in contrast to the previous one are both
from Arthur Lewis, a Nobel prize-winner for his pioneering studies in development economics. The first statement was written shortly before the
end of World War II when Lewis was a promising young academic from
St. Lucia who, after having won a scholarship to study at the London
School of Economics, had lectured there and taken an active part in
post-war planning committees in the Colonial Office (Lee and Petter,
1982). Discussing past, present and future colonial policy, Lewis suggested that:

> The principal object of colonial policy should be to enable the colonies to stand
> on their own legs as soon as possible. This can be done only through their rapid
> economic development. Expenditure on social services, e.g. on health and cer-
> tain types of education, assists and is necessary to economic development. But
> social services are not the whole, or even the principal content of an economic
> policy. (Lewis, 1944)

To establish the background of Lewis's critique, we need to briefly sketch
the tenets of colonial development theory and policy as they applied before the war. Hitherto there had been strong resistance within the metropolitan services in Britain and France alike to use economics as a conceptual and practical tool to plan the transformation of colonial societies.
Such resistance stemmed partly from the hegemony of laissez-faire liber-

alism and its concomitant vision of colonial self-sufficiency. But it also arose from the perception of economics as a "dismal science" associated with the colonial export trade whose chief purpose was profit and not the welfare of the natives. In truth, market forces were often viewed with mixed feelings by the stick-in-the-mud colonial officers who needed the daily cooperation of natives diversely affected by the impact of capitalism. In their view – labelled as "paternalist" by some historians – the object of "good government" was to provide administrative stability. Making a virtue out of necessity, they were in favour of preserving those native institutions which they viewed as capable of absorbing major disruptions arising from the contact of aggressive industrial civilization (Lee, 1967; Hetherington, 1978).

This social preservationism, however, became untenable during the era of the great slump when it stood to reason that most colonial societies had been drawn into the world economy and could no longer count on their native institutions alone to shield them from shocks, which, in some instances, were causing economic and social upheavals of enormous proportions. A more aggressive approach was deemed necessary. It was argued, in influential reports such as the formidable *African Survey* published by Lord Hailey in 1938, that the pace for *welfare* measures – e.g. education and health services – needed to be accelerated. In many quarters, however, the same argument nurtured the belief that industrialization was the root of the problem and should therefore not be too strongly pushed for in the colonies.

The rise of "development economics" as a new branch of social studies occurred in the United States and Britain during the Second World War. It was very much a by product of post-war reconstruction planning committees. The British "Colonial Economic Advisory Committee", in which Lewis took part, was merely one amongst numerous others set up on both shores of the Atlantic (Louis, 1986; Lee and Petter, 1982). The two driving forces behind the upsurge of development economics were American anti-colonial sentiment and Keynesian interventionism, which had proved so effective during the war. Anti-colonial sentiment provided the impetus to condemn British and French "paternal" administration, which, by focusing somewhat miserly on the provision of welfare services to the detriment of industrial growth, was viewed as a deliberate attempt to retain power. It was argued that the tenets of this ideology had created a Catch 22 situation: colonial propagandists would declare that the control of colonies was necessary until the natives were better equipped to come to terms with Western economic and social influences, but nothing would be done in earnest to speed up such progress. Keynesianism, on the other hand, provided the momentum to get down to business and carry out the programme.

As evidenced by Lewis's proposition, the self-proclaimed domain of development economics was appropriate government action in achieving *rapid* capital accumulation. In this respect, its pedigree can be traced further back to the old tradition of state economics – or the *economic* art of governing – which emerged in Western Europe in the early eighteenth century, taking the name of *police économique* in France and *Polizeiwissenschaft* in Germany. Priorities and techniques have obviously varied since then. But the main agenda has remained relatively constant, and this consists of providing rulers with a specific kind of *prudentia* or foresight, the object of which is to stimulate the growth of manufactures and raise the material living standards of the subjects.

It is important to stress that Lewis's insistence on the paramountcy of capital accumulation was considered progressive at that time. It anticipated the expectations of the throng of Asian and African colonial students who would come to study in Western universities in the 1950s. In effect, Lewis and other growth theorists were calling for *money* – to be invested in basic industries whose multiplier effect would lead to further industrialization. However, such calls for a "big push" (Rosenstein-Rodan), a "frontal attack" (Nurkse), a "critical minimum effort" (Leibenstein), a "take-off" (Rostow), a "big spurt" (Gerschenkron) were not matched by deeds. This begs the question as to why the gap between theory and practice has yawned so widely.

Scholarly and policy-oriented research in the economic aspects of development began in earnest in the aftermath of the Second World War under strong American pressure. It was dramatic evidence of the political and economic influence sought by the United States in those societies which were about to achieve, or were in the process of, independence from colonial rule. The basis on which such influence was grounded was and remains *development aid*. Now, one barely needs to scratch the veneer of this term to understand what went wrong. Though widely used by both policy-makers and academics, aid is perhaps one of the most misleading notions in the field of international relations. Undoubtedly, the semantics of it creates confusion between what *is* done and what *should* be done. It is a notion of hope and hopelessness that at once manages to console us – by conveying the idea that what *ought* to be done *could* be done if aid *were* aid – while initiating despair when the gap between words and deeds becomes all too obvious. It may be as well briefly to examine what kind of practices aid subsumes and the part it plays in the international development regime.

Though the pursuit of development was enshrined in the Charter, United Nations agencies have had no influence over bilateral aid programmes and practically none over multilateral institutions with money and muscle – such as the World Bank and the International Monetary

Fund – whose weighted voting systems allow the main donors to have the preponderant say in how funds should be used. Let us first consider *bilateral* concessional aid. As an axiom, it is never neutral nor entirely altruistic (there is indeed no such thing as a free lunch in international relations). It always subsumes transactions beneficial to the donor. Bilateral concessional aid enables donor countries to advance the interests of certain economic sectors by subsidizing them or opening up markets for them. It is a public redistributive enterprise living off the direct or indirect profits derived from a politically controlled trade. Direct profits stem from interest payments on previous loans, from purchases of national products when aid is "tied" (and these products are usually priced higher than their market value), or, more recently, from takeovers of public enterprises in recipient countries. Indirect profits arise from various forms of political and economic influence which can be exerted upon recipients (Petras and Veltmayer, 2002).

As for *multilateral* concessional aid, it has from its very inception been based on the following central principles: it should never compete with private capital when the latter is willing to lend monies on reasonable terms; it should be conditional on whatever is deemed to be appropriate economic policy by major "donors" at that particular time; it must be guaranteed by recipient governments; continued access depends on fulfilment of debt obligations by recipient governments; and only firms from donor countries should be eligible to participate in procurement financed by loans from the multilateral fund (Wood, 1986).

The functioning of the aid regime during the past half-century has merely confirmed an axiom formulated by Francis Bacon some four hundred years ago in his *Essays*: "There be but three things, which one nation selleth unto another; the commodity as nature yieldeth it; the manufacture; and the vecture, or carriage. So that if these three wheels go, wealth will flow as in a spring tide. And it cometh many times to pass, that *materiam superabit opus*; that the work and carriage is more worth than the material, and enricheth a state more". Aid has indeed been the "vecture" which industrialized countries have *sold* to LDCs in order to enable them to *buy* more goods and services than they could possibly afford.

This is not to say that some recipient countries have not faired relatively well. Conventional wisdom holds that while colonial powers had to draw revenues from their possessions to cover the costs involved in building up areas of security around their factories, decolonization inaugurated the age of "fenceless factories". Nothing can be less obvious or more open to dispute. South- and North-East Asian countries, which were regarded as vital to the strategic interests of the US, received fairly large amounts of soft loans and capital flows to fence in their factories from communist takeovers, and they were moreover given access to the American market. It is worthy of note here that in countries such as Korea or Taiwan, these capital flows did have, at that time, a multiplier effect on further investments.

The return of the repressed notion of mankind's patrimony in the management of southern hemisphere resources

Let us now consider one last quotation from a famous work by Arthur Lewis:

> It is sometimes argued that any expectation that all nations of the world can raise their standards of living continuously must be illusory, since the effect would be only to exhaust rapidly the world's accumulated stocks of minerals and fuels. This argument rests upon two uncertain assumptions. First it presumes that human ingenuity must in due course fail to find new substitutes for what is used up, an assumption which is rendered increasingly doubtful by what we are learning about the nature of the atom, and about the transformation of one element into another. And secondly it assumes that future generations have an equal claim to the world resources. Why should we stay poor so that the life of the human race may in some centuries to come be extended for a further century or so? Is there not as good a case for the present generations to make the best of the resources they find, and to leave the distant centuries to look after themselves? (Lewis, 1955: 424)

These words, especially when contrasted with the official definition of "sustainable development" referred to earlier, point to the paradigmatic shift which has occurred in development theory and policy over barely three decades. The shift is one from frontier economics to environmentalism (Kapur et al., 1997, II: 730). As exemplified in Lewis's statement, frontier economics is predicated upon the technocentric notion of human perfectibility and its unlimited capacity, nay its *duty* to conquer nature, particularly that very last "land frontier" which still remains. Frontier economics traces a process between a *terminus a quo* (uncultivated nature) and a *terminus ad quem* (industrial society), and this process corresponds to the gradual capacity of societies to transform nature regarded merely as raw material. Life in "primitive" or "backward" societies is held to be, following Hobbes's description of the state of nature, "poor, nasty, brutish, and short" – a disgrace when compared to life in industrial societies. This justifies the need for collective responsibility: every effort should be made to advance and enhance the civilizing process, regardless of ecological consequences which human ingenuity will anyway be capable of solving in the future.

Environmentalism, on the other hand, may or may not regard nature as valuable for its own sake. In eco parlance, the former perspective is la-

belled *preservationist* because of its bias in favour of "bio-centric" policies, even if the endangered species present no particular use to mankind
or are sufficiently abundant for survival. Conversely, the latter perspective, usually called *conservationist*, is said to be either "eco-centric" or
"anthropocentric" because ultimately it restricts conservation policies to
the utility the species presents to the survival of mankind. On the whole,
however, conservationism and preservationism both believe, in contradistinction to technocentrism, that there are biophysical *limits* to economic
growth which should, at some stage, take precedence over other considerations, particularly developmental ones. Environmentalism first began
as, and partly remains today, a "full stomach" movement. In overseas
territories, it stemmed, as we have seen, from a utilitarian logic of long-
term resource management, or was supported by groups of affluent individuals who sought abroad what they could not find at home, such as big
game or other wildlife species, or simply "things natural, wild and free".[6]
In environmentalism, the notion of the "frontier" connotes something
very different from what "frontier economics" makes of it. It refers to
a *heritage* (for preservationists) or a *valuable depleted resource* (for conservationists) threatened by the very process of civilization and which, as
a result, requires national or international stewardship.

Decolonization with its concomitant creation of numerous formally independent states did not stop the more outspoken conservationists and
preservationists from continuing to voice their support for the pursuit of
"public trust" schemes to protect the "endangered frontier" in former
colonies. Thus, as early as 1961, Julian Huxley – who in his capacity as
director-general of UNESCO played a major role in creating the International Union for the Protection of Nature (the future IUCN) in 1948 –
insisted that "Africa's wild life belongs not merely to the local inhabitants but to the world, not only to the present but to the whole future of
mankind". He was well aware that Africans could rejoinder that "You
white men have killed all your wolves and bears: why do you want us
Africans to preserve our lions and elephants?" But he went on to note
that "in the modern world ... a country without a National Park can
hardly be recognised as civilised" (Huxley, 1960: 24, 88, 94).

Conjoining the principles of national sovereignty and common heritage in the management of southern hemisphere resources: A genealogy of the Rio conventions

The making of a hybrid

Categories which have shaped earlier rounds of the debate on civilization
and/or conservation offer guidance to a better understanding of its latest

dimensions. International stewardship to solve environmental problems has been gaining momentum since the 1971 Stockholm Declaration enshrined the notion (known as Principle 21) that states would have to "ensure that activities within their jurisdiction or control do not cause damage to the environment of other States or of areas beyond the limits of national jurisdiction". However, because of fears on the part of LDCs that restrictive environmental agreements would stifle their attempts to industrialize, this recognition was amalgamated with its opposing principle (the sovereign right of states to exploit their own resources) to form a somewhat confusing hybrid.

Similar tensions were at work during the 1992 Rio Conference. Though all the agreements which were signed reaffirmed that states have the sovereign right to exploit their own resources, the notion of *common but differentiated responsibilities* (Principle 7 of the Declaration) – to which we shall come back – constituted yet another instance of the "common boat ideology". It has been slowly steering LDCs towards recognizing the existence of a superordinate environmental order consisting of a biosphere of interdependent ecosystems which do not necessarily respect artificial territorial boundaries between states. This is reflected in the two most significant documents signed at Rio, the Convention on Biological Diversity and the Framework Convention on Climate Change.

Climate change and biodiversity issues have shown that when industrialized countries do have a significant stake in a problem, there is concrete follow-up action. It would of course be entirely hazardous to conjecture as to whether these regimes in the making will eventually be implemented and enforced: at this stage, they merely appear as political processes involving groups which seek to advance their purposes against the opposition of other groups. Be that as it may, the growing agitation surrounding these two issues makes them all the more capable of revealing the major stakes and stakeholders in contemporary environmental politics. It is therefore justifiable to devote more than a few sentences to the discussion of the genesis of these conventions. Let us first examine the biodiversity issue.

Plant genetic resources: public or private goods?

Since colonial times, the notion of threatened or endangered animals and plants has gathered momentum. New arguments have emerged alongside the long-standing economic and recreational justifications used by colonial administrators, by nature entrepreneurs and by sport hunters, all of whom had a vested interest in conservation. Over the past decades, ideas such the aesthetic satisfaction provided by, or the ethical responsibility due to, or the ecosystemic functions performed by, endangered species have received increasing currency. These arguments have been mainly supported by vocal groups in affluent countries and have initiated practices aimed at preserving or conserving various endangered species on account of the luxury, the necessity or the asset they supposedly constitute (Smith, 1976).

Arguments stressing ecological necessity and economic interest have especially been used in the conservation of *phytogenetic* resources to which our discussion on biodiversity issues will be confined. It is a well-known fact that plant variability is crucial in agriculture and medicine which can both be conceived as dynamic technologies insofar as their activities aim at erecting defences against pests and predators which are likely to develop successful counter-strategies, hence necessitating the creation of new defences. Thus, from the viewpoint of evolutionary biology, the extinction of plant species results in an irreversible loss of genetic resources containing information (i.e. successful strategies) that may be needed for the future improvement of cultivars or pharmaceuticals.

In the field of agriculture in particular, where plant improvement has been strongly and somewhat simplistically equated with food security and the eradication of famine, LDCs were encouraged to allow access to their phytogenetic resources which were, from the 1960s onwards, collected and safeguarded in international agricultural research centres originally supported by foundations such as Rockefeller and Ford. Some of these centres coalesced in 1971 into the Consultative Group of International Agricultural Research (CGIAR), a consortium of donors set up under the auspices of the World Bank with the Food and Agricultural Organization (FAO) and the UN Development Programme (UNDP) as co-sponsors. In 2001, the CGIAR totalled 16 centres which together held approximately 600,000 germplasm accessions corresponding to 50 per cent of unduplicated seed samples from wild crop progenitors, semi-domesticated crop relatives, landraces, forage and pasture species (Wade, 1975; Barton, 1982; Plucknett et al., 1983; Plucknett, 1987; Brush, 1989; Falcon and Fowler, 2002; Koo, 2003). Until then, these centres, following their mission statement emphasizing food security and poverty eradication, made their collections freely available not only to national public institutions but also to private plant breeders – most of whom are located in OECD countries. But whereas the collected germplasm was considered a *public good* held in trust for the world community, the new commercial plant varieties possibly adapted from this material could be granted a special legal protection called Plant Breeders Rights (PBRs) – which are close to, though less stringent than, patents. Prior to the adoption of the Biodiversity Convention in 1992, this asymmetry was reflected in the existence of two divergent property rights regimes over biological diversity.

On the one hand, PBRs have been enforced *internationally*[7] since the 1961 Act of the International Union for the Protection of New Varieties of Plants (UPOV) – originally an inter-governmental club consisting of nine West European nations plus South Africa – came into force in 1968. UPOV has granted breeders an exclusive property right for plant varieties which are distinct (from any other variety), uniform (true to the original when propagated) and stable (true to the original when re-produced).[8] However, this monopoly right – conferred for at least fifteen years – was restricted in the 1961 and the revised 1978 Acts by two exceptions. First, the *breeders' exemption* provided that a protected variety should be made freely available as an initial source for the creation of new varieties.[9] Second, farmers were tacitly allowed to save the seed of harvested material and use it to grow a new crop, as well as to exchange seeds freely for non-commercial purposes (*farmers' privilege*).[10] Overall, the stated aim of the 1961–1978 UPOV regime was to balance the interests and needs of plant breeders and farmers, and consequently the objectives of technology innovation and commercialization on the one hand and of food security on the other. It provided plant breeders with an economic incentive for varietal development, but by allowing breeders to use protected seeds to create new lines, and farmers to store harvested seeds for the purpose of improving local varieties or providing for their own subsistence, UPOV PBRs did not extend to acts done for the purpose of crop improvement or food security (Barton, 1982; Kameri-Mbote and Cullet, 1999; Dutfield, 2000).

The notion of the farmers' *privilege* was further developed and extended by the FAO into one of *rights* – conceived in terms of compensating farmers in LDCs for their past contributions to conserving, improving, and making available plant genetic resources. Indeed, farmers' rights constituted one of the two main pillars of the International Undertaking On Plant Genetic Resources adopted by the FAO in 1983 – a non-binding *alternative* instrument to deal with phytogenetic management. In a Resolution adopted in 1989 and annexed to the Undertaking, it was specified that farmers' rights should be "vested in the International Community, as trustee for present and future generations of farmers, for the purpose of ensuring full benefits to farmers, and supporting the continuation of their contributions, as well as the attainment of the overall purposes of the International Undertaking". This was a *de lege ferenda* indication that farmers ought to be recognized as *breeders* for their role in the selection, conservation and domestication of folk crop varieties or landraces – and that they should be compensated for their contribution to plant variety improvement. However, no institutional and financial mechanism was devised in order to achieve the aims of the Resolution.[11]

The second and more controversial pillar of the FAO Undertaking consisted in affirming that plant genetic resources were a *heritage of mankind* which should be made available without restriction. The notion of *common good* was premised on the guiding principles of the international agricultural research centres which, as we have seen, held crop germplasm collections in trust for the world at large. By making phytogenetic material freely available to public researchers, commercial breeders and farmers alike, it was assumed that innovation, improvement – and, hence, food security – would be fostered. As stated in Article 1, the objective of the Undertaking was to ensure that plant genetic resources of economic and social interest, particularly for agriculture, could be explored, preserved, evaluated and made available for plant breeding and scientific purposes.

Widespread international acceptance of the *common heritage* status of phytogenetic resources proved impossible to obtain. For members of UPOV, the principle appeared to set a dangerous precedent against PBRs, as it tacitly implied common ownership and management of *all* plant genetic material, including new plant varieties. So as to facilitate the withdrawal of the reservations formulated by some UPOV contracting parties and to secure the adherence of others, the FAO endorsed in 1989 an agreed interpretation stating that PBRs were "not incompatible with the International Undertaking".[12] Though the same session of the FAO Conference endorsed the concept of farmers' rights to compensate LDCs for their recognition of PBRs, it stood to reason that the differences in property rights governing raw germplasm, on the one hand, and commercial seed varieties, on the other, were biased in favour of developed countries.

Against this background of asymmetrical property rights, the FAO recognized, in November 1991, that the concept of mankind's heritage was "subject to the *sovereignty* of the states over their plant genetic resources".[13] The principle of permanent sovereignty over phytogenetic resources reflected the claims of LDCs that in their capacity as primary suppliers of the original breeding materials they should receive compensation for past contributions and especially payments for future transfer and use. Yet, for all the talk about equity and benefit sharing, the Resolution lacked clarity by the fact of continuing to endorse PBRs and farmers' rights alongside this new recognition of state sovereign rights.[14]

Such were the overlapping property rights systems over phytogenetic resources when state delegations convened to complete negotiations over a United Nations Convention on Biological Diversity (CBD). The scope of this treaty was far more ambitious than the previous legal frameworks.

Indeed, the very notion of *biological resources* is a wide-ranging one as it includes "genetic resources, organisms or parts thereof, populations, or any other biotic component of ecosystems with actual or potential use or value for humanity". In theory, the Convention has three main objectives, namely, the conservation of biological diversity, the sustainable use of its components and the fair and equitable sharing of benefits arising out of the utilization of genetic resources. The first two objectives were sought by conservationists, but also and perhaps especially by pharmaceutical and biotechnology companies which had been claiming that a major source of potential profit was being lost at an alarming rate in the rainforests of southern hemisphere countries where more than half of all plant and animal species are thought to live. The third objective was pursued by LDCs who were well aware that many top-selling drugs worth billions of dollars in sales derived from natural products discovered within their jurisdictions (Fenwick, 1998).

The compromise was that signatory LDCs committed themselves to conservation but obtained recognition of sovereign rights over their genetic resources and, concomitantly, the authority to determine access. Article 15 of the CBD stipulates that any access, where granted, should be "subject to prior informed consent" and "on mutually agreed terms", meaning that countries providing resources should be notified and could demand payments or transfer of technology in exchange for access. Moreover, article 8(j) provides for respecting, protecting and rewarding the knowledge, innovations and practices of local communities. On the other hand, an important qualification was introduced to the principle of sovereignty, again in the form of an argument based on presupposed global commonalities of interest. Conservation of biological diversity was proclaimed a *common concern of humankind*, in effect implying that biodiversity loss constituted an international problem in regard to which all states had a standing whether or not they possessed the genetic resources in *in situ* conditions (Cullet, 2001, 2003).

LDC parties, however, demanded in return and obtained inclusion of another provision – Article 20(4) – stating that eradication of poverty and economic and social development remained their "first and overriding priorities", and that the extent to which they would carry out effective conservation depended on the implementation by developed country parties of their commitments related to financial resources and transfer of technology. It was agreed that the provision of these resources would have to be *new* and *additional* – and not simply taken from other ODA budgets. The financial interim arrangement designed for implementing the Convention consisted in the GEF – a fund established by developed countries in 1991 in order to steer LDCs to adhering to the Conventions on Biological Diversity and Climate Change.

Valuing and allocating public bads: greenhouse gases emissions

Before going on to deal with the GEF and discuss in more detail some problems relating to the international management of biodiversity, it is necessary to examine briefly the background to the negotiation of the other Convention which was opened for signature during the 1992 Earth Summit held at Rio, namely, the Framework Convention on Climate Change (FCCC). The first crucial step in the formation of the climate regime was the creation of the Intergovernmental Panel on Climate Change (IPCC) in November 1988. Set up jointly by two United Nations agencies, the World Meteorological Organization (WMO) and the United Nations Environment Programme (UNEP), the mandate of this intergovernmental group of experts – which has progressively included researchers from LDCs so as to ensure a wider international participation – consists in assessing the state of knowledge on the (i) science, (ii) impacts and (iii) policy responses to climate change in three Working Groups set up to examine separately each of these components (Agrawala, 1998, 1999; Skodvin, 2000; Andresen, Agrawala, 2002). The wording of IPCC assessments has followed a complex process involving government officials' approval, particularly the "summaries for policy makers" and "synthesis reports" which undergo a simultaneous expert and government review process, the latter reports having to be approved line-by-line at a special plenary meeting attended by hundreds of delegates from the participating countries. Characterized ironically by some scientists as a "literary circus" in which political appointees are given the authority to agree "on how a scientific study should be summarized", the panel's reports have nevertheless had an indisputable policy impact (Schrope, 2001). The conclusions of the first final Report of Working Group I in 1990 – that atmospheric concentrations of anthropogenic emissions of greenhouse gases (GHGs) were substantially increasing and would result in a corresponding increase in the global average temperature – came as a bombshell and boosted negotiations for a Climate Convention. Indeed, impacts of global warming appeared particularly dire: melting of polar caps, rising sea levels resulting in inundation of islands and coastlines, changes in ocean currents, overall increases of storms and precipitation, flooding in some areas, desertification in others, and so forth.

Yet for all that, there was insufficient agreement in 1992 to set binding targets in a UN Framework Convention. As a result, the objective of the FCCC was downscaled to a vague commitment by industrialized countries to stabilize their GHG concentrations in the atmosphere "at a level that would prevent dangerous anthropogenic interference with the climate system".[15] Article 4(2) required that countries listed in Annex

I of the FCCC – comprising OECD and some former East-European COMECON countries – should limit their emissions of GHGs and return to 1990 emission levels by 2000.

Article 4(1), on the other hand, obligated *all* parties to develop national inventories of anthropogenic emissions by sources and removals by sinks of GHGs, as well as to set up mitigating programmes. In this instance, however, commonalities of interest were more difficult to justify than in other multilateral environmental agreements. LDCs are estimated to have 80 per cent of the world's population while consuming only 30 per cent of global commercial energy (Martinot et al., 2002). Moreover, if it is true that anthropogenic GHG concentrations in the atmosphere are beginning to produce deleterious effects, there is no doubt that much of the blame is to be assigned to developed countries who owe their industrialization to past emissions of carbon from the burning of fossil fuels.[16] No amount of alarmist projections regarding future GHG emissions expected to emanate from fast industrializing countries such as China or India could justify at present that LDCs as a whole should share the burden of mitigation on an equal par with industrialized countries. This would indeed constitute a gross violation of the "polluter pays principle" to which we shall soon return.

As a result, the "common boat" argument used to integrate LDCs to the climate change regime was watered down into the phrase *common but differentiated responsibilities* as defined in Principle 7 of the Rio Declaration.[17] Commonalities of responsibility stemmed from acceptance of ecological interdependence. That responsibilities should however be *differentiated* was grounded in two acknowledgements referred to in the Preamble of the FCCC: one ethical, namely, that "the largest share of historical and current global emissions of greenhouse gases has originated in developed countries" while "per capita emissions in developing countries are still relatively low"; the other pragmatic, namely, that developed countries should anyway take the lead in combating climate change because of "the technologies and financial resources they command".

The 1995 Second Assessment Report of the IPCC – which was more assertive in its affirmation that there appeared to be a "discernable human influence" on climate change and that some action should be taken immediately – created quite a commotion and led the Conference of the Parties to agree on strengthening the FCCC vague commitments through a protocol. The Kyoto Protocol, which opened for signature in 1997, was the result of strenuous negotiations to define quantified and legally binding targets as well as timetables for the 38 countries included in FCCC Annex 1 (listed, somewhat confusingly, in Annex B of the Protocol). The quantified emission limitation or reduction objectives (QELROs, hereafter targets) finally agreed by these countries amounted to a 5.2

per cent overall reduction against a base year (1990 for most parties). This reduction had to be achieved by the end first commitment period between 2008–2012.

There was a good deal of bickering at Kyoto over whether or not additional "sinks", such as forests that absorb carbon dioxide from the atmosphere, should be deducted from national emission inventories. The European Community demanded that inventories be limited to sinks resulting from direct human-induced land use change such as afforestation, deforestation and reforestation. The argument was that reductions due to sinks are difficult to account for, because sinks lock up carbon during their life-cycle but release it when they decline. The American and Australian delegations nevertheless obtained that the Protocol provide for new categories for removals by sinks in agricultural soils, land use change, and forestry.[18] Moreover, owing to strong American pressure, the Kyoto Protocol allowed countries to use market-based approaches – called *flexibility mechanisms* – to achieve their targets. In exchange, the European Community obtained vague acknowledgement in the Protocol that any such carbon trading would be supplemental to domestic actions for the purposes of meeting commitments. Three main mechanisms were thus devised.

First, *International Emissions Trading* (IET) will enable an Annex 1 country that has achieved an overall emissions path *lower* than its target level to either bank or sell its unused *assigned amounts* to other Annex 1 countries which may need extra amounts to achieve their targets. Second, *Joint Implementation* (JI) consists in a project-based flexible instrument through which an investor who should fund an emission reduction project in a host country listed in Annex 1 may receive tradable *emission reduction units*. Third, the *Clean Development Mechanism* (CDM) is another project-based mechanism except that it will be hosted by a developing country (not listed in Annex 1), and the resulting reductions are termed *certified emission reductions*. The terminology used here is a clear indication of the stricter procedures required to verify CDM reductions (OECD, 1999; Michaelowa and Dutschke, 2000; Yamin, 2000; Ellis et al., 2006).

One of the main arguments advanced in favour of flexibility has been that it would enable developed countries to achieve their Kyoto commitments at the lowest possible cost because reducing GHG emissions at a source in another country may be cheaper than doing so domestically. Moreover, as global warming is thought to be the result of the total accumulation of GHGs in the atmosphere, it is quite irrelevant where these pollutants are in actual fact reduced. The tradable carbon credit approach would, so the argument goes, make optimal use of marginal cost differences in undertaking abatement measures. American negotiators have taken pains to stress that these confident claims test well against the evidence gathered from a similar public policy adopted in the USA under Title IV of the Clean Air Act Amendments of 1990 to deal with the control of emissions of sulphur dioxide (SO_2), the primary precursor of acid rain. The flexible system adopted is said to have been so successful that it has achieved more significant reductions in these depositions than was initially expected.[19] That conceded, it is one thing to use markets to internalize domestic externalities as in the case of sulphur dioxide emissions within the USA; it is an altogether different one to broaden the scope of market environmentalism to internalize transborder externalities as in the case of global GHG emissions.

The Kyoto Protocol was presented as a golden opportunity to provide LDC Parties with substantial capital and technological inflows through the Clean Development Mechanism, but also – and even more so – through the GEF. By way of being the financial mechanism of the FCCC, the GEF was to provide, as for the Convention on Biological Diversity, "new and additional financial resources" to help LDCs "meet the agreed full costs incurred by advancing the implementation of existing commitments", in particular the setting up of national inventories of anthropogenic emissions by sources and removals by sinks of GHGs.

The environment as a market niche: conjoining market environmentalism and ecological modernization

Global environment funding

The GEF was set up in the World Bank as a pilot programme by major donor governments in 1991 in order to induce LDCs to sign the Rio Conventions.[20] In April 1992, participants agreed that the structure and modalities of the facility should be modified so as to establish it as "one of the principal mechanisms for global environment funding" and to replenish its resources. The restructured GEF was established in an *Instrument* accepted by Participating States in 1994. Grants and concessional funds were to be made available for projects and other activities in recipient countries that addressed climate change, biological diversity, international waters, and depletion of the ozone layer. The new structure of the GEF was supposed to ensure a form of governance that would be "transparent and democratic in nature"[21]. In truth, besides publishing or putting online various reports which anyway conceal as much as they reveal, *transparency* has mainly consisted in allowing a select number of NGOs to sit in the Governing Council's meeting room and a few others to observe on closed circuit TV from a nearby room (Young, 2002). Selection of the

NGOs permitted to attend these meetings is entrusted to the GEF Secretariat which can use this leverage to ensure their active collaboration and preclude public criticism. As for *democratic governance*, it has been restricted to grouping the Governing Council in 32 constituencies, with 18 constituencies composed of recipient countries (including 2 from Central and Eastern Europe), and 14 constituencies of donor countries,[22] only G8 countries have permanent seats, while all other participants share their seats in constituencies. Many analysts have hailed the unique blend devised by the GEF between the Bretton Woods "one dollar one vote" and the UN "one state one vote" systems (Boisson de Chazournes, 2005). But surely this generous appreciation needs to be qualified, since contested votes within the Council require a *double* weighted majority of 60 per cent of countries by number *and* contribution. This precludes all possibility of beneficiary countries ever gaining majority control over the Facility.[23]

GEF funding can be provided through one of three Implementing Agencies, the World Bank, UNDP, and UNEP.[24] In reality, all "Full-Sized" projects (grants over US$1 million) – which account for more than 90 per cent of the GEF's portfolio as of 2001 – follow the World Bank's project cycle and standard procedures regardless of whether or not the Bank is the Implementing Agency.[25] It appears, furthermore, that from 1991 to 2005 the World Bank has received the lion's share of GEF funding (US$2,912 million), followed by UNDP (US$1,801 million) and UNEP (US$417 million).[26] Such overwhelming dominance of GEF-associated World Bank loans has attracted critical attention from some observers, such as Zoe Young, who views the facility as a means enabling the World Bank to *externalize* the environmental costs of its projects by getting the GEF to pay for "mitigating the damage done" (Young, 2002: 15, 136). This violates the "polluter pays principle" (PPP) adopted by the OECD in 1972 according to which "the polluter should bear the expenses of ... measures decided by the public authorities to ensure that the environment is in an acceptable state" (Schoenbaum, 1997: 296). The PPP was recognized in Principle 16 of the Rio Declaration and forms the basis of most environmental treaties. But whereas the GEF's funds were raised on a polluter pays principle in the first place, it is widely accepted that they have also been used for "greenwashing" purposes, i.e. precisely to avoid internalizing environmental externalities by making "the private sector party being leveraged ... the beneficiary or sponsor of the project" (Young, 2002: 137). When public funds are thus allocated by the GEF, it is not the entity which causes the polluting activity and benefits from it that has to bear the environmental costs, but society as a whole.

Two other important qualifications determine GEF grants. Firstly, allocations account for no more than 25 per cent of the total cost of

implemented projects. The remaining 75 per cent are *cofinanced* by multilateral banks (28 per cent), public monies (25 per cent), commercial
loans (21 per cent) and NGO grants (18 per cent).[27] Thus, from 1991 to
2006, the GEF has provided $4.5 billion in grants and generated $14.5
billion in cofinancing. As cofinancing can take various forms – grants,
loans, credits – it raises, according to a GEF Report, "different issues
for reporting and monitoring", and can create much confusion.[28] Another report noted that GEF-associated World Bank loans were particularly problematic because they led recipient government agencies to
"push for more activities in the project to generate foreign exchange
with which to repay the loan" – and these activities often collided with
the objectives pursued by the Conventions.[29]

Secondly, the GEF only funds *incremental* or additional costs associated with "transforming a project with national benefits into one with
global environmental benefits". An example like the following appears
with tedious frequency in GEF literature: "Choosing solar energy technology over coal or diesel fuel meets the same national development
goal (power generation), but is more costly. GEF grants cover the difference or "increment" between a less costly, more polluting option and a
costlier, more environmentally friendly option". This implies that the
GEF is mainly involved in valuing the environment, using monetary analysis to determine whether a project is "economically no-regret" or "economically regret", and in the latter case calculating the trade-off between
the "with GEF project" scenario on account of its "global" environmental benefits but economic costs, on the one hand, and, on the other, the
"without GEF project" or baseline scenario on account of its economic
cost-effectiveness but "global" environmental costs. Precisely because
they require this type of tedious economic analyses which can only be
performed by bureaucrats and technical experts familiar with multilateral aid jargon, incremental costs determinations are, according to Zoe
Young (2002: 151), "highly vulnerable to manipulation, artificiality and
arbitrariness". Not only have they excluded the local populations directly
concerned by environmental degradations who obviously lack representation in multilateral institutions, they have even, as has been acknowledged in a GEF Overall Performance Study (1998: xviii), "excluded the
participation of recipient country officials in most cases, because of the
lack of understanding of the concept and methodologies".[30]

Finally, a word should be said about how the GEF's financial resources
are obtained and spent. They are subject to pledges from donor governments and replenished approximately every four years, beginning with $1
billion in the pilot phase, $2 billion in 1994 for the GEF-1 period, $2.6 billion in 1998 for GEF-2, and $2.9 in 2002 for GEF-3. However, over the
past years, the United States, followed by other donors, have failed to

appropriate as much as their pledges, and have used these delays in payments to put the facility under sufficient pressure to ensure that conservation policies may be defined and carried out on their terms. According to the figures published in a Procurement Report of GEF projects since its inception till 2001, it appears that OECD countries have received 69 per cent of the money spent by the three Implementing Agencies in civil work, personnel, subcontracts, equipment training, and other goods and services. As the major donor, the US has received 31 per cent of procurement contracts.[31] This does not account for the remaining 75 per cent cofinanced by other means. It is more than probable that procurement contracts awarded yearly to American firms for GEF-funded projects, *inclusive of cofinance*, particularly via World Bank provisions, exceed US cumulative allocations to the facility.

The question immediately arises: could the GEF be a financial mechanism used mainly to subsidize various OECD interests abroad, particularly environmental investments? What then would its contribution be to the objectives of the two Conventions? Though other questions press themselves upon our attention, critical discussion will be limited to these issues.

The carving up of the commons by states and markets

In a world of sovereign states lacking compulsory redistributive mechanisms, treasuries are unlikely to finance activities that have no direct bearing on their perceived immediate interests. As alluded to earlier, "overseas development assistance" has always been tied by donor governments to various restrictions which aim at bringing specific returns – strategic or economic – to those interest groups whose views have prevailed. The potential of multilateral environmental agreements to avoid the "tragedy of the commons" has captivated the imagination of a wide variety of political scientists, environmentalists and economists alike. Many analysts have hastily concluded that the Earth Summit Conventions may well constitute boons for LDCs because it is in the interest of the industrialized nations to transfer resources and technology overseas so as to prevent both the removal of existing sinks and biodiversity reserves such as forests and the opening up of new sources of GHGs such as industrial plants that burn fossil fuels. What follows is an attempt to add some cautionary notes to this upbeat view. It appears all the more timely to treat present policies with scepticism as naive optimism can act as an eye blinder to ongoing processes of appropriation by a powerful minority. To illustrate this, let us first revert to the biodiversity issue.

It is essential to remember that in the early nineties, genetic engineering brought about a scientific revolution in the life sciences whereby it became possible to deliberately modify the characteristics of an organism by manipulating DNA material and transferring it from one organism to another by means of a technique called recombinant DNA (Uzogara, 2000; Lappe, Bailey, 1999; Hilder, Boulter, 1999). Until then, as mentioned previously, issues regarding the legal protection of phytogenetic resources had concerned *plant breeders* whose new varieties incorporated certain observed characteristics – or the *phenotype* – of other plants. From the nineties onwards, the possibility of using the biological coding or *genotype* of various resources, and of transferring this material from one species (say, a pig) to another (a carrot) resulted in the expansion of chemical and pharmaceutical companies into the life sciences. Through a series of strategic mergers and acquisitions, the value of which exceeded US$2 trillion in 1998, giant conglomerates such Monsanto, Du-Pont, Novartis, or Zeneca[32] now combine food, agrochemical, pharmaceutical and biotechnology industries, and assemble the intellectual property rights needed to develop their new products, effectively increasing barriers to entry into the germplasm industry massively confined to developed countries (Falcon, Fowler, 2002; Chataway, Tait, Wield, 2004; Adi, 2006). These new corporate interests, in alliance with the entertainment and informatics industries, have moreover endeavoured to obtain, and have had the power to lobby successfully for, the inclusion of intellectual property rights within the remit of WTO (May, 2000; Sell, 2003). As a result, they have secured exclusive commercial rights not only over plant varieties but more generally over life forms. This is reflected in article 27.3(b) of the Agreement on Trade-Related Intellectual Property Rights (TRIPs) which came into effect with the WTO in 1995. WTO contracting parties are now obliged to enact laws that provide patent protection for micro-organisms and for non-biological and microbiological processes. In addition, the article calls for protection of plant varieties by either patents or an effective *sui generis* system, or a combination thereof. It appears that *effective protection* of biodiversity has been altogether engulfed by the issue of the legal *protection* of plant variety and genetic resources.

The introduction of the *sui generis* concept for plant varieties – meaning, in this context, an alternative to patents – has been mainly directed towards LDCs. It gives them a margin of appreciation in determining how to set up plant variety protection, thus leading many governments to introduce both plant breeders' and farmers' rights. True, developed countries consider that an effective *sui generis* protection is provided by UPOV which, in 1991, extended the rights of breeders to the *harvested* material of the protected variety, thereby rendering the farmer's privilege merely optional.[33] Because they were given the possibility to join by April 1999, the milder 1978 UPOV regime, which does not include harvested material, some emerging and South American countries have hurried to ratify the treaty in order to abide by article 27.3(b) of the TRIPs and thus avoid countervailing trade measures restricting access to developed markets.

However, 1999 was also the year in which Article 27.3(b) of the TRIPS Agreement, particularly the *sui generis* options it provides for, was scheduled to be officially reviewed and was accordingly brought before the Committee on Trade and Environment. Many LDCs, led by Brazil and India, have taken up this opportunity to call for the harmonization of the TRIPS Agreement and the CBD which they consider could be achieved by amending Article 27.3(b) so as to require that applicants of life-form patents disclose: "(a) the source of any genetic material used in a claimed invention; (b) any related traditional knowledge used in the invention; (c) evidence of prior informed consent from the competent authority in the country of origin of the genetic material; and (d) evidence of fair and equitable benefit sharing".[34] As yet, none of these proposals has been accepted by developed countries delegations which to appear to be quite satisfied with the wording of Article 27.3(b) (Mukerji, 2000: 57). Switzerland has proposed to amend the Patent Cooperation Treaty (PCT) of the World Intellectual Property Organization (WIPO) so as to enable the Contracting Parties of the PCT to require patent applicants to declare the source of genetic resources and traditional knowledge, if an invention is based on or uses such resource or knowledge.[35] This concession however pales into insignificance before the fact that WIPO's stewardship has always been perceived as both under-subscribed and ineffectual on account of its lack of coercive means to sanction states, contrariwise to the WTO and its enhanced enforcement mechanisms (May, 2000: 68). LDCs would like the TRIPS Agreement to be amended precisely to help ensure compliance through the WTO dispute settlement.

The most powerful argument in favour of extending the CBD provisions which relate to access and benefit sharing of genetic resources is to put an end to "biopiracy" – the attempt by First World companies to patent natural resources based on traditional knowledge without prior consent. This is reflected in the "Bonn Guidelines" adopted by the Sixth Conference of the Parties to the CBD in 2002. Though merely voluntary in nature these guidelines invite states to enact legislation that (i) subjects access to genetic resources to the prior informed consent of the countries of origin; (ii) encourages users to disclose the origin or any relevant traditional knowledge when filing applications for IPRs; (iii) respects the rights and requires the approval and involvement of holders of traditional knowledge; (iv) sets up mechanisms ensuring equitable benefit-sharing with relevant stakeholders inclusive of indigenous communities (Tully, 2003; Verma, 2004: 776–777). An increasing number of LDCs, notably Brazil and India, have or are in the process of implementing Access and Benefit-Sharing legislation along these lines (Dross and Wolff, 2005).

Proposals to protect traditional knowledge have commonsensical appeal. It is a well-known fact that such knowledge can constitute a valuable source of leads for the development of commercial products and processes, thereby enabling users, notably biotechnology companies, to save time and money. Why should the knowledge holders not have a share in the benefits? All the more so as the contribution of natural products to the sales of the larger pharmaceutical companies is estimated to range from 10 per cent to more than 50 per cent, while 42 per cent of the 25 top-selling drugs worldwide in 1997 were derived from natural products (ten Kate and Laird, 1999; Laird, 2002). Yet, many questions still need to be seriously addressed. One particularly vexing problem stems from the fact that traditional knowledge is held collectively, which requires that appropriate protection recognizes and rewards *common* property rights. This hardly appears to be the case in the present context of privatization *and* nationalization of plant genetic materials – in other words, of overwhelming bias in favour of *private* and *sovereign* rights over *common* property rights. Other difficulties, some of which may well prove insoluble, pave the way for making traditional knowledge fall within the remit of conventional forms of IPRs: such knowledge is ancestral, whereas conventional legal systems grant IPR protection for innovative steps (see Kameri-Mbote and Cullet, 1999); it would require proper documentation in order to make prior art available to patent examiners, which implies disclosure of what often constitutes a form of trade secret; so as to ensure that those contributing resources or knowledge would share directly in the benefits that might flow from commercialization of the invention, there is need to empower the indigenous communities – an objective difficult to attain as such (insofar as it is effectively pursued by governments eager to capture some if not all of the accruing rent) and which may in certain circumstances lead to the breakdown of communities as it is in no way certain that the benefits will be subject to egalitarian communal rights of usufruct rather than distributed so unequally as to have an overall disintegrative effect.[36]

Other no less strong arguments may be raised against not so much the possibility as the *judiciousness* of expanding IPRs. With regard to *crop* genetic resources, Frisvold and Condon (1998) note that recognition of sovereign rights over this material, in and of itself, "will not necessarily allow developing countries to reap large financial gains". As property rights only apply to holdings collected *after* the CBD comes into force, breeders would hardly need to purchase newly collected material, as there is a vast supply of unused germplasm available either in their own collections or in other *ex-situ* centres. Furthermore, it is a well-known fact that wild species or landraces form only a marginal percentage of the germplasm used by seed companies in the development of new varieties contrariwise to modern varieties which, as we have seen, are allowed to be used freely for breeding purposes (Dutfield, 2000: 6). In short, the CBD will most likely have little effect on the asymmetrical rights governing raw germplasm, on the one hand, which will continue to be viewed as valueless, and commercial seed varieties, on the other. It did, however, contribute to initiate adoption by the FAO in November 2001 of the International Treaty on Plant Genetic Resources for Food and Agriculture which aims at setting up a Multilateral System composed of a collection of samples of 35 food and 29 feed crops. This system requires payment of royalties into a biodiversity fund for any new variety developed from samples obtained through the system. Details of how the treaty will be regulated remain unaddressed, so there is reason to fear that its fate may well parallel that of the International Undertaking (Falcon and Fowler, 2002; Meldolesi, 2002).

As for phytogenetic material of interest to the pharmaceutical, cosmetic and other biotechnology industries, expansion of IPRs may, according to Artuso (2002: 1356), generate rents only in so far as source country suppliers are able to provide "biological samples and derivative products which combine relatively rare ecological characteristics with associated cultural and scientific knowledge". Obviously bioprospectors are not interested in randomly collected samples. "Value-added bioprospecting", however, would require a costly national strategy aimed at setting up a legal and institutional framework capable of regulating intellectual property rights, foreign investment guidelines, tax treatment, import and export procedures, as well as enhancing scientific and technical training, project management, business development, and marketing skills.

Could the GEF be of any assistance here? Officially, one of the facility's mandates consists in "biodiversity enabling activities" – that is, activities aimed at preparing national inventories, formulating strategies and action plans, undertaking awareness-building programmes, and so forth. As of yet, however, GEF investments have concentrated on "enabling access to information about resources of value to bioprospectors, energy investors, ecotourism operators and so forth" (Young, 2002: 15).[37] This insistence on economic returns results in offering financial support to bioprospectors for their "gene rush" activities, or to financiers for their willingness to trade future carbon credits, or to nature entrepreneurs for their bid to charge a price for exhibiting the animals and wild plants they keep in custody.

A last, but by no means least, argument against extending patent protection over life forms is the social cost this will entail to consumers in all countries, including LDCs who will have to pay monopoly prices for the patented applications derived from genetic resources over which only meagre royalties may be obtained. Indeed, by providing patentees with the ability to prevent others from producing, marketing and using an application, patents create temporary monopolies, to the effect that a patented good, if marketed successfully, always sells at a higher price and in lower quantities until the patent expires (Ordover, 1991).

Most worrying, however, is the fact that the expansion of IPRs leaves largely unaddressed the underlying social and economic causes of biodiversity loss. The dominant paradigm shared by development policymakers and practioners in the West links decline in biodiversity mainly to unchecked population growth, and assumes that the solution lies in attaching economic value to nature conservation. This view, however, is clearly reductionist. In some countries, deforestation can be attributed to the expulsion or marginalization of rural populations forced to use underused land such as forest or scrub. In other parts of the world, in particular South America, large landholders and cattle ranchers, rather than small farmers, are predominantly responsible for forest destruction (Rappel and Thomas, 1998; Fearnside, 2005).

Several other industrial and technological causes are equally disregarded by the dominant paradigm. Little mention is usually made of how high-yielding hybrid seeds spread during the green revolution led to intensive monocropping of genetically uniform varieties, in effect causing thousands of landraces – previously freely exchanged between farmers and farming communities – to become extinct through disuse. Because of their uniformity, hybrid varieties are particularly vulnerable to pathogens and require extensive use of pesticides which can be considered as biodiversity-reducers. Moreover, to be efficiently exploited, these varieties need chemical fertilizers which again provoke biological loss. Attempts to protect scientific research in agriculture by means of patents can only aggravate these trends by imposing higher costs on farmers with spiralling effects on social marginalization and hence biodiversity loss. Widespread commercialization of transgenic seeds tolerant to herbicides and pests risks to further threaten crop heterogeneity. Not surprisingly, the input trait engineered into close to three-quarters of the transgenic crops actually cultivated aims at increasing the ability to withstand the use of herbicides patented by the life-science company (McAfee, 2003: 212–213). Also, the higher yields expected from the use of genetic technology require holdings large enough to compensate for the cost of the variety. This again will have negative spiralling effects on marginalization (Yapa, 1993; Uzogara, 2000). The whole issue of biodiversity loss demonstrates how an environmental problem has been presented in a language that suits the business sector. Obviously, such standards for valuing the environment are wholly insufficient to attack the root of the problem.

Much of what has been said about the Biodiversity Convention can be applied to the Climate Change Regime in the making. Indeed, enhancement of sinks by means of biodiversity reserves has been supported by powerful companies from the industrialized world that would prefer to set aside land for carbon sequestration in LDCs rather than clean up, let alone reduce, local production. The following examination will therefore be short and confined to the removal or limitation of sources of GHGs in LDCs through expansion of renewables.

From 1991 to 2005, the total climate change funding of the GEF amounted to US$1.75 billion, 37 per cent of which was spent on renewable energy and 28 per cent on energy efficiency projects. A more detailed study shows that as of 1999 the GEF approved $480 million in grants for 41 renewable energy projects in 26 less developed and transition countries. It leveraged an additional US$2 billion cofinancing from governments, regional development banks, implementing agencies and the private sector (Martinot et al., 2002: 313). It contributed decisively to expand markets for rural household and small industry energy using solar PV systems, biogas, small hydro, geothermal and wind power. In the absence of financial incentives, LDCs would have been reluctant to borrow for renewables from multilateral banks. GEF funds were used to overcome the main barrier, namely, the higher costs of renewables compared to conventional fuels. Moreover, from 1991 to 2000, the GEF approved US$90 million in grants for eight projects "designed to stimulate markets for energy-efficient products – lights, refrigerators, industrial boilers, and building chillers – in 12 developing and transitional countries". US$430 million in additional co-financing were leveraged (Martinot, 2000). Finally, the GEF financed enabling activities for climate change mitigation consisting mainly in setting up national inventories of emission by sources and removal by sinks.

Overall, as with CBD activities, the GEF appeared to subsidize Northern elite management of Southern resources, and to assist firms and NGOs involved in renewables and energy-efficient products to provide their environment-friendly goods and services to developing markets (Young, 2002: 217). Owing to their cost, renewable markets have had to target the richer segments of society, thereby demonstrating that policies carried out in the name of ecological commonalities do not necessarily benefit the poor who form the majority of world population. The "one earth, one future" rhetoric of global sustainability may appear self-evident in industrialized countries, but understandably it has little meaning to those who have no land to live off or much of a future to contemplate. In turn, the local day-to-day problems that the poor face are not sufficiently addressed, let alone understood, by environmental experts and administrators concerned with "global benefits". As Bartelmus (1994: 12) reminds us, "the depletion and degradation of natural resources (land/soil, water and forests) and their effects on food and energy supply, marginal conditions in human settlements, environmentally conditioned diseases and natural disasters are high-priority issues in LDCs. By contrast, industrialized countries are especially concerned about air, land and water pollution, global environmental phenomena of climate change and the depletion of the ozone layer".

That said, by contributing to both the privatization *and* the nationalization of environmental "goods" (genetic diversity) and "bads" (emissions of pollutants), the post-Rio agenda has transformed the environmental issue into an economic niche for states and corporations and for industrialized and less developed countries alike. It has created a semantic confusion between the effective and the legal protection of biodiversity, devised proprietary rights in pollutants to induce corporations to speculate on the profitability of reducing their emissions – hence, restricting the adoption of command and control standards-setting and enforcement regulations – subsidized relatively costly renewables and energy-efficient or pollution-reduction equipment so as to enable them to be sold off to LDCs. In so doing, it has contributed to the spread of the myth that "sustainable development" is a win-win objective which can only benefit both sides of any divide – rich and poor countries, states and corporations, transnational NGOs and indigenous populations. This disregards the fact that sustainable development is none other than an agenda-setting process which, by way of defining new rights and duties regarding the exploitation of nature, necessarily generates conflicts between groups that enjoy unequal resources, necessitating them to defend their interests so as to achieve beneficial outcomes.

Unresolved issues

In theory, the domain of international institutions involved in social and economic governance should be the resolution of collective problems through the use of moral rules and legitimate coercive devices to regulate behaviour. Moral rules should function as eye-openers capable of enhancing adequate external and domestic pressure to get the painful business done, and coercive devices as threats sufficiently convincing to induce states and their organizations to regulate effectively the behaviour of private actors operating within their jurisdictions.

The tacit aim of development is to narrow the equity gap between the rich and the poor. Almost always this is taken to mean raising the bottom rather than lowering the top by redistribution. If one is to address sustainable issues effectively, the latter option would appear to be more consistent. This obviously requires proactive policy action by LDCs and NGOs alike.

LDCs need to coordinate to ensure that their views are represented rather than manipulated by the carrot of aid and the stick of trade sanctions. It is a well-known fact that the more organized the subject groups in political processes, the more they are capable of sharing in the making of decisions with the power groups. True enough, the political and economic boundaries which mapped what used to be called the Third World have shifted or blurred so much that the notion itself appears today somewhat anachronistic or meaningless. Nevertheless, developing countries cannot remain content, as many at present appear to be, with simply demanding that industrialized countries open up their markets. Palmerston's celebrated formulation of the imperialism of free trade – "It is the business of government to open and secure the roads of the merchant" – still holds true today as it did in the past: such business is and will continue to be the privilege of powerful governments, not weak ones.

Indeed, globalization has not so far, and will not in the near future, sprinkle production facilities across all five continents uniformly. Most trade and investment is, and will remain, between advanced countries. And there is no doubt that a considerable number of LDCs will continue to move closer to the margins of international irrelevance. Three-quarters of the total world overseas investment is concentrated in North America, Western Europe and Japan. In other words, a small part of the globe accounting for some 15 per cent of the earth's population provides nearly all the world's technological innovations, and perhaps not more than half of the world population is able to buy these technologies. Surely, the enhancement of regional South–South trade is no less absurd a strategy than to continue to seek access to industrialized markets (see Yves Berthelot and Miguel Lengyel, this volume) – unless LDC governments consider it worthwhile to continue transferring over US$100 billion annually in debt servicing to wealthy states, as has been the case since the mid-1980s (World Bank, 2003). What good can possibly result from the lowest-income countries continuing to spend approximately half their export earnings on such debt servicing, which is itself the consequence of North–South trade and finance? Of course one may well retort that such a line of argument is cogent but for the following problem: it is a non sequitur to assume that whatever appears wise policy to concerned citizens far removed from the kitchens of power should appear equally wise and feasible to those heads of states and governments who are busy doing the cooking.

This is why many believe that non-profit organizations in the northern and southern hemispheres alike can be helpful. NGOs have been hailed by reformist planners for their capacity to involve local populations in development projects, to deliver welfare services, or to contribute to democratizing processes (Fisher, 1997). In the view of some observers, alternative trade organizations are a case in point. Seeking to re-embed international economic relations in less exploitative relations, these associational trade networks link producer cooperatives in the South, who provide various marketing, micro-lending, and distribution services, with retail venues in the industrialized world which sell these products to conscious consumers at a set premium above free market prices (Leclair, 2002). This, it is asserted, may be a good example of how "development" can be taken to mean lowering the top by voluntary redistribution, besides contributing directly to "sustainability", since many fair trade organizations market either organic or traditional products, notably handicrafts.

In the view of more radically minded theorists, however, such practices are but reminders of the extent to which NGOs have become active participants in integrating communities into world markets and why they are so often co-opted and hailed by development agencies. These theorists remind us that one should not eulogize NGOs indiscriminately. For all the talk about the democratization of international relations induced by the emergence of an "international civil society", NGOs remain unelected groups that use public money for their projects. Nor do all pursue progressive agendas. They may just as well represent powerful interest groups in domestic politics or constitute docile agents of the state and the status quo. Still, radical theorists assert that some non-profit NGOs can and do create a mood of policy activism and should be supported. Of particular interest to these authors are the groups involved in challenging local and governmental elites as part of a strategy perceived as an "insurrection of subjugated knowledges" (Fisher, 1997: 449).

However important, these strategies which aim at reducing the North–South equity gap and the global despoliation of the environment remain nevertheless voluntary and associational. When successful, they should eventually result in *institutional innovation* based on similar ethical principles but supported by compliance mechanisms. Anticipating such success, some analysts and politicians have called for the creation of a world environmental organization (WEO) – and it is not unlikely that discussions to that effect could begin in earnest in the near future (Simonis, 2002). Several arguments have been advanced over the years in support of establishing such an organization. Some underline the need for a global coordinating agency for the 200 or so issue-specific multilateral environmental treaties on account of the fact that they are often impaired by fragmentation. Others see the purpose of a WEO as providing a body capable of either solely or jointly setting rules, monitoring and enforcing compliance, settling disputes, coordinating technical assistance, facilitating the bargaining of deals whereby environmental commitments are exchanged by poorer countries for financial resources such as cash or write-offs of debt (Lodefalk and Whalley, 2002; Tussie and Whalley, 2002; Whalley and Zissimos, 2002).

The topic as to whether multilateral environmental agreements are really in need of further institutionalization is large one, and detailed examination would require a separate study. That said, there appears to be an equally strong case for considering that the ad hoc arrangements displayed by these treaties – which comprise a conference or meeting of parties with decision-making powers, a secretariat and technical subsidiary bodies – are adequately flexible, cost-effective and, following two scholars of international law, "innovative in relation to norm creation and compliance" (Churchill and Ulfstein, 2000: 625). It is doubtful anyway that a more centralized bureaucratic system would be equipped with more authority to develop, implement and enforce rules, as this would imply that states surrender their sovereignty to an unelected international body lacking general consent (Bodansky, 1999).

More importantly, one may well wonder how a WEO with tasks of the sorts described above could possibly ward off legitimate fears about developing countries being sold yet another pig in a poke. One source of disquietude is that such an organization would in all likelihood prioritize trans-boundary *global* environmental issues – indeed, as we have seen, a main concern for industrialized countries – to the exclusion or marginalization of local problems such as soil degradation, water and air pollution which affect LDC populations to a comparatively higher degree (Biermann, 2002: 304). Another worry is that compliance with the rules set by a WEO could only be effectively ensured by trade sanctions or conditional financial assistance, and would hence bear more heavily on the poorer countries (Lodefalk and Whalley, 2002: 613). The leverage that industrialized countries, as donors and bigger trading nations, have over LDCs would be further heightened by their capacity to provide the scientific expertise and the best available technologies. Of concomitant concern here is the strong likelihood that the GEF – that is, a mechanism whose funds are used to cover the incremental costs incurred through activities involving scientific expertise and best available technologies – may serve as a blueprint for the provision of financial resources by a prospective WEO. This, to quote Newell's words, would reinforce the trend of allowing countries that pollute the most to "buy themselves out of trouble" by merely subsidizing their products and services that achieve environmental additionality "while demanding changes in those countries without the economic clout to resist them" (Newell, 2002: 661).

This begs the question of what ought to be done. In all events, one institution, the GEF, through its fiduciary the World Bank, has proved incapable of addressing the social and political causes of biodiversity loss and global GHGs emissions, or of targeting ecosystems most at risk. As Chatterjee and Finger have argued, "the idea of *global* management hands over the policing of the commons and their sustainable development to a global establishment, its institutions and agreements" (Chatterjee, Finger, 1994: 26). As a result, resources are not spent on assisting needy communities living in depleted habitats, but rather on subsidizing various green business products, or paying for the services of international experts engaged in collecting, analysing, organizing and presenting their specialized knowledge.

Ideally, the GEF should be abolished in favour of specific multilateral funds – such as the one first established by the Montreal Protocol to deal with ozone-depleting substances – with equal voting rights and effective veto power for both donor and recipient parties directly concerned by the problem at stake. Within each fund an equivalent of the GEF's Small Grants Programme – which targets exclusively "community based organizations" – should be scaled up to assist populations who live in threatened ecosystems and who, in the absence of such assistance, have often no alternative but to pursue the depletion of scarce resources. There would be no need here to involve the World Bank, international NGOs or other consultants based in the industrial world which, according to an analyst, have so far been the "central formulators of the global environmental agenda" and have largely benefited from it (Jamison, 2001: 127).

More ambitious would be to follow up the call for the establishment and enforcement of the "polluter pays principle" (PPP) in all multilateral environmental agreements and/or to set up a system-wide international tax – for example, on currency and other speculative transactions, the proceeds of which could be used to fund these agreements (see Pierre de Senarclens, this volume). "Taxing", Garrett Harding (1968) wrote in his seminal article introducing the notion of the "tragedy of the commons", is a "good coercive device" to handle "the system of fouling our own nest" in which independent, rational, free but fundamentally selfish enterprisers using a common pool are allowed to be locked in. Such a prospect, however, appears unlikely in the near future: "Alas, the lords of finance throughout the world will have none of the Tobin Tax" – lamented recently the one after whom that tax has been named – no more than the lords of the polluting industries would allow the spread of PPP taxes without putting up a strong fight (Tobin, 2000: 1104).

As this chapter has sought to make clear, the much preferred alternative consists of creating legal scarcities and new proprietary products relative to commonalities like the biosphere, the atmosphere or life forms. It is assumed that by assigning market values to resources previously considered "common property", sufficient incentive will be provided to manage them adequately. The present author hopes to have gone some way towards showing that a globally positive outcome based on such principles is quite unlikely considering past and present trends. This applies especially to market environmentalism, but also, though perhaps to a lesser degree, to the kind of "ecological modernization" (Hajer, 1995; Stewart, 2001) which some LDC governments, such as those forming the group of mega-diverse countries, have so enthusiastically endorsed with the view of translating into commercial benefits either their abundance of environmental goods such as genetic biodiversity, or their scant emissions of environmental bads such as GHGs. Indeed, the two models appear to benefit both the corporate sphere in the North and the elite in the South, and are therefore more likely to work to the disadvantage of the poor.

It appears, therefore, that one urgent need would be to rescue the issue of "sustainable development" from the realm of economism where it is currently confined. Though its symbols serve to convey the impression that essential changes have occurred or are in the process of occurring in development policies, in effect new *mechanisms* have been set up merely to mediate fundamentally unchanged socio-economic relations which, as a result, continue to engender their familiarly uneven benefit streams. One step forward would be that analysts and practicians together venture as they did in the past in reformulating the idea of development as a bona fide *utopia* whose function in the political process is to induce changes in power patterns. How this can be achieved is obviously a daunting question, but it clearly requires powerful collective action and enhanced communication and coordination between fragmented social movements and issue networks who need to articulate protest all at once at the local, regional, national and international levels (Fisher, 1997).

Another prerequisite is that any claim in the industrialized world regarding the *collective-good* aspect of the environment in the southern hemisphere should be based on the prior acceptance that ecological degradation is intimately connected with what an astute observer called the "intensified exploitation of all forms of nature, human and non-human" (Goldman, 1997: 3), and that such exploitation has usually domestic *and* international sociopolitical factors as its main causal variables. Yet another prerequisite is to cast off those "fast fixes" which benefit mainly elite government and transnational business circles, such as selling clean technology to LDCs at subsidized prices. As this is not equivalent to providing them with the capacity to produce the technology locally, it will merely aggravate their debt burden while satisfying the expansionary demands of those industries in the North which have invested in renewables, energy efficiency or pollution abatement equipment. Similar inequitable effects are likely to result from converting the Southern commons into commercial goods by way of accelerating the eviction of the commons-dependent poor by the local elite (Goldman, 1997).

There is finally an image problem that plagues less developed societies. They are often viewed as one desolate waste, in which tyranny, oppression, mass poverty and resource depletion prevail. Such images fuel simplistic notions that "overseas development assistance" aims at helping these societies make a leap from darkness to light. Obviously, images of this sort require a great deal of shading. What is the use of "rescuing" southern hemisphere populations from "backwardness" only to subject them to the disintegrative influences of legal property relationships, usury capitalism or commercial agriculture? Are "marginalized people" insulated from change or victims of change? Considering the indisputable fact that production and consumption patterns in the North affect disproportionately the world's biomass and atmosphere, why is there comparatively more talk and study about the negative environmental effects produced by shifting cultivators or small-scale farmers in the South or by the emergence of new power plants and consumption habits in a few fast-industrializing countries such as China, India, Brazil, Mexico, the North and South-East Asian Dragons and Tigers? Though is evident that these countries will make increasingly significant contributions to future environmental degradation, it is crucial to resist the temptation to collapse LDCs into a single entity. Emerging countries form a small subgroup – though a significant one demographically – and it is safe to say that the vast majority of LDCs contribute comparatively little to global environmental problems.

These are merely a handful of the more obvious questions which require some serious thought. We need to be better armed with the multifaceted local facts in the South relating to production, consumption, distribution and exchange patterns, and their complex relations with various national, transnational and international demands of accommodation. We need to disentangle organic, capitalist and techno-scientific uses and misuses of nature. Let us not listen to the siren's song of "sustainable development" chanted by global resource managers whose business it is to convince decision-makers that the world's biophysical commons should be accommodated to a limited set of legal schemes, notably proprietary rights, or to sophisticated techno-scientific modes of production developed in the North, and that this process ought to begin being applied in the southern hemisphere. Such views contribute, perhaps more than any other, to sustain a form of collective denial supported by powerful vested interests (which so happen also to control the international institutions with sharp teeth and adequately filled coffers) even though this denial is increasingly challenged by activists and concerned citizens worldwide, namely, that the unsustainable use of resources should be dealt with *before all else* in the industrialized world where it is the most self-evident and unnecessary in terms of human survival because engendered mainly by over-consumption.

Notes

1. Development is considered sustainable when it "meets the needs of the present without compromising the ability of future generations to achieve their own needs".
2. In another passage, Lugard (1965 [1922]: 18) makes the positive claim even clearer: "The civilised nations have at last recognised that while on the one hand the abounding wealth of the tropical regions of the earth must be developed and used for the benefit of mankind, on the other hand an obligation rests on the controlling Power not only to safeguard the material rights of the natives, but to promote their moral and educational progress".
3. For a French version, cf. Leroy-Beaulieu (1908 [1874–1908], II: 686); for an American one, cf. Great Britain vs. United States (15 August 1893) in *Moore's International Arbitration Awards*, vol. 1, 1893, p. 853.
4. Convention destinée à assurer la conservation des diverses espèces animales vivant à l'état sauvage en Afrique qui sont utiles à l'homme ou inoffensives, London 19 May 1900 (in Stoerk, 1904).
5. Convention Relative to the Preservation of Fauna and Flora in their Natural State (London), 8 November 1933 (cf. Kiss, 1983; Hayden, 1942).
6. Following Aldo Leopold's definition of wilderness (Leopold, 1968: vii).
7. The UPOV convention requires each party to give the nationals of other parties the right to obtain protection as if they were nationals. Prior to the entry of force of the 1961 UPOV Convention, plant patent laws, like nearly all patent law, provided protection only within national territory (Barton, 1982: 1074).
8. International Convention for the Protection of New Varieties of Plants, Act of December 1, 1961, Art. 6.
9. "Authorization by the breeder or his successor in title shall not be required either for the utilization of the new variety as an initial source of variation for the purpose of creating other new varieties or for the marketing of such varieties. Such authorization shall be required, however, when the repeated use of the new variety is necessary for the commercial production of another variety". International Convention for the Protection of New Varieties of Plants, Act of December 1, 1961, Art. 5(3).
10. International Convention for the Protection of New Varieties of Plants, Act of October 3, 1978, Art. 5(1).
11. Annex II, Farmers' Rights, Resolution 5/89, Extract of Twenty-fifth Session of the FAO Conference, Rome, 11–29, November 1989.
12. Annex I, Agreed Interpretation of the International Undertaking, Resolution 4/89, Extract of the Twenty-fifth Session of the FAO Conference, Rome, 11–29, November 1989.
13. Annex III, Resolution 3/91, Extract of the Twenty-sixth Session of the FAO Conference, Rome, 9–27, November 1991 (italics added).

14. "Breeders' lines and farmers' breeding material should only be available at the discretion of their developers".
15. United Nations Framework Convention on Climate Change, opened for signature June 4, 1992, Art. 2.
16. The Beijing Ministerial Declaration on Environment and Development adopted by 41 developing countries in 1991 had stated: "While the protection of the environment is in the common interests of the international community, the developed countries bear the main responsibility for the degradation of the global environment. Ever since the industrial revolution, the developed countries have over-exploited the world's natural resources through unsustainable patterns of production and consumption, causing damage to the global environment, to the detriment of the developing countries" (cf. Matsui, 2002: 154–155).
17. "States shall cooperate in a spirit of global partnership to conserve, protect and restore the health and integrity of the Earth's ecosystem. In view of the different contributions to global environmental degradation, States have common but differentiated responsibilities. The developed countries acknowledge the responsibility that they bear in the international pursuit of sustainable development in view of the pressures their societies place on the global environment and of the technologies and financial resources they command".
18. Article 3.4 (cf. Begg, 2002; Boehmer-Christiansen and Aynsley Kellow, 2002, 73–74).
19. The approach consists in assigning annual caps on electricity generating units called "affected sources". A cap defines the number of emissions allowances for use each year by the electric utility. At the end of the year, all affected sources must deposit enough allowances to cover their recorded emissions or be subject to significant penalties. Unused allocated allowances can either be banked or freely sold to other sources. The law thus offers utilities flexibility in determining how they intend to comply with their obligations (cf. Joskow, 1998).
20. Besides Biodiversity and Climate Change, four other environmental issues have since then been included, namely: International Waters, the Ozone Layer, Persistent Organic Pollutants (POPs) and Land Degradation. That said, Biodiversity and Climate Change projects have received the lion's share of GEF funding, as they account for respectively 36 per cent and 33 per cent of total funding from 1991 to 2005, cf. *Third Overall Performance Study*, June 2005, p. 13.
21. Preamble, Instrument for the Establishment of the Restructured GEF (1994).
22. Ibid., Annex E.
23. Ibid., Art. 25(c)ii.
24. The African Development Bank, the Asian Development Bank, the European Bank for Reconstruction and Development, the Inter-American Development Bank, FAO, the United Nations Industrial Development Organization (UNIDO), the International Fund for Agriculture have also been recognized by the GEF Council as executing agencies. Officially, however, "UNDP is responsible for technical assistance activities, capacity building, and the Small Grants Programme. UNEP is charged with catalysing the development of scientific and technical analysis, advancing environmental management in GEF-financed activities, and managing the Scientific and Technical Advisory Panel, an independent advisory body. The World Bank, the repository of the Trust Fund, is responsible for investment projects, and mobilizing resources from the private sector" (GEF, *Operational Report on GEF Programs* 2000).
25. GEF, *Rapport annuel du FEM 2001*, p. 7.
26. GEF, *Third Overall Performance Study*, June 2005, p. 154.
27. GEF, *Rapport annuel du FEM 2001*, p. 6.
28. GEF Council, *Cofinancing*, 2002, GEF/C.20/6, p. 2.

29. GEF, *Overall Performance Study* (OPS-1), p. 72.
30. GEF, *Overall Performance Study* (OPS-1), 1998, xviii.
31. GEF/R.3/Inf.4/Rev.1, December 2001.
32. The latter two have merged their agri-businesses to form Syngenta, the largest conglomerate in the field to date.
33. "[E]ach Contracting Party may, within reasonable limits and subject to the safeguarding of the legitimate interests of the breeder, restrict the breeder's right in relation to any variety in order to permit farmers to use for propagating purposes, on their own holdings, the product of the harvest which they have obtained by planting, on their own holdings, the protected variety" (Art. 15(2), International Convention for the Protection of New Varieties of Plants, Act of 1991, 19 March 1991).
34. IP/C/W/368, 8 August 2002. Cf. in particular the position of India (IP/C/W/198) and of Brazil (IP/C/W/228 and IP/C/W/356).
35. IP/C/W/400/Rev.1, 18 June 2003.
36. Cf. India's note (IP/C/W/198).
37. A careful analysis of the massive *Operational Report on GEF Programs*, 2001, confirms these trends in GEF investments.

REFERENCES

Adi, Bondo (2006) "Intellectual property rights in biotechnology and the fate of poor framers' agriculture", *Journal of World Intellectual Property* 9(1): 91–112

Agrawala, Shardul (1998) "Context and early origins of the Intergovernmental Panel on Climate Change", *Climatic Change* 39: 605–620.

—— (1999) "Early Science – Policy Interactions in Climate Change: Lessons from the Advisory Group on Greenhouse Gases", *Global Environmental Change* 9: 157–169.

Andresen, Steinar and Shardul Agrawala (2002) "Leaders, pushers and laggards in the making of the climate regime", *Global Environmental Change* 12: 41–51.

Artuso, Anthony (2002) "Bioprospecting, benefit sharing, and biotechnological capacity building", *World Development* 30(8): 1355–1368, 2002.

Bartelmus, Peter (1994) *Environment, Growth and Development*, London: Routledge.

Barton, Gregory (2001) "Empire forestry and the origins of environmentalism", *Journal of Historical Geography* 27(4): 529–552.

Barton, John (1982) "The international breeder's rights system and crop plant innovation", *Science* 216(4550): 1071–1071.

Begg, K.G. (2002) "Implementing the Kyoto Protocol on Climate Change: Environmental integrity, sinks and mechanisms", *Global Environmental Change* 12: 331–336.

Biermann, Frank (2002) "Strengthening green global governance in a disparate world society", *International Environmental Agreements: Politics, Law and Economics* 2: 297–315.

Birner, Sabrina and Eric Martinot (2002) "The GEF Energy-Efficient Product Portfolio: Emerging Experience and Lessons", Monitoring and Evaluation Working Paper, 9 June.

Bowman, Michael and Catherine Redgwell (2000 [1996]) *International Law and the Conservation of Biological Diversity*, Boston, Mass.: Kluwer Law International, 1996/*International Affairs* 76(2) Special Biodiversity Issue, 2000.

Bodansky, Daniel (1999) "The legitimacy of international governance: A coming challenge for international environmental law?", *American Journal of International Law* 93(3): 596–624.

Bochmer-Christiansen, Sonja and Aynsley Kellow (2002) *International Environmental Policy: Interests and the Failure of the Kyoto Process*, Cheltenham: Edward Elgar.

Boisson de Chazournes, Laurence (2005) "The Global Environment Facility (GEF): A unique and crucial institution", *RECIEL* 14(3): 193–201.

Brush, Stephen (1989) "Rethinking crop genetic resource conservation", *Conservation Biology* 3(1): 19–29.

Chataway, Joanna, Joyce Tait and David Wield (2004) "Understanding company R&D strategies in agro-biotechnology: Trajectories and blind spots", *Research Policy* 33: 1041–1057.

Chatterjee, Pratap and Matthias Finger (1994) *The Earth Brokers: Power, Politics, and World Development*, London: Routledge.

Churchill, Robin R. and Geir Ulfstein (2000) "Autonomous institutional arrangements in multilateral environmental agreements: A little-noticed phenomenon in international law", *American Journal of International Law* 94(4): 623–659.

Cullet, Philippe (2001) "Property rights regimes over biological resources", *Environment and Planning C: Government and Policy* 19.

——— (2002) "Plant variety protection: Patents, plant breeders' rights and sui generis systems", International Environmental Law Research Centre Briefing Paper.

——— (2003) "Property rights regimes over biological resources", *art. cit.*; "The Convention on Biological Diversity", International Environmental Law Research Centre Briefing Paper.

Dross, Miriam and Franziska Wolff (2005) *New Elements of the International Regime on Access and Benefit-Sharing of Genetic Resources: The Role of Certificates of Origin*, Bonn: Budesamt für Naturschutz (BfN).

Dutfield, Graham (2000) *Intellectual Property Rights, Trade and Biodiversity: Seeds and Plant Varieties*, London: Earthscan and IUCN.

Ellis, Jane, Jan Corfee-Morlot and Harald Winkler (2006) "CDM: Taking stock and looking forward", *Energy Policy* 35(1): 15–28.

Falcon, W.P. and C. Fowler (2002) "Carving up the commons: Emergence of a new international regime for germplasm development and transfer", *Food Policy* 27: 197–222.

Fearnside, Philip M. (2005) "Deforestation in Brazilian Amazonia: History, rates and consequences", *Conservation Biology* 19(3): 680–688.

Fenwick, Simon (1998) "Bioprospecting or biopiracy?", *Drug Discovery Today* 3(9, September): 399–402.

Fisher, William (1997) "Doing good? The politics and antipolitics of NGO practices", *Annual Review of Anthropology* 26: 439–464.

Frisvold, George and Peter Condon (1998) "The convention on biological diversity and agriculture: Implications and unresolved debates", *World Development* 26(4): 551–570.

Goldman, Michael (1997) "Customs in common: The epistemic world of the commons scholar", *Theory and Society* 26(1): 1–37.

Grove, Richard H. (1990) "Colonial conservation, ecological hegemony and popular resistance: Towards a global synthesis", in John M. MacKenzie (ed.) *Imperialism and the Natural World*, Manchester: Manchester University Press, pp. 15–50.

———— (1995) *Green Imperialism: Colonial Expansion, Tropical Edens and the Origins of Environmentalism, 1600–1860*, Cambridge: Cambridge University Press.

Guha, Ramachandra (1989) *The Unquiet Woods*, Berkeley: University of California Press.

Guha, Ramachandra and Madhav Gadgil (1989) "State forestry and social conflict in British India", *Past and Present* 123: 141–177.

Hajer, Maarten A. (1995) *The Politics of Environmental Discourse: Ecological Modernization and the Policy Process*, Oxford: Clarendon Press.

Hailey, Malcolm (ed.) (1938) *An African Survey: A Study of Problems arising in Africa South of the Sahara*, London, Oxford University Press.

Hardin, Garrett (1968) "The tragedy of the commons", *Science* 162: 1243–1248.

Hayden, Sherman Strong (1942) *The International Protection of Wild Life. An Examination of Treaties and other Agreements for the Preservation of Birds and Mammals*, New York: Columbia University Press.

Hetherington, Penelope (1978) *British Paternalism and Africa 1920–1940*, London: Frank Cass.

Hilder, Vaughan and Donald Boulter (1999) "Genetic engineering of crop plants for insect resistance: A critical review", *Crop Protection* 18: 177–191.

Hirschman, Albert O. (1991) *The Rhetoric of Reaction: Perversity, Futility, Jeopardy*, Cambridge MA: Harvard University Press.

Huxley, Julian (1960) *The Conservation of Wild Life in Africa*, Paris: UNESCO.

Jamison, Andrew (2001) *The Making of Green Knowledge: Environmental Politics and Cultural Transformation*, Cambridge: Cambridge University Press.

Joskow, Paul L., R. Schmalensee and E.M. Bailey (1998) "The market for sulfur dioxide emissions", *American Economic Review* 88(4): 669–685.

Kameri-Mbote, Patricia and Philippe Cullet (1999) "Agro-biodiversity and international law: A conceptual framework", *Journal of Environmental Law* 11(2): 257–279.

Kapur, Devesh, John P. Lewis and Richard Webb (1997) *The World Bank: Its First Half Century*, Washington DC: Brookings Institution.

Kiss, A. (ed.) (1983) *Selected Multilateral Treaties in the Field of the Environment*, Nairobi, Kenya: UNEP.

Koo, Bonwoo, Philip G. Pardey and Brian D. Wright (2003) "The price of conserving agricultural biodiversity", *Nature* 21(February): 126–128

Laird, Sarah A. (ed.) (2002) *Biodiversity and Traditional Knowledge*, London: Earthscan.

Lappe, Marc and Britt Bailey (1999) *Against the Grain: The Genetic Transformation of Global Agriculture*, London: Earthscan.

Leclair, Mark S. (2002) "Fighting the tide: Alternative trade organizations in the era of global free trade", *World Development* 30(6): 949–958.

Lee, J.M. (1967) *Colonial Development and Good Government: A Study of the ideas expressed by the English official classes in planning decolonisation 1939–1964*, Oxford: Clarendon Press.

Lee, J.M. and Martin Petter (1982) *The Colonial Office, War, and Development Policy: Organisation and the Planning of A Metropolitan Initiative, 1939–1945*, London: Maurice Temple Smith.

Leopold, Aldo (1968) *A Sand County Almanac*, New York: Oxford University Press.

Leroy-Beaulieu, Paul (1908 [1874–1908]) *De la colonisation chez les peuples modernes*, Paris: Félix Alcan.

Lewis, Arthur (1944) "An economic plan for Jamaica", *Agenda* 3(4): 154–163.

———— (1955) *The Theory of Economic Growth*, Homewood: Richard D. Irwin.

Lodefalk, Magnus and John Whalley (2002) "Reviewing proposals for a World Environmental Organisation", *World Economy* 25(5): 601–617.

Louis, Wm. Roger (1986 [1977]) *Imperialism at Bay: The United States and the Decolonization of the British Empire, 1941–1945*, Oxford: Clarendon Press.

Lugard, Frederick (1965 [1922]) *The Dual Mandate in British Tropical Africa*, London: Cass.

McAfee, Kathleen (2003) "Neoliberalism on the molecular Scale: Economic and genetic reductionism in biotechnology battles", *Geoforum* 34: 203–219.

McCormick, John (1995) *The Global Environmental Movement*, New York: Wiley.

MacKenzie, John M. (1988) *The Empire of Nature: Hunting, Conservation and British Imperialism*, Manchester, Manchester University Press.

Martinot, Eric (2000) "Renewable energy markets and the global environment facility", *Financial Times Renewable Energy Report*, Issue 12, Feb., pp. 18–22.

Martinot, Eric, Akanksha Chaurey, Debra Lew, Jose Roberto Moreira and Njeri Wamukonya (2002) "Renewable energy markets in developing countries", *Annual Review of Energy and the Environment* 27: 309–348.

Matsui, Yoshiro (2002) "Some aspects of the principle of 'common but differentiated responsibilities'", *International Environmental Agreements: Politics, Law and Economics* 2: 151–171.

May, Christopher (2000) *A Global Political Economy of Intellectual Property Rights: The New Enclosures?*, London and New York: Routledge.

Meldolesi, Anna (2002) "CGIAR under pressure to support seed treaty", *Nature* 20(February): 103–105.

Michaelowa Axel, and Edward Dutschke (2000) *Climate Policy and Development: Flexible Instruments and Developing Countries*, Cheltenham: Edward Elgar.

Mukerji, Asoke (2000) "Developing countries and the WTO: Issues of implementation", *Journal of World Trade* 34(6): 33–74.

Nash, Roderick F. (1967) *Wilderness and the American Mind*, New Haven: Yale University Press.

Newell, Peter (2002) "A World Environmental Organisation: The wrong solution to the wrong problem", *World Economy* 25(5): 659–671.

Ordover, J.A. (1991) "A patent system for both diffusion and exclusion", *Journal of Economic Perspectives* 5: 43–60.

Organisation for Economic Co-operation and Development (OECD) (1999) *Contre le changement climatique. Bilan et perspectives du protocole de Kyoto*, Paris: OECD.

Petras, James and Henry Veltmayer (2002) "Age of reverse aid: Neo-liberalism as catalyst of regression", *Development and Change* 33(2): 291–293.

Plucknett, D.L. (1987) *Gene Banks and the World's Food*, Princeton: Princeton University Press.

Plucknett, D.L., Smith, N.J.H., Williams, J.T. and Murthi Anishetty, N. (1983) "Crop germplasm conservation and developing countries", *Science* 220(4593): 163–169.

Rappel, Ian and Neil Thomas (1998) "An examination of the compatibility of World Bank policies towards population, development and biodiversity in the Third World", *Environmentalist* 18: 95–108.

Raynolds, Laura T. (1993) *Revue française d'histoire d'outre-mer*, nos. 298, 299 (special issues on colonization and environment).

—— (2000) "Re-embedding global agriculture: The international organic and fair trade movements", *Agriculture and Human Values* 17: 297–309.

Schoenbaum, Thomas (1997) "International trade and protection of the environment: The continuing search for reconciliation", *American Journal of International Law* 91(2): 268–313.

Schrope, Mark (2001) "Consensus science, or consensus politics?", *Nature* 412(12 July): 112–114.

Sell, Susan K. (2003) *Private Power, Public Law. The Globalization of Intellectual Property Rights*, Cambridge: Cambridge University Press.

Simonis, Udo E. (2002) "Advancing the debate on a World Environment Organization", *Environmentalist* 22: 29–42.

Sivaramkrishnan, K. (1997) "A limited forest conservancy in Southwest Bengal, 1864–1912", *Journal of Asian Studies* 56(1): 75–112.

Skodvin, Tora (2000) *Structure and Agent in the Scientific Diplomacy of Climate Change*, Dordrecht: Kluwer.

Smith, Robert Leo (1976) "Ecological genesis of endangered species: The philosophy of preservation", *Annual Review of Ecology and Systematics* 7: 33–55.

Stewart, Keith (2001) "Avoiding the tragedy of the commons: Greening governance through the market or the public domain?", in Daniel Drache (ed.) *The Market or the Public Domain?*, London: Routledge.

Stoerk, Felix (1904) *Nouveau Recueil de traités et autres actes relatifs aux rapports de droit international: Continuation du grand recueil de Fr. de Martens 430* (2nd series, Vol. XXX).

Ten Kate, K. and Sarah A. Laird (eds.) (1999) *The Commercial Use of Biodiversity: Access to Genetic Resources and Benefit-Sharing*, London: Earthscan.

Thomas, Frédéric (2003) *La forêt mise à nu: Essai anthropologique sur la construction d'un objet scientifique tropical Forêts et bois coloniaux d'Indochine, 1860–1940*, Thèse de 3ème cycle: EHESS.

Tobin, James (2000) "Financial globalization", *World Development* 28(6): 1101–1104.

Tully, Stephen (2003) "The Bonn Guidelines on access to genetic resources and benefit sharing", *RECIEL* 12(1): 84–98.

Tussie, Diana and John Whalley (2002) "The functioning of a commitment based WEO: Lessons from experience with the WTO", *World Economy* 25(5): 685–695.

Uzogara, Stella (2000) "The impact of genetic modification of human foods in the 21st century: A review", *Biotechnology Advances* 18: 179–206.

Verma, Surinder Kaur (2004) "Protecting traditional knowledge: Is a *sui generis* system an answer?", *Journal of World Intellectual Property* 7: 765–805.

Wade, Nicholas (1975) "International agricultural research", *Science* 188(4188): 585–589.

Whalley, John and Ben Zissimos (2002) "An internalisation-based World Environmental Organisation", *World Economy* 25(5): 619–642

Wood, Robert E. (1986) *From Marshall Plan to Debt Crisis: Foreign Aid and Development Choices in the World Economy*, Berkeley: University of California Press.

World Bank (2003) *Global Development Finance, II: Summary and Country Tables*, Washington: IBRD.

Yamin, Farhana (2000) "Joint implementation", *Global Environmental Change* 10: 87–91.

Yapa, Lakshman (1993) "What are improved seeds?", *Economic Geography* 69(3): 254–273.

Young, Zoe (2002) *A New Green Order? The World Bank and the Politics of the Global Environment Facility*, London: Pluto Press.

10

Can global governance make globalization more legitimate?[1]

Jean-Marc Coicaud

At the centre of this book are three closely connected assumptions: first, the downsides that globalization generates call for regulations; second, an improved system of global governance can contribute to minimizing the ills of globalization; third, better global governance will enhance the legitimacy of globalization and the credibility of global governance.

The book unpacks these assumptions by examining the roles and relations of actors of global governance (states, international organizations, regional organizations and non-governmental organizations) and their possible improvement in the context of human rights, security, development, finance, and environment. In the process, it also explores the link between global governance, globalization and legitimacy. As a way to shed more light on these issues, this chapter aims to answer the following question: how can global governance contribute to a better regulation (normative and institutional) that could render globalization more legitimate?

The chapter touches upon four issues: first, it examines what links globalization, global governance and legitimacy. Second, it identifies some of the key criteria upon which rest the legitimacy of global governance and its ability to counteract the shortcomings of globalization. Here the chapter gives pride of place to human rights. Third, it shows that there is a very significant gap between these criteria and the reality of global governance and globalization. Fourth, and finally, the chapter explores ways in which the reality of global governance and globalization could be brought closer to the criteria of global legitimacy.

Regulating globalization: Critical approaches to global governance, de Senarclens and Kazancigil (eds), United Nations University Press, 2007, ISBN 978-92-808-1136-0

Globalization, global governance and legitimacy

Globalization understood as the existence of transnational relations affecting the lives of millions of people within specific societies is not a new phenomenon (Held, 2004: 1).[2] It has been at work for centuries (Gruzinksi, 2004). But there is a certain specificity of the current form of globalization. The bonds that it has established between societies lead to a reorganization of social life on a transnational basis that is much deeper than in any previous context. As such, it combines four characteristics: extensity of global networks, intensity of global interconnectedness, velocity of global flows, and impact propensity of global interconnectedness (Held, McGrew, Goldblatt and Perraton, 1999: 17; Montbrial and Moreau Defarges, 2005).

It is the economic dimension (which embraces diverse forms of international integration, including foreign trade, multinational direct foreign investment, movements of short-term portfolio funds, technological diffusion, and cross-border migration (Bhagwati, 2004) of globalization that has captured most of the attention in recent years (Stiglitz, 2003a). Yet globalization is so much more. It is a multilayered phenomenon that embraces all dimensions of organized human life. Beyond its economic aspects, it entails security (Held, McGrew, Goldblatt and Perraton, 1999: 87–148), normative (Delmas-Marty, 1994), political, environmental (Senarclens, 1998: 143–154), and cultural dimensions (Appadurai, 1996). The cumulative effect of this state of affairs can be seen in an intertwining of the local, national, regional and global levels (Rosenau, 2003: 11).

From globalization to global governance

The fact that the world is more and more interconnected goes hand in hand with the increasing importance of global governance. In this regard, global governance as it stands, is the product of a century-long development. Although the word "governance" and the expression "good governance" became widely used only in the 1980s, initially in the context of the World Bank (see Chapter 4, this volume, by Perret), the international reality to which they refer and try to depict can be traced back to the late nineteenth century. From then onwards it has proceeded in four successive waves. The goal of the first wave of global governance before World War I was mainly to facilitate and coordinate the economic opening of national polities in order to enhance growth (James, 2001: 11–13). Following World War I, the second wave of global governance added the pursuit of international security to this goal. Eventually, it failed on both accounts (ibid.: 25–30). After World War II, the third wave of global governance, while continuing to pursue economic growth and international security, made the monitoring of the economic downsides of globalization in particular economic instability, and a better protection of civil, political, social and economic human rights other aspects of its mandates (see chapter, this volume, by de Senarclens). Following the end of the Cold War, the fourth wave of global governance remained focused on these goals. In addition, it opened global regulation to the new area of environment. Moreover, it emphasized the need to pay more attention to the democratic requirements of global governance. In the process, non-governmental organizations acquired a very significant role. As a whole, the idea of an international rule of law emerged as the overarching goal of global governance.

Global governance entails three main levels: norms, actors (or agency) and mechanisms. The normative dimension involves a whole set of norms which, in the various sectors of international life, outlines in particular the basis for rule-bound multilateral order. Norms organize systems of regulation that guide, coordinate and constraint activities and interactions, and introduce forms of accountability. At the agency level, global governance encompasses a multiplicity of actors of different nature who intervene in different realms and at different levels, use different means, and pursue relatively different ends. They include supra-national organizations (international and regional organizations), transnational entities (corporations, international networks and non-governmental organizations) national entities (states) and sub-national agencies (local networks and non-governmental organizations). As for the mechanisms of global governance, they relate to how actors act and interact within the framework established by the norms of governance, in institutional or non-institutional (that is to say formal or informal) settings.

Global governance of globalization: a double quest for legitimacy

The norms, actors and mechanisms of global governance are not as articulated and as convergent as they are in a well-functioning polity. Hence the fact that the problem of global governance is, in the words of Robert O. Keohane, "one of how the various institutions and processes of global society could be meshed more effectively, in a way that would be regarded as legitimate by attentive publics controlling access to key resources" (Keohane, 2002: 15–16).

At stake here, however, is not only the question of the legitimacy of global governance. At stake is also the legitimacy of globalization. For, to a large extent, the purpose of global governance has come to be identified as the need to minimize, beyond its positive effects (Bhagwati, 2004), the ills that globalization supposedly generates. As such, the power to make globalization (more) legitimate and to secure a strong level of legitimacy for itself rests upon the ability of global governance to tame the pathologies of globalization, as well as to enhance its benefits.

Benchmarks for a good governance of globalization

If one of the key roles of good governance is, as it is assumed in this chapter, to contribute to a more legitimate globalization, then outlining its criteria is of essence. In this perspective, on the basis of the values (expressed and defended by international norms) and best practices recognized by current scholars as the foundation and ideal, of not only good governance but also, of good democratic governance, requirements can be identified within five areas. They concern: (1) the respect and implementation of human rights, and a sense of public good; (2) the imperative of consistency; (3) the recognition of the primary role of institutional actors (first and foremost states and international organizations); (4) the necessity to achieve a credible threshold of implementation, with a special burden of responsibility and accountability put on (powerful) states; (5) and the need for norms, and actors, of governance to cope with and monitor the evolution of what is considered just at the global level.

Human rights and the global public good

The respect and implementation of core human rights as defined and agreed upon by the international instruments put in place since 1945, outline the overall end of global governance in terms of the public good (Hollenbach, 2002, ch. 1). These core rights deal with the basic security and well-being of people. They are based on two fundamental principles: equal worth and dignity of individuals – in other words, the idea that humankind belongs to a single moral realm in which each person is equally worthy of respect and consideration (Beitz, 1994); and active agency, that is to say the capacity of human beings to be in control of their lives and, consequently, the imperative to realize and secure this capacity (Held, 2004: 172). International instruments of human rights look after these core rights and principles in two major ways. First, they do so by prohibiting inhuman acts. This is, for instance, the case of the convention against genocide, the convention abolishing slavery, the convention on the elimination of racial discrimination, the convention on the suppression of apartheid, the convention against torture, and the international jurisdictions recently established to sanction violations in these areas. Second, they look after core human rights and principles by promoting the respect for human dignity on a more day-to-days basis in various aspects of social life. The international covenants on economic, social and cultural rights, and on civil and political rights, for example, treat this aspect (Cassese, 1994: 287–316).

This centrality of human rights may appear at odds with the realist focus on self-interest to which states and market actors have traditionally given much attention internationally. Yet, the classical realist primacy of self-interest in the international realm is not per se a disqualification of people's welfare as an essential benchmark. It is simply, based on the national bent of international life, a particularist rather than a universalist understanding (Anghie, 2000). Therefore, it cannot be said that the realist approach undermines human rights as a key criterion for good governance at per se the global level. This is in line with the fact that, at the most general level, social organization is made by and for human beings with the aim of securing and enhancing human life as much as possible (Aristotle, 1992; Sen, 1999; Linklater, 1998).[3] In the post-Cold War context, this state of affairs has only been furthered by the spread of democratic values (Grant and Keohane, 2005).

The imperative of consistency

Consistency is another element to factor into good global governance and its ability to contribute to a more legitimate globalization. This condition is difficult to achieve considering that wanting to have it both ways (i.e. to focus on the self-serving aspects of governance and disregard the costly ones) is a well-known temptation, especially for states. Their dual identity, being independent states while UN member states, only serves as an encouragement to pursue this path. Given their might, the temptation is particularly strong for countries at the top of the international hierarchy. Against this adverse background, consistency has to be pursued at two levels: the substantive and procedural level.

Regarding the first point, the purpose of global governance policies has to match the substantial demands of human rights. In other words, the human rights dimension of the public good should always be featured in a pre-eminent manner in the initiatives and actions of global governance. It does not have to be at the top of the "to-do list" of all actors, but it has to be the aggregated goal of their efforts. As for the procedural requirement, it amounts to the need for global governance policies to follow the guidelines emanating from the values of human rights (Taylor, 1988). The values of universality, equality and empowerment, springing from equal worth and dignity and active agency, give much significance to consent, participation and representation in the modus operandi of governance (Held, 2005: 173–177). As such, collective decision-making and collective action are vital aspects of the accountability of good global governance and, ultimately, its contribution to a more legitimate globalization. One should add that crises also serve as a test of the extent to which the power holders of global governance take human rights seriously (Schmitt, 1988, 2003; Byers, 2004). In this context, following the right procedures demonstrates the legitimacy of global governance and functions as a tool for its reinforcement.

This does not mean that consistency should be absolute. A certain level of inconsistency is probably unavoidable. Furthermore, non-compliance does not erode support for and functioning of global governance relations as long as it remains, on the one hand, marginal and rather isolated and, on the other, within the limits of acceptable and at times required flexibility. But there is a threshold for tolerating inconsistency. This threshold boils down to the fact that when there is inconsistency, it must be justified. And here "justified" means motivated by factors which are as little as possible disconnected or foreign from the reasons and guidelines offered by global governance, including multilateral rights and obligations. The inconsistency is not justified if two similar situations generate different responses due to expedience considerations. The same reasoning applies to procedural consistency.

Institutional actors as key players of good global governance

Institutional actors (states, international organizations and, increasingly, regional organizations) play a key role in the search for a consistency in global governance. They are essential for three reasons.

First, although a large number of institutional actors tend to be outrun and overshadowed by non-institutional actors, they continue to have a commanding position, domestically and in the international arena. To this day, they are a key aspect of the management of social life, nationally and globally. Second, seeing to the respect and implementation of consistency is very much one of the key missions, if not the key mission, of institutional actors. The regulatory tools at their disposal (which include the power to interpret norms), at work before action (creating an incentive for actors to follow norms), during action (fulfilling a monitoring function) and after action (associated with sanctions), are largely designed to this effect. Third, the public scrutiny under which institutional actors find themselves, exemplified by the need to justify their policies, entrusts them all the more in the role of consistency guarantors. This is especially true when democratic values, as increasingly is the case, enter into their fabric and functioning. In this regard, good global governance puts a premium on the commitment to consent, participation and representation, internally and externally. The greater the proliferation of globalization, the more important it becomes.

From the implementation of human rights to the accountability of actors of global governance

Assessing the contribution of global governance to the implementation of core human rights is an important way to measure the extent to which it fulfils its responsibilities and consequently, to make it accountable on a result basis.

Following the principles of equal worth and dignity of individuals and of active agency, the realization of human rights is meant to be universal in its scope. Among the universal beneficiaries of human rights, it is towards the individuals in dire need that the universality of human rights is first and foremost oriented. This is an illustration and a subset of the fact that democratic justice at the most general level, while being for the benefit of each and everyone, particularly looks after those individuals whose rights are denied or in jeopardy. This state of affairs, which establishes justice on a worst-case scenario basis, happens to be one of the guarantees of its extensiveness. Knowing that if the need arises they can benefit from it, people buy into the system of justice; and by supporting it, they make it a regulatory tool applicable to all (Rawls, 2001: 15–16, 97–100).[4] In the process, the possibility of experiencing a sense of community is ensured. Of course, for this to work presupposes that attending to the individuals deprived from their rights does not generate new injustices.[5]

The depth of the implementation of human rights is as important as its scope. Here two elements come to the fore. Firstly, basic violations have to be concretely addressed as they emerge. This entails preventing them as soon as they arise, fighting them when they unfold and bringing about reparations once they have occurred. However, the depth of implementation does not stop here. Stopping here would only compound people to stay in a situation of non-equal value and dignity, and non-agency. Secondly, as a result, depth of implementation calls for providing the structure required to organize life above survival lines. This includes development policies, education policies and other (Pogge, 2004).

The implementation of human rights is supposed to take place on the basis of the respective capacity and mandates of the actors of global governance. In this regard, all actors are not equal. For some, concerns of human rights are a by-product or indirect product of their activity. For others it is a priority. In this contrasted landscape, institutional actors have a primary responsibility. The fact that they are the guarantors of the public good puts them in this position.

Weak, or weaker, institutional actors have a significant responsibility in the implementation of good global governance. Not recognizing this undermines their standing in the eyes of the powerful as well as in their own. It also hampers global governance as a whole. This being said, the burden of responsibility and accountability falls particularly on powerful democratic institutional actors, especially on powerful democratic states. Their mandates, including in principle their structural commitment to the public good, and their capacity to shape the overall directions of global governance and its regulation of globalization, give them a critical role (Coicaud, 2001: 4–5).

In this regard, the United States holds an unparalleled role and responsibility. It is also what makes it more globally accountable than any other state. The systemic consequences of this situation should be neither mistaken nor overlooked: the matchless power of the United States leads to the evaluation of global governance and of its impact on globalization amounting, to a certain extent, to an appraisal of the overall legitimacy of America's international standing and of the world order (including disorders and inequalities) that it largely endorses (Brzezinski, 2004).

As for international organizations and regional organizations (and regional groupings in one form or another), they may have acquired a growing importance in the global governance of globalization in recent decades. They may also increasingly constrain states. Nevertheless, states continue to call the shots. The fact that the influence of international organizations largely depends upon the backing that they receive from (powerful) states is a case in point. The same applies at the regional level of organization. Short of powerful countries serving as their backbones, regional organizations are destined to be rather ineffective (see chapter, this volume, by Ali Kazancigil).

Governance and the evolution of justice at the global level

Core human rights and people's expectations associated with them are products of history. What they are today is the outgrowth of a long evolution. This evolution is not going to stop. The ability of the norms and institutions of global governance to accompany this evolution is therefore a key component of their legitimacy (Coicaud, 2007a). This makes it imperative for governance, in its management of globalization, to factor in as much as possible the changing character of what is globally viewed as right or just.

This is easier said than done. The more challenging the situations that the norms and actors (especially institutional actors) of global governance have to tackle are, the more the questions arise: How to balance status quo and change? Where to place the cutting point between what can be brought to the global governance agenda, and what has to be left out? To what extent should the international community be firm or flexible in the interpretation and implementation of the rights associated with the values and goals of global governance? To what extent should it be firm or flexible so that, on the one hand, these rights are not betrayed and on the other, the actors of global governance, in particular member states, stay on board and continue to perceive themselves as stakeholders?

The socialization of the international realm pursued within the global governance framework of multilateralism introduces a dynamic of change which helps answering these questions. Arguably, the legitimizing principles of multilateral governance have a strong democratic outlook. The rights and obligations attached illustrate as well as feed and deepen this evolution. They initiate a process which calls for more legitimacy and empowerment. It serves as a guideline, first to identify how the sense of what is right (at the global level) is evolving and second to generate the political capital (political will) needed to back it up.

This is what accounts for the fact that, over time, the dynamics of legitimacy and empowerment has modified the sense of international justice embedded in the key criteria, and principles, of good global governance. The extension and deepening of mandates that can be noticed in the successive waves of global governance alluded to earlier are a case in point. And so is the fact that today states are no longer the sole and primary actors and rights carriers at the international level.

The rights that states enjoy and the duties and responsibilities that fall upon them more than before derive from the individual level, from the ability of states to respect and fulfil individual and human rights. From previously being quasi-absolute rights, neither challenged nor questioned, rights of nations (or rights of nation-states) are becoming conditional. They tend to partly depend upon the willingness and capacity of states to fulfil the duties and responsibilities that come with democratic rights, particularly with human rights.[6]

In the transformation of quasi-absolute rights into qualified and therefore challengeable rights, powerful democratic nations occupy a centre role. It is, by and large, under their political and normative leadership that this process has taken place and continues to unfold. Ultimately, as a result, whether or not powerful and democratically minded Western nations are consistent with, and abide by, the constraints of good global governance in the conduct of their foreign policy is of primary importance. It shapes the extent and limits of the validity of their claim to be the models, depositories and key instruments of (democratic) legitimacy and empowerment, nationally and internationally. Their attitude becomes an indication of the extent to which the world should or should not believe them and embrace the international order (including the system of global governance and globalization) that they underwrite.

Assessing the gap between reality and the benchmarks of good governance of globalization

The benchmarks of good global governance outlined above are far more prescriptive than descriptive. This is because the gap between them and the reality of governance of globalization is a very significant one. This is what comparing reality to the criteria of good global governance shows.

A low commitment to the global public good and human rights

At the global level, the sense of the public good is elusive. The shallow and loose character of the global community explains this state of affairs. Short of people socially integrated at the global level, short of individual identification with the idea of the global community, and short of channels of representation and participation and of decision-makers being held accountable at this level, the pursuit of the global public good suffers. The fact that institutional actors are unable (not surprisingly considering the lack of global community) to bring the variety of actors and activities of global governance together under one roof further accounts for the tenuous impact of the idea of the global public good. In this regard, international organizations, in principle one of the major tools and expressions of global governance, are largely under-equipped to play a regulating, let alone an integrating role efficiently. Three shortcomings are particularly imposing: lack of a straight line of representation, participation and accountability between international organizations and ordinary people (disconnecting those who are meant to be the ultimate beneficiaries from the policy-makers); disparity among the mandates of international organizations (the value goals of the United Nations are not, for instance, entirely compatible with the ones of the World Trade Organization); and relative scarcity of means (financial, logistic and other). These limitations are less at work in international organizations with technical (and therefore relatively narrow) mandates, but they are very much a factor for the ones with holistic and all-encompassing mandates, such as the United Nations.

The elusive character of the public good at the global level translates into a thin commitment to human rights. The ways in which humanitarian crises were handled in the 1990s is one illustration among many of the limited dedication to human rights.

The period created a pressure for the key actors of the United Nations Security Council – principally the United States, the United Kingdom and France. Unfolding humanitarian crises could no longer be ignored. Something had to be done. However, the incentive to address these crises remained relatively low. The de facto lack of international legal obligation to stop massive human rights violations turned out to be convenient (Schabas, 2000: 545–546).[7] It was echoed in the reluctance of the three Western powers to engage fully in the international realm for reasons other than mainstream international peace and security matters (Coicaud, 2007a). When confronted with extending solidarity and responsibility at the global level for non-traditional strategic reasons, they advocated international involvement. But their defence of human rights beyond borders never prevailed over national priorities, over what they felt they owed to their nationals. Balancing the moral, political and legal obligations, the three Western permanent members of the Security Council recognized the growing obligations that the international community holds towards individuals beyond borders, whoever and wherever they are. Yet, in the end, the community of the national realm continued to overshadow the universal community.

Inconsistency of global governance

Lack of consistency is a major weakness of global governance today. This is not surprising considering that the enforcement capacity of the norms and institutions of global governance is strong and seriously acted upon only in a few areas, such as trade, and by a few institutional actors, for example powerful states, powerful regional organizations (the European Union) and powerful international organizations (WTO). Beyond these few areas and actors, consistency tends to rely mainly on good will or on moral grounds not backed by systematically enforced law. This makes for weak guarantees, rarely met by deeds (Coicaud, 2007a).[8]

Furthermore, the areas where enforcement is strongest tend to be the ones in which powerful actors have vested interest to ensure compliance. This is in line with the fact that the restricted capacity of global governance to enforce consistency is deepened by the constant temptation facing its powerful backers to in their advantage conceive and implement consistency in a very inconsistent way. In this regard, the most powerful democratic states may have played a key role in the establishment of multilateralism and international organizations, including their democratic aspects. They may also continue to be essential to their development. But they are equally prone to bend multilateralism and international organizations in their favour. For powerful democratic states the practice of double standards, insisting to have less powerful countries abide by rules that they themselves overlook whenever suitable, is "fair play". As such, they both underwrite and undermine the principle of reciprocity, of equal rights and duties around which, the multilateral system is supposedly built.

The promotion of a double standard attitude in international trade is a telling example of this state of affairs. The most important expectation of poor countries in the Uruguay Round of international trade negotiations (1986–1994) was that rich countries would open their agriculture and textile markets. However, the results have been largely disappointing. Through a variety of instruments, protection in richer countries remains extremely high. Their trade policies are highly discriminatory against the agricultural and textile products produced in the poorest countries. Higher tariffs are applied to agricultural goods and simple manufactures, the very products that developing countries produce and export. For instance, Bangladesh exports about US$2.4 billion to the United States each year and pays 14 per cent in tariffs while France exports more than US$30 billion and pays 1 per cent in tariffs. The poorest countries often also face tariff escalation if they try to process their exports rather than simply export primary products (UNDP, 2003: 154–155). In other words, it is a system of generalized hypocrisy (Trade Imbalances, 2005).[9]

The inadequacies of the actors of global governance

One of the crucial shortcomings of global governance is the inability of institutional actors to cope with the downsides of globalization. They are on the defensive vis-à-vis the private economic forces which drive globalization forward. Not only are states and international organizations often unable to monitor globalization and contain its pathologies, but at times they are also accused of contributing to, and therefore being the accomplices of these pathologies. The anti-Seattle movement certainly has to be seen in this light (Pianta, 2001).[10]

In light of the limitations of the institutional actors of global governance, much importance has in recent years been given to the rise of non-governmental organizations (NGOs) and civil society at the global level. Institutional actors have themselves made an effort to make these part and parcel with their mechanisms. The United Nations is still looking for ways to improve its relationships with non-governmental actors (United Nations, 2004). The Global Compact initiative, aiming at making transnational corporations socially more responsible and the UN more relevant in the business world, has to be viewed as part of this effort (www.unglobalcompact.org/Portal/Default.asp). These developments are very laudable. But they tend to address the representation and participation problems of global governance more in the margins than at the core. Disenfranchisement continues to be a worldwide issue. This is especially the case since the attempts of bringing NGOs and civil society on board often leave hanging not only the question of their own representation, but also the one of their accountability (Bell and Coicaud, 2006; see also, the chapter, this volume, by Woods).

The thin (in scope and depth) implementation of the value-goals of global governance

Basic facts suffice to show how ample the gap is between the human right value-goals of global governance and reality. Development is a domain as good as any other to illustrate this point.

The preamble of the United Nations Charter makes the promotion of social progress and better standards of life one of the main objectives of the post-World War II order (Charter of the United Nations 1945). In this context, over time, the World Bank has identified the eradication of poverty as one of its key aims. The present situation tells us how far we still are from achieving these goals. Among the figures quoted by the 2003 *Human Development Report*, we can read that the richest 1 per cent of the world population receives as much as the poorest 57 per cent; or that the 25 million richest Americans have as much income as almost 2 billion of the world's poorest people. Moreover, in many countries inequality in assets, and especially income, appears to be on the rise. It is estimated, for instance, that between the 1980s and the mid- to late 1990s, inequality increased in 53 countries (Cornia, Addison and Kiiski, 2004: 41).

This state of affairs is partly due to misguided public policies although in principle, public policy is meant to look after the public good, including sustainable (or equitable) development taking the needs of the poorest into account. Analyses seem to indeed show that worldwide, particularly in developing countries, public spending in domains as essential as education and health is frequently geared towards the rich (or at least the middle class) rather than towards the poor (UNDP, 2002: 59–60; Stewart and Wang, 2003).

Global governance and the defence of the status quo

Finally, global governance does not demonstrate much adaptability, nor ability, to change. The apparent incapacity of the United Nations system to improve its functioning hampers its aptitude to achieve its self-assigned goals in terms of development (Millennium Development Goals). The last wave of institutional reform (including the reform of the Security Council) initiated by the UN Secretary-General is, following the disappointing outcomes of the UN World Summit of September 2005, failing to bring about a deep transformation of the United Nations. These are some of the signs that the norms and institutions of global governance are more committed to the status quo than to anything else.

This commitment of global governance to the status quo does not necessarily mean a rejection of any change. After all, global governance accompanies the profound transformations associated with globalization. But it certainly seems quite opposed to changes that would ease the existing political and economic global inequalities and, more decisively, challenge the privileged position of those benefiting from these inequalities.

Closing the gap between reality and the benchmarks of good governance?

The track record of the global governance of globalization is far from being entirely negative. In the past 50 years, if the multilateral system of global governance has shown much rigidity, it has also shown much flexibility and capacity to bring on board the evolving demands of international life. If it has had the tendency to align itself with the status quo, it has also been a formidable instrument of change. If it has been prone to support discriminatory and exclusionary policies, it has also been an embracing and inclusive mechanism of management of international life. Even though the progressive characteristics of the system of global governance may have taken place at times more from a normative point of view (with the caveat that not all the normative regulatory work of global governance has been progressive: certain aspects of the World Trade Organization are a case in point (Howse, 2001; Porter, Sauvé, Subramanian and Zampetti, 2001) than from a political and operational one, it is hard to deny their reality.

Despite this, however, as we just saw in the previous section, the gap between the criteria of good global governance and reality remains large. So the question is: what can be done to bridge the gap? To answer this question, one can envisage two types of changes: attitudinal changes, and greater pressure exercised on institutional actors to increase the likelihood of these attitudinal changes happening.

Attitudinal changes required

The attitudinal changes required are fourfold. They entail: furthering the public policy dimension of global governance, in particular its progressive aspects (with primarily the pursuit of human rights); making the case for a more legitimate global governance of globalization from a security point of view; harmonizing relations between the norms of governance and globalization; and balancing power and principles at the international level.

Strengthening the public policy dimension of global governance

Global governance is to some extent an exercise of public policy. Yet, global governance as an exercise of public policy suffers from a low level of implementation (from a legal and operational standpoint) mainly because of the national bent of international life and of the particularist rather than universalist policies that it favours. This is especially the case when it comes to human rights. The global governance support of human rights frequently ends up being only a matter of morally doing the right thing. While a moral impulse to act is better than nothing, it tends to be very weak. Indeed, when doing the right thing is essentially a matter of moral judgement, that is, when it does not benefit from a systematic application by law, its implementation is destined to be problematic. It does not profit from the social and political qualities associated with law. In particular, it does not proceed along a predictable course of action. One cannot count on the right thing happening. Its occurrence is largely a voluntary matter, and a question of choice where it is essentially up to international actors, especially state actors, to act morally or not. In this context, more often than not, inaction prevails over action. This is all the more the case considering that the controversies often generated by a moral justification for action (due to a lack of legal backing) lead institutional actors to adopt a rather conservative course. This is what happened with the humanitarian interventions of the 1990s.

This state of affairs is a far cry from a form of good governance which, as a public policy of solidarity, would not just build upon moral considerations but go beyond them, fully recognizing the need to have human rights structure a sense of solidarity at the global level. A form of good governance would also institutionalize and routinize the implementation of human rights in a significant manner through redistribution and enforcement mechanisms truly embedded in law[0] (Atkinson, 2005).

The quest for security and a more legitimate global governance of globalization

At a time when public policies of solidarity tend to be dismantled and replaced by "police" approaches in developed countries (Bauman, 2004: 51–52), how can we hope that global governance will become more of a public policy approach in the service of human rights? This is where calling for a better global governance by alluding to the link between rule of law and security come into play.

Although the link that a credible global rule of law establishes between greater solidarity and global security remains largely unexplored,[11] it is a rather straightforward one. Its initial appeal lies in the fact that obsession with security is, to this day, the most likely incentive to encourage member states to pay attention and rally together. Against this background, the link amounts to the fact that making solidarity a very secondary global concern, and not an integral part of international policy reasoning and implementation, puts global security itself at risk. For as much as it is the case at the national level, at the international level the rights of all are not secured when the rights of individuals are not fully recognized and protected. Unless an actor feels that the context in which he operates and through which he interacts with other actors attempts to look after his personal rights, as well as what is morally right, and does it reasonably well, the risk is that he will feel that he does not owe much to other actors and the social arrangements and political institutions that preside over their relations, except what prudence commands for his own survival. The feeling that hardly anything is owed will deepen if the social and political setting appears to unduly favour others. No "tranquillity of spirit" (Montesquieu, 1989: 157), so to speak, can be expected for each and everyone. Even the powerful are not immune in this state of affairs. As the power of the powerful gives them great responsibility in the shortcomings (unfairness) of the political and social arrangements, they (the powerful) are prone to be a target of resentment and acts of violence by those who feel cheated by the system. Thus the concentration of power tends to become self-defeating for the powerholder(s).

How economic inequality is prone to bring insecurity serves as a case in point. When economic growth is shared, when it is envisioned and implemented in solidarity terms, one of its aims is to reduce inequalities and widen as much as possible the circle of its beneficiaries. In the process, closing the gap between rich and poor generates a public good. This public good is at the same time both the good which is exchanged among people and the element that allows the actual exchange. Security, the relatively peaceful interactions among actors, is one aspect of this public good. The picture is quite different when economic growth is self-centred or minimally social, that is to say when it is more geared towards enduring discrimination than enhancing inclusion. Insecurity tends to be one of its by-products. The unsettling impact of inequalities leads to a contesting of the social arrangements that preside over them. Ultimately, insecurity, by preventing new stable markets to be established locally, diminishes the scope and fairness of economic growth, which in turn only further deepens insecurity. Over time, local tensions become a fertile ground for the nurturing and spread of threats. The violation of people's rights, made all the more visible by the dynamics of globalization itself, and the challenge of the "international order of things", go hand in hand. Being on the lookout within and among societies can turn into a full-time job, and a common fate.

Improving relations between the national and international norms of governance

The harmonization of relations between the norms of governance is destined to improve the global governance of globalization. Harmonization does not mean promoting the full integration of the normative regimes existing in the various areas (political, economic, cultural areas, and others) of activity worldwide. The fact that diversity of cultures and levels of development and national sovereignty shape international life, and that they will and should continue to do so, is a reason that militates against this. Nevertheless, global governance can certainly do better than the fragmented and disarticulated normative system currently displayed. Doing better implies revisiting the relations of competition, compatibility, juxtaposition and hierarchy between national and international norms.

Revisiting the relations of competition and compatibility between norms should not amount to choosing one over the other. Both are essential – that is, as long as their interactions are inhabited, beyond their specificities, by an overall convergence and coherence of purpose, especially when it comes to the core norms. The relationship of juxtaposition should not amount to a solo style of management, for this hampers interaction and, consequently, limits good global governance (Ost and van de Kerchove, 2002). As a whole, the relationships between norms should place the public good and human rights at the top of the global governance hierarchy, certainly more than is the case today. In this context, human rights should benefit from appropriate incentives and enforcement mechanisms. At a minimum, all regimes of norms should, in one way or another, contribute to the realization of this goal. Achieving this should not necessarily be the main concern of all the regimes of norms. But, to be seen as embodying a sense of legitimacy, none of them should be in contradiction with it, and each of them, based on their respective domains, should contribute to its realization.

Balancing power and principles at the international level

Bridging the gap between power and principles in the global realm is a manifold enterprise. As a start, it calls for having some of the key actors buying into the improvement of global governance agency and, as such, changing the ways in which they relate to the international realm. This is the case of the United States, the European Union, leading Asian countries, and developing countries. Developed nations have contributed in a very significant manner to the past and present shape of global governance and globalization. It is likely that they will continue to do so in the future. The extent to which global governance of globalization will respond to the demands of legitimacy better largely depends therefore on how these actors behave in the years to come. As for developing countries, their role has to go beyond being simply at the receiving end of global governance and globalization.

- Changing the ways of the United States vis-à-vis global governance and globalization: The overwhelming power of the United States also turns out to be a weakness. It leads to seeing the United States as a major cause of what is faulty in globalization and global governance. The necessity to rectify this perception, and the reality that it encompasses, calls for the introduction of at least three changes in US foreign policy. First, there is the need for a better balance between US national interests and global interests. A discretionary conception and use of its power leads the United States to deprive itself of one of the main instruments at its disposal in order to achieve what should be its principal goal: to generate a consensus based upon and around its preponderance. It deprives the US of the possibility to make its preponderance part of a system of international justice, and therefore projecting itself as just. Second, the United States has to take seriously the constraint that democratic values impose upon its foreign policy. A systematic self-serving American approach to global governance (and globalization) is an invitation to more one-sided attitudes. In the process, it is not only the validity claim of the structure of the international system that runs the risk of being undermined, it is also the democratic values and ideas which are meant to be part of its foundation (Coicaud, 2002: Preface).[12] Third, the American leadership should keep in mind that, at best, as envisioned in the most inclusive and democratic understanding of global governance, good governance makes for the promotion of a fair access to goods in connection with key international rights (be they political, economic and/or social rights) the overarching goal.
- Improving the European contribution to global governance: The European Union and its key countries are always eager to present themselves as the most committed to internationalist global policies (in the context of the UN system and beyond). This commitment is, however, not as genuine as it claims to be. First, there is a strong attachment to the status quo. Europe's insistence on negotiated solutions is at times a way of hiding its uneasiness with rapid and drastic changes. This has been proven time and again since the end of World War II. Somehow one could even argue that in the past 50 years it is essentially in the context of the European project that major Western European powers

have demonstrated and invested most of their historico-political imagination and boldness. Beyond this, Europe has shown much timidity.
Second, when it comes to global governance and the establishment of
fair rules of the game, the European Union is as eager as the United
States to put forward self-serving policies. The trade policies supported
by the European Union match those of the United States in terms of
global unfairness. Third, the tense relationship that has developed in
recent years between the US and the European Union may have less
to do with their differences in ways of envisioning and implementing
the global public good – the European vision of global governance and
globalization presents itself as more progressive and "selfless" than the
American one – and more with the pursuit of European self-interest.
Against this background, European attitudes need to be altered. One
way would be for Europe to play a more important role in bridging the
gap between the United States and the rest of the world. For instance,
rather than being simply another and less militaristic version of the contemporary West, compared to the US, could Europe bring the concerns
of the developing countries to the United States, and to the developing
countries the concerns of America? Could it help the two sides of the
development divide, in the context of the UN and others, to ease the
tensions that keep them apart?

- What role should Asia have in the future of global governance? Asian
  countries (above all the other leading ones) have a key role to play in
  the future of global governance. But the challenges that they are facing
  are somewhat different from those of the major Western powers. The
  conceptual, normative, political and operational management of the
  global realm is still very much a transatlantic affair. While it is not so
  much the case in global economic affairs, it is largely so in other areas
  – the United States and Europe together continue to enjoy the lion's
  share. If trying to realize the inclusive dimensions of global governance
  and globalization is going to become a truly global matter (not simply a
  Western project and projection), and a more legitimate one, Asia has
  to be increasingly involved. Asia serves as a bridge between developing
  and developed countries, the West and the non-West. The fact that it is
  the only other global region besides Europe and the USA puts it in an
  ideal position to make a significant contribution to the management of
  global order. The fact that the successful Asian countries have been
  able to make a comeback after having been rolled over by Western imperialism gives them this responsibility.

- The role of developing countries in global governance: Developing
  countries also have a card to play. This presupposes going beyond the
  combination of the victim and entitlement mentality, which is at times
  adopted. It is not enough for them to simply be either at the receiving

end of global governance and globalization or in a reactive mode to these, as it helps neither them nor the international community. Being weaker should not make them helpless and hopeless. It is often an up-hill battle for leaders of developing nations to make the case for their country, but the need to be respected should encourage them to redou-ble efforts. Both the fulfilment of their responsibilities at home and their international efforts to have the rights of their country taken into account are essential to their contribution to a better global gover-nance system. In particular, a great deal of progress will have been made when, in the developing world, rulers understand that taking the interests of their people truly to heart (i.e. respecting their civil, politi-cal, economic and social rights) is the best way to defend the national interest of their country, as well as to ensure their meaningful partici-pation to the globalizing world.

Democratic pressure as a tool for change

What are the chances for the changes recommended to take place? One has to concede that they are rather slim for three reasons: one concerns US foreign policy; another has to do with the attitude of UN member states; a third one concerns what seems to be the lack of overall view and thinking on the problems at hand.

US foreign policy in the post-Cold War era, and even more so since 2001, tends to be very far from the directions advocated here. Given the centrality of the United States, this can only have an impact on the evo-lution of the international system. In the short term, this will continue to make it difficult to mitigate the tensions existing between the United States and an inclusive conception and management of the norms and institutions of global governance and of their relations to globalization. Beyond 2008 and the second Bush administration, the evolution of American foreign policy is unlikely to give reasons for optimism. After all, Bush's foreign policy is not simply an aberration in the history of US foreign policy. To a certain extent, it is a radical version of the traditional characteristics of American foreign policy and its relations with the rest of the world, characteristics now "in our face".

The tendency of other member states to take the back seat is another obstacle. Ultimately, very few of them, including the Europeans, appear willing to invest much energy and capital to address the current short-comings of global governance and globalization at the collective level. At the level of the United Nations system in particular, there is hardly any serious desire to have the discussions on how to trigger profound change followed by real action. It seems that for most member states, in-cluding the critics of the current international situation, getting by is a good enough option. As the UN World Summit of September 2005 showed, it is difficult to find a common denominator on marginal changes and even more so on more central changes.

Finally, if a lot of people agree on the fact that there is something wrong with the multiple pathologies unfolding nationally and internationally, if a lot of people agree on the fact that the neo-liberal model of development has a role in the growing social, economic and political inequalities and disorders, few seem to have much of a clear and concrete vision on the ways to, in a comprehensive manner, address the problems. Surely the fact that the increased connectedness among societies and spheres of activity is adding levels of complexity is not making this task easy. Hence, it is as if we were living in the most knowledge-based society ever, and yet without the intellectual tools to figure out how to overcome the crisis-like situation that we are facing. It is as if experts and scholars, let alone politicians, were muted, more or less condemned to recognize that the situation is out of control and that they do not have much of a clue of how to fix it.

Does it mean that we should throw in the towel? Does it mean that we should accept the unfolding disorders as a fact of life, while concluding that nothing much can be done? The difficulty in comprehending the complexities of the mechanisms of global governance and globalization, and the problems associated with them, make it tempting to follow this route. On the other hand, running away from the crisis is hardly a solution. So, what to do?

Even though it cannot be seen in any way as a magic bullet, putting pressure on the key actors of governance and globalization, be it states, international organizations or corporations, as a way to force them as much as possible to abide by democratic norms and values, can help.

In that regard, civil society and non-governmental organizations have proved that they can play a decisive role. The fact that opposing the pathologies of globalization has become a key aspect of non-governmental organizations' work is making them a valuable contributor to a more democratic globalization. As such, NGOs turn out to be the beneficiaries of the world openness, a factor contributing to globalization, and a critic of its shortcomings. This is illustrated by the fact that trade and financial policies, and their social consequences, have been a particular concern for anti-capitalist oriented non-governmental organizations. Provided that non-governmental organizations address honestly their own problems of governance, this significant role is destined to grow stronger in the coming years. The reasons for this are multifold. They include the counter-balance function of non-governmental organizations, the type of collective mobilization that they constitute, their attractiveness for young people, the importance that women have in NGOs, and the alliance between new technologies and non-governmental organizations.

Conclusion

At the core of the ambitions of global governance and globalization is the idea of empowerment. In principle, both are about creating more opportunities for as many people as possible on a global scale. However, the limitations of global governance and the downsides of globalization hamper the realization of this idea. In the process, rather than being engines of a liberating movement, global governance and globalization run the risk of becoming the driving forces of a debilitating social arrangement, an arrangement all the more debilitating that it is often presented as without a viable alternative.

Global governance and globalization are not going away. In all likelihood, they will be among the shaping factors of the twenty-first century. Looking for ways to overcome their pathologies is consequently an essential task. This task amounts to make power at the global level, in whatever forms, responsible and accountable. It also amounts to putting capitalism at the service of democracy, and not the other way around.[13] In outlining criteria of a good global governance of globalization, indicating how the reality is far from implementing them seriously and offering some suggestions to close the gap, we have tried to identify areas in which global governance and globalization have to progress in order to achieve greater legitimacy and allow people to be more in control of their lives. Only the future can tell, if one is a pure idealist, or delusional, to think that this could happen.

Notes

1. This chapter has benefited from the comments of Pierre de Senarclens, Ali Kazancigil, Jibecke Jönsson, Laura Gomez and Hélène Gandois. The author also wishes to thank the two anonymous peer reviewers for their comments.
2. "Globalization, at its simplest, refers to a shift or transformation in the scale of human organization that links distant communities and expands the reach of power relations across the world's regions. This shift can be mapped by examining the expanding scale, growing magnitude, speeding up and deepening impact of transcontinental flows and patterns of interaction."
3. Historically and philosophically it is less the fact that the organization of the social realm aims at servicing people which has been a matter of debates and struggles, than the difficulty of agreeing upon how wide the circle of beneficiaries should be and how

the benefits should be shared. In this regard, the debates and struggles regarding the organization of society cannot be dissociated from an anthropological vision. The ways in which an anthropological vision influences the dilemmas of hierarchy and equality, of universality and particularism colour the political organization of society.

4. See John Rawls (2001) and his notion of "veil of ignorance" according to his theory of justice:

> In the original position, the parties are not allowed to know the social positions or the particular comprehensive doctrines of the person they represent. They also do not know persons' race and ethnic group, sex, or various native endowments such as strength and intelligence, all within the normal range. We express these limits on information figuratively by saying the parties are behind a veil of ignorance. One reason why the original position must abstract from the contingencies – the particular features and circumstances of persons – within the basic structure is that the conditions for a fair agreement for free and equal persons ... must eliminate the bargaining advantages that inevitably arise over time within society as a result of cumulative social and historical tendencies. 'To persons according to their threat advantage' (or their *de facto* political power, or wealth, or native endowments) is not the basis for political justice.

5. A well-functioning system of justice has a threefold benefit: it brings reparation to the victim; it allows the victim to move away from the temptation of becoming a perpetrator (when an injustice is not repaired, there is a chance that the victim will act on its own, encouraging as such the cycle of violence); each time justice is rendered, the system of justice is reinforced.

6. The qualification (conditionality) of rights of nations does not amount to advocating the liquidation and disappearance of these rights, or of nations themselves. Nation-states are going to remain for the time being one of the corner stones of international life and of the attempts to socialize it. Their rights constitute therefore an enduring value, and a key element of the socialization of international life, of international legitimacy and empowerment. Nevertheless, by no longer making the basic requirements of existence and coexistence of nation-states the sole pillar of international socialization, the conditionality of rights of nations deepens the impact of democratic legitimacy and empowerment within and among nations.

7. "Perhaps the greatest unresolved question in the Convention is the meaning of the enigmatic word 'prevent'. The title of the Convention indicates that its scope involves prevention of the crime, and, in article I, State parties undertake to prevent genocide. Aside from article VIII, which entitles State parties to apply to the relevant organs of the United Nations for the prevention of genocide, the Convention has little specific to say on the question. The obligation to prevent genocide is a blank sheet awaiting the inscriptions of State practice and case law. A conservative interpretation of the provision requires States only to enact appropriate legislation and to take other measures to ensure that genocide does not occur. A more progressive view requires States to take action not just within their own borders but outside them, activity that may go as far as the use of force in order to prevent the crime being committed. The debate on this is unresolved, and is likely to remain so, at least until the next episode of genocide, if there is no insistence that the subject be clarified."

8. As the reluctance to address humanitarian crises showed in the 1990s, doing the right thing is less likely to happen when it is primarily a matter of good will than when it is institutionalized.

9. Joseph Stiglitz (2003b) reminded the trade ministers preparing for their Cancún meeting in September 2003 that the average subsidy per cow "matches the two dollars per day

poverty level on which billions of people barely subsist", whereas America's four billion dollars worth of cotton subsidies paid to 25,000 well-off farmers "bring misery to ten million African farmers and more than offset the US's miserly aid to some of the affected countries".

10. What came to be known as the "battle of Seattle" epitomized the ability of civil society to challenge the "Washington consensus".

11. At a recent session of the United Nations System Chief Executives Board (CEB) for Coordination, a senior UN official was noting, rightfully so, that the importance of the connection between solidarity and security is not stressed enough at the global level.

12. From a general point of view, democratic values encourage and integrate as much as possible an evolving distribution of power. In democracy, legitimate power is not meant to be the property or monopoly of anyone. Power – political, economic, social power – is to circulate and to be, in principle, accessible to everyone. Asymmetry in the distribution of power and the benefits – political, economic, social – attached to it tend to be acceptable as long as those in power are not using them to create monopolies and prevent others, potential and real competitors, from mounting a challenge and empowering themselves. At the global level, taking democratic values, and rights, seriously calls for the most powerful actors, the United States to begin with, to abide by the policy and political implications of this state of affairs.

13. Putting democracy at the service of capitalism not only eliminates democracy but also weakens the progressive and positive aspects of capitalism.

REFERENCES

Anghie, Antony (2000) "Time present and time past: Globalization, international financial institutions, and the Third World", *New York University Journal of International Law and Politics* 32(2) Winter.

Appadurai, Arjun (1996) *Modernity at Large: Cultural Dimensions of Globalization*, Minneapolis MN: University of Minnesota Press.

Aristotle (1992) *The Politics*, Trevor J. Saunders and T.A. Sinclair (trans.), London, UK: Penguin Books.

Atkinson, A.B. (ed.) (2005) *New Sources of Development Finance*, Oxford: Oxford University Press (UNU-WIDER Studies in Development Economics).

Bauman, Zygmunt (2004) *Wasted Lives. Modernity and its Outcasts*, Cambridge, UK: Polity Press.

Beitz, Charles C. (1994) "Cosmopolitan liberalism and the states system", in Chris Brown (ed.) *Political Restructuring in Europe: Ethical Perspectives*, London, UK: Routledge.

Bell, Daniel A. and Coicaud Jean-Marc (eds.) (2006) *Ethics in Action*, Cambridge, UK: Cambridge University Press.

Bhagwati, Jagdish (2004) *In Defense of Globalization*, Oxford: Oxford University Press.

Brzezinski, Zbigniew (2004) *The Choice: Global Domination or Global Leadership*, New York NY: Basic Books.

Byers, Michael (2004) "Agreeing to disagree: Security Council Resolution 1441 and intentional ambiguity", *Global Governance: A Review of Multilateralism and International Organizations* 10(2) April–June.

Cassese, Antonio (1994) *International Law in a Divided World*, Oxford, UK: Oxford University Press.

Coicaud, Jean-Marc (2001) "Reflections on the extent and limits of contemporary international ethics", in Jean-Marc Coicaud and Daniel Warner (eds.) *Ethics and International Affairs: Extent and Limits*, Tokyo, New York, Paris: United Nations University Press.

————— (2002) "Legitimacy, democratic legitimacy and transition in China", Preface in Chinese edn., Dong Xinping and Wang Yuanfei (trans.) *Legitimacy and Politics: A Contribution to the Study of Political Right and Political Responsibility*, Beijing: Central Compilation and Translation Press.

————— (2007a) *The Politics of International Solidarity*, Toshiro Ikemura (Japanese trans.), Tokyo: Fujiwara Shoten.

————— (2007b) "Transcendence without transcendence: the historicity of international law and the quest for just order", in Hilary Charlesworth and Jean-Marc Coicaud (eds.) *Fault Lines of International Legitimacy* (forthcoming), Tokyo, New York, Paris: United Nations University Press.

Cornia, Giovanni, Andrea, Addison, Tony and Kiiski, Sampsa (2004) "Income distribution changes and their impact in the post-Second World War period", in Giovanni Andrea Cornia (eds.) *Inequality, Growth, and Poverty in an Era of Liberalization and Globalization*, Oxford, UK: Oxford University Press.

Delmas-Marty, Mireille (1994) *Pour un droit commun*, Paris: Ed. du Seuil.

Grant, Ruth W. and Keohane, Robert (2005) "Accountability and abuses of power in world politics", *American Political Science Review* 99(1) February.

Gruzinski, Serge (2004) *Les quatre parties du monde: Histoire d'une mondialisation*, Paris: Ed. La Martiniére.

Held, David (2004) *Global Covenant: the Social Democratic Alternative to the Washington Consensus*, Cambridge UK: Polity Press.

Held, David, McGrew, Anthony, Goldblatt, David and Perraton, Jonathan (1999) *Global Transformations: Politics, Economics and Culture*, Stanford CA: Stanford University Press.

Hollenbach, David S.J. (2002) *The Common Good and Christian Ethics*, Cambridge UK: Cambridge University Press.

Howse, Robert (2001) "The legitimacy of the World Trade Organization", in Jean-Marc Coicaud and Veijo Heiskanen (eds.) *The Legitimacy of International Organizations*, Tokyo, New York, Paris: United Nations University Press.

James, Harold (2001) *The End of Globalization: Lessons from the Great Depression*, Cambridge MA: Harvard University Press.

Keohane, Robert O. (2002) *Power and Governance in a Partially Globalized World*, London UK: Routledge.

Linklater, Andrew (1998) *The Transformation of Political Community: Ethical Foundations of the Post-Westphalian Era*, Columbia SC: University of South Carolina Press.

Montbrial, Thierry de and Moreau Defarges, Philippe (2005) *Les faces cachées de la mondialistation (Rapport annuel mondial sur le système économique et les stratégies)*, Paris: Ed. Dunod.

Montesquieu (1989) *The Spirit of the Laws*, Anne M. Cohler, Basia C. Miller and Harold Stone (trans.), Cambridge UK: Cambridge University Press (reprint).

Ost, François and Kerchove, Michel van de (2002) *De la Pyramide aux réseaux? Pour une théeorie dialectique du droit*, Brussels: Publications des Facultés universitaires de Saint-Louis.

Pianta, Mario (2001) "Parallel summits of global civil society", in Helmut Anheier, Marlies Glasius and Mary Kaldor (eds.) *Global Civil Society 2001*, Oxford UK: Oxford University Press.

Pogge, Thomas W. (2004) *World Poverty and Human Rights: Cosmopolitan Responsibilities and Reforms*, Cambridge UK: Polity Press.

Porter, Roger B., Sauvé, Pierre, Subramanian, Arvind and Zampetti, Americo Beviglia (eds.) (2001) *Efficiency, Equity, and Legitimacy. The Multilateral Trading System at the Millennium*, Washington DC: Brookings Institution Press.

Rawls, John (2001) *Justice as Fairness: A Restatement*, Erin Kelly (ed.), Cambridge MA: Harvard University Press.

Rosenau, James N. (2003) *Distant Proximities: Dynamics beyond Globalization*, Princeton NJ: Princeton University Press.

Schabas, William A. (2000) *Genocide in International Law*, Cambridge UK: Cambridge University Press.

Schmitt, Carl (1988) *Crisis of Parliamentary Democracy: Studies in Contemporary German Social Thought*, Ellen Kennedy (trans.), Cambridge MA: MIT Press.

Schmitt, Carl (2003[1952]) *Nomos of the Earth in the International Law of Jus Publicum Europeaum*, G.L. Ulmen (trans.), New York NY: Telos Press.

Sen, Amartya (1999) *Development as Freedom*, New York NY: Random House.

Senarclens, Pierre de (1998) *Mondialisation, Souveraineté et théories des relations internationales*, Paris: Armand Colin.

Stewart, Frances and Wang, Michael (2003) "Do PRSPs empower poor countries and disempower the World Bank, or is it the other way around?", *Queen Elisabeth House Working Papers Series, No. 108*, Oxford UK: Oxford University.

Stigliz, Joseph E. (2003a) *Globalization and its Discontents*, New York NY: Norton.

———— (2003b) "Trade imbalances", *Guardian*, 15 August.

Taylor, Charles (1988) "Le juste et le bien", *Revue de Métaphysique et de Morale* 1(January–March).

United Nations Development Program (UNDP) (2002) *Human Development Report 2002: Deepening Democracy in a Fragmented World*, New York NY: Oxford University Press for UNDP.

———— (2003) *Human Development Report 2003: Millennium Development Goals: A Compact Among Nations to End Human Poverty*, New York NY: Oxford University Press for UNDP.

United Nations (2004) *We the peoples: Civil Society, the United Nations and Global Governance*, Report of the Panel of Eminent Persons on UN-Civil Society Relations (A/58/817, June), New York NY: United Nations.

11

Conclusion

Pierre de Senarclens and Ali Kazancigil

This book does not call into question globalization as such. Its dynamics, with their political roots, are the result of material and technical changes, which are, to some extent, uncontrollable. The consequences of these changes remain controversial, although they may be the source of economic, social and cultural progress. The authors of this work recognize the positive aspects of exchange liberalization, which, under certain conditions, should lead to better resource allocation, increased productivity and economic growth, which favours social progress. They are, nevertheless, concerned by the rapid and unstructured growth of transnational corporations and by the deregulation of the short-term movement of capital, which undermines the ability of states to effect social regulation. They are equally concerned by the expansion of a financial capitalism which favours the distribution of dividends to shareholders over productive investment.

The future of globalization remains uncertain, but the neo-liberalism which drives it tends to neglect the mechanisms for distributive justice and social protection as well as public policies which could hinder the functioning of the free market. As a result, the way in which globalization is spreading today increases both social polarization and the risk of political violence. It also has serious consequences for the natural environment. Governments, which do not exercise control over market forces, are unjust because they confer enormous power on the already privileged to the detriment of the most vulnerable. Such a situation affects the OECD countries, but, above all, the poorest countries, which are

Regulating globalization: Critical approaches to global governance, de Senarclens and Kazancigil (eds), United Nations University Press, 2007, ISBN 978-92-808-1136-0

struggling to break free from the dominant economic and political structures that reflect the policy orientations of the major commercial and financial powers.

Today, these criticisms have gathered a fairly wide consensus among those who are concerned by the way in which international society is developing. They inspire a wide range of normative theories about global governance, some of which are extremely abstract and idealistic. Within this range, there are countless ethics-based approaches to the changes, which need to be made to the numerous and various regulatory bodies – those of the state, of international organizations, of civil society, including transnational corporations. This vision reflects a certain type of thinking that is fashionable within international organizations. It is the product of apolitical reasoning, which is essentially normative and destined to promote a general desire for "global governance". It should, nevertheless, be recognized, in a more realistic perspective, that regulatory mechanisms are the outcome of political choices made by governments and, in particular, those of the major powers. As a result, the weaknesses of global governance do not arise from the irrational management of multilateralism, but rather from the configurations of political forces, in which the governing powers of all states participate. In other words, the lack of international order is a consequence of the action or inaction of the major powers.

V. Perret expresses this very well. "The political struggle for comparative advantage of the major powers has greatly contributed to the creation of a propitious environment for the emergence and the consolidation of the 'structural power' of private or quasi-private authorities." These weaknesses reflect power relationships, which are hard to modify and all the more so because they benefit those who support the status quo. For this reason, Jean-Marc Coicaud stresses the need for a fundamental review of the political and strategic orientations of the United States, of the European Union and of the major Asian powers in order to restore legitimacy to globalization through acceptable mechanisms of global governance.

In any event, the future remains uncertain. The interests of states are both heterogeneous and contradictory. The conflicts and crises, which are inherent to these political realities, could in fact create a climate of rapid and unexpected changes, which would favour the evolution or even the transformation of the mechanisms for international regulation. In this context, A. Kazancigil compares the chances for success of a reformist approach to global governance, which he likens to reinforced multilateralism, with that of a process of transformation, going well beyond this perspective and implying the active participation of actors from civil society and from citizens' groups. He describes the conditions necessary for embarking on such a process and puts forward recommendations concerning its mechanisms and its financing. In fact, as both he and V. Perret point out, the non-state actors and above all the NGOs play an important part in the opening up of a new space of contestation and public deliberation at the transnational level. Such contestation could well contribute to the emergence of radically new regulatory mechanisms, all the more so because international society is facing problems so grave and so complex that it is unable to resolve them in a peaceful and organized manner.

Whatever the case may be, the authors of this work recognize with A. Kazancigil that, for better or worse, states remain the principal actors in globalization and that the erosion of their sovereignty amounts to nothing less than the erosion of their democratic legitimacy. This is equally a major preoccupation for V. Perret, who demonstrates to what extent the lack of regulation of short-term capital movements undermines the very foundations of democracy. M. Lengyel also stresses the importance for developing countries to establish their own new procedures for political participation, with a view to negotiating the principal dossiers of the WTO to their advantage. It requires "the construction of rule-based participatory instances for decision-making that bring together relevant public officials and socio-economic actors with the aim of enabling interactive and iterative learning and, therefore, nurturing the capacities for collective problem-solving".

It is states, and in particular the major powers, that exercise a decisive influence on the setting up and development of regulatory mechanisms. However, international organizations have an important part to play in this respect, since they are the guardians of principles, of norms, of decision-making procedures and of a whole range of diverse and varied programmes that affect the evolution of international society. In other words, it is not possible to think about the dynamics of globalization without taking into account the mandates and the commitment of international organizations, which can have either a positive or negative effect on these dynamics.

The authors of this book place considerable emphasis on the weaknesses of intergovernmental cooperative mechanisms at both the regional and global levels. These institutional arrangements do not have the capacity to ensure that globalization develops in a positive fashion, because they are not in a position to resolve major world problems such as mass poverty, irreversible damage to the natural environment, the emergence of new pandemics and the increasing number of violent conflicts in the southern hemisphere. Following the same logic, the bureaucratic and opaque management methods of the international organizations, and the structural constraints which undermine the effectiveness of their development programmes, also have a negative effect on regimes for regional and international cooperation.

P. de Senarclens proposes a fundamental transformation of the UN in order to accommodate within its structures both the participation of the major powers and a fair representation of more vulnerable countries, while giving a voice to representatives of a selective number of influential NGOs. The Security Council would be enlarged, with additional permanent representation for the major powers and a rotating selection of representatives from the developing world, but the European Union would have only one representative. A new *Trusteeship Council*, would be established for the reconstruction of countries in the aftermath of a period of civil war or persistent violent upheaval. It would also examine cases brought by minority groups or indigenous peoples and draw the attention of the Security Council to internal conflicts that threaten the integrity of a state. He envisages a new *Economic and Social Security Council* that would take over the G8 negotiations, expanding them to a broader representation on a regional basis. Most of the specialized agencies and their independent governing bodies would be abolished and replaced by specialized organizations answering to the Economic and Social Security Council. The mandate of the Council would be *inter alia* to increase international liquidity, harmonize regional monetary systems, oversee balance of payment difficulties and manage the thorny problem of debt crisis, taking into account the responsibilities of the lender countries. It would be responsible for the management of a new *fund for sustainable development* whose budget would be financed, to a certain extent, by contributions from the member states, but mainly by international tax contributions.

The future mechanism of international governance will have to be based on new debating procedures. N. Woods and V. Perret underline the need to reform the Bretton Woods institutions. They point, in particular, to the authoritarian manner in which they work and to the fact that representatives from the countries most concerned by their decisions have practically no influence over their policies and strategies. The reform of these institutions would need to include a considerable improvement in their working methods, in the sense that there is a need for much greater transparency in their decision-making processes. It would also need to establish a mechanism that guaranteed full accountability from the top management. The reform would need to increase the number of states represented on the Executive Boards of these institutions with a view to ensuring a fair representation of poor countries, which are the principal "beneficiaries" of the financial aid and the measures for structural adjustment or stability decided upon by these institutions.

The complex relationships between organizations for cooperation on a global scale and those which are sector-based continue to provoke lively debate within the United Nations system. In his analysis of approaches to environmental problems, Y. Ariffin is resolutely opposed to the idea of setting up a *World Environmental Organization* (WEO) that would act as a coordinating agency for the 200 or so issue-specific multilateral environmental treaties and would set rules, monitor and enforce compliance, settle and coordinate technical assistance. He much prefers the ad hoc arrangements employed by these treaties – which comprise a conference or meeting of parties with decision-making powers, a secretariat and technical subsidiary bodies – because they are sufficiently flexible and cost-effective. He doubts that a more centralized bureaucratic system would be endowed with more authority to develop, implement and enforce rules, as this would imply that states surrender their sovereignty to a non-elected international body lacking general consent. Moreover, such an organization would in all likelihood give priority to cross-border global environmental issues to the exclusion or marginalization of local problems such as soil degradation, water and air pollution, which affect populations in the poorest countries to a comparatively higher degree.

The authors of this work subscribe to the idea of strengthening levels of regional governance and to the encouragement of better representation of regional or sub-regional groups of states within international organizations. As L. Fawcett emphasizes, regionalism is part of the fabric of global governance, conditioning its structure and development. It can help to strengthen weaker states, especially in the area of conflict prevention. It can also protect the cultural identity and political aims of sovereign states in a way that global institutions cannot. Y. Berthelot, who argues in favour of stronger UN regional commissions, points out that, in a regional framework, it is possible to ensure food security. At the same time, he indicates that the opening up of agriculture to world markets can have extremely negative effects on peasant farmers, who find themselves in unfair competition with the giants of the agribusiness. He is also in favour of developing regional monetary systems and establishing regional development funds along the lines of the European model. International organizations are "well placed for agreeing on general principles", but it is at the regional level that these principles have to be implemented and this must be done within a framework that takes regional specificities into account. The mandates of the UN's regional commissions need to be revised. The OECD which examines the economic and social policies of its member states and provides advice to governments on the management of public policies – in particular, in the fields of education, health and sustainable development – could be a model in this context. This provides for the scrutiny of the economic and social policies of its member states and for the provision of advice to governments on the management of public policies. M. Lengyel is equally convinced that it is within regional frameworks that developing countries will be best placed to adapt to the constraints of multilateral forces. In order to ensure ideological and doctrinal pluralism within such an institutional system, new consultative mechanisms need to be established at regional levels. One of their main functions would be to promote the participation of NGOs in the very conception and subsequently in the supervision of the system. The experience of the European Union is probably inimitable. It is, nevertheless, most likely to be at the regional level that integrative mechanisms, with a capacity to combat globalization, based on neo-liberalism, will emerge in the future.

Index

accountability
  concept 94–6
  data collection 112
  enforcement mechanisms 112–13
  evaluations 110–11
  in global governance 94–5, 253–4, 255–6
  and human rights 256
  and media 93, 94, 98, 99, 108, 111, 112
  monitoring and transparency 110–12
  political 95–6
Adjustment with a Human Face (UNICEF)
    21
Afghanistan 24
African countries
  conflicts 165
  debt crisis 21
  international aid 23, 55
  and regionalism 162, 173, 174
  trade flows 179, 180
African Development Bank 193
African Survey (Hailey) 211
African Union (AU) 160, 166, 165, 169,
    170, 173, 203n11
  Constitutive Act (May 2001) 166
  Strategic Plan (2004–2007) 167
Agenda for Peace (Boutros-Ghali) 162
Aglietta, Michel 3
agriculture
  agrochemical industry 228

crop genetic resources 230–1
  farmers' privilege/rights 218, 219
  food trade liberalization 189
  and genetic technology 232–3
  international research centres 217
  international trade 124–5
  monocropping 232
  plant improvement 217
  protectionist measures 51
  regional policies 189–90
  UR agreement 121, 124
  see also biodiversity
Algeria 100
Alliance for Peace project 17
American Chemistry Council 97
Americas
  civil society networks 156
  and regionalism 155, 161, 162
Amnesty International 54, 101
Andean Common Automotive Policy 122
Andean Community of Nations (ACN)
    137–8, 139
Andrews, D.M. 75
Angell, Norman 158
Angola 100
Annan, Kofi (UN Secretary-General) 55,
    57, 191–2
anti-personnel mines 57
Antidumping Agreement (AD) 126

281

Arab League 165
Argentina 86, 122, 126, 129, 140
Aron, Raymond 49
Artus, Patrick 65n1
Artuso, Anthony 231
Asia 170, 174, 199
  financial crisis (1997) 50, 86, 163, 192
  global governance role 267
  trade flow 179, 180
Asia-Europe Meeting (ASEM) 152, 164
Asia-Pacific region 61, 161
Asian, Caribbean and Pacific countries
    (ACP) 120, 186
Asian Development Bank (ADB) 138
Asian Monetary Fund (AMF) 192, 197
Asian Pacific Economic Cooperation
    (APEC) 196
Association of South East Asian Nations
    (ASEAN) 138, 157, 160, 164, 165, 170,
    184
  ASEAN "Plus Three" (APT) 164, 197
  development 185
  Trans-Regional EU–ASEAN Trade
    Initiative (TREATI) 195
Australia 51, 61, 85, 103
  and Kyoto Protocol 223
Austria 77
Azerbaijan 100

Bacon, Francis 213
Bangladesh 260
banks/banking 43
  credit ratings 73–4
  development banks 88, 159, 163, 233
  disintermediation/securitization 71, 73–4,
    75, 76
  Glass–Steagall Act (US 1933) 70–1
  internationalization 72–3
  securities business 70–1, 75–6
  see also investments/investment market
Barnier, Michael 105
Bartelmus, Peter 234
Belgian Congo 209
Belgium 77
Bertrand, Doris 25
Bertrand, Maurice 27
biodiversity 209, 216, 217, 220
  biopiracy 229
  enabling activities 231–2
  international management 221
  losses 232–3

patents/protection 228–9, 231–2, 234
plant breeders' rights (PBRs) 217–18
reserves 227
Biological Diversity Convention
    (1992) 217, 220
biotechnology industry 228, 231
Bodin, Jean 44
Boutros-Ghali, Boutros 162, 170
"Brahimi Report" (UN) 162
Brandt, Willy 199, 200
Brazil 50, 51, 57, 63, 86, 128, 135, 229
  and IPRs 140
  regional trade agreements 140
  and TRIPS 229, 230
  and UR agreements 122, 123, 126
Brazilian Business Coalition 128
Bretton Woods agreement (1944) 69, 70–1
Bretton Woods institutions (BRI) 10, 12,
    16, 22, 35, 52
  economic strategies 29
  and globalization 43, 158
  governance 225
  reform 62, 63, 161, 278
  structural adjustment policies 21
Britain 82
  Colonial Economic Advisory
    Committee 211
  see also United Kingdom
Bruntland Commission 57

Cairns Group 125
Campbell, Kurt M. 196
Canada 187
capital movement 180–1, 190–1, 212,
    213–14, 277
  controls 71, 72
  deregulation 21, 47, 54, 71, 82, 118, 180,
    275
  markets 21, 71, 72, 73, 75, 78, 80, 87
capitalism 2, 39, 40, 41, 270
  and First Development Decade 17–18
  regulation 40, 47
  see also shareholders' capitalism
Cardoso, Fernando Enrique 55
Caribbean Community and Common
    Market (CARICOM) 183–4
Caribbean regional groupings 196
Carter, President Jimmy 20
Central America 165, 195
Central Asia 161, 163, 170
Central Treaty Organization (CENTO) 159

Cerny, P.G. 76–7
Chad-Cameroon 99
chemical industry 97, 228
Chemical Weapons Treaty 101
Chile 122, 125, 126, 127
China 50, 170, 185, 197, 222
  economic liberalization 22
  and regionalism 163, 179
  and UN 33, 63
civil society 44, 155, 158
  global 94, 101, 236
  and global governance 260, 269, 276–7
  organizations (CSOs) 201
  and UR involvement 128–9
climate change 58, 101, 206–7, 209, 216
  conventions 206–7, 216, 220
  and energy use/sustainability 233–4
  funding 233
  and LDCs 222
Climate Change Convention see UN
    Framework Convention on Climate
    Change (FCCC)
Codex Alimentarius Commission
    (CAC) 55, 132
Cold War 12, 13, 17, 22, 159
  and regionalism 160, 161
  see also post-Cold War era
Colombia 99, 100
  and UR effects 122, 126, 127, 128
colonialism 19
  colony definition 208
  decolonization 215
  and development 207–10
  wildlife conservation convention 209–10
Commission on Global Governance 78
Commission on Intellectual Property 141
Committee on Trade and Environment 229
common property rights 227–34
Communaute des Etats d'Afrique de
    l'Ouest (CDEAO) 186
communications 128, 184
  improvements 135, 152, 239
  Internet 98
  strategies 41
  technology/ICTs 2, 22, 38
  telecommunication 55, 107, 180, 186
Communist regime 2, 47, 185
Compliance Adviser/Ombudsman
    (CAO) 113
Condon, Peter 230
Conference/Organization of Security and

Cooperation in Europe (CSCE/OSCE)
    160, 164, 166, 171
conflicts 8, 9, 43, 64, 165, 276, 277
  and development 234
  and multinational companies 100
  and regionalism 165, 167, 169, 279
  southern hemisphere/Third World 17,
    277
  and UN 34, 51, 57, 278
conservation 209–10
  ecocentric/anthropocentric 215
  and exploitation 206, 207–10, 234, 239
  of phytogenetic resources 217–20
  wildlife 209–10
  see also forests/forestry
Constant, Henjamin 47
Constitutive Act of the African Union
    (May 2001) 166
Consultative Group of International
    Agricultural Research (CGIAR) 217
Convention on Biological Diversity
    (CBD) 206, 216, 219–20, 224, 229–30
  Bonn Guidelines 229
Convention on Climate Change
    (CCC) 206–7, 216, 233
Convention on the Prevention and
    Punishment of the Crime of
    Genocide 13
Council of Europe 12
Council for Mutual Economic Assistance
    (CMEA) 182, 185
Crédit Lyonnais 48
Cruz, Hernan Santa 16

de Guiringaud, Louis 19
de Seynes, Philippe 16
decentralization 76, 81, 133, 161
decision-making
  and global governance 55, 253–4
  international 127–31, 149
  UN/WTO processes 28–9, 134–5, 137
democracy/democratization 5, 44, 47, 64,
    102, 167, 236
  concept 81–2
  early systems 58–9
  erosion 77–8, 862
  European 59, 60
  and globalization 83–4, 93–4
  institutional 166, 171
  public/private divide 69, 78–9, 80, 85
  and regionalism 172

Deutsch, Karl 49, 159
developing countries 107, 119, 132
  and accountability 94, 111–12, 136–7
  and agricultural policies 189–90
  governance 98, 265–6, 267–8
  and indigenous/traditional
    knowledge 133, 229–30
  learning and information exchange
    135–6
  Point IV Program (US) 14
  public–private interaction 130–1, 135
  regional groupings 183–5
  technical assistance 132–3
  trade issues 135–6, 179
  and UR agreements 120–1, 123–4, 125
development issues 17–18, 165, 207, 261
  colonial period 207–10
  concept, theory and policy 77, 214
  dirigisme 118–19
  and environmental policies 205–41
  equity gap 49, 63, 83, 200, 207, 219,
    234–5, 236, 269
  funding 16, 24–5, 152, 163, 279
  and industrialization 15, 17
  international aid 20, 23, 24, 25, 55, 212
  policies 6, 9, 102, 118, 184, 190, 232, 239,
    255
  post-colonial 210–14
  and regionalism/integration 123, 156,
    184–5
  sustainability 34, 200, 205–6, 207, 214,
    233–4, 235, 239, 261, 278
  and UN projects 14, 15–16
  unresolved problems 234–41
  see also economic development
diamond industry 94, 100
Doha Development Round 6, 24, 51
drugs issues 55, 173, 220, 230
  trafficking 165, 167
Dual Mandate in British Tropic Africa
  (Lugard) 208

Earth Summit *see* UN Conference on
  Environment and Development
  (1992)
East African Common Market 186
East Asia 122, 153, 193
East Timor 170
Eastern Economic Association 85
ecological issues 214, 222, 228
  degradation/exploitation 239–40

ecosystems 205, 216, 220, 224, 238,
  242n17
endangered species 215, 216–17
germplasm collections/resources 217–20,
  228, 230–2
landraces 217, 218, 231, 232
modernization 224–34, 239
property rights regimes 217
see also biodiversity; conservation
Economic Community of West African
  States (ECOWAS) 157, 160, 165, 166,
  168–9, 170
Economic Cooperation Organization
  (ECO) 164
economic development 2, 45, 51, 210,
  212–13
  and biophysical limits 215
  and conservation policies 210–11
  First Development Decade 17–18
  and interventionism 45–6
  models 75
  and regionalism/regionalization 153,
    181
  Second Development Decade 198
economic issues 13, 22, 45, 78, 119
  accountability 5, 108–9
  cooperation/integration 165, 184, 187,
    250
  interdependence 42, 75, 113–14, 118,
    158, 180
  manufacturing trade 179–81
  policies 18, 40
  and regionalism 168–9, 178–80, 202
  see also capital movement; foreign direct
    investments (FDIs); regulation issues;
    world economy
education issues 21, 24, 211
  funding 25, 46
  illiteracy 14, 18
Elysée Treaty (1963) 183
environmental issues/environmentalism 3,
  5, 6, 9, 58, 206, 209, 214–15, 216
  agreements/treaties 206–7, 237, 279
  and developmental link 205–41
  funding 107
  global warming 221, 223
  and globalization/governance 207, 275
  market environmentalism 224–34, 239
  NGO activity 155, 165
  polluter pays principle (PPP) 198, 222,
    225, 238

pollution 8, 182, 195, 198–9, 234, 237,
    240, 279
sustainable development 205–6, 207, 239
WEO proposal 236–7, 279
see also climate change; ecological issues;
    Global Environmental Facility (GEF);
    greenhouse gas emissions
Essays (Bacon) 213
Europe 161, 162, 164, 172, 174
European Central Bank (ECB) 105
European Coal and Steel Community 182
European Commission 78, 188
European Common Market 186
European Court of Justice 60, 188
European Economic Community
    (EEC) 12, 18, 159, 171, 182–3, 187
development 185
European Free Trade Association
    (EFTA) 160, 183, 185
European Human Rights Court 60
European Monetary Union (EMU) 105
European Parliament 59–60, 188
European Regional Development
    Fund 193
European Union (EU) 33, 51, 59–60, 85,
    161, 170, 181, 196
    Common Agricultural Policy (CAP) 187
    Constitution/Treaty 60, 166, 188
    creation/development 182–3, 187
    and global governance 265, 266–7, 280
    and globalization 152–3
    governance rationale 103 4, 105
    institutions 168
    membership 178, 182
    and regionalism 152–3, 164, 167–8
    trade agreements/partnerships 141, 164,
    186
European Union-ACP (EU-ACP) 164, 186
European Union-MERCOSUR (EU-
    MERCOSUR) 164
Expanded Programme of Technical
    Assistance (EPTA) 14–15

Falk, Richard 172
financial issues
    capital controls 71
    corporate profits 40–1, 46, 54, 213
    crises/management 41, 76, 86, 87, 122,
    163, 192–3
    decompartmentalization 71
    deregulation measures/effects 48, 52, 71

devaluation 76
disintermediation/securitization 71–3, 74,
    75–6
exchange rates 71, 72, 73, 75, 76
Federal Reserve 193
flows and markets 2, 71, 74–7, 75, 83, 211
globalization 74–5, 76–7, 82, 85
institutions 86
international monetary system 69, 70–1,
    72, 73
models 107–8
monetary policies 70, 71, 75
and political economy 82–4
private sector/privatization 72–7
regional approaches 192–4
see also capital movement; International
    Monetary Fund (IMF); investments/
    investment market; regulation issues
Financial Leaders Group 107
Financial Services Agreement (1997) 107
Financial Stability Forum (FSF) 103
Food and Agriculture Organization
    (FAO) 15, 189, 217, 231
food production/supplies
    agricultural policies 189
    famine eradication 217
    food aid 189–90
    food security 190, 217, 218, 219, 279
    hunger issues 18, 189–90
    malnutrition 42
foreign direct investments (FDIs) 20–1,
    125, 180
    decline 73
    multinational 250
forests/forestry 234
    as carbon sinks 223, 227
    conservation 209
    deforestation 209, 220, 223, 232
France 44, 48, 64–5, 186, 187, 188, 209
free trade 50, 62, 132, 196, 235
    and networks/regimes 52, 155
    regional 165, 183, 195
Free Trade Agreements (FTAs) 128, 136,
    137–41, 141, 195, 196
    Arab/Pan-Arab 156, 160
    EU 141, 164, 186
    Latin America 122, 126–8
    Mercosur 195–6
    NAFTA 122, 160, 172, 179, 187, 196
Free Trade Area of the Americas
    (FTAA) 128, 136, 141, 196

Frieden, J.A. 77
Frisvold, George 230
Fukuyama, Francis 45
functionalism 187–8

Geertz, Clifford 44
General Agreement on Tariffs and Trade
   (GATT) 12, 18, 52, 158, 185
General Agreement on Trade in Services
   (GATS) 106–7
genetic engineering 227–8
genocide 51, 252
   prevention 271n7
Germany 41, 44, 57, 209
Global Compact *see* UN Global Compact
   Initiative
global corporations *see* transnational
   corporations (TNCs)
Global Environmental Facility (GEF) 7,
   28, 207, 220, 221, 238
   funding 224–7, 233–4, 238
   governance 225
   grant qualifications 225–6
   Implementing Agencies 225–7, 238
   Overall Performance Study (1998) 226
   Projects Procurement Report 227
global governance 2–3, 4, 5, 10, 31
   and accountability 94–6, 108–14, 253–4,
      255–6
   agricultural policies 189–90
   authority 78–90, 81–2, 85
   consistency/inconsistency 253–4, 259–60
   and democracy/democratization 60, 61,
      64, 114, 268–70
   and disenfranchisement 260–1
   and empowerment 270
   and erosion of democracy 69–77
   funding 64–5
   and globalization 250–2
   institutional actors/inadequacies 254,
      260–1
   and interdependence 8, 14
   and international justice 256–7
   legitimacy 7, 58–63, 250–2, 254, 262,
      263–5
   mechanisms 25, 112–13, 251, 259
   and non-state actors 77–9
   power/principles balance 265–8
   private sector role 98–9, 109–10
   prospects 32–5
   public/private divide 69, 70, 78–9, 80

reformist process 37, 56–7, 261–2
regional approaches 189–94
and regionalism 152, 155, 157, 173–4,
   202
and regions/organizations 61, 194–201
and statehood 39, 44
and status quo 261–2
structure, rules, funding 4, 5, 60–1, 64–5
transformative process 37, 56, 58–63
value-goals implementation 261–2
Global Reporting Initiative 54
global trading system 105–6
globalization 38, 74, 78
   and accountability 93–4
   cross-border migration 250
   and developing countries 41–2
   EU model 152–3
   and governance 250–62
   and interconnectedness 250
   and international organizations 93
   and legitimacy 250–2, 263–5, 276
   neo-liberalism 2, 3, 4, 20–35, 37, 38,
      39–50, 275–6
   post-Cold War 161–3
   and sovereignty 38, 42–50
   as Westernization 171
good governance 77, 86, 250
   accountability 253–4
   benchmarks 252–70
   consistency imperative 253–4
   human security and wellbeing 252–3
Goodman, J.B. 84
governance
   and coexistence 173–4
   concept/definition 77, 79
   national/international norms 265–70
   networks 103–4, 106–7, 250
   output rationale 103–4
   private sector 78, 94, 96, 97, 98–9,
      109–10
   subsidiarity principle 60, 195
   technocratic 102–8
   see also global governance; good
      governance; regional governance
governmental NGOs (GONGOs) 54
Great Britain 209
   see also Britain; United Kingdom
Greater Arab Free Trade Area 156
Greece 193
greenhouse gas emissions (GHGs) 211–14
   carbon sinks 223, 227

Clean Development Mechanism (CDM) 223, 224
and global warming 221
International Emissions Trading (IET) 223–4
national targets (QELROs) 222–3
Gregg, Robert W. 184
Group of 6 (G-6) 51
Group of 7 (G-7) 22, 41, 85, 97
Group of 8 (G8) 31, 32, 49, 53, 55, 63, 188
Group of 10 (G10) 31
Group of 20 (G-20) 32, 51, 120
Group of 77 (G-77) 18, 160
Guatemala 166
Gulf Cooperation Council (GCC) 160
Gulf States 164

Hailey, Malcolm 211
Haiti 166
Harmes, A. 76
Haufler, V. 80
health issues 14, 22, 25, 211, 279
disease/eradication 18, 234
funding 46, 189, 210, 261
HIV/AIDS programmes 28
pandemics 24
private provision 48, 189
public provision 15, 21, 26, 45, 46, 52, 211
UN resolutions 24
highly indebted poor countries (HIPCs) 41
debt alleviation/cancellation 55, 87, 189, 235, 240
Hirschman, Albert 133, 207
Hobbesian models 44–5
Hoffman, Stanley 151
Hong Kong 85, 103, 129
Human Development Report (2003) 261
human rights 7, 13, 20, 22, 51–2, 62
and good governance 252, 255–6, 258–9, 263
institutions 166
and multinational companies 99–100
and NGO activity 155, 165
racial discrimination 19
violations 99, 252, 255, 259, 264
Human Rights Watch 54, 99–100
Human Security Report (2005) 174
humanitarian issues 3, 20, 165
aid 23, 34
human trafficking 167

and international organizations 258–9
interventions 166, 170
Hurd, I. 78
Huxley, Julian 215

India 50, 51, 126, 222, 229
and TRIPS 229, 230
and UN 33, 57, 63
industrialization 6, 118
and colonialism 211
and development 14, 15, 211
and environmental degradation 240
fenceless factories 213–14
and GHG emissions 222
Middle East 179
and over-consumption 241
and trade flows 180–1
Institute for International Finance 97
Institute of Social and Ethical Accountability 54
institutions/institutionalization 127–8, 166, 168, 170
accountability 109
communications 128
and development policies 119–20
global/international 4, 109, 172
and governance 94, 254
inter-state 96
post-Cold War 161, 169
public 95
see also regional institutions/ organizations
intellectual property rights (IPRs) 120, 123, 125, 127, 131, 138, 140, 141
applications 229–30
and common property rights 230
and industrial conglomerates 228
and Mercusor 140
Inter-American Development Bank (IADB) 138
interdependence 8, 14, 152
ecological 222
economic/financial 42, 75, 113, 180
and governance 157
and regionalism 188
intergovernmental organizations (IGOs) 2, 5, 6, 39, 49, 50, 59, 159
cooperative mechanisms 277–8
funding 63
international politics/rules 8–9, 49, 190–1
and TNCs 55

International Accounting Standards
  Committee 97
international aid
  agencies 101, 160
  bilateral concessional 213
  development 20, 23, 24, 25, 55, 212
  multilateral 14, 213
  programmes 28, 45, 86–8, 189, 212–13
International Chamber of Commerce
  (ICC) 96
International Commission on Intervention
  and State Sovereignty 156
International Committee of the Red Cross
  (ICRC) 34
International Court of Arbitration 97
International Court of Justice 52, 95
International Covenant on Civil and
  Political Rights (1966) 51
International Covenant on Economic,
  Social and Cultural Rights (1966) 51
International Criminal Court 43, 51, 57
International Development Strategy
  (1972) 18
International Federation of the Red Cross
  and Red Crescent (IFRC) 34
International Finance Corporation
  (IFC) 113
International Financial Services London
  (IFSL) 106–7
International Fund for Agricultural
  Development (IFAD) 189
International Labor Organization
  (ILO) 11, 15, 22, 54, 132
  Fundamental Principles on Rights at
  Work 99
international law 13, 26, 237
  and accountability 95
  courts/tribunals 43, 51, 52, 57, 95, 97
  crimes against humanity 51
  criminal law 3
  development 44, 52
  humanitarian law 44, 51
  and international relations 95, 171
  justice system 256–7, 266
  and US 57
International Monetary Fund (IMF) 6, 10,
  18, 31, 49, 52, 53, 55, 56, 188
  accountability 87, 97, 104–5, 109–13
  aid programmes 86–8, 212–13
  Article of Agreement 71
  and globalization 93

and governance 103–4
  Guidelines on Conditionality 111
  Independent Evaluation Office
  (IEO) 110–11
  Office of Internal Audit and Inspection
  (OIA) 111
  reform 86
International Organization of Securities
  Commissions (IOSCO) 80
International Organization for
  Standardization (ISO) 54, 132
international organizations 29, 33, 138
  accountability 94, 95–6, 109–13, 258–9
  democratic deficit 108–9, 277–8
  development policies 118
  and global governance 69, 77, 93, 251,
  252, 256
  and humanitarian crises 258
  transnational nongovernmental 101, 155,
  160
international relations 78–9, 151
  democratization 236
  and development aid 212
  functionalism 187
  and globalization 85
  theory 42
International Road Transport (TIR) 199
International Standardization Organization
  (ISO) 132
International Telecommunication Union
  (IUT) 55
International Trade Organization (ITO) 12
International Treaty on Plant Genetic
  Resources for Food and
  Agriculture 231
International Undertaking On Plant
  Genetic Resources 218, 219, 231
International Union for the Protection of
  Nature (IUCN) 215
International Union for the Protection of
  New Varieties of Plants (UPOV) 218,
  228–9
Internet Corporation for Assigned Names
  and Numbers (ICANN) 98
interstate space (ISS) 50–5
interventionism 71, 211
investments/investment market 122, 182,
  235
  agencies/credit ratings 73–4
  hedge funds 76
  portfolios 73, 73–4, 76, 250

Iran 163, 170
Iraq: US/UK invasion 44, 45, 171
Ireland 44, 193
Islamic Conference Organization
    (ICO) 160, 165, 170
Italy 209

Japan 41, 48, 51, 57
    intra-regional trade 179, 196–7

Kennedy, President John F. 17
Kenya 186
Keohane, Robert 251
Keynesianism 71, 211
King, Andrew 97
Korea 214
Kosovo 24, 60
Kurzer, P. 77
Kyoto Protocol 57, 222, 223, 224

Lamy, Pascal 197
Latham, R. 79
Latin America 174
    Alliance for Peace project/Peace
        Corps 17
    debt crisis 21
    and EU 196
    Group of Friends of Development 140
    institutions 127–8, 170
    integration 137
    intra-regional trade 179, 180
    regionalism 186, 195
    trade agreements 122, 126–8
    and USA 171
Latin American Free Trade Association
    (LAFTA) 160
Latin American Trade Network
    (LATN) 142n6, 143n22
League of Nations 33, 151, 157, 158
    Permanent Mandates Commission 208
Lennox, Michael 97
less/least developed countries (LDCs) 21,
    41
    and climate change 222
    conservation/exploitation of
        resources 206, 219–20
    and globalization 6–7, 23
    and TRIPS harmonization 229
    and UN system 31–2
    and Uruguay Round 120
Lewis, Arthur 16, 210–12, 214

liberalism/liberalization 45, 71, 106, 107,
    181
    of capital movements 180
    and colonialism 210–11
    in OECD countries 21
    promotion 13–17, 22
    of trade 86, 119, 121–2, 137, 178, 189
    see also neo-liberalism
Liberia 169
"London Convention Relative to the
    Preservation of Fauna and Flora..."
    (1933) 209–10
Lugard, Frederick 208

Maddison, Angus 180
Malaysia 50, 122
Manuel, Trevor 170
market forces 44, 48, 65, 275
    and colonialism 211
    and developing countries 21
    and global governance 37–8
    post-Cold War 22
Marshall Plan 12, 15, 182, 185
Mauritius 127
media 3, 9, 30
    and accountability 93, 94, 98, 99, 108,
        111, 112
    and public opinion 20, 42, 53, 54
Médicin Sans Frontières (MSF) 34, 54
Mediterranean region 199
Meltzer, Alan 86
Mercosur 137–8, 139, 140, 141, 156, 164–5,
    169, 170, 172
    and trade agreements 195–6
Mercosur Automotive Regime 122
Mexico 122, 123, 125, 187
Middle East/Gulf region 19, 164, 167, 171,
    179
Mill, John Stuart 47
Mitrany, David 187
Mitterand, François 75
Monroe Doctrine 170
Montreal Protocol 238
Moody's Investors Service (Moody's) 74
Moravesik, Andrew 187
A More Secure World (UN report) 27
Moses, J.W. 77
Mosley, Layna 83
Motta Veiga, Pedro da 140
Multilateral Investment Guarantee Agency
    (MIGA) 113

multilateralism 13, 43
  environmental agreements 206–7
  global governance 56, 257, 276
  and international aid 14, 213
  and regionalism 137, 140
  and trade 22, 24, 127–8, 129–30
  and UN 14, 29–30, 33
  and US 32, 57
multinational corporations 99–100, 160
  accounting mechanisms 191
Myrdal, Gunnar 16, 151, 182, 187

Nash, Roderick 209
natural resources
  biological 219–20
  conservation 206, 209
  depletion/degradation 234
  exploitation 208–9
  global commons 208–9
  management 207–24
  as public/private goods 216–20
  and sovereignty 208, 215–24
neo-liberalism 2, 3, 4, 20–35
  and economic issues 45
  and globalization 37, 38, 39–50
the Netherlands 77, 103
networks 42, 94, 107, 156
  regional/international 155, 250, 251
  technocratic 103–4
New Economic Partnership for African
    Development (NEPAD) 165
New International Economic Order
    (NIEO) 19, 20–35, 160
New Partnership for African Development
    (NEPAD) 192
New Zealand 61
Newell, Peter 237–8
Nigeria 57, 170
Non-Aligned Movement 160
non-governmental organizations (NGOs) 2,
    5, 30, 99, 101–2, 160
  and accountability 102
  and civil society networks 155, 236
  consultative status 165
  and democratization 102
  and developing countries 136
  global governance role 100–2, 251, 260,
    269–70, 280
  and globalization 93
  and regionalism 164, 165–6

roles 165–6
  and security issues 166
  and sovereignty 42
  and transnational corporations
    (TNCs) 53, 58, 101
  and UN 32–5, 159, 260
  and WTO 106
non-profit organizations 236
non-state actors 277
  and global governance 50, 52, 77–9, 80,
    276
  and regionalism 155, 172
  and UN 3, 62
North America 46, 107, 153, 180, 235
North American Free Trade Agreement
    (NAFTA) 122, 160, 172, 179, 187, 196
North Atlantic Treaty Organization
    (NATO) 60, 159, 171
  Partnerships for Peace (PfPs) 164
North–South divide
  environmental issues 206–7
  equity gap 236, 240
  and governance 51, 167
Northeast Asia 213
northern hemisphere 7, 50, 207, 240
Norway 178

oil industry 19, 72–3, 99–100
Organization of African Unity (OAU) 159,
    161
  Mechanism for Conflict Prevention,
    Management and Resolution
    (1993) 166
Organization of American States
    (OAS) 155, 159, 170
  Declaration on the Collective Defense of
    Democracy (1991) 166
  Inter-American Democratic Charter
    (2001) 166
Organization of Arab Petroleum Exporting
    Countries (OAPEC) 160, 168
Organisation for Economic Co-operation
    and Development (OECD) 18, 22, 279
  aid policies 23, 54
  and economic growth 20–1, 49
  and financial crises 86
  funding 24–5
  and governance 77–8, 275
Organization for European Economic
    Cooperation (OEEC) 12

Our Global Neighbourhood (Brandt) 199, 200
Overseas Development Aid (ODA) 23, 24
Oxfam 53–4, 101

Palan, R. 81
Pan-Arab Free Trade Area (PAFTA) 160
Paraguay 166
Patent Cooperation Treaty (PCT) 229
Pauly, L.W. 84
peacekeeping/peacebuilding operations 23–4, 152, 155, 166
  and regionalism 156, 165, 201
Peru 128, 135, 166
Petersmann, Ernst-Ulrich 104
pharmaceutical industry 228, 231
the Philippines 122
Polanyi, Karl 47
politics/political issues 62, 84, 102, 216
  international 8–9, 49, 150, 158
  national 105, 106, 109, 236
population issues 22, 23, 232
  Bucharest conference (1974) 20
  ECAFE work 198, 199
  and environmental degradation 232, 237, 279
  and governance/representation 59, 101, 226
  local/indigenous 234, 236, 238, 240
  poor/underprivileged 24, 41–2, 49, 53, 210, 233, 237
  wealthy/overprivileged 222, 235, 261
Portugal 193, 195, 209
post-Cold War era 161–3, 166, 174
  institutions 161, 169
  social organization 253
poverty issues 22–5, 37, 119, 199
  eradication 217, 220, 261
  and globalization 42
  reduction programmes 86
  and UN strategy 200
Poverty Reduction Strategy Papers (PRSPs) 27
Prebisch, Raoul 16, 17, 18
private sector/privatization 5–6, 48, 97, 230
  and financial issues 74–7
  and governance 78, 94, 96, 97, 98–9, 109–10
  and public services 46, 118
Purcell, M. 81

Rao, M.K. 16
Reagan, President Ronald 20
reformism 40, 56–8, 207
regional economic commissions *see* UN Regional Commissions
regional governance 152, 153, 155, 156, 173–4
  and global fora 153, 163, 279
  monetary funds/development banks 193–4
  obstacles 167–71
regional institutions/organizations 61, 138, 140, 153, 160–1, 172, 185, 188
  constitutional changes 166–8
  and global finance 192–4
  and global governance 194–5, 256
  growth in numbers/membership 163–4
  tasks and roles 164–6
Regional Social Fora 63–4
regionalism 6, 61, 156, 161, 162
  background/history 156–61
  benchmarking criteria 138–9
  capacity and performance 168–9
  collaboration/cooperation 139–40, 173
  concept/definitions 154–5, 178
  and development 156, 169, 173
  economic integration 168–9
  and globalization 165, 167, 202, 279
  interdependence 188
  and interregionalism 152, 164, 195–8
  knowledge exchange 139
  and multilateralism 137, 140
  "new" 163–7
  potential/limitations 153, 164–6, 168–9, 171–4
  roles 151–2, 155
  security issues 154, 156, 161–2, 165
  social and economic programmes 140
  sovereignty and hegemony 140, 167, 168, 169–71
  theory and practices 150–4
  trade agreements 137–41
regionalization 6
  definition 177–8
  in developing countries 183
  dynamism 201–2
  external influences 185–6
  and globalization 43, 202
  and integration/interdependence 30, 61, 188

regionalization (cont.)
  post-Cold War 161–3
  statistics 177–81
  theoretical background 186–9
  underlying factors 181–9
regions
  agricultural policies 189–90
  definitions 154, 177–8
  and development 184–5
  economic integration 168–9, 202
  and global governance 192–201
  institutions 185
  integration 120, 137, 140, 160, 168,
    180–1, 184, 186, 188
  inter-relations 188–9
  intra-trade flows 178–80
  networks 155
regulation issues 5, 6, 37, 70
  concept/theory/models 80, 81–2, 85, 94
  deregulation policies 47, 82–3, 180
  global goverance 42, 98, 192
  institutions 80
  norms 251
  processes 80–2
  regulatory mechanisms 70–1, 96–100,
    276
  see also self-regulation
resources
  as common property 239
  and sovereign rights 216
  see also natural resources
The Responsibility to Protect (ICISS
  report) 156
Righter, Rosemary 35n3
Rio Conference/Principles *see* UN
  Conference on Environment and
  Development (1992)
Russia 86, 170, 192
Rwandan genocide 110

Said, Edward 172
San Francisco Conference (1945) 10
Sanitary and Phytosanitary Measures
  (SPS) 138
Santayana, George 206
Saudi Arabia 170
Scholte, Jan Aart 101, 167
Schultz, Theodore W. 16
Schumpterian processes 40
security issues 2, 23, 158, 166
  collective/cooperation 3, 165

and good governance 252, 262, 263–5
and inequality 264–5
and NGOs' roles 165
post-9/11 agenda 166–7
and regionalism 154, 156, 161–2, 165, 201
terrorism 42, 44–5, 165, 167
self-regulation 93
  and global economy 96–100
  private sector 94, 112
shareholders' capitalism 2, 39–42
  corporate profits 40–1, 46, 54
  corporate social responsibility (CSR) 41,
    54, 55
Sierra Leone 157, 169
Singapore 85, 103
Singer, Hans 16
socio-economic issues 48, 58, 62, 105, 236
  developments/reform 12, 40, 47–8
  and globalization 40, 45–6, 76–7, 85
  and regionalization 181, 183
  social welfare 2, 8, 9, 10, 46, 76–7, 211
  Thatcher/Reagan era 20, 102
  and UN 13–14, 22, 105
  unemployment 119
Soros, George 76
South Africa 57, 63, 170, 218
  apartheid 19, 170, 185, 252
South America 165, 169
South Asian Association for Regional
  Cooperation (SAARC) 160
South East Asian Treaty Organization
  (SEATO) 159
South Korea 197
Southeast Asia 162, 170, 213
Southern African Development Community
  (SADC) 166, 170, 184
Southern Cone Common Market
  (MERCOSUR) 156, 184
  see also Mercosur
southern hemisphere 14, 41, 50, 236
  resources management 207–24, 239–40
sovereignty 12, 61
  concept 2, 44
  and globalization 38, 42–50
  and resources management 215–24
Soviet Union 12, 19, 165, 182, 185
Spain 195, 209
Spero, J.E. 70
Standard and Poor's Ratings Group
  (S&P) 74
statehood 2–3

and global governance 39, 51, 59, 64
state–citizen relations 80–2
states
  and compulsory redistributive
    mechanisms 227
  failed 45, 46
  and global governance 59, 108–9, 277,
    279
  and globalization 42–50, 85
  and independence 17
  inequalities 37, 46, 48
  and regionalism 162–3
  regulatory/competitive 44, 48, 53, 66n1
  sovereign 2, 42, 43, 49, 59, 279
Stiglitz, Joseph 3
Stockholm Declaration (1971) 216
sub-Saharan Africa 33, 86
Sweden 77
Switzerland 85, 178, 229

Taiwan 214
Tanzania 186
taxation 46, 85, 85–6, 184, 238
  global/international 55, 64–5, 238–9, 278
*Technical Assistance for Economic
  Development* (UN) 14
Thailand 122
Thatcher, Margaret 20, 48–9, 102, 187
Third World countries
  conflicts 17, 277
  contestation of 17–20
  Group of 77 18
  regional groupings 181, 186
  and UN 17–19, 18
Tobin, James 85, 238
trade agreements 57, 121–2, 125–6
  bilateral 57, 186, 196
  regional 127 8, 137–41
  see also Free Trade Agreements (FTAs)
trade issues
  accounting and competition 191–2
  agricultural products 185–6
  barriers and development issues 24–5
  cooperatives 236
  decision-making mechanisms 130
  dispute settlement mechanisms 121
  double standards 260
  export subsidies 123, 138
  international 16, 17–18, 72, 121, 127–31
  and IPRs 120, 123, 125, 127, 131, 138, 140
  multilateral 22, 24, 127–8, 129–30

organizations 236
patents 125–6
protectionism 50, 51, 260
public–private interaction 128–9, 130
regional/intra-regional 178–80, 192, 235
self-regulation 20–1
tariffs 121, 122–3, 140, 142n7 124–5, 180,
  195, 260
unilateral reform 121–3
see also free trade; market forces
Trade Related Intellectual Property Rights
  (TRIPs) 52, 123, 124, 133, 139, 141,
  228
Trade-Related Investment Measures
  (TRIMs) Agreement 122
transnational corporations (TNCs) 2, 3, 5,
  42, 54–5, 72, 101
  and Global Compact 260
  and globalization 47–8, 58
  and NGOs 53, 169
  and regulation/rules 97, 190–2
transnational public space (TPS) 54, 57
  and interstate space (ISS) 50, 52–4
transportation 2, 198, 199
Truman, President Harry S. 14
Turkey 23, 126, 170

Uganda 186
UN Commission on Sustainable
  Development 55
UN Conference on Environment and
  Development (Rio de Janeiro,
  1992) 99, 215, 221, 224, 227
UN Conference on Trade and
  Development (UNCTAD) 18, 26, 123,
  138, 180, 198
  First Development Decade 17–18
  Foreign Direct Investment Report 180
  Second Development Decade 198
  Trade and Development Reports 21
UN Convention on Biological Diversity
  (CBD) 206, 216, 219–20, 224, 229–30,
  233
UN Council for Economic and Social
  Security, proposal 56
UN Development Group (UNDG) 27
UN Development Programme (UNDP) 11,
  16, 18, 23, 25, 217
  and GEF funding 225
  and governance 78
  Human Development reports 22, 261

UN Economic Commission for Africa
(ECA) 192, 198
UN Economic Commission for Asia and
the Far East (ECAFE) 198, 199
UN Economic Commission for Europe
(UNECE) 181–2, 185, 187, 198, 199
UN Economic Commission for Latin
America and the Caribbean
(ECLAC) 138, 159
UN Economic Commission for Latin
America (ECLA) 17, 198
UN Economic and Social Commission for
Asia and the South Pacific
(ESCAP) 138, 199
UN Economic and Social Commission for
Western Asia (ESCWA) 198, 199
UN Economic and Social Council
(ECOSOC) 11, 13, 19, 29, 63, 165
restructuring 114
UN Educational, Scientific and Cultural
Organization (UNESCO) 21, 25, 215
UN Environment Programme (UNEP) 221,
225
UN Food and Agriculture Organization
(FAO) 15, 189, 217, 231
UN Framework Convention on Climate
Change (FCCC) 216, 220, 221–2
UN Fund for Population Activities
(UNFPA) 25
UN Global Compact Initiative (1991) 5, 23,
41, 54, 55, 99, 165, 192, 260
UN High Commissioner for Refugees
(UNHCR) 11, 23, 24
UN High-Level Panel Report (2004) 153,
162, 173
UN Human Rights Commission 54, 57
UN Intergovernmental Panel on Climate
Change (IPCC) 221
Kyoto Protocol 57, 222, 223, 224
Second Assessment Report (1995) 222
UN International Children's Emergency
Fund (UNICEF) 11, 15, 23, 25
UN Millennium Summit (2000) 199
millennium development goals
(MDGs) 24, 261
UN Non-Governmental Liaison Service
(NGLS) 201
UN Regional Commissions (RCs) 6, 11, 15,
158–9, 193, 198–200, 279
UN Relief and Works Agency
(UNWRA) 11

UN Security Council 4, 10, 22, 159, 173
enlargement 57
and humanitarian crises 258–9
inconsistency 9, 259–60
reform 33–4, 56, 63, 278
and regionalism 201
UN Social and Economic Council 55
UN Temporary Social Commission on
Social Affairs 13
UN Universal Declaration on Human
Rights (1948) 13, 51–2, 99
UN World Summits 31, 57
2005 meeting 3, 5, 151, 165, 261, 269
Union des Etats d'Afrique Centrale
(UDEAC) 186
Union Montaire Ouest Africaine
(UMOA) 186
United Kingdom (UK) 21, 41, 44, 258
and Doha Round 51
and regionalization 186
United Nation Special Funds 16
United Nations Charter 4, 13, 51, 155, 158,
159, 170, 261
Article 55 10
and development 212–13
revision 31
United Nations General Assembly 11, 33,
159
enlargement 18
and Third World policies 17–19
United Nations Secretariat 14, 16
development reports 16
international conferences 20
reform 26, 28
United Nations Secretary-General
reform proposals 27–8, 57
see also UN Global Compact Initiative
United Nations (UN) 14, 20, 22, 158, 161
budgeting/funding 19, 24–5, 26, 30–1,
199
decision-making process 28–9
and global governance 198–200, 268–70
global/regional interactions 198–200
and globalization 43, 93
institutions 10–11
and multilateralism 29–30
partnerships 165
peacekeeping functions 60, 173
politics 11–13, 20
reform 25–32, 56–7, 62, 63, 200–1,
261–2, 278

and regionalism 153, 164, 198
resolutions 19–20, 22, 24, 26–7
role and limitations 9–11
United States (USA) 12, 41, 44, 51, 82, 258
anti-colonialism 211
bilateral agreements 186, 196
Bush administration 57, 268
Clean Air Act Amendments (1990) 224
Coalition of Services Industries
(USCSI) 106
development aid 213–14
and Doha Round 51
foreign and trade policies 185, 266
Glass–Steagall Act (1933) 70–1
and governance 97, 98, 256, 265–6
hegemony 20–1
and international justice 266
and IPRs 125
and Kyoto Protocol 223
and multilateralism 32, 57
and NAFTA 187, 196
Nixon administration 72
Trade Representative (USTR) 125
and UN 12–13, 16, 21, 32
unilateralism 153, 171, 173
Uruguay Round (UR) 6, 119, 260
Agreement on Subsidies and
Countervailing Measures
(ASCM) 122, 133
Agriculture Agreement (AA) 121, 124
Antidumping Agreement (AD) 126
benefits and concessions/gains and
losses 120–4, 126, 127
export/import activities 122, 123, 126
investment policies 122
outcome 120–7
special and differential approach
(S&D) 121
tariffication 121, 122–3, 124–5, 126
Textiles and Clothing Agreement
(ATC) 121
Trade-Related Investment Measures
(TRIMs) Agreement 122
UR Agreements (URAs) 119–27
USSR see Soviet Union

Venezuela 122
Ventura-Dias, Vivianne 137
Via Campasina network 155
Vienna Convention 57
Vietnam 185

Warsaw Pact (1955) 159
Washington Consensus 41, 86
welfare services see socio-economic issues
Western Europe 179, 180, 183
Western European Union (WEU) 165
Wolf, Martin 48
women's issues 199, 270
conferences 20, 22, 199
groups/movements 158, 178n2
A Working Peace System (Mitrany) 187
World Bank 6, 10, 16, 18, 23, 25, 49, 52, 53,
55, 56, 188
accountability 87, 97, 109–13
Annual Review of Evaluation Results
(ARDE) 111
Compliance Adviser/Ombudsman's office
(CAO) 113
development/funding aid
programmes 45, 86–8, 189, 212–13
Global Environment Facility 224–7, 238
and globalization/governance 77, 93, 252
Inspection Panel 112–13
Operations Evaluation Department
(OED) 110
reform 86
World Commission on Dams 98–9
World Commission on Environment and
Development, 1987 report 205
World Diamond Council 100
World Economic Fora, Davos (2001) 53
World Economic Outlook 2005 (IMF) 49
world economy 38–9, 46, 211
and interdependence 42, 75, 113–14, 118,
180
population/income ratios 49–50
purchasing-power parities 50
regulating models 94
World Education Forum, Dakar (2002) 25
World Food Programme (WFP) 27
World Health Organization (WHO) 15, 28
World Intellectual Property Organization
(WIPO) 132, 140, 229
World Meteorological Organization
(WMO) 221
world politics 8
and globalization 42–4
and regionalism 150
Thatcher/Reagan effects 20
World Social Fora (WSF) 53, 54, 63–4
World Trade Organization (WTO) 22, 43,
53, 93, 119, 141

Agreement on Subsidies and
   Countervailing Measures
   (ASCM) 125–6
Agreement on Textiles and Clothing
   (ATC) 121
Agreement on Trade-Related Intellectual
   Property (TRIPs) 52, 123, 124, 133, 139,
   141, 228
Agreement on Trade-Related Investment
   Measures (TRIMs) 96
Agriculture Agreement (AA) 121
Basic Telecommunications and Financial
   Services Agreements 107
Committee on Trade and
   Environment 229
decision-making processes 134–5, 137
and global governance 103–4, 105–6, 262
Ministerial Conference (Cancun,
   Mexico 2003) 50, 86, 119, 120, 124,
   134, 160, 185

Ministerial Conference (Hong
   Kong 2005) 51, 119, 134
Ministerial Conference
   (Seattle 1999) 50, 53, 86, 106, 119,
   120, 260
reform 62, 106, 131–4, 137, 138, 161
and regionalism 158, 164
rule-making procedures 123–4, 131–41
Settlement of Disputes organization
   52
Subsidies and Countervailing Measures
   Agreement (SCM) 122, 133
World Wildlife Fund 101

Young, Zoe 225, 226
Yugoslavia 23
   former Yugoslavia 165

Zeneca 228
Zionism 19